Lecture Notes in Computer Science 16471

The series Lecture Notes in Computer Science (LNCS), including its subseries Lecture Notes in Artificial Intelligence (LNAI) and Lecture Notes in Bioinformatics (LNBI), has established itself as a medium for the publication of new developments in computer science and information technology research, teaching, and education.

LNCS enjoys close cooperation with the computer science R & D community, the series counts many renowned academics among its volume editors and paper authors, and collaborates with prestigious societies. Its mission is to serve this international community by providing an invaluable service, mainly focused on the publication of conference and workshop proceedings and postproceedings. LNCS commenced publication in 1973.

Jianfeng Zhan · Wei Wang · Fanda Fan ·
Yushan Su
Editors

Evaluation Science and Engineering

17th BenchCouncil International Symposium, Bench 2025
Guanghan, China, December 3–5, 2025
Revised Selected Papers

Editors
Jianfeng Zhan
Institute of Computing Technology, Chinese Academy of Sciences
Beijing, China

Fanda Fan
Institute of Computing Technology, Chinese Academy of Sciences
Beijing, China

Wei Wang
East China Normal University
Shanghai, China

Yushan Su
Waymo LLC
Mountain View, CA, USA

ISSN 0302-9743 ISSN 1611-3349 (electronic)
Lecture Notes in Computer Science
ISBN 978-981-95-9693-5 ISBN 978-981-95-9694-2 (eBook)
https://doi.org/10.1007/978-981-95-9694-2

This Springer imprint is published by the registered company Springer Nature Singapore Pte Ltd.
The registered company address is: 152 Beach Road, #21-01/04 Gateway East, Singapore 189721, Singapore

Preface

This volume contains the papers presented at the 17th BenchCouncil International Symposium on Evaluation Science and Engineering (Bench 2025), held on December 3–5, 2025, in Guanghan, Sichuan Province, China.

Evaluation is a fundamental activity that underpins scientific discovery, technological innovation, and societal decision-making. Yet across many disciplines, evaluation has long been conducted in fragmented, experience-driven, or ad hoc ways, lacking unified principles and systematic engineering methodologies. To address this challenge, the International Open Benchmark Council has pioneered Evaluatology—the Science and Engineering of Evaluation—aiming to establish evaluation as a rigorous, interdisciplinary, and reproducible scientific domain.

Bench 2025 marks a significant milestone in this transition. Centered explicitly on Evaluatology, the symposium was organized to promote unified evaluation principles, methodologies, and engineering practices across disciplines, including computer science, artificial intelligence, systems and infrastructure, aviation, energy, education, and the social sciences. By bringing together researchers, practitioners, and standardization experts, Bench 2025 sought to bridge theoretical foundations and real-world evaluation needs.

The conference program reflected this holistic vision. The opening sessions featured keynote talks on next-generation AI cyberinfrastructure, data-driven intelligence automation, and emerging challenges in evaluation from both system and methodological perspectives. A series of official releases introduced major Evaluatology initiatives, including the launch of Evaluatology monographs in Chinese and English, the establishment of the Editorial Advisory Board for the Evaluatology Book Series, and the introduction of BenchCouncil Press as an AI-powered open publishing platform.

A distinctive feature of Bench 2025 was its strong emphasis on evaluation engineering and standardization. The symposium presented achievements from multiple Evaluatology-based standard working groups, covering CPUs, large language models, vector databases, mobile-side AI systems, and open-source software. These efforts highlight how Evaluatology principles are translated into concrete standards, benchmarks, and evaluation systems, enabling fair comparison, reproducibility, and transparent decision-making.

Another key component of Bench 2025 was the comprehensive Bench Conference Report sessions. Across two full-day tracks, the conference showcased peer-reviewed research contributions spanning benchmarking methodologies, open-source evaluation, AI system performance analysis, compiler and system optimization, sustainability and aviation evaluation, scientific and technological evaluation, and emerging application domains. These presentations demonstrate the breadth of Evaluatology applications and the growing maturity of evaluation as a cross-cutting scientific discipline.

In addition, Bench 2025 featured open tutorials on Evaluatology, designed to systematically introduce its theoretical foundations, methodological frameworks, and engineering practices to a broader audience. These tutorials further reinforced the conference's mission of knowledge dissemination and community building.

All papers included in this proceedings volume were selected through a rigorous peer-review process conducted by an international program committee. The accepted contributions represent both methodological advances and practical insights, collectively advancing the development of evaluation science and engineering.

Bench 2025 received 42 submissions, of which 19 were accepted for presentation and inclusion in this volume, yielding an acceptance rate of 45.24%. All submissions underwent a double-blind peer-review process, and each paper was reviewed by at least three independent reviewers, followed by program committee deliberation to ensure fairness and rigor in the selection process.

We extend our sincere gratitude to all authors for their high-quality contributions, which form the intellectual foundation of this volume. We also thank the program committee members, reviewers, keynote speakers, panelists, and working group contributors for their dedication and professionalism. Their collective efforts ensured the academic rigor and practical relevance of Bench 2025.

We hope that this proceedings volume will serve as a valuable reference for researchers, practitioners, and policymakers, and will contribute to the long-term goal of establishing Evaluatology as a unified, systematic, and impactful science of evaluation.

December 2025

Jianfeng Zhan
Wei Wang
Fanda Fan
Yushan Su

Organization

General Chair

Weiping Li	Oklahoma State University, USA and Civil Aviation Flight University of China, China

Organizing Committee Chair

Lin Zou	Civil Aviation Flight University of China, China

Program Chairs

Jianfeng Zhan	BenchCouncil and Chinese Academy of Sciences, China
Wei Wang	East China Normal University, China

Program Committee Vice-chairs

Fanda Fan	ICT, Chinese Academy of Sciences, China
Yushan Su	Waymo LLC, USA

Award Committee

D. K. Panda	Ohio State University, USA
Geoffrey Fox	Indiana University, USA
Jianfeng Zhan	University of Chinese Academy of Sciences, China
Tony Hey	Rutherford Appleton Laboratory, UK
David J. Lilja	University of Minnesota, Twin Cities, USA
Jack J. Dongarra	University of Tennessee, USA
John L. Henning	Oracle, USA
Lieven Eeckhout	Universiteit Gent, Belgium

Sponsorship Chair

Fei Ling	Anlink, China

Publication Chair

Zhengxin Yang	University of Chinese Academy of Sciences, China

Publicity Chair

Wanling Gao	University of Chinese Academy of Sciences, China

Program Committee

Ana Gainaru	Oak Ridge National Laboratory, USA
Bin Hu	Institute of Computing Technology, Chinese Academy of Sciences, China
Biwei Xie	Institute of Computing Technology, Chinese Academy of Sciences, China
Ce Zhang	ETH Zurich, Switzerland
Chen Zheng	Institute of Software, Chinese Academy of Sciences, China
Chunjie Luo	Institute of Computing Technology, Chinese Academy of Sciences, China
Chundian Li	Meta, USA
Emmanuel Jeannot	Inria, France
Fei Sun	Meta, USA
Gang Lu	Tencent, China
Gregory Diamos	Baidu, China
Guangli Li	Institute of Computing Technology, Chinese Academy of Sciences, China
Khaled Ibrahim	Lawrence Berkeley National Laboratory, USA
Krishnakumar Nair	Facebook, USA
Lei Wang	Institute of Computing Technology, Chinese Academy of Sciences, China
Mario Marino	Leeds Beckett University, UK
Miaoqing Huang	University of Arkansas, USA

Contents

An On-Device Evaluation Framework for LLMs with Budget-Constrained Subsets

Minghao Wang[1(✉)], Enqi Liu[1], Ping Zhang[2], Jianhua Huang[2], Dongdong Zhang[2], and Rui Zhang[1]

[1] China Academy of Information and Communications Technology, Beijing, China
wangminghao@caict.ac.cn

[2] China Certification and Inspection Group Beijing Co., Ltd., Beijing, China

Abstract. Evaluating LLMs on mobile devices presents challenges, as standard benchmarks like MMLU comprise thousands of questions requiring substantial time and resources. This paper adapts item response theory (IRT) subset selection for on-device evaluation. We present an end-to-end framework for Android smartphones that integrates automated testing via ADB with comprehensive performance monitoring. Using an IRT-sampled subset of 300 questions, we validate that our approach achieves accuracy within 0.13% of full MMLU results while reducing evaluation time. Testing across 12 mobile devices reveals substantial performance variations—up to 2.78× in latency—demonstrating that thermal design, memory configuration, and system optimization are as critical as hardware specifications for practical LLM deployment.

1 Introduction

Large language models (LLMs) are increasingly deployed on edge devices such as smartphones, offering reduced latency, enhanced privacy, and offline capability [6]. However, evaluating LLMs on resource-constrained devices presents unique challenges. Standard benchmarks like MMLU [2] comprise thousands of questions, requiring substantial time and computational resources to execute on mobile hardware. Efficient evaluation methods are essential for iterative development and hardware optimization.

Recent work has addressed benchmark efficiency through subset selection. tinyBenchmarks [3] demonstrates that IRT-based subsets of 100 examples can estimate full benchmark performance with under 2% error, primarily targeting cloud-based evaluation to reduce GPU hours and API costs. While efficient for high-performance environments, executing thousands of questions on resource-constrained mobile devices still requires hours to days. We adapt subset selection to enable practical evaluation within mobile device time and thermal constraints.

However, existing subset evaluation frameworks primarily target cloud-based inference via APIs. On-device evaluation imposes distinct challenges: device

J. Zhan et al. (Eds.): Bench 2025, LNCS 16471, pp. 1–11, 2026.
https://doi.org/10.1007/978-981-95-9694-2_1

power and thermal constraints limit sustained workload, execution time impacts development workflow, and hardware-specific optimizations (NPU acceleration, quantization support) necessitate device-native testing. Remote API-based evaluation cannot assess these device-specific characteristics critical for real-world mobile deployment.

Contributions. This paper operationalizes subset-based evaluation for on-device LLM assessment. We present an end-to-end framework for Android smartphones that integrates tinyBenchmarks' subset strategies with automated testing via Android Debug Bridge (ADB):

- **On-Device Adaptation:** While tinyBenchmarks targets cloud-based evaluation to reduce GPU costs, we adapt its IRT-based subset selection for resource-constrained mobile devices, enabling practical evaluation within time and thermal constraints through ready-to-use CSV datasets.
- **Automated Pipeline:** We develop an ADB-based framework integrating data preprocessing, inference execution, comprehensive resource monitoring (memory, power, temperature), and performance analysis.
- **Empirical Validation:** Using the unquantized Qwen2.5-3B model [4], we validate that IRT-sampled subsets of 300 questions achieve 58.70% accuracy, differing from the full MMLU result (58.83%) by only 0.13%.

2 Related Work

2.1 Efficient Evaluation via Subset Selection

Standard LLM benchmarks like MMLU [2] comprise thousands of questions, requiring substantial computational resources. tinyBenchmarks [3] addresses evaluation cost through IRT-based subset selection, where 100-item subsets yield under 2% error while reducing GPU hours and API expenses. This work targets cloud-based evaluation, whereas we adapt subset selection to enable practical evaluation on resource-constrained mobile devices where full benchmarks require hours to days.

2.2 Model Quantization Techniques

Post-training quantization reduces model memory footprint and accelerates inference by lowering precision of weights and activations. GPTQ [1] introduces approximate second-order information to achieve accurate 3-bit and 4-bit weight quantization for generative transformers, enabling deployment on resource-constrained hardware without significant accuracy degradation. Modern quantization strategies extend these techniques to support various bit-widths and mixed-precision schemes, making large models feasible for edge deployment.

2.3 On-Device LLM Deployment

Advances in mobile hardware have enabled LLM deployment on edge devices [6]. Compact models with parameter sizes under 4 billion, combined with quantization techniques, enable inference within typical mobile memory constraints of 8-12GB RAM.

Complementing deployment tools, MobileAIBench [5] provides comprehensive performance analysis of LLMs on mobile devices, measuring latency, throughput, and resource utilization. While MobileAIBench employs dataset down-sampling to enable mobile evaluation, it does not leverage statistically principled subset selection methods. We bridge this gap by integrating IRT-based subset selection with automated on-device testing infrastructure, ensuring representative evaluation with minimal sample sizes.

3 Methodology

Our benchmark framework consists of six key components designed to evaluate quantized large language models on edge devices. We validate our methodology using Qwen2.5-3B quantized models deployed on mobile platforms. For data preparation, we use a preprocessing pipeline (Algorithm 1) that converts MMLU dataset into subject-wise prompt files. The model inference (Algorithm 2) is monitored by a resource tracking daemon (Algorithm 3) to capture real-time memory usage. Results are evaluated using our analysis pipeline (Algorithm 4), which computes both accuracy and performance metrics.

Figure 1 illustrates the complete benchmark framework, integrating software components and evaluation metrics.

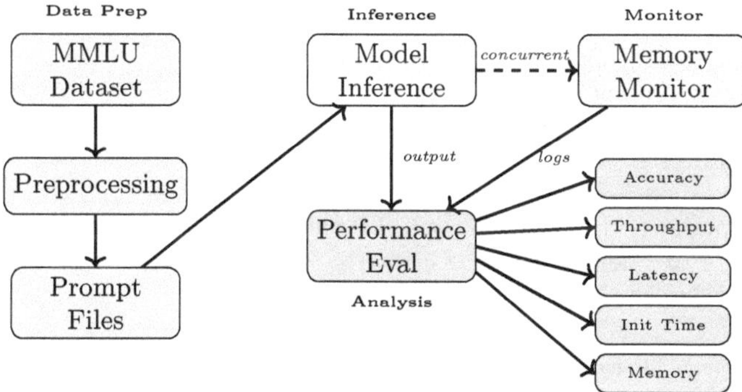

Fig. 1. Benchmark framework overview showing data preparation, inference execution with concurrent monitoring, and comprehensive performance evaluation

3.1 Dataset Preprocessing

We employ an IRT-sampled subset [3] derived from the MMLU benchmark to enable efficient on-device evaluation while maintaining representativeness. The subset comprises 300 questions across 45 academic subjects, with question distribution ranging from 1 to 19 per subject. This compact size allows complete evaluation within reasonable time and resource budgets on mobile devices, while the IRT-based selection ensures consistent subject coverage and difficulty characteristics compared to the full MMLU dataset.

The raw MMLU dataset is provided in CSV format with columns for questions, multiple-choice options (A-D), correct answers, and subject categories. The preprocessing pipeline, as detailed in Algorithm 1, first converts the CSV structure into two primary outputs: (1) a prompts file containing formatted question blocks with subject metadata, and (2) an answers file storing ground truth labels for subsequent evaluation. Each prompt block includes a separator, subject identifier, question index, question text, and formatted options. Additionally, the pipeline groups questions by subject into separate files, enabling parallel processing across different knowledge domains. To validate the representativeness of our sampling strategy, we conducted preliminary experiments using the original (unquantized) Qwen2.5-3B model. The results demonstrate that the subject-weighted accuracy on the IRT-sampled [3] subset1 (58.70%)

Algorithm 1. MMLU Dataset Preprocessing

Require: MMLU dataset CSV file F_{csv} with columns: Question, A, B, C, D, Answer, Subject
Ensure: Prompts file $F_{prompts}$, Answers file $F_{answers}$, Subject-wise prompt files $\mathcal{P}_{subj}$
1: $F_{prompts} \leftarrow$ create output file
2: $F_{answers} \leftarrow$ create output file
3: **for** each row r_i in F_{csv} **do**
4: Extract $\{idx, q, opt_a, opt_b, opt_c, opt_d, ans, subj\} \leftarrow r_i$
5: Construct prompt block P_i:
6: P_i.separator $\leftarrow$ separator marker
7: P_i.subject $\leftarrow$ subj
8: P_i.question $\leftarrow$ "$idx.\ q\ (subj)$"
9: P_i.options $\leftarrow \{A : opt_a, B : opt_b, C : opt_c, D : opt_d\}$
10: Write P_i to $F_{prompts}$
11: Write "$subj\ idx\ ans$" to $F_{answers}$
12: **end for**
13: Close $F_{prompts}$, $F_{answers}$
14: Parse $F_{prompts}$ using pattern matching to extract question blocks
15: Group blocks by $subj$ into dictionary $\mathcal{D}$
16: **for** each subject $s \in \mathcal{D}$.keys() **do**
17: Create subject prompt file F_s
18: Write all blocks in $\mathcal{D}[s]$ to F_s
19: **end for**
20: **return** $\{F_{prompts}, F_{answers}\} \cup \{F_s \mid s \in \mathcal{D}.\text{keys}\}$

---

closely matches that of the full MMLU dataset (58.83%), confirming that the sampled questions maintain consistent subject distribution and difficulty characteristics.

3.2 Model Inference Execution

The inference execution framework orchestrates model evaluation by integrating prompt construction, model invocation, and comprehensive output parsing. Each inference request begins with formatting the prompt using the model's chat template, which structures the conversation with system and user role markers. The framework supports resumable execution by tracking completed questions per subject, enabling evaluation across multiple sessions.

Algorithm 2. Model Inference Execution with Monitoring

Require: Subject prompt files $\mathcal{P}$, Model executable M, Config C, Finished subjects $\mathcal{F}$
Ensure: LLM answer files $\mathcal{A}_{LLM}$, Process log $\mathcal{L}_{proc}$
1: Initialize monitoring: start memory monitor daemon, PID file P_{all}
2: **for** each prompt file $P_s \in \mathcal{P}$ **do**
3: Extract subject s from filename
4: Read finished count $f_s \leftarrow \mathcal{F}[s]$
5: **if** $f_s ==$ total questions in P_s **then**
6: Skip completed subject
7: continue
8: **end if**
9: Parse P_s to extract question blocks $\{Q_1, \ldots, Q_n\}$
10: **for** each question Q_i, where $i \geq f_s$ **do**
11: Format prompt using model's chat template with system and user roles
12: Record start timestamp t_{start}
13: Execute model M with configuration C and prompt asynchronously
14: Record PID: $p_{inf} \leftarrow$ PID of M
15: Write p_{inf} to P_{all}
16: Wait for completion: wait p_{inf}
17: Record end timestamp t_{end}
18: Parse output O_i:
19: Extract answer block A_i from delimiters
20: Extract metrics $\{t_{init}, t_{prompt}, r_{prompt}, t_{token}, r_{token}\}$ from performance markers
21: Write structured result to answer file A_s:
22: record with delimiters, question_index, timestamps, metrics
23: Update $\mathcal{F}[s] \leftarrow i + 1$
24: **end for**
25: **end for**
26: Stop monitoring, compute total runtime
27: Convert answer files to structured format $\mathcal{A}_{LLM}$
28: **return** $\mathcal{A}_{LLM}, \mathcal{L}_{proc}$

As shown in Algorithm 2, the execution process launches the model with specified configuration and prompt parameters, then monitors the process until completion. The output parser extracts three critical components: (1) the answer block delimited by markers, (2) the final answer choice from structured patterns, and (3) detailed performance metrics including initialization time, prompt processing time, and token generation rates.

3.3 System Resource Monitoring

Accurate resource consumption measurement requires continuous monitoring throughout the inference execution. We implement a monitoring daemon that operates concurrently with inference tasks, capturing system memory usage at high temporal resolution. The monitoring framework distinguishes between baseline system consumption and LLM-specific resource utilization.

Algorithm 3 describes the monitoring process, which samples memory usage at high-frequency intervals by reading from the system memory interface. The framework integrates inference process detection via process scanning, enabling precise correlation between memory spikes and active inference periods. Each log entry includes timestamp, inference activity status, and system memory metrics, facilitating post-hoc analysis of memory patterns during inference workload execution.

Algorithm 3. System Resource Monitoring

Require: Sampling interval Δt, Log file L_{mem}
Ensure: Memory log with inference activity status
1: Clear log file L_{mem}
2: **while** monitoring active **do**
3: Record timestamp $t \leftarrow$ current time
4: Scan processes: $procs \leftarrow$ detect inference process
5: Read memory info from system interface:
6: $mem_{total}, mem_{avail} \leftarrow$ total and available memory
7: $mem_{used} \leftarrow mem_{total} - mem_{avail}$
8: Determine inference status:
9: **if** $procs$ is not empty **then**
10: $active \leftarrow$ true
11: **else**
12: $active \leftarrow$ false
13: **end if**
14: Sleep(Δt)
15: **end while**
16: **return** L_{mem}

3.4 Performance Evaluation and Analysis

Performance evaluation encompasses both accuracy assessment and efficiency metric extraction. We compute two distinct accuracy measures: subject-weighted accuracy, which follows the standard MMLU evaluation protocol by averaging performance across subject categories, and question-weighted accuracy, which aggregates performance across all individual questions. The subject-weighted metric ensures balanced evaluation given the varying question counts across subjects in our subset (ranging from 1 to 19 questions per subject).

The evaluation pipeline, presented in Algorithm 4, employs structured data parsing to extract model answers from inference outputs. For each question, the pipeline normalizes answer choices, compares against ground truth labels, and accumulates correct/wrong/not-found counts. Efficiency metrics including initialization time, prompt processing throughput, and token generation rates

Algorithm 4. Performance Evaluation and Analysis

Require: LLM answers $\mathcal{A}_{LLM}$, Ground truth $\mathcal{G}$, Power/memory report R_{pm}
Ensure: Subject results $\mathcal{R}$, Final report R_{final}
1: Initialize $\mathcal{R} \leftarrow \emptyset$
2: **for** each subject file $A_s \in \mathcal{A}_{LLM}$ **do**
3: Load LLM answers $data_s \leftarrow A_s$ using JSON parsing
4: Load ground truth $gt_s \leftarrow \mathcal{G}[s]$
5: Initialize counters: $correct \leftarrow 0$, $wrong \leftarrow 0$, $notfound \leftarrow 0$
6: Initialize metric lists: $\mathcal{T}_{init}, \mathcal{T}_{prompt}, \mathcal{R}_{prompt}, \mathcal{T}_{token}, \mathcal{R}_{token}$
7: **for** each answer entry $a \in data_s$.answers **do**
8: Extract $idx, ans, metrics \leftarrow a$
9: Collect metrics: append $metrics$ values to respective lists
10: **if** ans indicates not found **then**
11: $notfound \leftarrow notfound + 1$, $wrong \leftarrow wrong + 1$
12: **else**
13: Compare: $gt \leftarrow gt_s[idx]$
14: **if** normalize(ans) == normalize(gt) **then**
15: $correct \leftarrow correct + 1$
16: **else**
17: $wrong \leftarrow wrong + 1$
18: **end if**
19: **end if**
20: **end for**
21: Compute statistics:
22: $acc \leftarrow correct/(correct + wrong)$
23: $\bar{r}_{token} \leftarrow$ average of $\mathcal{R}_{token}$
24: Store result $r_s \leftarrow \{subject, correct, wrong, acc, metrics\}$
25: Append r_s to $\mathcal{R}$
26: **end for**
27: Compute aggregate metrics:
28: $acc_{question} \leftarrow \sum correct / \sum total$
29: $acc_{subject} \leftarrow$ average of accuracies across subjects
30: Extract power/memory data from R_{pm}:
31: $mem_{baseline}, mem_{peak}, mem_{model}, P_{soc}, E_{inference}$
32: Generate final report R_{final} with all metrics
33: **return** $\mathcal{R}, R_{final}$

are aggregated from individual inference results. The final output includes per-subject statistics and aggregate metrics for comprehensive analysis.

4 Experimental Results

We evaluated the performance of Qwen2.5-3B quantized models across 12 mobile devices spanning three SoC types. The results demonstrate clear performance hierarchies both within and across chip groups, with newer SoC Type 1 and SoC Type 3 platforms showing superior efficiency compared to SoC Type 2.

4.1 Evaluation Metrics

Subject-Weighted Accuracy calculates the mean accuracy across all MMLU subjects using the formula:

$$\text{Accuracy} = \frac{1}{N}\sum_{i=1}^{N}\frac{\text{correct}_i}{\text{total}_i} \tag{1}$$

where N is the number of subjects, and correct_i and total_i represent the number of correctly answered questions and total questions in subject i, respectively. The baseline accuracy is 58.70%, derived from the original unquantized Qwen2.5-3B model. Accuracy loss is calculated as the difference between this baseline and the quantized model accuracy.

Token Throughput measures the average number of tokens generated per second during inference, reflecting the model's generation speed after the first token is produced. Higher values indicate better performance for streaming applications and long-text generation tasks.

First Token Latency quantifies the time-to-first-token generation, representing the responsiveness perceived by users in interactive applications. This metric is critical for chat-based interfaces where quick initial response enhances user experience.

Initialization Time captures the model loading overhead, calculated as the difference between the general first token time and actual first token time. Lower values enable faster cold-start scenarios and reduce waiting time for model loading.

Model Memory indicates the RAM footprint required for model loading and inference, measured in megabytes. Lower memory consumption enables deployment on memory-constrained devices and allows allocation of larger context buffers.

4.2 In-Group Performance Comparison

Within each SoC group, devices using identical quantization profiles exhibit performance variations due to thermal design, memory configuration, and software optimization. Tables 1, 2 and 3 present detailed intra-group comparisons, including five performance metrics: First Token Time, Init Time, Model Memory, Token Throughput and Test Duration, which represents the total wall-clock time for completing the benchmark test across all questions. While Test Duration is not a performance metric, it reflects the combined effect of throughput, latency, and system stability during prolonged inference tasks.

Table 1. SoC Type 1 Group Performance Comparison

Device ID	Test Duration (ms)	First Token Time (ms)	Init Time (ms)	Model Memory (MB)	Token Throughput (tokens/sec)
DUT-1	**583200**	**163.5**	**1268.7**	**2430.4**	**34.01**
DUT-9	936373	170.1	2332.3	3295.1	31.88
DUT-4	751958	171.6	1497.9	3109.8	31.48
DUT-3	662440	176.0	1450.7	2828.2	29.39

Table 2. SoC Type 2 Group Performance Comparison

Device ID	Test Duration (ms)	First Token Time (ms)	Init Time (ms)	Model Memory (MB)	Token Throughput (tokens/sec)
DUT-2	**688432**	**187.6**	**1140.3**	**2310.3**	**30.87**
DUT-11	1092334	199.3	2220.2	3239.5	27.96
DUT-10	703749	304.2	1323.2	3155.0	26.72
DUT-12	1201496	512.7	2182.2	3171.1	18.45

Table 3. SoC Type 3 Group Performance Comparison

Device ID	Test Duration (ms)	First Token Time (ms)	Init Time (ms)	Model Memory (MB)	Token Throughput (tokens/sec)
DUT-7	1434175	**106.2**	3433.9	2862.1	**37.98**
DUT-5	1220452	109.8	2690.8	**2339.1**	37.57
DUT-6	**1208508**	123.4	**2548.3**	2647.5	37.19
DUT-8	1243412	127.5	2629.0	2788.3	36.20

The intra-group variations demonstrate that thermal management and system integration significantly impact performance, even when using identical hardware and quantization profiles. For instance, within the SoC Type 2 group,

DUT-12 exhibits 2.78x longer first token latency compared to DUT-2, despite sharing the same SoC platform and quantization profile. This substantial variance underscores the critical influence of thermal design, memory subsystem configuration, and system-level software optimization on actual inference performance. Manufacturers seeking to optimize LLM deployment must therefore look beyond raw SoC specifications and consider holistic system integration.

4.3 Test Device Specifications

Table 4 summarizes the hardware specifications of all tested devices, referred to as Device Under Test (DUT). All devices feature 11 GB of RAM and run Android 14–16.

Table 4. Specifications (all devices feature 11 GB RAM)

			SoC Type 1	**SoC Type 2**	**SoC Type 3**
Device ID	Ver.	Device ID	Ver.	Device ID	Ver.
DUT-1	16	DUT-2	15	DUT-5	16
DUT-3	16	DUT-10	15	DUT-6	16
DUT-4	16	DUT-11	15	DUT-7	16
DUT-9	16	DUT-12	14	DUT-8	16

5 Conclusion

This paper presents an end-to-end framework for evaluating on-device large language models using budget-constrained subsets adapted from tinyBenchmarks. Our empirical validation demonstrates that IRT-sampled subsets of 300 questions achieve subject-weighted accuracy within 0.13% of full MMLU results, enabling efficient evaluation without sacrificing representativeness.

The evaluation across 12 mobile devices reveals three key insights. First, substantial intra-group performance variations (up to 2.78x in first token latency) demonstrate that thermal design, memory subsystem configuration, and software optimization are as critical as raw SoC specifications. Second, different SoC architectures exhibit distinct performance profiles—SoC Type 3 excels in low-latency interactive scenarios, while SoC Type 1 leads in initialization efficiency suitable for batch processing. Third, the 43% memory overhead variation indicates significant optimization potential in runtime memory allocation and buffer management.

Future work includes extending subset selection to multimodal benchmarks, exploring quantization-aware training for mobile inference, and incorporating cross-platform support for embedded systems.

References

1. Frantar, E., Ashkboos, S., Hoefler, T., Alistarh, D.: GPTQ: accurate post-training quantization for generative pre-trained transformers (2022). arXiv preprint arXiv:2210.17323
2. Hendrycks, D., Burns, C., Basart, S., Critch, A., Li, J., Song, D., Toma, D.: Measuring massive multitask language understanding (2020). arXiv preprint arXiv:2009.03300
3. Polo, F.M., Weber, L., Choshen, L., Sun, Y., Xu, G., Yurochkin, M.: tinyBenchmarks: evaluating LLMs with fewer examples (2024). https://arxiv.org/abs/2402.14992
4. Team, Q.: Qwen2.5 technical report (2024). arXiv preprint arXiv:2412.10115
5. Zhang, Y., et al.: MobileAIBench: benchmarking LLMs and LMMs for on-device use cases (2024). arXiv preprint arXiv:2406.10290
6. Zhang, Y., et al.: A review on edge large language models: design, execution, and prospects. ACM Comput. Surv. **57**(3), 1–34 (2025)

GeoClaim: Programmable Geoscientific Fact Verification and Judge-Guided Evaluation for Open-Ended Mineral Exploration QA

Yuang Zhang[1,3], Pu Zhao[4], Fanyu Han[5], Jiaheng Peng[5], and Qinjun Qiu[2,3](✉)

[1] School of Geography and Information Engineering, China University of Geosciences, Wuhan, China
zhangyuang@cug.edu.cn

[2] School of Computer Science, China University of Geosciences, Wuhan, China
qiuqinjun@cug.edu.cn

[3] State Joint Local Engineering Laboratory of Geographic Information System, Beijing, China

[4] School of Information Engineering, Shanghai, China

[5] School of Data Science and Engineering, East China Normal University, Shanghai , China

Abstract. Geoscientific and mineral-exploration question answering (QA) requires high factual accuracy, as answers frequently involve spatial topology, coordinate reference systems, and quantitative units. However, widely used automatic metrics such as BLEU and ROUGE rely on surface-level lexical overlap and fail to capture domain-specific factual correctness, resulting in weak alignment with expert judgments for long and professional answers. We propose GeoClaim, a programmable fact-based evaluation framework for open-ended mineral-exploration QA. GeoClaim decomposes both model-generated and reference answers into atomic geoscientific facts (geo-claims) and verifies each claim along three core dimensions: spatial topology, coordinate reference systems and geodesic computations, and unit and numeric equivalence. On this basis, we introduce GeoClaim-F1 and GeoClaim-ROUGE, which measure answer quality at the factual level by assessing claim coverage and consistency, explicitly decoupling semantic correctness from lexical similarity. We further propose Geo-Judge, an evidence-guided LLM-as-Judge mechanism that incorporates structured fact-verification results into the judging process and improves reliability through multi-judge consistency calibration and stability testing. Experiments on a curated dataset of 200 professional mineral-exploration QA pairs show that GeoClaim metrics achieve substantially higher correlation with expert assessments than BLEU and ROUGE, and more accurately reproduce expert model rankings for system comparison and selection. GeoClaim establishes a fact-centric, interpretable, and practically deployable evaluation paradigm for geoscientific QA, supporting reliable assessment and model selection in geological and mineral-resource applications.

Y. Zhang and P. Zhao—These authors contributed equally.

J. Zhan et al. (Eds.): Bench 2025, LNCS 16471, pp. 12–26, 2026.
https://doi.org/10.1007/978-981-95-9694-2_2

Keywords: Question answering · Large language models · Evaluation metrics · Mineral exploration

1 Introduction

Geoscientific question answering (QA) systems demand a high level of factual accuracy, as correct answers often depend on spatial topology, coordinate reference systems, units, and precise quantitative relationships. In mineral exploration QA, even minor factual errors—such as incorrect spatial relations, coordinate misinterpretation, or unit inconsistencies—can render an otherwise fluent answer practically invalid.

Despite recent advances, large language models (LLMs) frequently generate answers that are linguistically polished yet factually incorrect in domain-specific contexts. This issue is exacerbated by the limitations of existing automatic evaluation metrics. Traditional text-based metrics such as BLEU and ROUGE rely on surface-level lexical overlap and fail to capture factual correctness under paraphrasing, numeric reformulation, unit conversion, or coordinate and geodesic reasoning. As a result, these metrics exhibit weak correlation with expert judgment and are insensitive to small but critical factual errors.

Evaluating geoscientific QA presents additional challenges, including spatial reasoning, multi-CRS relationships, and sensitivity to numerical and grade parameters. Accurate evaluation therefore requires domain-aware mechanisms capable of reasoning over spatial, numerical, and unit-based facts, rather than relying on textual similarity alone.

To address these challenges, we propose GeoClaim, a programmable evaluation framework for open-ended geoscientific question answering. GeoClaim verifies domain-specific facts in a structured manner and evaluates answers at the claim level, enabling precise assessment of factual correctness. The framework integrates three-axis geoscientific fact verification, evidence-guided multi-judge LLM evaluation (Geo-Judge), and novel fact-level metrics (GeoClaim-F1 and GeoClaim-ROUGE). Together, these components provide a reliable, interpretable, and expert-aligned evaluation paradigm tailored to mineral exploration QA.

2 Related Work

Automatic evaluation of natural language generation has traditionally relied on text-based metrics such as BLEU and ROUGE, which measure lexical overlap between generated outputs and reference texts [1]. These metrics have been widely adopted in tasks such as machine translation and summarization, where surface similarity often correlates with semantic adequacy [2]. However, prior studies have shown that lexical overlap is a poor proxy for factual correctness, particularly in open-ended question answering tasks [3].

In geoscientific and mineral exploration QA, this limitation is especially pronounced. Equivalent facts may be expressed through paraphrasing, numerical reformulation, unit conversion, or alternative spatial descriptions, leading to low overlap despite factual correctness [4]. Conversely, answers containing small but critical factual errors, such as incorrect coordinates, spatial inversions, or order-of-magnitude mistakes, may still receive high BLEU or ROUGE scores [5]. As a result, text-based metrics exhibit weak correlation with expert judgment and fail to capture domain-critical factual errors [6].

Recent work has explored the use of large language models as judges to evaluate open-ended generation tasks [7]. LLM-as-Judge approaches leverage the reasoning and language understanding capabilities of LLMs to provide holistic assessments that go beyond lexical similarity [8]. While promising, these approaches suffer from well-documented issues, including sensitivity to prompt phrasing, stochastic variability, and susceptibility to being misled by fluent but incorrect answers [9].

In fact-sensitive domains, such as geoscientific QA, unguided LLM judges often overemphasize surface fluency and narrative coherence while underweighting factual correctness [10]. Prior studies have reported substantial inter-judge variability and limited reproducibility, raising concerns about reliability and objectivity [11]. These limitations motivate the need for mechanisms that constrain LLM-based judging with explicit, domain-grounded evidence.

To address the shortcomings of lexical metrics, several fact-centric evaluation approaches have been proposed [12]. Among them, FActScore represents a notable step toward fine-grained factual evaluation by decomposing generated answers into atomic claims and verifying them against external knowledge sources [13]. This claim-based paradigm improves factual sensitivity and interpretability compared to token-level metrics.

However, existing fact-centric metrics are primarily designed for general-purpose factual QA and do not explicitly account for the unique characteristics of geoscientific reasoning [14]. In particular, they lack systematic support for spatial topology, coordinate reference systems, geodesic computation, and unitquantity normalization, which are central to mineral exploration QA [15]. Moreover, prior approaches typically focus on metric design and do not address the instability of LLM-based judging in open-ended evaluation settings [16].

3 The GeoClaim Framework

3.1 Overview of GeoClaim

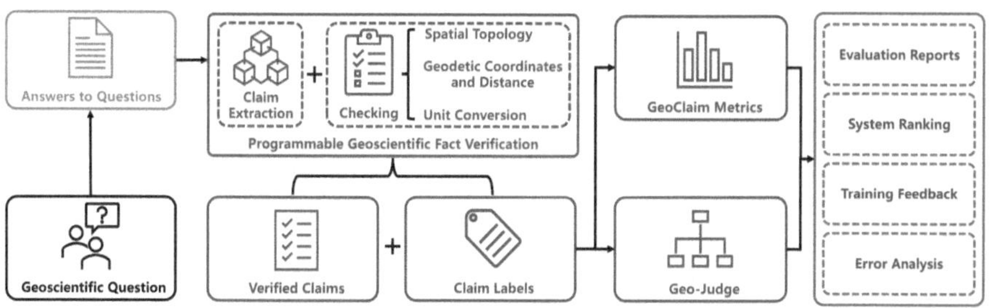

Fig. 1. Overview of the GeoClaim Framework

GeoClaim follows the fine-grained, fact-centric evaluation paradigm exemplified by FAc tScore, and extends it to geoscientific question answering by incorporating domain-critical verification dimensions—most notably spatial reasoning and unitquantity consistency—that are typically absent from general-purpose factuality metrics [17].

Figure 1 summarizes the GeoClaim architecture for factual assessment in open-ended geoscientific QA. For each model-generated answer, GeoClaim pairs it with the corresponding reference answer and applies a programmable fact-verification pipeline consisting of structured geo-claim extraction and domain-aware verification along three dimensions: (i) spatial topology, (ii) coordinate reference systems with geodesic computation, and (iii) unit and quantity normalization.

Verified geo-claims and their structured labels support GeoClaim metrics that quantify semantic and factual agreement beyond surface-level overlap. In parallel, the same verified evidence is injected into an evidence-guided LLM-as-Judge module, Geo-Judge [18], via evidence strips that constrain the judging process to the verification outcomes, reducing hallucinated judgments and improving inter-judge consistency [19].

Finally, outputs from the metric-based branch and the evidence-guided judging branch are combined to produce downstream evaluation artifacts, including system ranking, model diagnosis, training feedback, and error analysis [20]. Collectively, GeoClaim provides an interpretable, reliable, and domain-aligned evaluation framework for geoscientific and mineral exploration QA.

3.2 Programmable Atomic Fact Verification

Definition of Geo-Claims Given a model-generated or reference answer in natural language, programmable fact verification first extracts a set of geo-claims that capture the answer's factual content, converting unstructured text into atomic, verifiable assertions for downstream domain-specific verification.

In GeoClaim, claim extraction follows semantic faithfulness rather than linguistic completeness [21]: it focuses on concrete geoscientific relations, properties, and quantities that determine factual correctness, while excluding explanatory discourse, rhetorical structure, and speculative interpretations [22].

Extraction is implemented as a controlled semantic parsing process that identifies candidate geo-claims from geoscientific entities, relational predicates, and quantitative expressions [23], and then normalizes them into the structured representation defined in Sect. 3.2.1 to ensure consistent encoding of semantically equivalent facts.

To accommodate open-ended variability, GeoClaim adopts a hybrid strategy that combines rule-based components with large language model assistance [24]. Rules detect numerical expressions, units, and coordinate formats, while LLM-assisted extraction handles paraphrased or implicit assertions [25]; the LLM is restricted to claim identification and normalization, not factual verification. Typical extraction targets include: (1) spatial relationships between geographic entities; (2) explicit coordinates, distances, angles, depths, or elevations; and (3) numerical attributes of geological or mineral entities with units [28].

Extraction errors are inherent in claim-based evaluation [26,29]. GeoClaim reduces their impact by applying the same extraction pipeline to reference and model-generated answers and verifying claims independently, so spurious claims are labeled as incorrect or unverifiable rather than biasing evaluation.

The output is an unordered set of normalized geo-claims for each answer [27, 30], which underpins the three-axis verification process described in the following section.

Three-Axis Verification. After geo-claims are extracted and normalized, GeoClaim verifies each claim with a programmable procedure that targets common high-impact factual errors in geoscientific QA. Instead of full geological reasoning, it uses three checkable axes—spatial topology, CRS/geodesic computation, and unitquantity consistency.

Verification is rule-based and modular, using authoritative geospatial data, coordinate system definitions, and numerical rules. Topology checking validates qualitative relations (e.g., containment, adjacency, direction) [31]. CRS/geodesic checking normalizes coordinates and measurements and recomputes derived quantities to detect CRS mismatches or calculation errors. Unitquantity checking converts values to canonical units to recognize equivalent expressions and flag conversion errors, incompatibilities, or order-of-magnitude discrepancies.

Axes are selected by claim type, and each claim is labeled correct, incorrect, or unverifiable when required reference data are missing. This decomposition provides transparent, extensible verification that supports claim-level metrics and evidence-guided judging.

3.3 GeoClaim Metrics

Based on the verified geo-claims produced by the programmable fact verification pipeline, GeoClaim defines a fact-level evaluation paradigm that assesses answer quality in terms of geoscientific correctness rather than surface textual similarity. Under this paradigm, both reference answers and model-generated answers are represented as sets of normalized geo-claims annotated with verification labels (correct, incorrect, or unverifiable), and evaluation is performed by measuring factual coverage and consistency between these claim sets.

Within this unified framework, we instantiate two complementary metrics, GeoClaim-F1 and GeoClaim-ROUGE, which correspond to precisionrecallbased and recall-oriented views of factual agreement, respectively [32,33]. Let $C_r$and $C_m$denote the verified geo-claim sets extracted from the reference answer and the model-generated answer. A model claim is considered a true positive only if it matches a semantically equivalent reference claim and is verified as correct. Claims that contradict reference facts or are verified as incorrect reduce precision, while missing reference claims reduce recall. Claims labeled as unverifiable are excluded from positive contributions.

Formally, claim-level precision and recall are defined as:

$$\text{Precision} = \frac{|C_m \cap C_r|}{|C_m|} \tag{1}$$

$$\text{Recall} = \frac{|C_m \cap C_r|}{|C_r|} \tag{2}$$

GeoClaim-F1 is then computed as the harmonic mean of precision and recall:

$$\text{GeoClaim-F1} = \frac{2 \cdot \text{Precision} \cdot \text{Recall}}{\text{Precision} + \text{Recall}} \tag{3}$$

While GeoClaim-F1 balances factual correctness and hallucination control, GeoClaim-ROUGE emphasizes factual coverage. Analogous to recall-oriented ROUGE metrics, GeoClaim-ROUGE measures the extent to which the reference answer's factual content is covered by the model-generated answer at the claim level. Let $S_{ref}$and S_{pred}denote the ordered sequences of verified geo-claims in the reference and model answers, respectively. Claim-level longest common subsequence (LCS) is used to quantify factual overlap:

$$R_{\text{LCS}} = \frac{\text{LCS}(S_{\text{ref}}, S_{\text{pred}})}{|S_{\text{ref}}|} \tag{4}$$

$$P_{\text{LCS}} = \frac{\text{LCS}(S_{\text{ref}}, S_{\text{pred}})}{|S_{\text{pred}}|} \tag{5}$$

GeoClaim-ROUGE is defined in an F-score form as:

$$\text{GeoClaim-ROUGE} = \frac{(1+\beta^2)\, R_{\text{LCS}} \cdot P_{\text{LCS}}}{R_{\text{LCS}} + \beta^2 P_{\text{LCS}}} \tag{6}$$

where β=1, yielding an F1-style ROUGE-L variant at the claim level.

The fundamental distinction between GeoClaim metrics and traditional automatic metrics such as BLEU and ROUGE lies in the level of comparison. While BLEU and ROUGE operate on tokens or n-grams and implicitly assume that lexical overlap correlates with factual correctness, GeoClaim metrics perform comparison after normalization and verification at the claim level [34]. This shift allows semantically equivalent facts, such as paraphrased spatial descriptions or unit-converted quantities, to be treated consistently, while explicitly penalizing small but critical factual errors that token-level metrics overlook.

By grounding evaluation in verified geoscientific facts, GeoClaim metrics offer a more faithful and interpretable assessment of answer quality for mineral exploration QA and other fact-sensitive scientific applications, where factual accuracy, rather than stylistic similarity, determines practical usefulness and safety.

3.4 Geo-Judge: Evidence-Guided LLM-as-Judge

While GeoClaim metrics provide reliable and interpretable automatic evaluation at the factual level, open-ended geoscientific question answering also requires holistic judgment of structure, coherence, and usefulness. However, naïvely applying large language models as judges is known to produce unstable and biased evaluations, particularly in fact-sensitive domains where fluent but incorrect answers may be overvalued [35]. GeoClaim therefore introduces Geo-Judge, an evidence-guided LLM-as-Judge mechanism that injects programmable fact-verification results into the judging process.

Geo-Judge constrains subjective scoring by grounding the judge in verified evidence via evidence strips, which summarize extracted geo-claims together with their labels (correct, incorrect, or unverifiable). These strips are embedded in the prompt as mandatory evidence, discouraging judgments driven by surface fluency while preserving the flexibility of holistic evaluation.

To further enhance reliability, Geo-Judge adopts a multi-judge evaluation strategy in which multiple independent judging runs are performed under the same evidence-guided protocol [36]. Judge agreement is quantified with rank-based correlations, outliers are detected, and stability is tested under controlled perturbations (e.g., prompt phrasing, initialization, and evidence order). Together, evidence guidance and multi-judge calibration make Geo-Judge a robust complement to GeoClaim metrics for fact-sensitive, open-ended geoscientific QA.

4 Experiments and Results

4.1 Experimental Setup

We design the experimental evaluation around three questions—validity, reliability, and usefulness—to assess GeoClaim for open-ended mineral exploration QA (Fig. 2). These dimensions capture alignment with expert judgment, robustness under uncertainty, and practical utility for model comparison and selection.

Specifically, the experiments aim to answer:

Fig. 2. Experimental Design and Evaluation Questions

(1) Validity: Do GeoClaim's scores align more closely with geoscience experts' judgments than traditional automatic metrics?
(2) Reliability: Are GeoClaim's conclusions more stable under different judges and controlled perturbations?
(3) Usefulness: When used for model selection or tuning, does GeoClaim lead to choices that are preferred by human experts?

Accordingly, we conduct human evaluation, compare against baseline metrics, and test stability under multi-judge and perturbation settings.

We curate 200 mineral-exploration QA pairs covering spatial relations, coordinates, numerical measurements, and unit-based quantitative reasoning, with expert reference answers as ground truth. We generate answers using four LLMs with diverse backgrounds: GeoGPT, DeepSeek-V3.2, Qwen3-Max, and GPT-5.1, spanning domain-specialized and general-purpose behaviors.

Three geoscience graduate students independently score model outputs using a rubric for factual accuracy, completeness, and professionalism. Scores are averaged across evaluators to form reference judgments for system-level comparison.

We compare GeoClaim with BLEU and ROUGE-L as surface-overlap baselines, and include GeoClaim-F1 and GeoClaim-ROUGE (Sect. 3) for fact-level evaluation based on verified geo-claims. We report correlations with expert scores using Spearman's rank correlation and Kendall's τ for ranking agreement.

We assess reliability under judge inconsistency and input perturbation. Vanilla LLM-as-Judge is compared with Geo-Judge using inter-judge agreement, score variance, and correlation with human mean scores across repeated runs. Controlled perturbations (e.g., prompt phrasing and evaluation order) test whether GeoClaim and Geo-Judge remain stable under superficial changes.

All experiments are conducted under a unified software and hardware environment to ensure reproducibility. The software stack includes Python 3.11, Transformers 4.51.1, and PyTorch 2.5.1 (CUDA-enabled). Experiments are executed on a high-performance computing platform equipped with an Intel i9-14900KF CPU, 128 GB of memory, and an NVIDIA RTX 4090 D GPU.

4.2 Correlation with Human Judgments

To evaluate validity, we analyze correlations between automatic metrics and expert judgments on the curated 200-question mineral-exploration QA benchmark. For each question, the four model outputs are evaluated using both human scoring and automatic metrics.

Each (question, reference answer, model answer) instance is independently assessed by three geoscience graduate students using the rubric in Sect. 4.1, covering factual accuracy, completeness, and professionalism. Human scores are averaged to produce system-level reference judgments. On the same outputs, we compute the metrics described above and include FActScore to compare lexical overlap metrics, prior fact-based approaches, and GeoClaim.

Figure 3 compares model performance across metrics. BLEU and ROUGE-L show limited discriminative power and do not reliably reflect factual quality, whereas GeoClaim-F1 and GeoClaim-ROUGE better separate the four systems, highlighting differences in factual correctness that are obscured by lexical overlap.

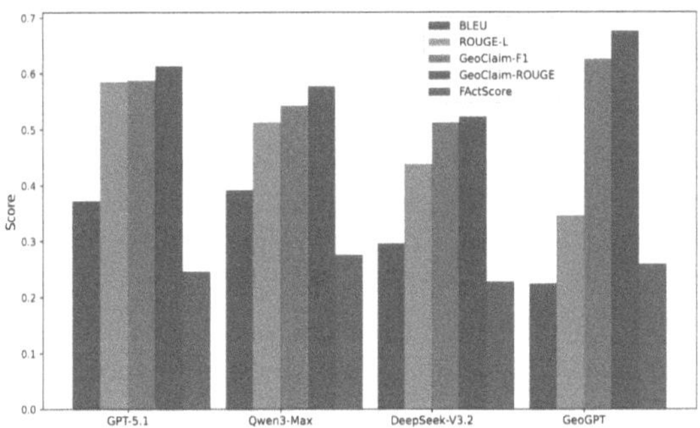

Fig. 3. Comparison of Model Performance Across Different Evaluation Metrics

Figure 4 reports system-level Spearman rank correlations between automatic metrics and human judgments on factual accuracy, completeness, and professionalism. BLEU and ROUGE-L show weak or negative correlations, and FActScore is only modestly correlated. In contrast, GeoClaim-F1 and GeoClaim-ROUGE exhibit consistently high positive correlations across all three dimensions, indicating strong alignment with expert assessment.

These results confirm that GeoClaim metrics more faithfully reflect expert evaluation criteria than traditional text-based metrics. In particular, the high correlation with factual accuracy underscores the effectiveness of claim-level verification, while the strong alignment with completeness and professionalism suggests that fact-centric evaluation also captures broader aspects of answer quality valued by domain experts. Overall, this experiment provides clear evidence that GeoClaim achieves superior validity as an automatic evaluation framework for mineral exploration QA.

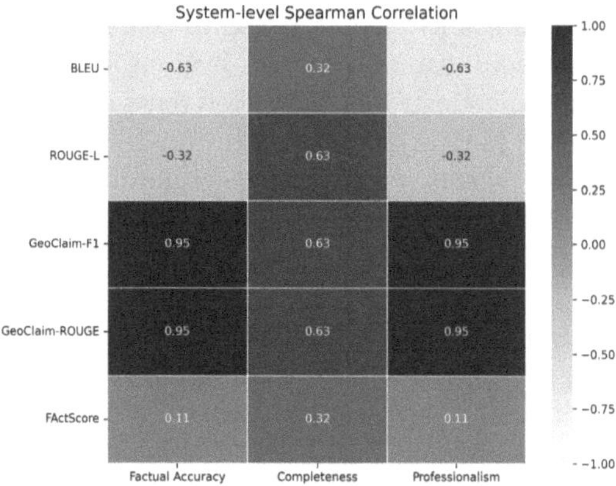

Fig. 4. System-Level Spearman Correlation Between Automatic Metrics and Human Judgments

4.3 Judge Consistency and Stability

To evaluate the reliability of Geo-Judge, we conduct a series of multi-judge and stability experiments comparing Geo-Judge with a vanilla LLM-as-Judge baseline and human evaluators. The goal of these experiments is to assess whether evidence-guided judging produces evaluations that are more consistent with human experts, more coherent across judges, and more stable under stochastic variation.

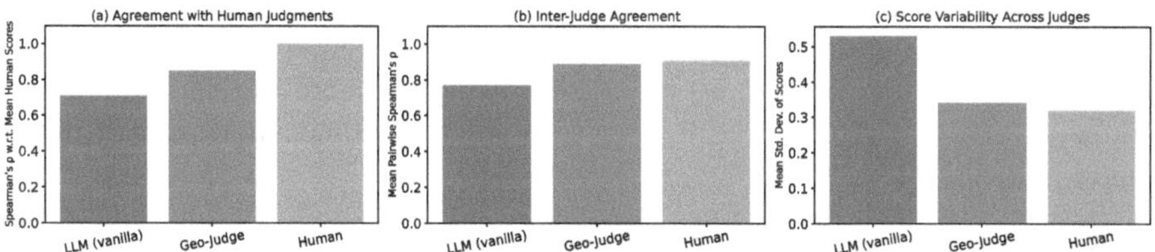

Fig. 5. Judge consistency and stability across three evaluation criteria: (a) agreement with human judgments measured by Spearman's ρ w.r.t. mean human scores; (b) inter-judge agreement measured by mean pairwise Spearman's ρ; and (c) score variability across judges measured by mean standard deviation of scores (lower indicates higher stability).

We first examine how closely different judging approaches align with human expert judgments. Specifically, we compute Spearman's rank correlation (ρ) between judge-assigned scores and the mean human scores, aggregated at the system level across models.

As shown in Fig. 5(a), the vanilla LLM-as-Judge exhibits only moderate agreement with human experts. In contrast, Geo-Judge achieves a substantially higher Spearman's ρ, indicating that evidence-guided judging produces evaluations that are significantly closer to expert consensus. Although a small gap remains between Geo-Judge and human evaluators, the improvement over unguided LLM judging demonstrates the effectiveness of incorporating verified factual evidence into the judging process.

This result supports the hypothesis that grounding judgments in explicit fact-verification outcomes reduces the tendency of LLM judges to overemphasize fluency or stylistic factors that are less relevant to expert assessment in geoscientific QA.

Next, we analyze inter-judge agreement, quantified by the mean pairwise Spearman's ρ among multiple independent judging runs. This metric captures the extent to which different judges produce consistent relative rankings of model performance.

Figure 5(b) shows that vanilla LLM judges achieve only moderate inter-judge agreement, reflecting substantial variability in their evaluations. Geo-Judge markedly improves agreement, with mean pairwise Spearman's ρ approaching that of human evaluators. This indicates that evidence strips effectively constrain the judging process, reducing subjective interpretation and variability across judges.

The improved inter-judge agreement demonstrates that Geo-Judge not only aligns better with experts on average, but also produces more coherent and reproducible evaluations across independent judging instances.

Finally, we examine score variability as a direct measure of evaluation stability. For each judging method, we compute the mean standard deviation (Std. Dev.) of scores assigned across judges, where lower dispersion indicates higher stability.

As shown in Fig. 5(c), vanilla LLM-as-Judge exhibits the highest score variability, indicating unstable and inconsistent ratings across judges. Geo-Judge substantially reduces score dispersion, resulting in more stable evaluations. Human evaluators remain the most consistent, providing an empirical upper bound on achievable stability.

This reduction in dispersion highlights a key advantage of evidence-guided judging: by anchoring decisions to verified factual evidence, Geo-Judge narrows the range of plausible judgments and mitigates stochastic fluctuations inherent to generative models.

4.4 Model Ranking Consistency

Beyond system-level correlation, an evaluation metric must support practical model comparison and selection in geoscientific QA. We therefore test whether different automatic metrics induce model rankings consistent with human expert judgments.

We construct a human overall quality ranking by aggregating expert scores across rubric dimensions, and compare it with rankings produced by BLEU, ROUGE-L, GeoClaim-F1, GeoClaim-ROUGE, and FActScore. Agreement is quantified using Spearman's rank correlation (ρ) and Kendall's τ, capturing monotonic and pairwise consistency.

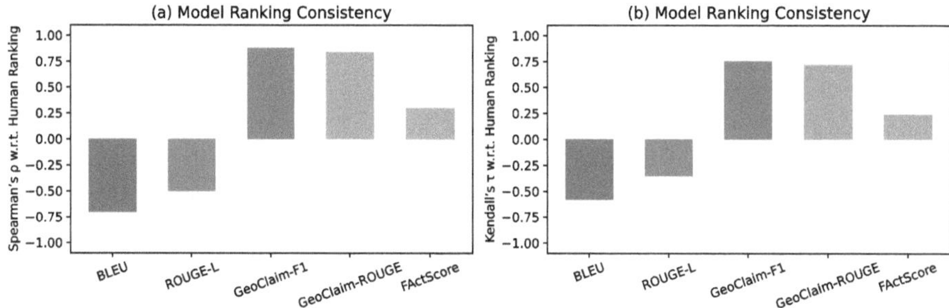

Fig. 6. Model ranking consistency with human judgments: (a) Spearman's ρ and (b) Kendall's τ.

Figure 6(a) and Fig. 6(b) report the ranking agreement results. BLEU and ROUGE-L perform poorly, producing rankings inconsistent with expert judgments and exhibiting negative correlation under both measures (BLEU: $\rho = -0.70$, $\tau = -0.58$; ROUGE-L: $\rho = -0.50$, $\tau = -0.35$), indicating that surface-level similarity is unreliable for model comparison in fact-sensitive geoscientific QA. In contrast, GeoClaim-F1 and GeoClaim-ROUGE achieve strong ranking agreement with human experts (GeoClaim-F1: $\rho = 0.88$, $\tau = 0.75$; GeoClaim-ROUGE: $\rho = 0.84$, $\tau = 0.72$), demonstrating that claim-level evaluation preserves the relative strengths and weaknesses of models. FActScore shows only weak positive correlation ($\rho = 0.30$, $\tau = 0.24$), suggesting limited but insufficient ranking signal.

Overall, this experiment confirms that GeoClaim provides reliable guidance for model selection in geoscientific QA by grounding evaluation in verified domain facts rather than surface textual overlap.

5 Discussion and Conclusion

We introduce GeoClaim, a fact-centric evaluation framework that shifts geoscientific QA assessment from surface-level overlap to verifiable factual correctness. By decomposing answers into atomic geo-claims and verifying them with domain computation, GeoClaim supports spatial and quantitative precision. Geo-Judge further operationalizes this idea by injecting verified evidence into LLM-based judging, improving consistency and stability. Together, these results suggest a general paradigm for high-stakes evaluation: decompose outputs into factual units, verify them, and integrate verification outcomes into both metrics and judging.

GeoClaim remains limited by knowledge-base coverage and residual LLM bias. Our current verification focuses on topology, CRS, and unit consistency, while higher-level geological reasoning (e.g., structural evolution and ore genesis) is still difficult to validate automatically. Future work will expand knowledge sources (e.g., survey APIs), incorporate uncertainty-aware scoring for unverifiable claims, strengthen evidence-grounded judge training, and extend verification modules to richer geological logic.

Acknowledgment. This work was supported by the National Key R&D Program of China (No. 2022YFF0711601) and the National Natural Science Foundation of China (No. 42301492).

Disclosure of Interests. The authors declare no competing interests.

References

1. Schmidtová, P., et al.: Automatic metrics in natural language generation: a survey of current evaluation practices. arXiv preprint arXiv:2408.09169 (2024)
2. Samad, A. S., Sushma, R., Mohan, G. B., et al.: Advancing abstractive summarization: evaluating GPT-2, BART, T5-Small, and Pegasus models with baseline in ROUGE and BLEU metrics. In: Proceedings of the International Conference on Innovations in Cybersecurity and Data Science (ICICDS), pp. 119–131. Springer, Singapore (2024)
3. Chinthalapelly, P.R., Selvaraj, A., Murthy, C.J.: Evaluating LLM outputs for legal contracts using BLEU, ROUGE, and BERTScore. Am. J. Data Sci. Artif. Intell. Innov. **4**, 229–262 (2024)
4. Smee, B. W., Bloom, L., Arne, D., et al.: Practical applications of quality assurance and quality control in mineral exploration, resource estimation and mining programmes: a review of recommended international practices. Geochem. Explorat. Environ. Anal. **24**(2), geochem2023–046 (2024)
5. Fu, Y., Wang, M., Wang, C., et al.: GeoMinLM: a large language model in geology and mineral survey in Yunnan Province. Ore Geol. Rev. 106638 (2025)
6. Chen, Z., Wang, X., Zhang, X., et al.: GeoFactory: an LLM performance enhancement framework for geoscience factual and inferential tasks. Big Earth Data –33 (2025)
7. Chang, Y., Wang, X., Wang, J., et al.: A survey on evaluation of large language models. ACM Trans. Intell. Syst. Technol. **15**(3), 1–45 (2024)
8. Zhou, P., Peng, X., Song, J., et al.: OpenING: a comprehensive benchmark for judging open-ended interleaved image-text generation. In: Proceedings of the IEEE/CVF Conference on Computer Vision and Pattern Recognition (CVPR), pp. 56–66 (2025)
9. Liu, S., Gemp, I., Marris, L., et al.: Re-evaluating open-ended evaluation of large language models. arXiv preprint arXiv:2502.20170 (2025)
10. Li, D., Jiang, B., Huang, L., et al.: From generation to judgment: opportunities and challenges of LLM-as-a-judge. In: Proceedings of the 2025 Conference on Empirical Methods in Natural Language Processing (EMNLP), pp. 2757–2791 (2025)
11. Cao, Z., Ma, Z., Chen, M.: An evaluation system for large language models based on open-ended questions. In: Proceedings of the 2024 IEEE 11th International Conference on Cyber Security and Cloud Computing (CSCloud), pp. 65–72. IEEE (2024)
12. Zhao, W., Liu, Y., Niu, T., et al.: DIVKNOWQA: assessing the reasoning ability of LLMs via open-domain question answering over knowledge base and text. In: Findings of the Association for Computational Linguistics: NAACL 2024, pp. 51–68 (2024)

13. Shafayat, S., Kim, E., Oh, J., et al.: Multi-fact: assessing factuality of multilingual LLMs using FActScore. arXiv preprint arXiv:2402.18045 (2024)
14. Chen, Y. S., Jin, J., Kuo, P. T., et al.: LLMs are biased evaluators but not biased for fact-centric retrieval augmented generation. In: Findings of the Association for Computational Linguistics: ACL 2025, pp. 26669–26684 (2025)
15. Zhou, B., Li, K.: Fusing geoscience large language models and lightweight RAG for enhanced geological question answering. Geosciences **15**(10), 382 (2025)
16. Li, H., Dong, Q., Chen, J., et al.: LLMs-as-judges: a comprehensive survey on LLM-based evaluation methods. arXiv preprint arXiv:2412.05579 (2024)
17. Yu, B., Shen, T., Na, H., et al.: MineAgent: towards remote-sensing mineral exploration with multimodal large language models. arXiv preprint arXiv:2412.17339 (2024)
18. Dorner, F.E., Nastl, V.Y., Hardt, M.: Limits to scalable evaluation at the frontier: LLM as judge will not beat twice the data. arXiv preprint arXiv:2410.13341 (2024)
19. Jayakumar, E., Dash, N. S., Mukherjee, D.: Large language model agent personality and response appropriateness: evaluation by human linguistic experts, LLM-as-judge, and natural language processing models. arXiv preprint arXiv:2510.23875 (2025)
20. Zhou, X., Kim, K., Zhang, T., et al.: An LLM-as-judge metric for bridging the gap with human evaluation in SE tasks. arXiv preprint arXiv:2505.20854 (2025)
21. Xu, A., Bansal, S., Ming, Y., et al.: Does context matter? ContextualJudgeBench for evaluating LLM-based judges in contextual settings. arXiv preprint arXiv:2503.15620 (2025)
22. Dechtiar, M., Katz, D. M., Jaume, S., et al.: LLM as a judge for evaluating contract graphs: multi-judge benchmarking and agentic uncertainty-aware refinement. SSRN 5937996 (2025)
23. Hu, L., Li, W., Xu, J., et al.: GeoEntity-type constrained knowledge graph embedding for predicting natural-language spatial relations. Int. J. Geogr. Inf. Sci. **39**(2), 376–399 (2025)
24. Raz, T., Luchini, S., Beaty, R., et al.: Automated scoring of open-ended question complexity: a large language model approach (2024)
25. Zhang, K., Wu, P., Yu, B., et al.: Logical rule-constrained large language models for document-level relation extraction. In: Proceedings of the CCF International Conference on Natural Language Processing and Chinese Computing, pp. 132–145. Springer, Singapore (2025)
26. Dmonte, A., Oruche, R., Zampieri, M., et al.: Claim verification in the age of large language models: a survey. arXiv preprint arXiv:2408.14317 (2024)
27. Wang, H., Pan, Y., Song, X., et al.: F2RL: factuality and faithfulness reinforcement learning framework for claim-guided evidence-supported counterspeech generation. In: Proceedings of the 2024 Conference on Empirical Methods in Natural Language Processing (EMNLP), pp. 4457–4470 (2024)
28. Dagdelen, J., Dunn, A., Lee, S., et al.: Structured information extraction from scientific text with large language models. Nat. Commun. **15**(1), 1418 (2024)
29. Cui, M., Huang, R., Hu, Z., et al.: Semantic rule-based information extraction for meteorological reports. Int. J. Mach. Learn. Cybern. **15**(1), 177–188 (2024)
30. Zhao, X., Deng, Y., Yang, M., et al.: A comprehensive survey on relation extraction: recent advances and new frontiers. ACM Comput. Surv. **56**(11), 1–39 (2024)
31. Li, F., Hogg, D. C., Cohn, A. G.: Advancing spatial reasoning in large language models: an in-depth evaluation and enhancement using the StepGame benchmark. In: Proceedings of the AAAI Conference on Artificial Intelligence, vol. 38, no. 17, pp. 18500–18507 (2024)

32. Sykes, B., Simon, L., Rabin, J.: Unifying and extending precision–recall metrics for assessing generative models. arXiv preprint arXiv:2405.01611 (2024)
33. Diaz, F., Ekstrand, M.D., Mitra, B.: Recall, robustness, and lexicographic evaluation. ACM Trans. Recommend. Syst. (2025)
34. Davoodijam, E., Alambardar Meybodi, M.: Evaluation metrics on text summarization: a comprehensive survey. Knowl. Inf. Syst. **66**(12), 7717–7738 (2024)
35. Choi, J.H.: Large language models are unreliable judges. SSRN 5188865 (2025)
36. Tang, Y., Feng, K., Wang, Y., et al.: Learning an efficient multi-turn dialogue evaluator from multiple judges. arXiv preprint arXiv:2508.00454 (2025)

PerfMamba: Performance Analysis and Pruning of Selective State Space Models

Abdullah Al Asif[1(✉)], Mobina Kashaniyan[1], Sixing Yu[1], Juan Pablo Muñoz[2], and Ali Jannesari[1(✉)]

[1] Iowa State University, Ames, IA, USA
{aaasif,mobina,yusx,jannesar}@iastate.edu
[2] Intel Labs, Santa Clara, CA, USA
pablo.munoz@intel.com

Abstract. Recent advances in sequence modeling have introduced selective SSMs as promising alternatives to Transformer architectures, offering theoretical computational efficiency and sequence processing advantages. A comprehensive understanding of selective SSMs in runtime behavior, resource utilization patterns, and scaling characteristics still remains unexplored, thus obstructing their optimal deployment and further architectural improvements. This paper presents a thorough empirical study of Mamba-1 and Mamba-2, systematically profiled for performance to assess the design principles that contribute to their efficiency in state-space modeling. A detailed analysis of computation patterns, memory access, I/O characteristics, and scaling properties was performed for sequence lengths ranging from 64 to 16384 tokens. Our findings show that the SSM component, a central part of the selective SSM architecture, demands a significant portion of computational resources compared to other components in the Mamba block. Based on these insights, we propose a pruning technique that selectively removes low-activity states within the SSM component, achieving measurable throughput and memory gains while maintaining accuracy within a moderate pruning regime. This approach results in performance improvements across varying sequence lengths, achieving a 1.14x speedup and reducing memory usage by 11.50%. These results offer valuable guidance for designing more efficient SSM architectures that can be applied to a wide range of real-world applications.

Keywords: Selective State Space Models (SSMs) · Model Profiling · Performance Optimization

1 Introduction

Large language models (LLMs) have revolutionized natural language processing, yet their computational efficiency remains a critical challenge. While

J. Zhan et al. (Eds.): Bench 2025, LNCS 16471, pp. 27–44, 2026.
https://doi.org/10.1007/978-981-95-9694-2_3

Transformer-based architectures dominate the field [22], their quadratic attention mechanism has spurred research into alternative architectures. Selective State Space Models (SSMs) have emerged as a promising direction, offering theoretical advantages through their linear scaling properties and efficient sequence modeling capabilities [11].

SSMs represent a fundamental shift in sequence modeling, replacing attention mechanisms with state space dynamics that capture long-range dependencies and local patterns. Recent implementations, including Mamba-1, Mamba-2 [7], and other variants, have demonstrated 5x higher throughput and 1.7x lower memory usage compared to similarly sized Transformer models during inference [11]. This property makes them attractive for applications in natural language processing, speech, and time series, where long-range dependencies are common. Despite their growing adoption, however, the computational behavior of SSMs remains underexplored. In particular, it is unclear which internal components dominate runtime costs and how these costs scale with sequence length, leaving open questions about where to direct optimization efforts.

In this work, we present **PerfMamba**, a study of the computational characteristics of Mamba-1 and Mamba-2. We profile their components across a range of sequence lengths (64–16k) and identify the SSM update as the significant cost driver, consistently accounting for more than half of the total computation and memory. This finding highlights a specific target to improve the efficiency of SSMs without altering their expressive power. Motivated by this observation, we propose *Δ-guided structured state pruning*, a novel method that exploits a signal unique to SSMs. Each Mamba layer computes an input-dependent continuous-time gate, Δ, which modulates how strongly state channels retain or overwrite information. We show that averaging Δ values across data provides a simple but effective activity measure for each state channel. By removing channels with consistently low activity and introducing a lightweight bridging linear to preserve compatibility, we reduce the dimensionality of the SSM state space in a structured way. Unlike weight sparsification or unstructured pruning used in other architectures, our method directly targets the state dimension of SSMs, making it both principled and architecture-specific.

We evaluated this technique on Mamba-2-130M with sequence lengths up to 16k. Our experiments show that Δ-guided pruning improves throughput and reduces memory footprint at long sequences. Accuracy remains stable in a moderate pruning regime ($\leq$ 30% of states pruned), while more aggressive pruning exposes clear trade-offs across tasks. Beyond efficiency, this analysis also reveals how state activity is distributed across layers and datasets, providing additional interpretability into SSM dynamics.

This paper makes three key contributions:

1. We conduct the first component-level profiling study of Mamba-1 and Mamba-2, identifying detailed resource consumption patterns for the core components of Mamba blocks. This breakdown provides actionable insights to guide optimization priorities and highlights components requiring further enhancements to improve both temporal and spatial efficiency.

2. We present empirically derived best practices for deploying State Space Models (SSMs), showing how effective hardware–software co-optimization can preserve accuracy while delivering substantial efficiency gains across diverse sequence lengths.
3. Building on these insights, we demonstrate that the proposed optimizations improve inference throughput by up to 1.14× compared to baseline implementations, while also achieving memory savings of up to 11.5% in the state update phase for long sequences.

The remainder of this paper is organized as follows: Sects. 2 and 3 provide the necessary background on SSMs and related work in sequence model profiling. Section 4 describes our profiling methodology and presents detailed findings and analysis. Section 5 discusses the implications of our profiling results and presents an efficient pruning method for the state of the SSM, along with its implementation. Section 6 presents the results and evaluation of our pruning approach. Finally, Sect. 7 concludes with recommendations for future research and development.

2 Background

Mamba [11] is a sequence model that replaces the quadratic-cost attention in Transformers [22] with selective state space models (SSMs). This gives linear-time complexity in sequence length while retaining strong modeling accuracy.

2.1 State Space Models

An SSM maintains a hidden state $h(t)$ that summarizes past inputs. It updates $h(t)$ linearly from the previous state and the current input, and produces an output $y(t)$:

$$h'(t) = Ah(t) + Bx(t), \tag{1}$$

$$y(t) = Ch(t). \tag{2}$$

Here, A is the transition matrix, B and C are input/output projections, N is the number of state channels, and D is the hidden size.

2.2 Discretization and Gating

To make this computable, Mamba discretizes the equations using a learnable timescale Δ_t:

$$A_t = \exp(\Delta_t A), \tag{3}$$

$$B_t = (\Delta_t A)^{-1}(\exp(\Delta_t A) - I)\,\Delta_t B. \tag{4}$$

The parameter Δ_t acts as a gate: large values down-weight past states, while small values preserve them [10].

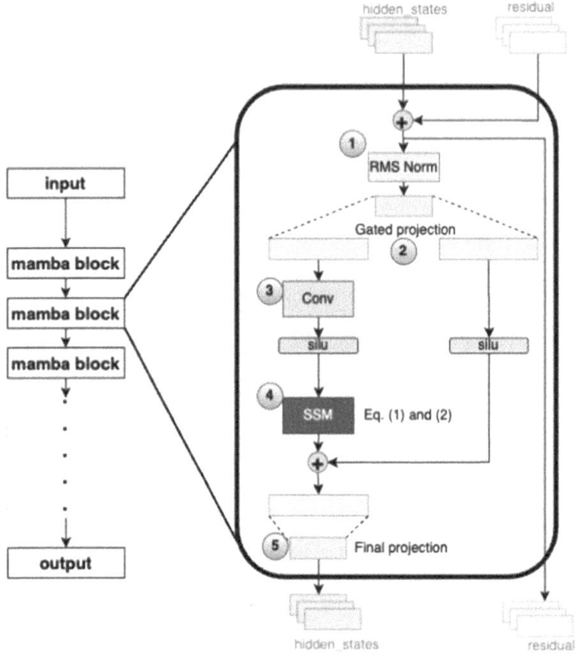

Fig. 1. Mamba block. Input is normalized, gated, convolved, and passed through a selective SSM, then projected back to the hidden size with residual connections.

2.3 Mamba-2: State Space Duality

Mamba-2 extends this with *state space duality* (SSD) [15], which provides two complementary views:

$$h_t = A_t h_{t-1} + B_t x_t, \qquad y_t = C_t^\top h_t, \tag{5}$$

$$y = (L \circ QK^\top)V. \tag{6}$$

The first (recurrent) form is efficient ($O(N)$), while the second (quadratic) form shows attention-like behavior. Together, SSD combines efficiency with expressiveness.

2.4 Block Design

Each Mamba block (Fig. 1) applies normalization and gating, then a convolution and the SSM, before projecting back to the hidden dimension with residuals. Variants like the multi-input SSM (MIS) and extra normalization layers [7,20] improve efficiency and stability.

As the model is channelized (N states) and each state is modulated by Δ_t, we can measure the activity of individual channels and prune the inactive ones, motivating our method in Sect. 5.

3 Related Work

Structured State Space Models. Linear State-Space Layers (LSSLs) unify RNNs, CNNs, and continuous-time models for scalable sequence learning and strong long-range dependence modeling [13]. More broadly, Structured State Space Models (SSMs) provide an effective alternative to Transformers via structured dynamics [12]. Building on time-variant selectivity, Mamba introduces input conditioned state updates to retain or discard information efficiently, achieving state-of-the-art results across modalities with near-linear scaling [11,23]. Surveys summarize Mamba's advances and open problems [31]. Mamba-2 further connects SSMs and attention through State Space Duality (SSD) and structured semiseparable matrices, yielding 2–8× speedups while remaining competitive for language modeling [7].

Network Pruning. Pruning removes less important parameters to cut compute, memory, and energy [14]. Complementary tooling supports profiling/monitoring of deep learning workloads and GPU performance analysis, including top-down methodologies and HPCToolkit for scalable bottleneck diagnosis [2,28,33]. Unstructured pruning yields sparse weights that often require specialized hardware, whereas structured pruning removes channels/filters/layers for hardware-friendly speedups [27]. Comprehensive surveys cover taxonomies, timing (pre-/post-training), and combinations with other compression (e.g., quantization) [5]. Scheduling matters: policy-based early structural pruning can reduce cost while preserving accuracy [19]; forward-pass-only structured pruning enables practical LLM compression without backpropagation [9]. Structured pruning can also improve generalization [25]. For LLMs, formulating pruning as a Multiple Removal Problem improves post-training efficiency [32]. In SSMs, fine-grained token reduction exploiting importance and similarity boosts efficiency for models like Mamba-2 [30]. Mamba-specific compression achieves up to 1.4× inference speedup while maintaining accuracy [17]. Analyses show Mamba exhibits emergent attention-like behavior that supports long-range dependencies [3]; hardware co-design such as MARCA delivers reconfigurable, energy-efficient acceleration [16]. Extensions include MambaTree for tree-structured long-range modeling [26] and MambaSpike, which integrates spiking front-ends for low-power temporal processing [18].

4 Component-Level Performance Analysis

This section evaluates Mamba components (Mamba-1 and Mamba-2) on memory cost, Time-to-First-Token (TTFT, Prefill), Time-per-Output-Token (TPOT, Decoding), and overall performance. We measure FLOPs, execution time, memory usage, and I/O parameters. All profiling runs use NVIDIA A100 (40 GB) with the PyTorch profiler [1]; traces are exported as JSON and parsed. To reduce non-systematic noise, we perform three warm-up runs and then repeat measurements multiple times, reporting means. Experiments span sequence lengths around the 64 and 2048 token regimes at a fixed batch size of 8, to probe varying compute/memory regimes.

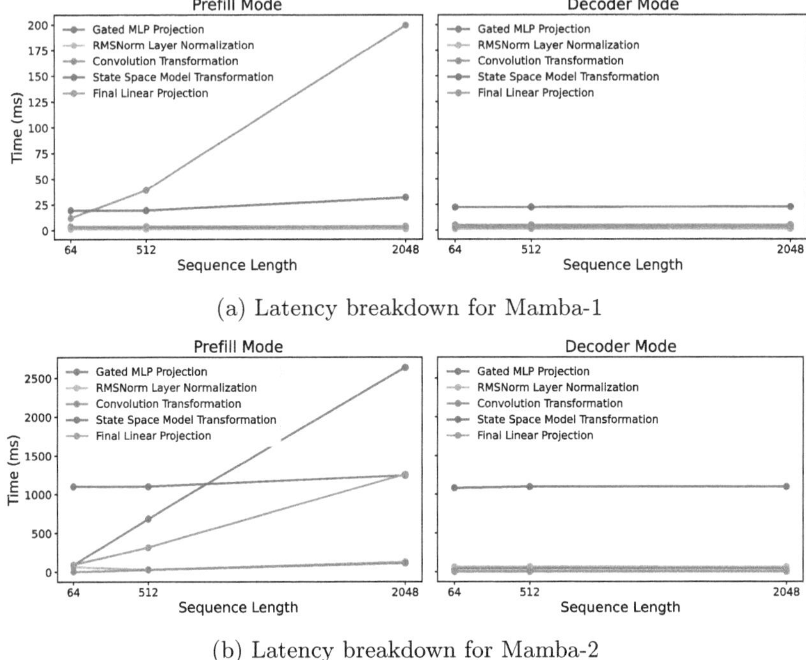

(a) Latency breakdown for Mamba-1

(b) Latency breakdown for Mamba-2

Fig. 2. Latency breakdown of individual components in Mamba-1 and Mamba-2 across Prefill and Decoder modes.

We analyze Gated MLP, Convolution, SSM Transformation, Final Projection, and Normalization—key stages in Mamba's pipeline [11]. Gated MLP supplies nonlinear feature transforms; Convolution captures local structure; SSM Transformation replaces attention for long-sequence modeling; Final Projection maps to output space; Normalization stabilizes training. For both Mamba-1 and Mamba-2, we extract per-layer time and memory by matching kernel launches to GPU allocations; the script iterates trace events to aggregate layer metrics. Total FLOPs are estimated from theoretical counts of matrix multiplies, activations, and convolutions [8], using the HuggingFace implementations of Mamba-1/2 [24].

Our goal is to locate optimization opportunities—e.g., eliminating redundant computation, refactoring memory access, and improving parallel execution. From component-level cost profiles, we identify bottlenecks and candidate improvements; the following subsections report detailed results and their implications for Mamba efficiency.

4.1 Latency Analysis

Latency in Mamba arises in two modes: *Prefill* and *Decoder*. Prefill processes the entire sequence at once to initialize states, while Decoder generates tokens one by one using these states. Prefill is length-dependent and costly; Decoder is length-independent and dominates real-world inference such as autoregressive generation.

In Prefill, Mamba-1 is bottlenecked by the convolution:

$$y_t = \sum_{i=0}^{k-1} W_i x_{t-i},$$

which scales as $O(kL^2)$ with sequence length L due to sequential dependencies (Fig. 2a). Mamba-2 reduces this cost using 2D scanning,

$$y_t = \text{Conv2D}(X_{t,s}) + \text{SSM}(\text{Scan}(X_{t,s})),$$

achieving $O(kL)$ complexity (Fig. 2b). The main prefill bottleneck then shifts to the gated MLP, where

$$[z_x \,\|\, B \,\|\, C \,\|\, \Delta_t] = W_{\text{proj}} x_t,$$

requires $O(\gamma DNL)$ operations, with state dimension N and expansion factor γ.

In Decoder mode, costs change fundamentally. Convolution and projection overheads vanish because only one new token is processed at a time. Each step requires a single SSM recurrence,

$$h_t = A_t h_{t-1} + B_t x_t,$$

whose $O(N)$ cost is independent of L. As a result, the SSM is always the dominant component in Decoder latency. Other layers (normalization, output projection) add constant, negligible overhead.

In summary, Prefill bottlenecks differ by architecture (convolution in Mamba-1, gated MLP in Mamba-2), but in Decoder mode—the critical path for practical inference—the SSM consistently dominates latency. This makes SSM optimization the most effective route to real-world speedups.

4.2 Memory Analysis

Memory usage in Mamba is dominated by the State Space Model (SSM) component. At a sequence length of 2048, Mamba-2's SSM consumes 33.5% more memory than Mamba-1 (115.68 GB vs. 86.64 GB) due to block-wise state materialization, which improves cache efficiency but increases memory demand. Localized state transitions in Mamba-2 reduce redundant updates, partly offsetting this cost. The Gated MLP in Mamba-2 achieves 11.6% lower memory usage (10.32 GB vs. 11.52 GB) via parallel parameter generation, optimizing layout and reducing overhead for large sequences. Smaller layers such as RMSNorm scale predictably with $O(BLD)$, e.g., from 0.5 GB at length 64 to 15.75 GB at 2048 in Mamba-2, mainly for per-channel statistics. While minor in overall usage, they help explain scaling trends in larger components (Table 1).

Table 1. Component-wise Resource Utilization in Mamba-1 and Mamba-2 Architectures

Seq	Component	FLOPs (G)		Memory (GB)		I/O (GB/s)		Latency (ms)	
		M-1	M-2	M-1	M-2	M-1	M-2	M-1	M-2
64	RMSNorm	0.06	0.06	0.75	0.5	0.0016	0.08	3.20	2.90
	Gated MLP	2.42	29.03	0.24	0.48	0.0039	0.45	4.08	3.99
	Conv. Transform	0.60	0.26	0.48	0.24	0.0032	0.19	9.40	0.21
	State Space	68.63	48.95	6.24	7.44	0.042	0.31	16.76	45.88
	Final Linear	28.99	14.50	0.96	0.48	0.0024	0.23	3.13	2.18
512	RMSNorm	0.45	0.45	6.25	4.0	0.01	0.6	2.02	1.37
	Gated MLP	19.37	232.23	2.64	0.2	0.03	1.87	26.16	28.51
	Conv. Transform	4.83	2.11	1.92	2.16	0.03	1.51	9.59	1.23
	State Space	548.49	391.64	22.08	29.76	0.34	2.47	23.73	35.87
	Final Linear	231.93	115.96	7.44	2.88	0.02	1.02	15.12	13.20
2048	RMSNorm	1.81	1.81	25.18	15.75	0.05	2.42	7.65	5.53
	Gated MLP	77.45	928.92	10.32	11.52	0.13	6.73	98.58	109.83
	Conv. Transform	19.33	8.46	7.44	8.4	0.10	6.04	12.81	4.78
	State Space	2193.73	1566.55	86.64	115.68	1.35	9.87	74.82	51.79
	Final Linear	927.71	463.86	23.04	5.04	0.08	3.74	59.99	52.35

4.3 Computational Complexity Analysis

The SSM is the most computationally intensive component, dominating FLOPs across both architectures. At a sequence length of 2048, Mamba-2 reduces FLOPs by 28.6% compared to Mamba-1 (1566.55G vs. 2193.73G) through block-wise processing, which minimizes redundant matrix multiplications and improves scalability without sacrificing throughput. The Gated MLP also benefits from parallel parameter projection, resulting in a 20.3% reduction in FLOPs at 2048 tokens and improved GPU utilization. Other layers, including RMSNorm and Convolutional Transformations, contribute only 5–10% of total FLOPs and remain consistent across models. These results underscore how targeted design choices in the SSM and Gated MLP significantly enhance computational efficiency.

4.4 Data Flow and Hardware Utilization

I/O bandwidth analysis reveals how computational components interact with memory hierarchies and GPU resources. The State Space Model (SSM) has the highest I/O demand due to recurrent state updates for long-range dependencies. Unlike standard matrix multiplications, its sequential data dependencies cause complex memory access patterns. Block-wise state transfers group states into contiguous regions, improving cache efficiency and reducing global memory fetches. This enables peak bandwidth of 9.87 GB/s at sequence length 2048—a

26.3% gain over a sequential layout—showing that localized state materialization better leverages GPU memory.

The Gated MLP, responsible for token embedding transformations, exhibits dense parameter reads and processes tokens independently, enabling parallelization. Its I/O bandwidth increases by over 51% for long sequences, underscoring the role of parallel parameter loading in minimizing stalls.

$$P_{\text{parallel}} = \left[x_t \parallel \Delta_t \parallel B_t \parallel C_t\right] \in \mathbb{R}^{B \times L \times (D+3N)} \tag{7}$$

Here, x_t are input embeddings, Δ_t the learned time-step scalars, and B_t, C_t the selective gating parameters; B, L, D, and N denote batch size, sequence length, hidden dimension, and state channels. Concatenating these allows simultaneous retrieval, exploiting GPU memory coalescing and reducing latency. RMSNorm, though minor in footprint, scales predictably with $O(BLD)$ and provides a baseline for I/O efficiency. Despite having few parameters, the SSM still dominates FLOPs, memory, and I/O usage, as confirmed by manual analysis from official code. Results may vary with GPU configurations.

5 Pruning Mamba's State Representation

Profiling in Sect. 4 identified the State Space Model (SSM) component as the primary computational bottleneck in both Mamba-1 and Mamba-2, accounting for 60–70% of total runtime and memory usage. Mamba-1 implements SSM via the Selective Structured State Space (S6) formulation, while Mamba-2 enhances this with the State Space Duality (SSD) framework [15]. Both variants employ a selective update mechanism for sequence processing, as described in Eqs. (1) and (2). The gating factor Δ_t is computed as:

$$\Delta_t = \text{softplus}(W_\Delta x_t), \tag{8}$$

and controls the balance between retaining the previous state h_{t-1} and incorporating new input x_t [11]. In practice, Mamba parameterizes A *diagonally* (state-wise) for efficiency; thus $A_t = \exp(\Delta_t A)$ is computed as per-state exponentials $a_{t,s} = \exp(\Delta_t a_s)$ rather than a dense matrix exponential [11]. Given that A is initialized with negative entries, large Δ_t values drive the corresponding exponentials toward zero, suppressing the recurrent term $A_t h_{t-1}$, allowing $B_t = \Delta_t B$ to dominate and yielding $h_t \approx B_t x_t$ (current input dominance). Conversely, when Δ_t is small, $A_t \approx I$ and $B_t \approx 0$, so $h_t \approx h_{t-1}$, preserving past state information with minimal new input influence.

Here, $A_t \in \mathbb{R}^{N \times N}$ is the state transition, $B_t \in \mathbb{R}^{N \times 1}$ is the input projection, $C \in \mathbb{R}^{1 \times N}$ is the output projection, and $N = d_{\text{state}}$ denotes the number of *state channels*. The hidden state vector $h_t \in \mathbb{R}^N$ consists of N scalar components, each representing one state s. A "state" in this context corresponds both to the s-th component of h_t and to the associated row and column in A_t, as well as the s-th entries in B_t and C.

For each layer l, we maintain a *state activity matrix*:

$$S_l \in \mathbb{R}^{d_{\text{state}} \times n_{\text{samples}}},$$

where $d_{\text{state}} = N$ and n_{samples} equals the total number of time steps evaluated (sequence length L times the number of sequences processed during profiling). The average activity of state s in layer l is:

$$\text{activity}(l, s) = \mathbb{E}_{x \sim \mathcal{D}} \left[\Delta_t^{(l,s)} \right], \tag{9}$$

where $\Delta_t^{(l,s)}$ is the s-th entry of the Δ_t vector in layer l. In Mamba-2's multi-head configuration, states are grouped into clusters of size $d_{\text{state}}/n_{\text{heads}}$ per head, enabling head-specific importance analysis (Sect. 2).

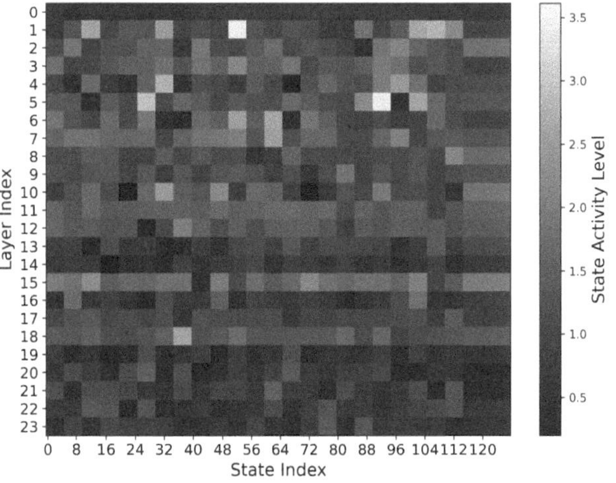

Fig. 3. State Importance Heatmap for Mamba2-130M: brighter colors indicate higher average Δ_t activity.

Figure 3 shows that certain states maintain low activity across most inputs, especially in early and late layers, while others are consistently high-activity. This suggests redundancy that can be exploited through pruning.

Pruning Approach. From Eq. (1), removing a state s entails zeroing the s-th row and column of A_t and the corresponding entries in B_t, C, and h_t. This effectively eliminates the recurrent and input/output contributions of that state without requiring the entire A_t to vanish. As states are parameterized independently by channel, pruning operates at the *channel level* and removes full (A, B, C) contributions for state s, avoiding the ambiguity of element-wise masking.

Algorithm 1 selects the $k = \lfloor N(1 - r) \rfloor$ most active channels for a pruning ratio r, using the activity scores from Eq. (10). After pruning, the state dimension is reduced from N to N', and the input projection W_{proj} is updated so

Algorithm 1. Activity-Based SSM State Selection (per layer l)

1: **Input:** input $X \in \mathbb{R}^{B\times L\times D}$, SSM parameters (A, B, C, Δ), state dimension N, pruning ratio r
2: **Output:** pruned hidden state $h_{t,\text{bridge}} \in \mathbb{R}^N$
3: **Step 1: Score states**
4: Initialize activity scores $s \in \mathbb{R}^N$
5: **for** $s = 1 \dots N$ **do**
6: Compute gating values $\Delta_t^{(s)}$ for X (Eq. 9)
7: $s[s] \leftarrow \mathbb{E}[\Delta_t^{(s)}]$ (Eq. 10)
8: **end for**
9: **Step 2: Select active states**
10: $k \leftarrow \lfloor N(1-r) \rfloor$
11: $I_{\text{keep}} \leftarrow \text{Top-}k(s)$
12: **return** I_{keep}

that it no longer produces parameters for the removed channels. Because later layers are implemented to expect the original size N, we add a *bridging layer* $W_{\text{bridge}} \in \mathbb{R}^{N\times N'}$. This layer takes the reduced hidden state $h_{t,\text{keep}} \in \mathbb{R}^{N'}$ and maps it back to $h_{t,\text{bridge}} \in \mathbb{R}^N$. In this way, normalization and output projections can operate without any change to their dimensions.

We evaluate three configurations: (1) a dense baseline; (2) a sparse variant with pruned states zeroed but retained in memory; and (3) an optimized variant with pruned states physically removed, reducing FLOPs and memory usage. All evaluations use a 10-iteration warm-up followed by 100 measured iterations with explicit CUDA synchronization to minimize measurement variance.

6 Evaluation and Results

6.1 Experimental Setup

We evaluate pruning on the Mamba2-130M model, chosen for its improved SSM state management, computational efficiency, and balanced capacitycost trade-off. This scale enables detailed state dynamics analysis, scales to other model sizes, and supports extensive pruning experiments within practical resource limits. Zero-shot performance is measured on four diverse benchmarks—PIQA [4], Arc Easy [6], Hellaswag [29], and OpenBookQA [21]—without task-specific fine-tuning, assessing reasoning and comprehension under varying pruning ratios.

6.2 Impact of Pruning on Model Accuracy

The baseline (unpruned) model demonstrates varying levels of competence in performing diverse tasks. Among these, PIQA has the highest baseline accuracy of 65%, followed by Arc Easy with 57%, Hellaswag with 37%, and OpenBookQA with 22%. The variation in baseline performance highlights the intrinsic challenge and reasoning requirements of each task. Under increasingly stricter pruning, each task exhibits a particular trend of degradation. PIQA remains the most robust, achieving high performance despite aggressive pruning, dropping by only five percentage points (to 60%) at a pruning ratio of 0.9. Arc Easy is the most susceptible to pruning, with its accuracy dropping significantly from 57% to 25% at a 0.9 pruning ratio. Hellaswag shows a consistent but modest decline from 37% to 28%, while OpenBookQA is remarkably stable, remaining nearly constant at around 20–22% across all pruning ratios (Fig. 4).

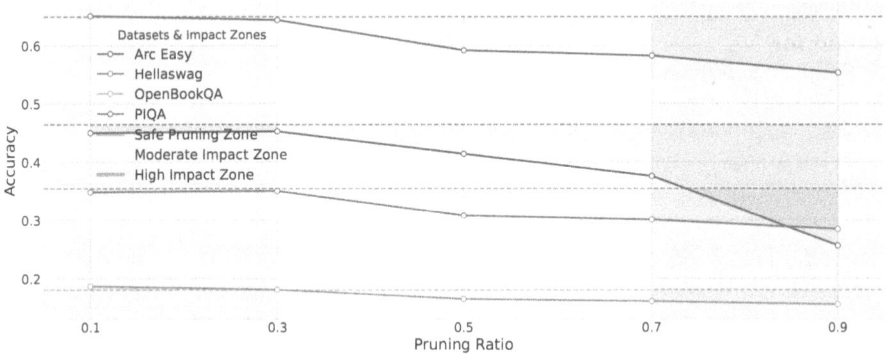

Fig. 4. Effect of state pruning on model accuracy across various datasets. Dotted lines indicate baseline accuracies, while solid lines represent the performance of the pruned model. The background is divided into three pruning zones based on average performance degradation.

Based on the observed performance patterns, we recognized three distinct operational regions that characterize the effect of pruning:

- **Safe Pruning Region** (≤ 0.3 pruning ratio): This is the range within which the model's performance is almost as good as the baseline for every task, with a mean accuracy loss of merely 0.7%. This region implies that roughly 30% of the model's states can be pruned without much performance loss. Therefore, it reflects a high computational redundancy in the original model.
- **Moderate Impact Zone** (0.3–0.7 pruning ratio): This zone marks the onset of quantifiable drops in performance, with a mean 12.2% reduction in accuracy for all tasks. The different breakdown rates observed across this zone, ranging from no visible effect on PIQA to precipitous declines for Arc Easy, illustrate task-specific dependencies for model capacity and computational heuristics.
- **High Impact Zone** (pruning ratio > 0.7): This zone demonstrates pruning conditions of high impact that result in extensive performance degradation for most tasks, as expressed by an average accuracy loss of 22.3%. Still, the stark contrasts in degradation trends, from PIQA's high resilience to Arc Easy's sharp decline, provide insight into the spread of task-specific computational demands across different model states.

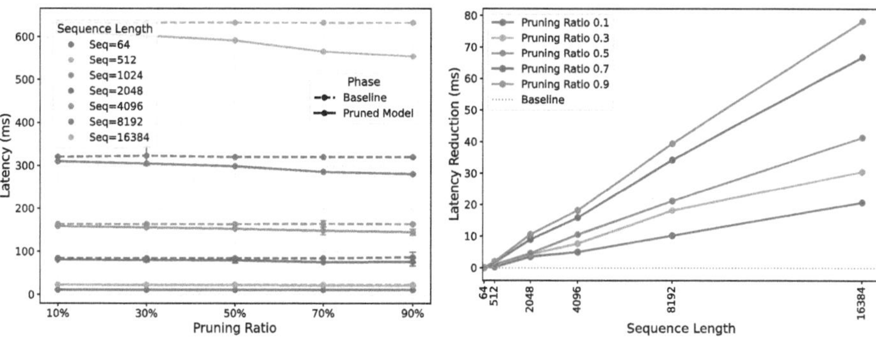

(a) Latency versus pruning ratio for various sequence lengths.

(b) Latency reduction across sequence lengths compared to baseline.

Fig. 5. (a) Latency versus pruning ratio and (b) Latency reduction across sequence lengths.

This zoning analysis is critical for deploying pruned models in high-performance computing environments. The Safe Zone defines clear boundaries for optimization without performance degradation, and the Moderate and High Impact Zones provide flexible trade-offs between computational efficiency and task-specific performance needs. These observations are particularly useful in resource-constrained deployments that require the optimal balance between computation and accuracy.

6.3 Resource Efficiency Improvements

To evaluate the efficiency gains from our pruning method, we performed latency measurements across sequence lengths of 64 to 16,384 tokens and pruning ratios of 0.1 to 0.9. Our findings reveal a complex relationship between sequence length and pruning effectiveness (in Fig. 5a). For short sequences ($\leq$ 512 tokens), pruning minimally affects latency, with base times around 15 ms for 64 tokens and 45 ms for 512 tokens. This suggests that state management overhead is negligible for short sequences. The impact of pruning becomes more evident for medium-length sequences (2,048 to 8,192 tokens). For 4,096-token sequences, latency decreases from 300 ms to 280 ms as the pruning ratio increases to 0.9. Similarly, for 8,192-token sequences, latency improves from 400 ms to 370 ms. The most significant gains occur with longer sequences (16,384 tokens), where pruning reduces latency from 630 ms to 560 ms at a pruning ratio of 0.9, resulting in approximately an 11% improvement. This suggests that pruning is more effective with longer sequences, where computational savings are more pronounced. Overall, the effectiveness of state pruning increases with sequence length, indicating that pruning strategies should be dynamically adjusted to optimize resource utilization and processing efficiency in distributed computing scenarios.

To showcase the significant benefits of our pruning method in high-performance computing, we evaluated computational speedup and memory sav-

Table 2. Impact of Pruning on Computational Efficiency: The table presents the speedup factor (×) and memory reduction (%) for different sequence lengths and pruning ratios. The speedup factor quantifies the relative decrease in latency compared to the baseline model, while the memory reduction percentage indicates the relative decrease in memory usage.

Seqlen	Metric	Pruning Ratio				
		0.1	**0.3**	**0.5**	**0.7**	**0.9**
64	Speedup (×)	1.01×	1.00×	1.01×	1.00×	1.00×
	Mem. Red. (%)	0.82%	2.58%	4.35%	6.05%	7.82%
512	Speedup (×)	1.01×	1.03×	1.05×	1.08×	1.10×
	Mem. Red. (%)	0.84%	2.07%	4.79%	7.99%	10.30%
2048	Speedup (×)	1.04×	1.05×	1.06×	1.12×	1.14×
	Mem. Red. (%)	0.88%	3.45%	6.08%	8.31%	10.97%
4096	Speedup (×)	1.03×	1.05×	1.07×	1.11×	1.13×
	Mem. Red. (%)	1.32%	3.66%	6.21%	8.87%	11.20%
8192	Speedup (×)	1.03×	1.06×	1.07×	1.12×	1.14×
	Mem. Red. (%)	1.18%	3.82%	6.35%	8.88%	11.50%
16384	Speedup (×)	1.03×	1.05×	1.07×	1.12×	1.14×
	Mem. Red. (%)	1.40%	3.59%	6.38%	8.78%	11.47%

ings across various sequence lengths and pruning ratios in Table 2. For very short sequences (64 tokens), our method achieves memory reduction of up to 7.82% at a 0.9 pruning ratio, demonstrating efficient memory optimization even in scenarios where computational overheads dominate. As sequence length increases, the advantages of pruning become even more pronounced. For medium lengths (512–2048 tokens), we observe consistent speedup ratios ranging from 1.10× to 1.14×, accompanied by substantial memory savings of 10.30% to 10.97%. These results highlight the growing importance of state management and the effectiveness of our method in optimizing longer sequences. Our method delivers sustained improvements for longer sequences (4096 tokens to 16,384 tokens), achieving speedup ratios of up to 1.14× and memory savings of 11.50% . This plateauing at a high level of optimization reflects the robustness of our approach, which maximizes computational efficiency without compromising model performance. Notably, the relationship between pruning ratio and efficiency gains is carefully balanced. While aggressive pruning (0.7–0.9) demonstrates diminishing returns, it further underscores the versatility of our method in maintaining a balance between efficiency and model accuracy. Overall, Table 2 highlights these compelling trends in resource utilization, demonstrating that pruning becomes increasingly impactful as sequence lengths grow, making it a valuable tool for high-performance distributed computing scenarios.

6.4 Accuracy–Latency Trade-Off

Figure 6 illustrates the accuracy–latency behavior across pruning ratios. For pruning up to 0.4–0.5, latency decreases steadily (5.09 ms to 10.61 ms) while accuracy remains relatively stable (0.65 to 0.60), indicating removal of mostly redundant states. Beyond this point, accuracy drops more sharply (0.59 to 0.55) despite further latency gains (reaching 18.27 ms), showing that pruning starts affecting states essential for selective scanning and long-range mixing. This identifies ∼0.5 as a practical threshold: lower ratios suit accuracy-critical tasks, whereas higher pruning favors throughput-oriented or resource-limited deployments.

To quantify this shift, we use the marginal accuracy drop,

$$\Delta_{\text{acc}} = \frac{\text{Acc}(r+\delta) - \text{Acc}(r)}{\delta},$$

where r is the pruning ratio and δ is a small increment (here, 0.1). Empirically, $|\Delta_{\text{acc}}| < 0.01$ for $r \leq 0.5$ but exceeds 0.03 beyond it, confirming nonlinear degradation past the threshold.

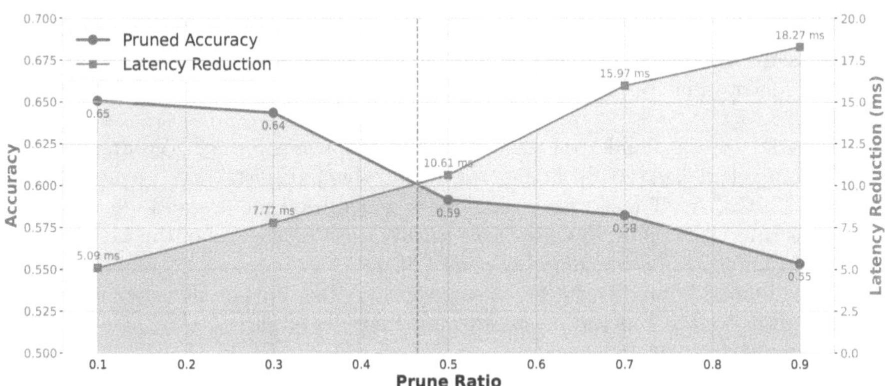

Fig. 6. Accuracy-latency trade-off across pruning ratios, highlighting optimal balance at moderate pruning levels for efficient deployment.

7 Conclusion and Future Work

This work profiled the Mamba architecture and showed that the state space module is the dominant bottleneck in both latency and memory. We introduced an activity-based pruning approach that reduces redundant states and improves efficiency while preserving functionality. Future directions include dynamic cache allocation, cross-layer cache sharing, hardware-optimized sparse-state computation, and extending the pruning evaluation to larger datasets and longer-sequence workloads to validate scalability.

Acknowledgments. We extend our gratitude to Intel Labs for supporting this project. This work utilized the Delta system at the National Center for Supercomputing Applications (NCSA) through allocation CIS240626. We also acknowledge support from the National Science Foundation under grants 2138259, 2138286, 2138307, 2137603, and 2138296.

References

1. Pytorch profiler. https://pytorch.org/tutorials/recipes/recipes/profiler_recipe.html
2. Adhianto, L., et al.: HPCTOOLKIT: tools for performance analysis of optimized parallel programs. Concurrency Compututation: Pract. Experience, **22**(6), pp. 685–701 (2010). http://hpctoolkit.org
3. Ali, A.A., Zimerman, I., Wolf, L.: The hidden attention of mamba models. In: Proceedings of the 63rd Annual Meeting of the Association for Computational Linguistics, vol. 1, pp. 1516–1534 (2025)
4. Bisk, Y., et al.: PIQA: reasoning about physical commonsense in natural language. In: Proceedings of the AAAI conference on artificial intelligence, pp. 7432–7439 (2020)
5. Cheng, H., Zhang, M., Shi, J.Q.: A survey on deep neural network pruning: taxonomy, comparison, analysis, and recommendations. IEEE Trans. Pattern Anal. Mach. Intell. pp. 10558–10578 (2024). https://doi.org/10.1109/TPAMI.2024.3447085
6. Clark, P., et al.: Think you have solved question answering? Try arc, the AI2 reasoning challenge (2018). https://arxiv.org/abs/1803.05457
7. Dao, T., Gu, A.: Transformers are SSMS: generalized models and efficient algorithms through structured state space duality. In: Proceedings of the 41st International Conference on Machine Learning (2024)
8. Dehghani, M., Arnab, A., Beyer, L., Vaswani, A., Tay, Y.: The efficiency misnomer. In: International Conference on Learning Representations (2022). https://arxiv.org/abs/2110.12894
9. Dery, L., Kolawole, S., Kagy, J.F., Smith, V., Neubig, G., Talwalkar, A.: Everybody prune now: structured pruning of LLMs with only forward passes. arXiv preprint arXiv:2402.05406 (2024)
10. Gao, Y., Glowacka, D.: Deep gate recurrent neural network. In: Proceedings of the 8th Asian Conference on Machine Learning, pp. 350–365 (Nov, 2016)
11. Gu, A., Dao, T.: Mamba: linear-time sequence modeling with selective state spaces. In: First Conference on Language Modeling (2024). https://openreview.net/forum?id=tEYskw1VY2
12. Gu, A., Goel, K., Ré, C.: Efficiently modeling long sequences with structured state spaces. In: International Conference on Learning Representations (2022). https://arxiv.org/abs/2111.00396
13. Gu, A., et al.: Combining recurrent, convolutional, and continuous-time models with linear state space layers. Adv. Neural Inf. Process. Syst. pp. 572–585 (2021)
14. Le Cun, Y., Denker, J.S., Solla, S.A.: Optimal brain damage. In: Proceedings of the 3rd International Conference on Neural Information Processing Systems, pp. 598–605 (1989)

15. Lenz, B., et al.: Jamba: Hybrid transformer-mamba language models. In: The Thirteenth International Conference on Learning Representations (2025). https://openreview.net/forum?id=JFPaD7lpBD
16. Li, J., et al.: Marca: Mamba accelerator with reconfigurable architecture. In: 2024 ACM/IEEE International Conference On Computer Aided Design (ICCAD) pp. 1–9 (2024). https://api.semanticscholar.org/CorpusID:272704058
17. Munoz, J.P., Yuan, J., Jain, N.: Mamba-shedder: post-transformer compression for efficient selective structured state space models. In: Proceedings of the 2025 Conference of the Nations of the Americas Chapter of the Association for Computational Linguistics: Human Language Technologies, vol. 1, pp. 3851–3863 (2025)
18. Qin, J., Liu, F.: Mamba-spike: enhancing the mamba architecture with a spiking front-end for efficient temporal data processing. Comput. Graph. Int. Conf. pp. 323–334 (2024)
19. Shen, M., Molchanov, P., Yin, H., Alvarez, J.M.: When to prune? A policy towards early structural pruning. In: Proceedings of the IEEE/CVF Conference on Computer Vision and Pattern Recognition, pp. 12247–12256 (2022)
20. Shleifer, S., Weston, J., Ott, M.: NormFormer: improved transformer pretraining with extra normalization. CoRR (2021). https://arxiv.org/abs/2110.09456
21. Sun, K., Yu, D., Yu, D., Cardie, C.: Improving machine reading comprehension with general reading strategies. In: North American Chapter of the Association for Computational Linguistics (2018). https://api.semanticscholar.org/CorpusID:53109787
22. Vaswani, A., et al.: Attention is all you need. Adv. Neural Inf. Process. Syst. (2017)
23. Waleffe, R., et al.: An empirical study of mamba-based language models (2024). https://arxiv.org/abs/2406.07887
24. Wolf, T., et al.: Transformers: state-of-the-art natural language processing (2020). https://github.com/huggingface/transformers
25. Xia, M., Zhong, Z., Chen, D.: Structured pruning learns compact and accurate models. In: Proceedings of the 60th Annual Meeting of the Association for Computational Linguistics, pp. 1513–1528 (2022)
26. Xiao, Y., et al.: Mambatree: tree topology is all you need in state space model. In: The Thirty-eighth Annual Conference on Neural Information Processing Systems (2024)
27. Yang, Z., Zhang, H.: Comparative analysis of structured pruning and unstructured pruning. Front. Comput. pp. 882–889 (2022)
28. Yousefzadeh-Asl-Miandoab, E., Robroek, T., Tozun, P.: Profiling and monitoring deep learning training tasks. In: Proceedings of the 3rd Workshop on Machine Learning and Systems, pp. 18–25 (2023). https://doi.org/10.1145/3578356.3592589
29. Zellers, R., Holtzman, A., Bisk, Y., Farhadi, A., Choi, Y.: Hellaswag: Can a machine really finish your sentence? In: Annual Meeting of the Association for Computational Linguistics (2019). https://api.semanticscholar.org/CorpusID:159041722
30. Zhan, Z., et al.: Rethinking token reduction for state space models. In: Conference on Empirical Methods in Natural Language Processing (2024). https://api.semanticscholar.org/CorpusID:273501765

31. Zhang, H., et al.: A survey on visual mamba. Appl. Sci. (2024)
32. Zhao, P., et al.: Pruning foundation models for high accuracy without retraining. In: Conference on Empirical Methods in Natural Language Processing (2024). https://api.semanticscholar.org/CorpusID:273501976
33. Zhou, K., Krentel, M.W., Mellor-Crummey, J.: Tools for top-down performance analysis of GPU-accelerated applications. In: Proceedings of the 34th ACM International Conference on Supercomputing (2020). https://doi.org/10.1145/3392717.3392752

OpenChartInsight: Lightweight Automatic Interpretation of GitHub Charts

Siyi Xie, Yantong Wang, and Wei Wang(✉)

East China Normal University, Shanghai, China
{51275903081,51265903115}@stu.ecnu.edu.cn, wwang@dase.ecnu.edu.cn

Abstract. Visual analytics for GitHub repositories, including star events, activity, and contributor growth, are widely available through dashboards and plugins. Yet these visualizations often lack explanatory text, requiring users to interpret trends manually. This work presents OpenChartInsight, a lightweight AI framework that generates natural language interpretations directly beneath GitHub project charts. The framework introduces a Hierarchical Metric Interpretation method that structures repository indicators into three levels: basic metrics such as star count and forks, composite metrics such as activity and contributor retention, and trend-oriented metrics such as anomalies and long-term growth. These indicators are computed through metric templates and aligned with natural language generation. The framework is implemented with lightweight models such as Flan-T5, supported by retrieval-augmented context and a self-reflection mechanism to ensure alignment with underlying data while reducing hallucinations. To assess generation quality, we design a compact evaluation pipeline that integrates Execution Accuracy for numerical consistency, FactCC for faithful alignment, SummaC for faithful consistency checking, and BLEURT-tiny for fluency assessment. Scores from these modules are normalized and aggregated into a single composite quality score, enabling systematic and reproducible evaluation without human annotation. Experiments on GitHub repository data demonstrate that OpenChartInsight produces accurate and interpretable chart explanations, providing a practical extension to existing visualization tools for open-source project analysis.

Keywords: chart-to-text · GitHub · repository analytics · automatic interpretation

1 Introduction

With the continuous expansion of the global open-source ecosystem, platforms such as GitHub [1] and Gitee [2] have accumulated vast amounts of collaboration and development activity data over long-term evolution. These data not only reflect the organizational structure and collaboration patterns of open-source

J. Zhan et al. (Eds.): Bench 2025, LNCS 16471, pp. 45–53, 2026.
https://doi.org/10.1007/978-981-95-9694-2_4

communities but also provide crucial support for studying their evolutionary patterns and ecological health.

In recent years, both industry and academia have proposed various visualization and analysis tools targeting the open-source ecosystem [3]. Gitlights applies natural language processing (NLP) methods to perform topic recognition on commits and issues, combined with AI-generated project analysis reports [6]. However, its system is closed-source and relies on GitHub API calls, which are limited by rate restrictions and authorization constraints, making real-time interactive visualization difficult. Analytics & Reports by Screenful [4] provides mature charting and cross-platform data integration features, supporting automated periodic report generation. Yet, it is also a closed system, relatively expensive, and oriented toward task management scenarios. RepoSense, as an open-source tool, can accurately track contributors' commits and code change trends, but its visualization is relatively conventional, lacking intelligent explanations and adaptive analysis mechanisms [5]. Overall, existing tools still exhibit significant limitations in openness, intelligence, and deep platform integration, making it difficult to meet the demands for multidimensional, dynamic, and interpretable analysis of open-source projects [8,10]. This "visible but not understandable" state limits the practical value of open-source data in project governance and operational decision-making.

Against this backdrop, this paper addresses the question of "how to make GitHub charts interpretable" and proposes the OpenChartInsight framework. The framework is implemented as a browser extension embedded into GitHub pages. While preserving the original chart display, it integrates lightweight large language models (LLMs) to automatically explain chart data, transforming numerical changes into structured, natural-language insights. This reduces comprehension costs and enhances the usability and actionable value of open-source data.

2 Functional Design

To address the deficiencies in openness, intelligence, and interpretability of existing tools, OpenChartInsight does not aim to replace native charts but instead builds an intelligent explanation layer on top of them. This design shifts data insights from "passive reading" to "automatic understanding."

The overall system architecture is illustrated in Fig. 1. As shown, the pipeline processes raw data through Metric Computation and a Retrieval-Augmented Module, utilizing an LLM with a Self-Reflection [11] mechanism to generate the Final Output. The system embeds directly into GitHub and Gitee pages via a browser extension, displaying project and developer metrics while preserving users' existing interaction habits.

The core objectives of the platform include:

- **Automatic explanation of chart trends:** Transform time-series data (e.g., Stars, Forks) into natural language descriptions through the Metric Computation module, revealing growth, fluctuations, and anomalies.

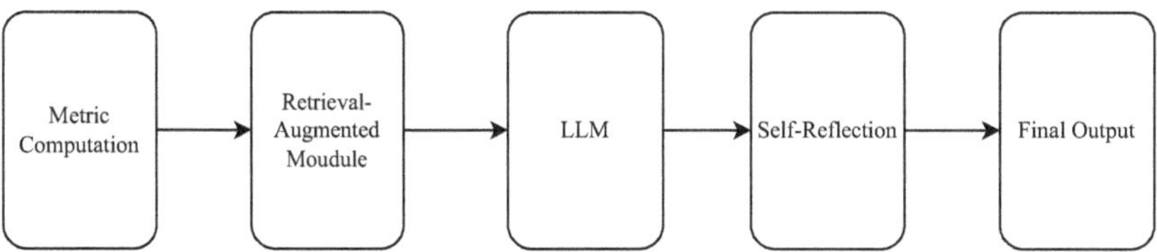

Fig. 1. The overall architecture of OpenChartInsight. The workflow integrates Metric Computation, Retrieval-Augmented Generation (RAG), and Large Language Models (LLM) with a Self-Reflection mechanism to produce reliable Final Output.

- **Lightweight and embeddable:** Through on-demand loading, analysis functions and visualization elements are dynamically injected into pages, reducing computational overhead and ensuring high responsiveness.
- **Controllable intelligent generation:** By combining lightweight LLMs with rule constraints and Retrieval-Augmented Generation (RAG) [14], the system ensures outputs are grounded in real data. Furthermore, the Self-Reflection module iteratively verifies the content to minimize hallucination risks before the Final Output.

Through this design, OpenChartInsight provides multidimensional, dynamic insights into open-source data directly on the native interface, supporting users in quickly understanding project status and developer behavior while keeping the system lightweight and efficient.

3 Implementation

3.1 Data Acquisition and Metric Foundation

OpenChartInsight relies on the OpenDigger [7] platform as its data foundation. OpenDigger continuously collects and processes GitHub global log data to compute and publish a series of standardized project and developer metrics, including basic indicators like Stars, Forks, Commits, and Issues, as well as composite indicators such as Activity [12] and OpenRank [13]. All metrics are stored and publicly released as static data files, ensuring stability and reproducibility.

During operation, OpenChartInsight operates without directly invoking the GitHub API. Instead, it dynamically constructs data requests based on the browsing context. As detailed in Table 1, when a user accesses a repository or developer profile, the system parses the page URL structure and key DOM elements to extract the repository name or developer ID. It then generates data paths consistent with the OpenDigger repository to load the relevant metrics on demand.

This approach effectively avoids GitHub API rate and authorization limitations while ensuring consistent results across time points, providing a stable data foundation for subsequent automated explanations and evaluation experiments.

Table 1. Mapping Rules for Context-Aware Data Request Construction

Category	URL Pattern
Repository	`https://~/{owner}/{repo}/*.json`
Developer	`https://~/{owner}/*.json`

3.2 Feature Injection and On-Demand Loading

On the front-end, OpenChartInsight adopts a browser extension architecture, dynamically injecting analytical features into GitHub native pages via content scripts. The front-end is built with React, and the UI design reuses GitHub's native elements wherever possible to maintain visual consistency and reduce cognitive load.

Feature injection is triggered by page structure detection. Modules are injected only when specific charts or target container nodes are detected. A unified feature manager registers, schedules, and manages the lifecycle of modules. Each feature checks its activation state and running conditions before execution, skipping modules that do not meet requirements.

This on-demand loading mechanism reduces unnecessary computation and rendering overhead, enabling intelligent explanations while maintaining low performance impact, satisfying the lightweight requirements of a browser extension.

3.3 Metric Modeling and Layered Structure

To support stable and interpretable text generation, OpenChartInsight employs a layered modeling approach for project metrics, dividing them into three abstraction levels to clarify their semantic roles in explanation generation.

Basic Metrics Layer: Includes Stars, Forks, Commits, Pull Requests, and Issues, reflecting project activity and community feedback over time. This layer describes surface-level activity changes.

Composite Metrics Layer: Built on top of basic metrics, e.g., Activity and OpenRank, measuring overall project activity and influence in the open-source ecosystem. These metrics combine multiple basic indicators to capture higher-level collaboration efficiency and ecosystem status.

Trend Metrics Layer: Analyzes time-series data to capture long-term growth trends, anomalies, and periodic patterns. Segment comparisons and rate-of-change analysis extract semantically meaningful trend features, providing structured input for natural language explanations.

This layered approach enables the system to understand project status across multiple abstraction levels, avoiding narrow interpretations based on single metrics.

3.4 RAG-Based Explanation Generation

For text explanation, OpenChartInsight uses retrieval-augmented generation (RAG) to constrain and guide model outputs. Before generation, relevant knowledge is retrieved from a dedicated knowledge base, including metric definitions, computation methods, standard templates, and rules to prevent improper inferences.

Retrieved content is injected into the model context along with current time-series data, ensuring that generation remains grounded in real data and predefined semantic rules. A template-guided strategy aligns metric changes, trend judgments, and explanation text structure, producing consistent outputs that help users quickly understand differences and similarities between charts.

3.5 Lightweight Model and Self-Reflection Process

Considering the extension's constraints on response speed, computation, and deployment cost, OpenChartInsight uses Flan-T5 as the core generation model. This model maintains good generation quality with relatively low inference cost, suitable for lightweight applications.

The workflow first generates a draft explanation based on the current context. A self-reflection process is then triggered to validate outputs, checking for numerical consistency, trend accuracy, and unreasonable causal or overinterpretations. Detected issues are corrected or regenerated until all validation criteria are met, improving reliability and consistency without significant additional computational overhead.

4 Evaluation

4.1 Goals and Setup

OpenChartInsight aims to generate accurate, interpretable, and trustworthy natural-language explanations for GitHub charts. Evaluation focuses not on subjective text quality but on faithfulness to chart data and readability.

Evaluation criteria include:

- **Numerical and factual consistency:** Does the text match actual chart data?
- **Semantic faithfulness:** Does it accurately reflect chart trends without introducing irrelevant or speculative information?
- **Language fluency:** Is the text readable while maintaining accuracy?

A fully automated evaluation pipeline ensures reproducibility and avoids subjective, costly manual evaluation.

4.2 Dataset and Experimental Samples

Data come from OpenDigger's GitHub project metrics. Samples cover projects of varying size and activity, including high-growth, stable, and periodic-fluctuation projects. Star, Commit, and Issue time-series are selected, and explanations are generated under consistent model configurations and prompts.

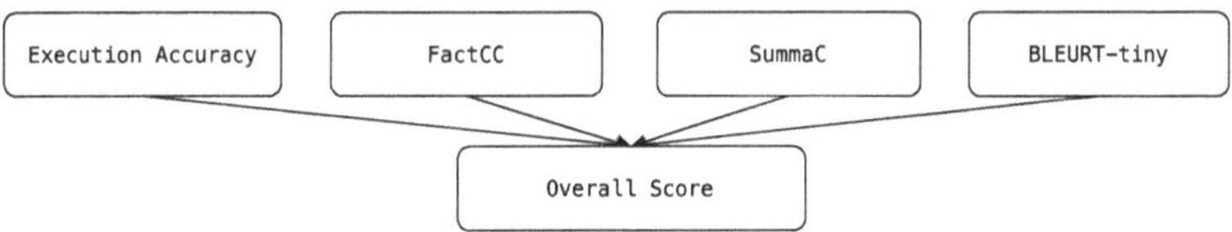

Fig. 2. Overview of the HyperEval pipeline. The system computes an aggregated Overall Score based on four independent dimensions: Execution Accuracy, FactCC, SummaC, and BLEURT-tiny.

4.3 Automated Evaluation Method

To ensure rigorous and efficient benchmarking, we introduce HyperEval, a compact automated evaluation pipeline illustrated in Fig. 2. This framework aggregates four complementary metrics to produce a comprehensive Overall Score, ensuring a holistic assessment of the generated explanations:

- **Execution Accuracy (EA)** [15]: Performs rule-based and programmatic checks to verify numeric and trend correctness.
- **FactCC (FC)** [16]: Utilizes a pretrained model to evaluate the factual consistency of the content.
- **SummaC (SC)** [17]: Measures the semantic alignment between the generated text and the input chart data.
- **BLEURT-tiny (BL)** [18]: Assesses language fluency and naturalness to ensure readability.

As depicted in the pipeline, all modules operate independently from the generation model, allowing for fully automated and unbiased evaluation.

4.4 Composite Quality Score

Metric scores are normalized to [0, 1] and combined using weighted summation:

$$Q = w_1 \cdot EA + w_2 \cdot FC + w_3 \cdot SC + w_4 \cdot BL$$

Weights reflect higher priority for numerical consistency and factual faithfulness, while language fluency acts as a supporting factor.

4.5 Results and Analysis

The quantitative evaluation results are presented in Fig. 3. As observed, OpenChartInsight consistently generates explanations that closely match the chart data across diverse projects (e.g., TensorFlow and PyTorch). Specifically, the high scores in Execution Accuracy (EA) and FactCC demonstrate that the RAG and self-reflection mechanisms significantly enhance numerical and factual reliability.

Furthermore, the BLEURT-tiny metric remains stable across all datasets, confirming that the generated text maintains high fluency and satisfies readability requirements. These results collectively validate the feasibility of reliable chart explanation under lightweight constraints.

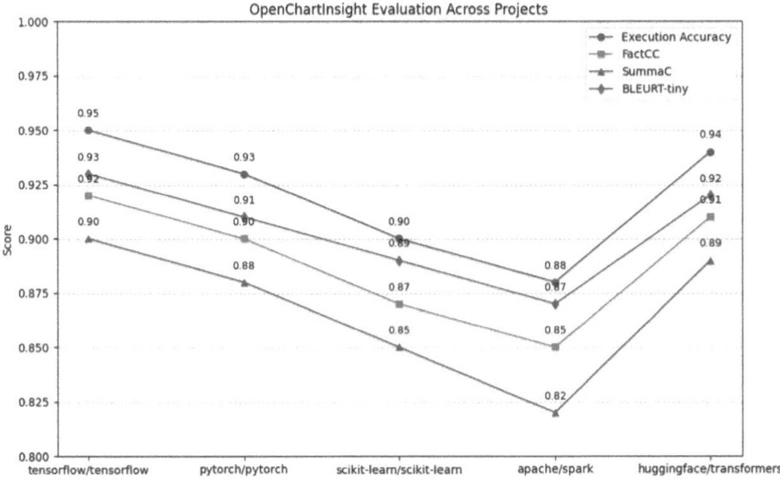

Fig. 3. Performance evaluation of OpenChartInsight across five representative open-source projects. The metrics include Execution Accuracy, FactCC, SummaC, and BLEURT-tiny.

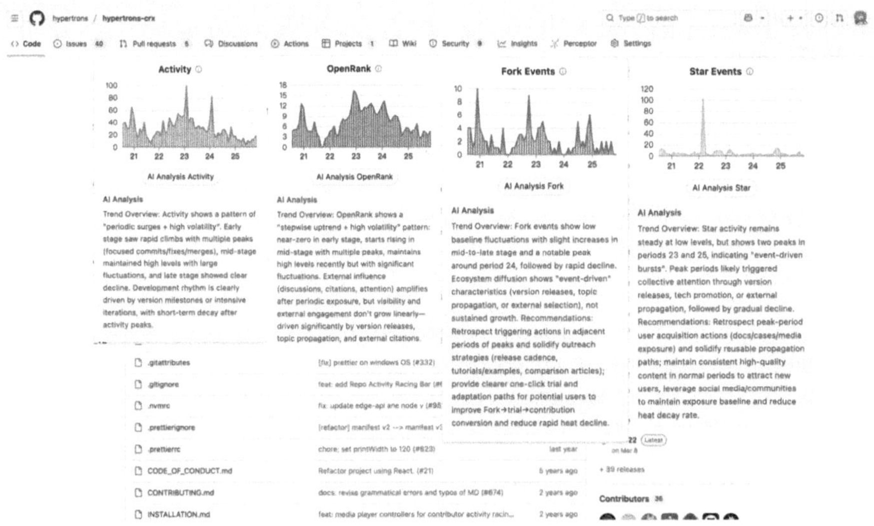

Fig. 4. A real-world case study of OpenChartInsight deployed on the *hypertrons-crx* [9] repository. The system overlays AI-generated analysis panels directly onto the GitHub interface, providing detailed trend interpretations for four key metrics: Activity, OpenRank, Fork Events, and Star Events.

5 Conclusion and Future Work

OpenChartInsight explores the feasibility of introducing lightweight LLMs for GitHub chart explanation. As demonstrated in the real-world deployment scenario in Fig. 4, OpenChartInsight successfully integrates with the GitHub UI to provide intuitive, multi-dimensional insights. By leveraging layered metrics, retrieval-augmented generation (RAG), and self-reflection mechanisms, the system is capable of generating context-aware, data-driven explanations that are both controllable and reliable, even under limited computational resources. This approach not only enhances the interpretability of GitHub charts for developers and project maintainers, but also reduces cognitive load and facilitates more informed decision-making in open-source project management. The lightweight design ensures minimal disruption to existing user workflows while providing timely and actionable insights, demonstrating a practical balance between usability, efficiency, and intelligence in real-world applications.

Future work will focus on:

- Optimizing model and retrieval strategies for real-time interaction.
- Extending to additional open-source hosting platforms for cross-ecosystem applicability.
- Enhancing the metric system to support complex project governance and operational decisions.

References

1. GitHub. https://github.com. Accessed 03 Jan 2026
2. Gitee. https://gitee.com. Accessed 03 Jan 2026
3. Lungu, M., Pfeiffer, R.-H., D'Ambros, M., Lanza, M., Findahl, J.: Can git repository visualization support educators in assessing group projects? In: Working Conference on Software Visualization (VISSOFT 2022), pp. 187–191. IEEE, Limassol (2022). https://doi.org/10.1109/VISSOFT55257.2022.00030
4. Screenful: Analytics & Reports by Screenful. GitHub Marketplace (2025). https://github.com/marketplace/analytics-reports. Accessed 03 Jan 2026
5. RepoSense Team: RepoSense: Visualize programmer activities across Git repositories. Official Website (2025). https://reposense.org. Accessed 03 Jan 2026
6. Gitlights: Gitlights: AI-Powered GitHub Analytics. GitHub Marketplace (2025). https://github.com/marketplace/gitlights-analytics. Accessed 03 Jan 2026
7. Xia, X., Zhao, S., Han, F., Bi, F., Wang, W.: OpenDigger: Data Mining and Information Service System for Open Collaboration Digital Ecosystem. CoRR abs/2311.15204 (2023). https://doi.org/10.48550/arXiv.2311.15204
8. Scheibel, W., et al.: Integrated visual software analytics on the Github platform. Comput. **13**(2), 33 (2024). https://doi.org/10.3390/computers13020033
9. Wang, Y., et al.: HyperCRX 2.0: a comprehensive and automated tool for empowering Github insights. In: 47th IEEE/ACM International Conference on Software Engineering (ICSE Companion), pp. 49–52. IEEE (2025). https://doi.org/10.1109/ICSE-Companion66252.2025.00022

10. Ko, A.J., Myers, B.A., Coblenz, M.J., Aung, H.H.: An exploratory study of how developers seek, relate, and collect relevant information during software maintenance tasks. IEEE Trans. Softw. Eng. **32**(12), 971–987 (2006). https://doi.org/10.1109/TSE.2006.116
11. Asai, A., Wu, Z., Wang, Y., Sil, A., Hajishirzi, H.: Self-RAG: learning to retrieve, generate, and critique through self-reflection. In: International Conference on Learning Representations (ICLR). OpenReview.net (2024). https://openreview.net/forum?id=hSyW5go0v8
12. Xia, X., Weng, Z., Wang, W., Zhao, S.: Exploring activity and contributors on GitHub: who, what, when, and where. In: 29th Asia-Pacific Software Engineering Conference (APSEC), pp. 11–20. IEEE (2022). https://doi.org/10.1109/APSEC57359.2022.00013
13. Zhao, S., et al.: OpenRank leaderboard: motivating open source collaborations through social network evaluation in Alibaba. In: 46th International Conference on Software Engineering: Software Engineering in Practice (ICSE-SEIP), pp. 346–357. ACM (2024). https://doi.org/10.1145/3639477.3639734
14. Lewis, P., et al.: Retrieval-augmented generation for knowledge-intensive NLP tasks. In: Advances in Neural Information Processing Systems (NeurIPS), vol. 33, pp. 9459–9474. Curran Associates, Inc. (2020). https://proceedings.neurips.cc/paper/2020/hash/6b493230205f780e1bc26945df7481e5-Abstract.html
15. Kim, H., Jeon, T., Choi, S., Choi, S., Cho, H.: FLEX: Expert-level False-Less EXecution Metric for Reliable Text-to-SQL Benchmark. arXiv preprint arXiv:2409.19014 (2024). https://doi.org/10.48550/arXiv.2409.19014
16. Kryscinski, W., McCann, B., Xiong, C., Socher, R.: Evaluating the factual consistency of abstractive text summarization. In: Conference on Empirical Methods in Natural Language Processing (EMNLP), pp. 9332–9346. Association for Computational Linguistics (2020). https://doi.org/10.18653/v1/2020.emnlp-main.750
17. Fabbri, A.R., Wu, C.-S., Liu, W., Xiong, C.: QAFactEval: improved QA-based factual consistency evaluation for summarization. In: North American Chapter of the Association for Computational Linguistics (NAACL), pp. 2587–2601. Association for Computational Linguistics (2022). https://doi.org/10.18653/v1/2022.naacl-main.187
18. Sellam, T., Das, D., Parikh, A.P.: BLEURT: learning robust metrics for text generation. In: Annual Meeting of the Association for Computational Linguistics (ACL), pp. 7881–7892. Association for Computational Linguistics (2020). https://doi.org/10.18653/v1/2020.acl-main.704

Dynamic Multi-view RAG: Mitigating Hallucinations of Large Language Models in Education

Weijun Zhao and Qiwen Dong(✉)

East China Normal University, Shanghai, China
qwdong@dase.ecnu.edu.cn

Abstract. Nowadays, LLMs are increasingly used in education. However, hallucination severely undermines the reliability and pedagogical value of their responses. While Retrieval-Augmented Generation (RAG) helps to mitigate hallucinations with external knowledge, existing methods not only rely on limited retrieval sources, but also lack mechanisms to verify whether generated answers are sufficiently supported by retrieved evidence. To address these limitations, we propose a Dynamic Multi-View RAG (DMVR) framework. First, DMVR dynamically rewrites each original query from textbook and example perspectives to perform multi-view retrieval. In addition, a verification mechanism generation process encourages cross-checking across multi-view sources and explicitly grounds answers in supporting evidence. Experiments on question answering tasks show that DMVR outperforms baselines in answer accuracy, showing its effectiveness in mitigating hallucinations.

Keywords: Hallucination · Dynamic Multi-View Retrieval · Education · LLMs · RAG

1 Introduction

The emergence of Large Language Models (LLMs) is driving a paradigm shift in the field of personalized education [1]. LLMs are capable of providing students with immediate feedback, generating customized learning materials, and adapting to different learning paces, showcasing immense application potential [2]. However, despite this promising outlook, LLMs possess a fundamental flaw: Hallucination. Hallucination refers to content generated by the model that appears fluent and coherent but is factually inconsistent or entirely fabricated [5]. This defect severely hinders their reliable application across various scenarios. In the education sector, which is the focus of this paper, there is an exceptionally high requirement for answer accuracy. An erroneous explanation or a fictitious formula can seriously mislead a student's cognitive understanding and disrupt the entire learning process, making hallucination an unacceptable failure mode. Surveys indicate that the accuracy of answers and potential biases are the primary concerns for educators and students when using LLMs [3].

J. Zhan et al. (Eds.): Bench 2025, LNCS 16471, pp. 54–65, 2026.
https://doi.org/10.1007/978-981-95-9694-2_5

To anchor the content generated by LLMs to reliable knowledge sources, Retrieval-Augmented Generation (RAG) has become a recognized standard solution in the industry [6]. RAG utilizes a "retrieve-then-generate" mechanism, extracting relevant information from external knowledge bases as context for the model before generating an answer, thereby significantly reducing the occurrence of hallucinations [9].

However, in complex educational scenarios, the traditional "Naive RAG" architecture exposes limitations. The system of educational knowledge is often not single-dimensional but is composed of normative theoretical narratives and contextualized application instances. Specifically, in teaching scenarios within the humanities and social sciences, students learning a concept need to not only memorize macro-definitions from textbooks but also identify the mapping relationships of that concept within specific micro-scenarios. Simply mixing these heterogeneous knowledge sources into a flat text repository leads to two core challenges for Naive RAG systems:

Contextual Misalignment. Student questions often imply specific assessment contexts, while retrieving only textbooks may return large amounts of background preamble lacking focus on the specific point of inquiry. This results in retrieved content that, while semantically related, fails to precisely hit the core of the question.

Unverified Association. There are often subtle similarities between numerous knowledge points in questions. Textbooks relatively lack "Example-Answer" strong association pairs as references. Consequently, LLMs tend to confuse concepts when synthesizing information—failing to distinguish between general descriptions and critical features—thus producing plausible but incorrect hallucinatory explanations.

To address the aforementioned problems, this paper proposes a Dynamic Multi-View RAG (DMVR) framework designed specifically for educational scenarios, directly addressing the deficiencies of traditional RAG:

Dynamic Multi-view Retrieval. The framework first analyzes the student's original inquiry to understand their underlying intent. It then dynamically decomposes the query into two targeted sub-queries and dispatches them to different knowledge bases partitioned by "view" (perspective). This architectural design aligns the retrieval process with the intrinsic structure of teaching materials, thereby maximizing the relevance of retrieved content.

Verified Generation. The generation phase is not a passive synthesis of information but actively cross-references evidence from two different views, assigning higher scores to claims verified by multiple perspectives. The framework introduces a verification model to test for a factual entailment relationship between every claim in the generated answer and its cited source evidence [23]. The final generated answer is not only reliable but also accompanied by explicit, traceable citations, greatly enhancing the system's trustworthiness and explainability.

To validate the effectiveness of this framework, we utilized three educational QA datasets. Experimental results indicate that compared to baseline models, our proposed DMV-RAG framework significantly improves answer accuracy.

2 Related Work

2.1 Applications of Large Language Models in Education

LLMs are reshaping the educational ecosystem. They are widely used in various roles, including as real-time learning assistants for students, providing Q&A and immediate feedback; as auxiliary tools for teachers, assisting in curriculum planning and content creation; and as core engines for adaptive learning platforms, providing personalized learning paths [1]. Although LLMs excel in improving teaching efficiency and interactivity, their application entails risks such as academic plagiarism, over-reliance on technology, and issues with hallucinations and potential bias in generated content [3]. These challenges highlight the importance of improving the reliability of LLMs in educational settings, which is the starting point of this study.

2.2 Hallucinations in Large Language Models

Hallucination—where an LLM generates content that is inconsistent with facts or fabricated—is currently the main obstacle hindering its application in critical fields. The causes of hallucinations are complex, potentially stemming from noise and bias in training data, defects in the model's parametric knowledge, or randomness in the decoding process [5]. The academic community has proposed various mitigation strategies, broadly categorized into three types: data-driven methods, model-driven methods, and inference-time methods. Among all inference-time methods, Retrieval-Augmented Generation (RAG) has become the preferred paradigm for handling knowledge-intensive tasks and mitigating hallucinations due to its flexibility and effectiveness [6].

2.3 Frontier Architectures in Retrieval-Augmented Generation

To overcome the limitations of Naive RAG, researchers have explored extensive optimizations in both the retrieval and generation phases.

Query Transformation Strategies. The RRR (Rewrite-Retrieve-Read) framework [4] introduces a small rewriting model trained via reinforcement learning, designed to adjust query formulation to maximize retrieval performance. RQ-RAG [10] further formalizes this process by proposing the concept of "Learning to Refine Queries". This approach goes beyond simple rewriting by endowing the model with explicit capabilities for query decomposition and disambiguation. Based on the context retrieved in the previous round, the model recognizes deficiencies in the current query and automatically generates a new, more targeted one.

Techniques such as Step-Back Prompting [11] abstract specific user questions into higher-level conceptual queries. This method effectively retrieves more generalized background or theoretical information, preventing the loss of key context due to overly specific queries. RAG-STAR [12] adopts a tree-based search structure, utilizing retrieved information to guide the decomposition process and prune invalid reasoning paths. MindSearch [13] proposes a multi-agent framework mimicking human cognitive processes, comprising two core components: *WebPlanner* and *WebSearcher*. These components are responsible for constructing the user's complex intents into a dynamic graph structure and executing these queries to acquire information from the Internet, respectively. LevelRAG [14] focuses on leveraging natural language processing techniques for the hierarchical deep decomposition of queries. It integrates multiple Low-level Searchers to incrementally acquire high-value information, deepening problem understanding through continuously accumulated information to generate query sequences that better align with logical chains.

Attributable and Verifiable Generation. To ensure the trustworthiness of Large Language Models (LLMs), recent research has primarily diverged into two attribution paradigms: Generation-Time Citation (G-Cite) and Post-hoc Citation (P-Cite) [15].

G-Cite methods integrate citation generation directly into the model's reasoning and decoding processes, aiming to generate both text and attribution information simultaneously [16]. CoT Citation [17] incorporates Chain-of-Thought reasoning to improve the logical alignment between claims and evidence, while LongCite [18] introduces a "coarse-to-fine" mechanism, particularly for generating precise sentence-level citations in long-context scenarios.

P-Cite methods decouple content generation from attribution, meaning citations are added or verified after the initial response is generated. This paradigm allows for the use of specialized verification modules without altering the underlying generative model. Pioneering works such as RARR [19] adopt a "research and revise" workflow, retrospectively finding evidence and correcting unsupported claims. Recent P-Cite frameworks focus more on efficiency and granularity: Sancheti et al. [20] and Ramu et al. [21] propose decomposition-based strategies to handle post-hoc attribution in long documents, while CiteFix [22] utilizes a post-processing correction mechanism to rectify incorrect citations based on retrieved evidence. VeriCite [23] introduces a rigorous three-stage verification framework, utilizing Natural Language Inference (NLI) models to perform dual verification and filtering on initially generated answer claims and retrieved evidence, ultimately generating highly credible responses by integrating verified information.

3 The Dynamic Multi-view RAG Framework

This section details the architectural design and workflow of the framework. The core idea is to align the retrieval and generation processes with the intrinsic structure of educational knowledge, utilizing strategies of "divide and conquer" and "cross-verification" to enhance answer reliability.

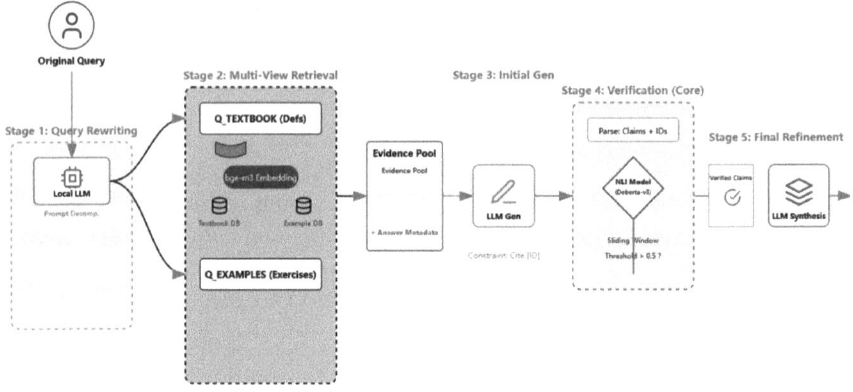

Fig. 1. The overall workflow of the DMVR framework.

3.1 Framework Overview

The overall workflow of the DMVR framework is shown in Fig. 1. The process consists of five stages: Query Rewriting, Multi-View Retrieval, Initial Generation, Verified Generation and Final Refinement. These can be summarized into two core phases: the Dynamic Multi-View Retrieval Phase and the Verified Generation Phase.

3.2 Knowledge Source Representation

The heterogeneity of educational knowledge is the starting point for this design. We categorize sources into two distinct Views:

Textbook View ($V_{textbook}$): Contains structured, formal knowledge from authoritative textbooks, such as definitions, theorems, and axioms.

Example View ($V_{examples}$): Contains questions, answers, and subject sources, providing similar problems and key concepts.

For the data source of each view $v \in V$, which $V = \{V_{textbook}, V_{examples}\}$, we adopt a Chunking Strategy with a fixed size of 1000 tokens and a 15% overlap between adjacent chunks to prevent key information from being severed at boundaries.

3.3 Dynamic Multi-view Retrieval Phase

This phase aims to transform an original student query into a series of precise retrieval instructions pointing to the correct knowledge types.

1. **View-Specific Query Rewriting:** Given an original student query q_{origin}, we use an LLM to dynamically rewrite it into a set of sub-queries targeted at different knowledge views: $q_{textbook}$ and $q_{examples}$.
2. **Multi-View Retrieval:** For each view $v \in V$, the system uses the corresponding sub-query q_v to retrieve the top-k most relevant text chunks from its exclusive vector database D_v. This outputs a structured evidence set $E = \{E_{textbook}, E_{examples}\}$.

3.4 Self-Verified Generation Phase

The core of this phase is the introduction of a rigorous verification loop to ensure the faithfulness of the generated content to mitigate the hallucination of LLMs.

1. **Initial Answer Generation:** All evidence chunks E are merged and provided as context to the LLM. The model generates an initial answer $A_{initial}$ with a key instruction: every statement must explicitly cite the ID of the source evidence chunks it relies on, it can be one or more.
2. **Cross-Source Verification:** To address the noise introduced by expanded retrieval, we decompose $A_{initial}$ into independent claims $C = \{c_1, c_2, \ldots, c_n\}$. For each claim c_j, we identify its supporting evidence set E_j. We use a pre-trained Natural Language Inference (NLI) model to calculate the entailment probability $P(\text{entailment}|\text{premise} = e, \text{hypothesis} = c_j)$ for each evidence block e. A Verification Score $S(c_j)$ is calculated to reward high entailment and multi-view support:

$$S(c_j) = \max_{e \in E_j} P(\text{entailment}|e, c_j) \times \log(1 + \text{unique\_views}(E_j)) \quad (1)$$

   In this formula, the maximization operation is employed because, within the logic of fact verification, the existence of a single piece of conclusive evidence is sufficient to validate the claim. The function $\text{unique\_views}(E_j)$ denotes the cardinality of distinct perspectives covered by the evidence sources supporting claim c_j. Also, the logarithmic term acts as a weighting factor, explicitly assigning higher relevance scores to claims that benefit from multi-source perspectives of both a textbook view and an example view.
3. **Final Answer Refinement with Citations:** We filter claims where $S(c_j) \geq \tau$ (threshold) to form a verified set $C_{verified}$. The LLM then synthesizes these verified claims into a final answer A_{final}.

4 Experimental Setup

4.1 Evaluation Benchmarks

We evaluate effectiveness using three benchmarks:

OpenStaxQA [24]: is a multilingual educational QA dataset built from 43 open-source college textbooks across business, humanities, social sciences, science and math. It can be used for evaluating LLMs on college-level subject understanding. We concentrate on the side of history, sociology and business.

MMLU [25]: is a widely used benchmark for general knowledge and reasoning, consisting of 57 multiple-choice tasks spanning subjects with college-level. Among these tasks, history, sociology and business can also be filtered out.

AGI Eval [26]: includes questions from human-centric standardized exams such as the SAT and LSAT. We evaluate the English multiple-choice tasks with five options each in LSAT.

4.2 Baselines

- **Vanilla** [16]: It serves as a baseline by directly feeding the top-k retrieved passages into the large language model's context window and instructing it to generate answers with corresponding citations. While this approach is simple and achieves strong performance close to the best strategies, it is inherently constrained by the model's context window, limiting the number of passages that can be processed at one time.
- **Summary** [16]: Retrieved passages undergo summarizationbased compression prior to model input. These summarized compressions are concatenated with the original query and processed through identical task-specific instructions and in-context learning mechanisms to guide the generation of answers with integrated citations. This approach intentionally mitigates textual redundancy in model inputs, enhancing focus on salient information.
- **HyDE** [27]: This method first utilizes an LLM to generate a "hypothetical document" based on the query. Although this document is fictional and may contain factual errors, it captures relevant text patterns. Subsequently, the hypothetical document is encoded into an embedding vector, and real documents are finally retrieved from the corpus based on vector similarity.
- **RAG-Fusion** [28]: This is a method that optimizes retrieval results by generating multiple queries. It first utilizes an LLM to expand the user's original question into multiple search queries from different perspectives, then executes vector retrieval for each generated query separately. Finally, it uses the Reciprocal Rank Fusion (RRF) algorithm to merge and rerank all retrieved documents, prioritizing highly relevant documents for input into the LLM.

4.3 Implementation Details

In our experiments, we use Qwen2.5-7B-Instruct [29] and Llama3-8B-Instruct [30] as the backbone Large Language Models (LLMs) to handle query rewriting, initial generation, and final generation tasks. For the retrieval phase, we utilize BAAI/bge-m3 [31] as the dense retriever and maintain two distinct vector indexes within ChromaDB for 'textbooks' and 'examples'. To maintain experimental consistency, we standardize the retrieval volume across all methods. For both the proposed DMVR and all baselines, we retrieve the top-k = 3 passages from each of the two views, resulting in a total of 6 reference chunks per query. Regarding citation verification, we adopt cross-encoder/nli-deberta-v3-base [32] as the Natural Language Inference (NLI) model, with the verification threshold set to $\tau = 0.5$. In terms of generation configuration, we use Nucleus Sampling (top-p=0.9) and set the temperature parameters for initial generation and final refinement to 0.6 and 0.7, respectively.

4.4 Main Results

Table 1. Comparison of Accuracy on OpenStaxQA, MMLU, and AGI Eval

Method	OpenStaxQA					MMLU					AGI Eval
	Hist.	Soci.	Gover.	Busi.	Avg	Hist.	Soci.	Gover.	Busi.	Avg	
						Qwen2.5-7b					
Vanilla	65.91	84.62	63.64	48.48	67.79	82.35	80.10	86.53	78.00	82.23	63.33
Summary	72.73	74.36	63.64	51.52	66.44	81.37	83.08	87.05	76.00	82.66	62.94
HyDE	81.82	82.05	57.58	54.55	70.47	84.31	82.59	88.08	80.00	84.24	64.51
RAG-Fusion	68.18	**89.74**	60.61	51.52	68.46	**84.80**	80.60	88.08	76.00	83.24	61.96
DMVR	**84.09**	84.62	**66.67**	**60.61**	**75.17**	81.86	**84.08**	**89.64**	**81.00**	**84.52**	**67.45**
						Llama3-8b					
Vanilla	68.18	76.92	57.58	48.48	63.76	59.80	66.17	69.43	**67.00**	65.33	33.92
Summary	72.73	82.05	57.58	45.45	65.77	69.12	73.13	76.68	**67.00**	72.06	38.43
HyDE	**75.00**	76.92	**66.67**	57.58	69.80	66.18	67.16	71.50	66.00	67.91	34.71
RAG-Fusion	72.73	79.49	54.55	**60.61**	67.79	70.10	70.65	69.43	57.00	68.19	37.25
DMVR	70.45	**89.74**	**66.67**	54.55	**71.14**	**73.53**	**78.11**	**83.42**	65.00	**76.36**	**45.10**

As shown in Table 1, DMVR demonstrates significant improvements across all three benchmarks. On Qwen2.5-7B, it achieved average scores of 75.17%, 84.52%, and 67.45% on OpenStaxQA, MMLU, and AGI Eval respectively, consistently outperforming the strongest baselines. This advantage is even more pronounced on Llama3-8B, where DMVR achieved a 6.67% improvement over the Summary baseline on AGI Eval, highlighting its capability to enhance general cognitive reasoning.

Beyond aggregated metrics, DMVR also exhibits superior effectiveness in specific domains. While occasionally scoring slightly lower than the best baseline on specific tasks, it maintains superior performance across the vast majority of subjects. Notably, in the Business subject of OpenStaxQA (Qwen2.5-7B), it surpassed the HyDE baseline by a margin of 6.06%. Similarly, in the Government subject of MMLU on Llama3, it outperformed the baseline by 6.74%. This indicates that our multi-view verification mechanism not only enhances broad cognitive capabilities but also effectively filters noise in knowledge-intensive domains.

5 Analysis

5.1 Ablation Study

Table 2. Ablation study of DMVR on OpenStaxQA tasks.

Method	OpenStaxQA				
	Hist.	Soci.	Gover.	Busi.	**Avg**
DMVR	**84.09**	84.62	**66.67**	**60.61**	**75.17**
w/o rewrite	68.18	**89.74**	60.61	**60.61**	70.47
w/o tx_view	65.91	84.62	63.64	54.55	67.79
w/o ex_view	70.45	87.18	60.61	51.52	68.46
w/o NLI	75.00	87.18	63.64	54.55	71.14

To validate the effectiveness of DMVR, we conducted a comprehensive ablation study on its key components using the OpenStaxQA dataset. As shown in Table 2, compared to the full framework, all variants exhibited performance degradation.

Specifically, the *w/o tx_view* (without textbook view) variant resulted in the most significant decline, with the average accuracy dropping by 7.38% from 75.17% to 67.79%. Notably, the History subject saw a sharp drop of 18.18%, demonstrating that definitions in textbooks are foundational sources for answering such academic questions. Similarly, the *w/o ex_view* (without example view) variant led to a 6.71% decrease in the average score, with a particularly substantial impact on the Business subject (a 9.09% drop). This indicates that practical exercises are crucial for complementing theoretical knowledge and enhancing application capabilities.

The *w/o rewrite* and *w/o NLI* variants caused average score drops of 4.70% and 4.03%, respectively. Although the magnitude of these drops is slightly smaller than that of directly removing data sources, they still constitute significant performance losses. This proves that dynamic query rewrite is vital for targeted retrieval across different data sources, while NLI verification effectively filters retrieval noise to ensure answer faithfulness. These results confirm that the completeness of data sources and the rigor of processing mechanisms must work synergistically to achieve superior performance.

6 Conclusion and Future Work

6.1 Conclusion

This paper addresses the reliability challenge caused by hallucinations in LLMs within educational scenarios by proposing the Dynamic Multi-View Retrieval-Augmented Generation (DMVR) framework. To align the traditional RAG architecture with the intrinsic structure of educational knowledge, our framework employs dynamic view-specific query rewriting at the retrieval stage to achieve precise and comprehensive retrieval from view of textbooks and examples. On the generation side, we introduce a cross-source verification mechanism based on NLI models, ensuring high factual consistency and robust multi-view support for the generated answers. To validate the effectiveness of the framework, we conducted experiments on three educational question-answering benchmarks: OpenStaxQA, MMLU, and AGI Eval. The results demonstrate that DMVR significantly improves answer accuracy compared to base LLMs and various RAG baselines. This provides a feasible and effective technical path for building safer and more trustworthy educational LLM applications.

6.2 Limitations

Despite the promising results achieved in this study, several limitations still remain:

- **Single Knowledge Modality:** The current framework primarily processes instructional materials in plain text format. It has not yet incorporated multimodal knowledge sources prevalent in educational scenarios, such as diagrams, images of formulas, and video lectures.
- **Computational Latency:** Compared to Naive RAG, DMV-RAG introduces multiple LLM invocations for query rewriting and answer generation, along with the inclusion of NLI model verification. These components collectively increase the system's computational overhead and response latency [33], which may pose challenges for deployment in real-time interactive applications, particularly under high-concurrency scenarios.

6.3 Future Work

In light of these limitations, future research should focus on the following strategic directions:

- **Fusion of Multimodal Knowledge Sources:** We plan to extend the framework into the multimodal domain, investigating methods to extract structured information from diagrams in textbooks, retrieve key audio segments from video lectures, and design cross-modal verification mechanisms.

- **Performance Optimization:** We aim to leverage high-quality synthetic data generated by large models like GPT-4 to train specialized, lightweight NLI models that maintain comparable performance with significantly fewer parameters [34]. Concurrently, deeper research will be conducted into caching strategies and parallel computing techniques. These optimization strategies are intended to reduce the inference latency of the DMVR framework, facilitating its deployment in educational dialogue systems that require real-time responsiveness.

References

1. Wang, S., et al.: Large language models for education: a survey and outlook. arXiv preprint arXiv:2403.18105 (2024)
2. Xu, H., et al.: Large language models for education: a survey. arXiv preprint arXiv:2405.13001 (2024)
3. Gan, W., et al.: Large language models in education: vision and opportunities. In: 2023 IEEE International Conference on Big Data (BigData). IEEE (2023)
4. Ma, X., et al.: Query rewriting in retrieval-augmented large language models. In: Proceedings of the 2023 Conference on Empirical Methods in Natural Language Processing. Association for Computational Linguistics (2023)
5. Dang, H.A., Tran, V., Nguyen, L.M.: Survey and analysis of hallucinations in large language models: attribution to prompting strategies or model behavior. Front. Artif. Intell. **8**, 1622292 (2025)
6. Li, Y., et al.: Mitigating Hallucination in Large Language Models (LLMs): an application-oriented survey on RAG, reasoning, and agentic systems. arXiv preprint arXiv:2510.24476 (2025)
7. Tonmoy, S.M.T.I., et al.: A comprehensive survey of hallucination mitigation techniques in large language models. arXiv preprint arXiv:2401.01313 (2024)
8. Sharma, C.: Retrieval-Augmented Generation: a comprehensive survey of architectures, enhancements, and robustness frontiers. arXiv preprint arXiv:2506.00054 (2025)
9. Gao, Y., et al.: Retrieval-augmented generation for large language models: a survey. arXiv preprint arXiv:2312.10997 (2023)
10. Zhong, Y., et al.: Reasoning-enhanced query understanding through decomposition and interpretation. arXiv preprint arXiv:2509.06544 (2025)
11. Zheng, H.S., et al.: Take a step back: evoking reasoning via abstraction in large language models. arXiv preprint arXiv:2310.06117 (2023)
12. Jiang, J., et al.: Rag-star: enhancing deliberative reasoning with retrieval augmented verification and refinement. In: Proceedings of NAACL-HLT 2025 (Volume 1: Long Papers). Association for Computational Linguistics (2025)
13. Chen, Z., et al.: MindSearch: mimicking human minds elicits deep ai searcher. arXiv preprint arXiv:2407.20183 (2024)
14. Zhang, Z., Feng, Y., Zhang, M.: LevelRAG: enhancing retrieval-augmented generation with multi-hop logic planning over rewriting augmented searchers. arXiv preprint arXiv:2502.18139 (2025)
15. Saxena, Y., et al.: Generation-Time vs. Post-hoc Citation: a holistic evaluation of LLM attribution. arXiv preprint arXiv:2509.21557 (2025)

16. Gao, T., et al.: Enabling large language models to generate text with citations. arXiv preprint arXiv:2305.14627 (2023)
17. Ji, B., et al.: Chain-of-thought improves text generation with citations in large language models. In: Proceedings of the AAAI Conference on Artificial Intelligence, vol. 38, no. 16 (2024)
18. Zhang, J., et al.: LongCite: enabling LLMs to generate fine-grained citations in long-context QA. In: Findings of the Association for Computational Linguistics: ACL 2025. Association for Computational Linguistics (2025)
19. Gao, L., et al.: RARR: researching and revising what language models say, using language models. In: Proceedings of the 61st Annual Meeting of the Association for Computational Linguistics (Volume 1: Long Papers). Association for Computational Linguistics (2023)
20. Sancheti, A., Goswami, K., Srinivasan, B.: Post-hoc answer attribution for grounded and trustworthy long document comprehension: task, insights, and challenges. In: Proceedings of the 13th Joint Conference on Lexical and Computational Semantics (*SEM 2024). Association for Computational Linguistics (2024)
21. Ramu, P., et al.: Enhancing post-hoc attributions in long document comprehension via coarse grained answer decomposition. arXiv preprint arXiv:2409.17073 (2024)
22. Maheshwari, H., Tenneti, S., Nakkiran, A.: CiteFix: enhancing RAG accuracy through post-processing citation correction. arXiv preprint arXiv:2504.15629 (2025)
23. Qian, H., et al.: VeriCite: towards reliable citations in retrieval-augmented generation via rigorous verification. arXiv preprint arXiv:2510.11394 (2025)
24. Gupta, P.: OpenStaxQA: a multilingual dataset based on open-source college textbooks. arXiv preprint arXiv:2510.06239 (2025)
25. Hendrycks, D., et al.: Measuring massive multitask language understanding. arXiv preprint arXiv:2009.03300 (2020)
26. Zhong, W., et al.: AGIEval: a human-centric benchmark for evaluating foundation models. In: Findings of the Association for Computational Linguistics: NAACL 2024. Association for Computational Linguistics (2024)
27. Gao, L., et al.: Precise zero-shot dense retrieval without relevance labels. In: Proceedings of the 61st Annual Meeting of the Association for Computational Linguistics (Volume 1: Long Papers). Association for Computational Linguistics (2023)
28. Rackauckas, Z.: RAG-Fusion: a new take on retrieval-augmented generation. arXiv preprint arXiv:2402.03367 (2024)
29. Yang, A., et al.: Qwen2.5 technical report. arXiv preprint arXiv:2412.15115 (2024)
30. Grattafiori, A., et al.: The Llama 3 herd of models. arXiv preprint arXiv:2407.21783 (2024)
31. Chen, J., et al.: BGE M3-embedding: multi-lingual, multi-functionality, multi-granularity text embeddings through self-knowledge distillation. arXiv preprint arXiv:2402.03216 (2024)
32. He, P., Gao, J., Chen, W.: DeBERTaV3: Improving deBERTa using ELECTRA-style pre-training with gradient-disentangled embedding sharing. arXiv preprint arXiv:2111.09543 (2021)
33. Liu, Z., et al.: E-Verify: a paradigm shift to scalable embedding-based factuality verification. In: Findings of the Association for Computational Linguistics: EMNLP 2025. Association for Computational Linguistics (2025)
34. Leemann, T., et al.: Auto-GDA: automatic domain adaptation for efficient grounding verification in retrieval-augmented generation. arXiv preprint arXiv:2410.03461 (2024)

Systematic Evaluation of Miniaturized Lunar Navigation and Communication Satellite Constellation Systems

Siyuan Han[1], Yan Kang[1], Lei Gao[1], Yanli Shao[1], Maodeng Li[2,3](✉), Yichen Jiang[2], Bowen Dong[2], Haidong Xia[4], and Hua Zhang[2]

[1] Lunar Exploration and Space Engineering Center, Beijing, China
[2] Deep Space Exploration Laboratory, Beijing, China
[3] Beijing Institute of Control Engineering, Beijing, China
mdengli@foxmail.com
[4] Chang'e Lunar Spaceflight Technology (Beijing) Co., Ltd., Beijing, China

Abstract. With the resurgence of lunar exploration, sustainable communication and navigation infrastructure has become critical. This paper addresses the trade-off between miniaturized and large-platform architectures for lunar constellations by proposing a systematic evaluation framework. The core idea of this framework is to separate design constraints from performance metrics: first, engineering models are used to place different schemes under unified equivalent resource constraints, ensuring a fair comparison; then, a hierarchical threshold-based ("pyramid") evaluation method is employed. This model sequentially filters schemes based on (1) a qualification threshold (basic service availability), (2) a reliability threshold (N-1 fault tolerance), and finally (3) ranks geometric dilution of precision (GDOP) and daily data throughput in a performance optimization layer. This framework is applied to evaluate typical configurations with varying satellite numbers and individual satellite masses. Simulation results validate the effectiveness of the evaluation framework, revealing potential limitations of the "large-platform" scheme in basic availability, while the all-miniaturized configuration demonstrates robust availability and reliability. The research findings not only provide a systematic evaluation framework and quantitative basis for the engineering design of lunar positioning, navigation, and timing (PNT) and communication systems but also lay a theoretical foundation for the evolution of advanced technologies such as the global coverage extension of lunar communication and navigation constellations.

Keywords: Performance Evaluation · Lunar Satellite Constellation · Architecture Trade-off

1 Introduction

With the rapid development of aerospace technology, deep space exploration has become the commanding height of global technological competition [1]. Cislunar space, as a strategic gateway and outpost for humanity's expeditions into

J. Zhan et al. (Eds.): Bench 2025, LNCS 16471, pp. 66–81, 2026.
https://doi.org/10.1007/978-981-95-9694-2_6

the deeper solar system, is rapidly becoming a new strategic frontier for competition among global space-faring nations [2]. Against this backdrop, major space-faring countries and agencies worldwide have either formulated or implemented corresponding lunar exploration programs, such as the International Lunar Research Station [3], the Artemis program [4], and the Moon Village initiative [5], aiming to establish long-term, sustainable lunar bases to lay the foundation for the large-scale exploitation of lunar resources and cutting-edge scientific research.

These programs have created an urgent demand for lunar communication and positioning, navigation and timing (PNT) services. Firstly, long-term lunar stays and the large-scale development of lunar resources will generate massive amounts of scientific data, necessitating high-bandwidth, low-latency data return links. In particular, for regions such as the lunar farside and poles, which lack direct line-of-sight communication with Earth, reliance on relay communication services is essential. Secondly, precise rendezvous and docking of spacecraft in lunar orbit, autonomous hazard avoidance and precision landing of landers in complex terrain, path planning and coordinated operations of lunar surface mobile units, and even the safety of astronaut extravehicular activities, all require meter-level or even higher-precision real-time PNT services. Therefore, constructing a lunar orbital constellation to provide integrated communication and navigation services has become a core foundation for future lunar exploration activities.

How to economically and efficiently build a lunar communication and navigation constellation is an architecture trade-off problem worthy of in-depth study. Traditional deep space exploration missions typically rely on powerful, high-reliability large satellite platforms. While this architecture is technologically mature with excellent single-satellite performance, it is plagued by inherent drawbacks, including long development cycles, high launch costs, and poor on-orbit deployment flexibility. Concurrently, the "all-miniaturized constellation" scheme offers another possibility. This approach leverages the advantages of small satellites—low cost, mass production, and rapid, flexible deployment—to achieve service coverage and system resilience through constellation networking. However, this architecture also faces severe technical challenges: miniaturized platforms are strictly limited in terms of payload power, antenna gain, and other aspects. Whether such platforms can satisfy the service requirements for lunar exploration remains a critical question that demands urgent empirical validation.

In response to the technical challenges in the aforementioned architecture trade-offs, this paper proposes a systematic evaluation framework to comprehensively assess the effectiveness of lunar communication and navigation constellations. This framework first disaggregates design constraints from performance metrics and places different schemes under unified equivalent resource constraints (e.g., total mass constraint) based on engineering approximation models, thereby ensuring a fair comparative analysis. On this basis, a hierarchical threshold-based ("pyramid" model) comprehensive evaluation method is constructed, which conducts sequential screening from basic service availability and fault tolerance to navigation and communication performance metrics.

Through this method, this paper can not only ensure that the selected schemes meet the basic requirements and reliability standards of the mission, but also identify the optimal performing solution among the qualified schemes, providing a solid scientific basis for architecture design of lunar communication and navigation constellations. Finally, by applying this framework, this paper conducts a quantitative evaluation of different constellation configuration schemes (such as varying satellite counts and individual satellite masses) under the same total mass constraint through simulation analysis.

2 System Architecture and Design Constraints

2.1 Mission Background and Challenges

The current lunar exploration paradigm has shifted from single missions to establishing a sustainable human presence, driven by water ice resources in permanently shadowed regions (PSRs) such as the Shackleton crater [6]. A significant portion of planned missions will be concentrated in the lunar south pole region. To meet the demands of these continuous, high-intensity missions, how to construct a lunar communication and navigation constellation system has become a core issue in architecture design.

As mentioned in the introduction, the architectural framework faces a trade-off between the two paths of traditional large satellite platforms and all-miniaturized constellations. The former relies on powerful, high-reliability large satellites with strong single-satellite performance but faces challenges of long development cycles and high launch costs. The latter leverages the advantages of small satellites—low cost, mass production, and rapid, flexible deployment—to achieve service coverage and system resilience through constellation networking. This architectural trade-off is not a simple opposition between "performance" and "cost." For example, miniaturized constellations attempt to compensate for a lack of "quality" with "quantity," but whether this can meet the demanding PNT accuracy and high-bandwidth communication needs of specific areas such as the lunar south pole is a critical question that needs to be answered.

2.2 Constellation Orbit Schemes

Common orbits for lunar communication and navigation constellations include Elliptical Lunar Frozen Orbits (ELFO), Earth-Moon libration point orbits (such as Halo orbits and Near-Rectilinear Halo Orbits, NRHO), and Distant Retrograde Orbits (DRO) [7–9]. The choice of different orbit types is a core trade-off point in constellation design, primarily reflected in coverage characteristics, operational costs, and mission flexibility.

The key advantage of ELFO is its orbital stability. By balancing various perturbation effects, it can minimize the fuel (ΔV) required for station-keeping and provide persistent, stable coverage for a single polar region (such as the lunar south pole). This makes it an ideal choice for supporting long-term static missions at specific locations (e.g., the south pole), especially suitable for building "small-satellite" constellations. The main advantages of Earth-Moon libration point orbits include continuous visibility to Earth (critical for communication and ground-based time transfer) and the potential to build large-area or even global coverage. However, these orbits are inherently less stable than ELFO and typically require more orbit station-keeping maneuvers. DRO orbits are extremely stable, requiring almost no orbit maintenance, but they are far from the Moon. Therefore, the choice of orbit scheme is essentially a fundamental trade-off between "operational efficiency" (such as the low maintenance cost of ELFO) and "mission flexibility" (such as the coverage range and Earth visibility of Halo/NRHO).

Given the limitations of single orbit types in meeting coverage, navigation accuracy, and cost constraints, adopting hybrid orbit schemes has become an important development direction. For instance, a combination of ELFO, NRHO, and Halo was proposed in [9] to achieve phased, combined coverage from polar regions to global coverage. In this phased construction roadmap, an ELFO constellation is typically the core of the first phase, used to prioritize initial communication services for key areas such as the lunar south pole. Therefore, the research focus of this paper is consistent with the "first phase" goal of the aforementioned phased construction. We must first address the core architectural trade-off faced when building this basic ELFO constellation: i.e., under a total resource constraint, should a miniaturized scheme (many satellites, small individual mass) or a large-platform scheme (few satellites, strong individual performance) be adopted?

Based on these considerations, to isolate variables and ensure the effectiveness of the comparison, this paper will temporarily not consider complex hybrid orbits but will focus on the comparison of this basic architecture. The subsequent simulation analysis will only target ELFO orbits, conducting a quantitative evaluation of configuration schemes with different satellite numbers and individual satellite masses under the same total mass constraint, aiming to provide a decision-making reference for the initial architecture selection of the lunar communication and navigation constellation.

3 Performance Evaluation System and Models

3.1 Hierarchical Performance Requirements

To systematically evaluate different architectures of lunar communication and navigation constellation schemes, a hierarchical quantitative metric system is established based on existing research (such as the NASA Service Requirements Document (SRD) [10], LNS proposals [8,11]), considering system-level, navigation service, and communication service dimensions comprehensively.

System-level metrics primarily consider the overall resource consumption and mission adaptability of the constellation. The focus is on the constellation's total deployment cost (including launch), orbit maintenance cost during its on-orbit lifetime, and the mapping relationship with total mass.

Navigation service metrics are used to quantify the quality and reliability of PNT (Positioning, Navigation, and Timing) services. They mainly include basic service availability, service robustness, and service accuracy. Service availability generally refers to the availability and continuity of obtaining a valid navigation solution (usually requiring ≥ 4 visible satellites) within the target area. Service robustness considers the ability to provide service when some satellites fail, used to evaluate the system's robustness under abnormal conditions. Service accuracy evaluates the final positioning accuracy achievable by the user through the GDOP and User Equivalent Range Error (UERE) models.

Communication service metrics focus on data transmission capability. This dimension assesses the availability of the communication link (usually requiring ≥ 1 visible satellite), the achievable peak data rate, and the most core total daily data volume. Similarly, it is also necessary to evaluate the service degradation and fault tolerance of the communication service in the event of a single-satellite failure.

The specific definitions of the above metrics are shown in Table 1.

3.2 Constraint Equivalence Modeling

As stated in the introduction, the core of this research lies in scientifically evaluating the performance trade-off between "large-platform" and "all-miniaturized" architectural paths. To ensure a fair comparison, different schemes must be placed under unified resource constraints (e.g., the same total mass). However, different schemes have varying single-satellite masses and satellite numbers. Therefore, before conducting a system-level evaluation, it is essential to establish a "constraint equivalence model" or "scaling relationship" between key performance metrics (such as communication rate) and single-satellite resources (such as mass). This section aims to establish this model, laying a theoretical foundation for the fair comparison of the total communication capabilities of different constellations under equal mass constraints. To establish this model, we analyze the relationship between communication capability (represented by data rate d_{Ka}) and satellite mass (represented by dry mass m_{dry}). The actual communication data rate is inherently a complex link budget problem influenced by multiple engineering factors, such as transmitter power, antenna gain, receiver G/T value, communication distance (causing significant path loss), and modulation/coding. However, in the mission-level architecture trade-offs explored in this paper, the focus is on the scaling relationship between communication capability and the satellite platform (specifically mass) rather than performing a precise decibel-level link budget.

According to the Friis transmission formula and the Shannon-Hartley theorem, the data transmission rate d_{Ka}, given a communication distance and

Table 1. Navigation and Communication Metric Definitions and Reference Values.

Service & Metric	Metric Description	Reference Value
Navigation Service Coverage (Availability)	Percentage of time a user in the target area has $\geq$ 4 visible satellites	$\geq$98%
Navigation Service Accuracy (GDOP)	Measures the impact of constellation geometry on positioning accuracy, a core metric	<6.0
Navigation Robustness (Fault Tolerance)	Navigation service availability when any single satellite in the constellation fails	$\geq$98%
Communication Service Coverage (Availability)	Percentage of time a user in the target area has $\geq$1 visible communication satellite	$\geq$75%
Communication Robustness (Fault Tolerance)	Communication service availability when any single satellite in the constellation fails	$\geq$75%
Communication Trans. Perf. (Data Rate)	The maximum communication rate supported between the user and satellite (Proximity), and between the satellite and Earth(Trunk)	Proximity $\geq$ 10 Mbps Trunk $\geq$ 100 Mbps
Communication Trans. Perf. (Daily Data Volume)	The total amount of data a single user can transmit/receive per day	>500 GB/day

receiver conditions, is primarily driven by two key parameters: transmission power (P_{tx}) and transmission antenna gain (G_{tx}), i.e.,

$$d_{Ka} \propto P_{tx} \cdot G_{tx} \tag{1}$$

We establish the following two key engineering approximations to relate P_{tx} and G_{tx} to the satellite dry mass m_{dry}. First, the available transmission power P_{tx} for the satellite is strictly constrained by the power subsystem (e.g., solar array area, battery capacity). In engineering practice, a larger satellite dry mass m_{dry} can support a larger and heavier power subsystem, thus providing higher P_{tx}. Therefore, we assume P_{tx} is proportional to m_{dry}:

$$P_{tx} \approx C_P \cdot m_{dry} \tag{2}$$

Here, $m_{dry} = m/E_i$ is the satellite dry mass, m is the total satellite mass, and E_i is the wet-to-dry mass ratio.

Similarly, a larger m_{dry} allows for carrying a larger (i.e., larger physical aperture A_{ant}), heavier high-gain antenna. Antenna gain G_{tx} is proportional to its physical aperture area A_{ant}. We assume the achievable G_{tx} (and the required antenna structure) is limited by the mass and space allocable by the satellite platform, and thus is also positively correlated with m_{dry}:

$$G_{tx} \approx C_G \cdot m_{dry} \tag{3}$$

where C_G is a constant, representing the conversion coefficient from unit dry mass to achievable antenna gain.

Substituting the two approximate relationships above, we obtain the key scaling model for communication rate d_{Ka} and m_{dry}:

$$d_{Ka} \approx (C_P \cdot m_{dry}) \cdot (C_G \cdot m_{dry}) = K_{total} \cdot m_{dry}^2 \tag{4}$$

where $K_{total} = C_P \cdot C_G$ is a comprehensive link constant, summarizing the efficiency of converting satellite platform "mass" into "communication capability" at a specific technology level. This quadratic relationship model is the constraint equivalence model adopted in this study.

Notably, while Table 1 provides reference peak data rates for context, the current simulation focuses on the relative scaling of communication capacity. The specific verification of these absolute rate thresholds requires detailed link budgets and is reserved for future high-fidelity studies.

3.3 Key Performance Metric Calculation Models

Navigation Performance Metrics Navigation performance metrics primarily include service availability, navigation service robustness, and navigation positioning accuracy. Let the navigation service availability be $P_{avail,nav}$ (in %), which can be obtained by the following formula:

$$P_{avail,nav} = \frac{T_{avail}}{T_{total}} \times 100\% \tag{5}$$

where T_{total} is the total duration considered, and T_{avail} is the duration of navigation service availability, i.e., the duration when at least 4 satellites are visible. If T_{total} is divided into K equal time steps Δt, then:

$$T_{avail} = \sum_{k=1}^{K} S(t_k) \cdot \Delta t$$

where $S(t_k)$ is the service status function, which is 1 when the number of visible satellites $N_{vis}(t_k) \geq 4$, and 0 otherwise.

This involves determining satellite visibility. The elevation angle of the i-th satellite at time t_k is denoted as $\alpha_i(t_k)$ and is given by:

$$\alpha_i(t_k) = \arcsin\left(\frac{\mathbf{r}_u \cdot (\mathbf{r}_{s,i} - \mathbf{r}_u)}{|\mathbf{r}_u||\mathbf{r}_{s,i} - \mathbf{r}_u|}\right) \tag{6}$$

where $\mathbf{r}_u$ and $\mathbf{r}_{s,i}$ are the position vectors of the user and the i-th satellite, respectively, in the Moon-centered coordinate system. When $\alpha_i(t_k) \geq \alpha_{mask}$, the satellite is visible to the user, where α_{mask} is the minimum elevation angle threshold.

Let the navigation service robustness metric be $P_{tolerant}$. This metric requires that when 1 satellite in the constellation fails, at least 4 satellites are still visible to maintain basic positioning capability, quantifying the system's ability to maintain service under single-satellite failure. It is calculated as follows:

$$P_{tolerant} = \frac{T_{tolerant}}{T_{total}} \times 100\% \tag{7}$$

where $T_{tolerant}$ is the service availability duration after a single satellite failure, given by:

$$T_{tolerant} = \sum_{k=1}^{K} F(t_k) \cdot \Delta t$$

$F(t_k)$ is the fault tolerance status function, which is 1 when $N_{vis}(t_k) \geq 5$, and 0 otherwise.

Let the navigation positioning accuracy be σ_{pos}. It is primarily determined by the GDOP and the equivalent ranging error:

$$\sigma_{pos} = \text{GDOP} \times \sigma_{\text{UERE}} \tag{8}$$

where σ_{UERE} is the User Equivalent Range Error. In the architecture trade-off comparison of this study, it is assumed that σ_{UERE} is at the same level for all compared parties. Under this assumption, the GDOP value becomes the core metric for directly comparing the PNT accuracy performance of different schemes. The GDOP value is determined by the geometric configuration of the visible satellites and is given by:

$$\text{GDOP} = \sqrt{\text{Tr}(G)} = \sqrt{G_{11} + G_{22} + G_{33} + G_{44}} \tag{9}$$

where Tr is the trace operator, G_{ii} is the i-th diagonal element of the matrix G, and G is the covariance matrix, which can be calculated from the geometric observation matrix H:

$$G = (H^T H)^{-1} \tag{10}$$

Here, the geometric observation matrix H reflects the Jacobian matrix of the measurements with respect to the state. For navigation positioning, the measurements can be represented by pseudoranges, and the state variables refer to the user's position, so H can be written as:

$$H_i = \left[\tfrac{x_{s,i}-x_u}{R_i}, \tfrac{y_{s,i}-y_u}{R_i}, \tfrac{z_{s,i}-z_u}{R_i}, 1\right] \tag{11}$$

where (x_u, y_u, z_u) and $(x_{s,i}, y_{s,i}, z_{s,i})$ are the coordinates of the user and the satellite, respectively, in the Moon-centered coordinate system, and $R_i = \sqrt{(x_{s,i} - x_u)^2 + (y_{s,i} - y_u)^2 + (z_{s,i} - z_u)^2}$ is the distance between the user and the i-th satellite.

Communication Service Performance Metrics Similarly, communication service performance metrics include communication service availability, communication service robustness, and daily data throughput. The communication service availability, denoted as $P_{avail,comm}$, can be given by:

$$P_{avail,comm} = \frac{T_{avail,comm}}{T_{total}} \times 100\% \quad (12)$$

where $T_{avail,comm}$ is the total communication availability duration, as follows:

$$T_{avail,comm} = \sum_{k=1}^{K} S_{comm}(t_k) \cdot \Delta t \quad (13)$$

In the above equation, $S_{comm}(t_k)$ is the communication service status function, which is 1 when the number of visible communication satellites $N_{vis,comm}(t_k) \geq 1$, and 0 otherwise.

Communication service robustness is given by the communication service fault tolerance ($P_{tolerant,comm}$), which measures the system's ability to maintain a communication link after a single communication satellite failure, as follows:

$$P_{tolerant,comm} = \frac{T_{tolerant,comm}}{T_{total}} \times 100\% \quad (14)$$

where $T_{tolerant,comm} = \sum_{k=1}^{K} F_{comm}(t_k) \cdot \Delta t$ is the communication fault tolerance duration, and $F_{comm}(t_k)$ is the communication fault tolerance status function, which is 1 when $N_{vis,comm}(t_k) \geq 2$, and 0 otherwise. The total daily data volume (D_{Ka}) is determined by the data rate and the daily available duration [8]:

$$D_{Ka} = d_{Ka} \cdot t_{Ka} \quad (15)$$

where d_{Ka} is the communication data rate calculated using the engineering scaling model established in Sect. 3.2, which relates link performance to satellite dry mass. The parameter t_{Ka} represents the sum of the daily available durations of all communication satellites, given by:

$$t_{Ka} = \sum_{i=1}^{N_{comm}} T_{avail,comm,i} \quad (16)$$

where $T_{avail,comm,i}$ is the total daily duration that the i-th communication satellite has a line-of-sight connection with Earth, given by Eq. 13.

3.4 Comprehensive Evaluation Method for Navigation and Communication Performance

To systematically evaluate the merits of different lunar communication and navigation constellation schemes, this paper first uses the system-level metrics from the "hierarchical performance requirements" as the top-level design constraint for the evaluation. This paper uses equal mass constraints as the core benchmark. All compared schemes are converted to approximately the same total mass constraint; if the total mass of the schemes is inconsistent, an approximate performance scaling relationship (as given by Eq. 4) is used to normalize the different schemes to a unified constraint baseline for comparison.

Under this unified constraint, a hierarchical threshold-based comprehensive evaluation framework ("pyramid" model) is adopted to conduct a detailed evaluation and screening of the navigation and communication service performance of each scheme. This framework draws on the hierarchy of needs theory, organizing the evaluation metrics into a pyramid structure with clear priority orders and progressive relationships between levels. This evaluation logic ensures that the finally selected scheme is not only superior in performance but also possesses the continuity and reliability necessary for actual missions. As shown in Fig. 1, the evaluation framework is divided into three levels, from bottom to top: Qualification Threshold Layer, Reliability Threshold Layer, and Performance Optimization Layer. The lower layer is the admission condition for the upper layer; only schemes that pass the lower-level threshold can enter the higher-level evaluation.

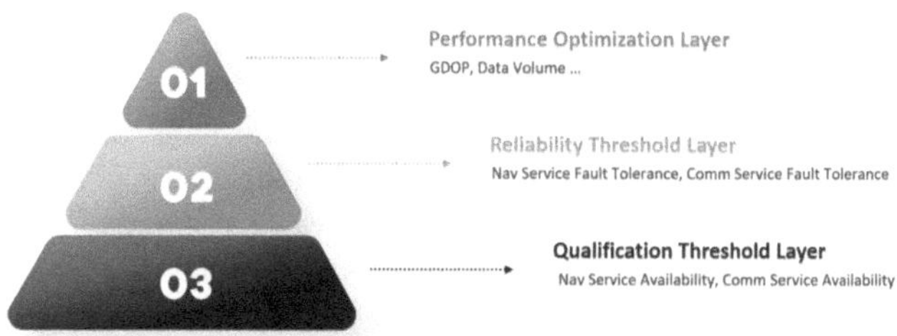

Fig. 1. Pyramid Evaluation Architecture

The Qualification Threshold Layer has "one-vote veto power." This layer uses two core metrics, navigation service availability ($P_{avail,nav}$) and communication service availability ($P_{avail,comm}$), to assess whether the constellation scheme can provide the most basic service coverage in the target area (e.g., the lunar south pole). The specific evaluation criteria are setting navigation service availability $P_{avail,nav} \geq 98\%$ and communication service availability $P_{avail,comm} \geq 75\%$ as the minimum standards for scheme selection. Any scheme that fails to meet both of these conditions simultaneously will be considered to have basic service defects and will not proceed to higher-level evaluation.

On the premise of ensuring basic service coverage, the Reliability Threshold Layer evaluates the constellation's ability to maintain service continuity in the event of a single-point failure (N-1), which is crucial for critical missions. This layer uses navigation service fault tolerance ($P_{tolerant}$) and communication service fault tolerance ($P_{tolerant,comm}$) metrics. The specific evaluation criterion is: for schemes that have passed the first-level threshold, set navigation fault tolerance $P_{tolerant} \geq 98\%$ and communication service fault tolerance $P_{tolerant,comm} \geq 75\%$ as the reliability assessment standard. Schemes that fail to meet the fault tolerance standard will be considered "fragile" designs, and their priority should be lower than that of schemes with high fault tolerance.

The Performance Optimization Layer is the final performance comparison stage, used to select the "best of the best" from the qualified schemes that have passed the first two threshold layers. This layer uses the 98% GDOP value and the total daily data volume as evaluation metrics. The specific evaluation criterion is: for all schemes that have passed the first two threshold layers, directly compare their GDOP values and daily data volumes. The scheme with a lower GDOP and a larger daily data volume is considered the final preferred design.

Based on the pyramid model described above, the comprehensive evaluation process in this paper is a strict hierarchical screening process: first, eliminate basic service non-compliant schemes through the "Qualification Threshold Layer"; then, identify high-risk designs through the "Reliability Threshold Layer"; finally, rank the qualified schemes that passed both rounds of screening according to the "Performance Optimization Layer" metrics, providing a scientific, rigorous, and engineeringly persuasive decision-making basis for the architecture design of lunar communication and navigation constellations.

This hierarchical threshold-based evaluation method avoids the problem of using a single comprehensive score, which can obscure the inherent differences in importance among various metrics. It makes the logic of scheme comparison clearer and more rigorous, and the conclusions more persuasive from an engineering perspective. This evaluation framework not only ensures that the selected schemes meet the basic requirements and reliability standards of the mission but also identifies the best performer among the qualified schemes, providing a scientific basis for decision-making in the design of lunar communication and navigation constellations.

4 Simulation Analysis and Results

4.1 Scenario Setup

To conduct an objective, quantitative evaluation of different constellation architectures, this section constructs a unified simulation analysis scenario. First, the target service area is clarified. Given the high priority of exploration at the lunar south pole, the core evaluation area (i.e., user points) is set to the lunar polar region from $-90°$ to $-85°$ south latitude, covering all longitudes from $-180°$ to $+180°$. The minimum elevation angle threshold for satellite visibility is set to $5°$.

Under the unified scenario above, to ensure the fairness of the architectural trade-off, this study applies the aforementioned equivalent constraint evaluation method, setting the system-level metric (represented by total mass) as the unified design baseline. The total on-orbit satellite mass for all compared scenarios is set to 3600 kg. To focus on analyzing the performance differences of constellation configurations during the on-orbit operational phase, the deployment cost differences due to variations in insertion velocity among different schemes are temporarily not considered.

As shown in Fig. 2 and Table 2, four different constellation configurations (A, B, C, and D) are compared. Configurations A, B, and D represent miniaturized schemes, while configuration C represents a large-platform scheme. All scenarios use ELFO orbits, with orbital parameters drawn from [8]. The link constant K_{total} in the simulation is set to 0.001766 for all cases, and the satellite wet-to-dry mass ratio is taken as 1.25.

Table 2. Simulation scenarios and constellation configuration parameters.

Config.	N_{sat}	Mass (kg)	a (km)	e	i (deg)	ω (deg)	Ω (deg)	M (deg)	Relay Config. (numbers)
A	12	300	6143	0.6	51.7	90	0:180:180	0:54:270	4 (Idx 1, 6, 7, 12)
B	12	300	6143	0.6	51.7	90	0:90:270	0:120:240	4 (Idx 1, 4, 7, 10)
C	6	600	6143	0.6	51.7	90	0:180:180	0:135:270	2 (Idx 1, 4)
D	16	225	6143	0.6	51.7	90	0:180:180	0:45:315	4 (Idx 1, 6, 7, 12)

4.2 Simulation Results and Analysis

To follow the hierarchical threshold-based ("pyramid") evaluation framework proposed in this paper, we first conduct a comprehensive simulation of the four configuration schemes. A summary of their core performance metrics is shown in Table 3. The subsequent analysis will strictly follow the order of "Qualification Threshold," "Reliability Threshold," and "Performance Optimization" to progressively screen and discuss the data in Table 3.

The simulation results conducted under the unified total mass constraint reveal significant differences in navigation and communication performance among the different constellation architectures. For the multi-satellite miniaturized schemes (Configurations A, B, D), they all meet the set minimum threshold ($\geq$98%) for navigation service availability, while also maintaining communication service availability above 75%, demonstrating robust coverage capabilities. In contrast, the large-platform scheme (Configuration C), while having strong single-satellite performance, fails the navigation availability requirement (88.27% $<$ 98%), although its communication availability marginally meets the threshold (76.10% $>$ 75%).

Further reliability analysis shows that miniaturized constellations can still maintain high navigation fault tolerance ($\geq$98%) even with a single-satellite failure, and communication links also have some redundancy, thus ensuring the continuity of critical missions. The large-platform scheme, however, shows a lack of robustness when a single satellite fails, with service continuity significantly declining, making it difficult to meet the demands of high-reliability missions. This result highlights the advantage of miniaturized constellations in terms of system robustness.

In the performance optimization layer comparison, the 98% GDOP values show that the multi-satellite miniaturized schemes have a greater advantage in

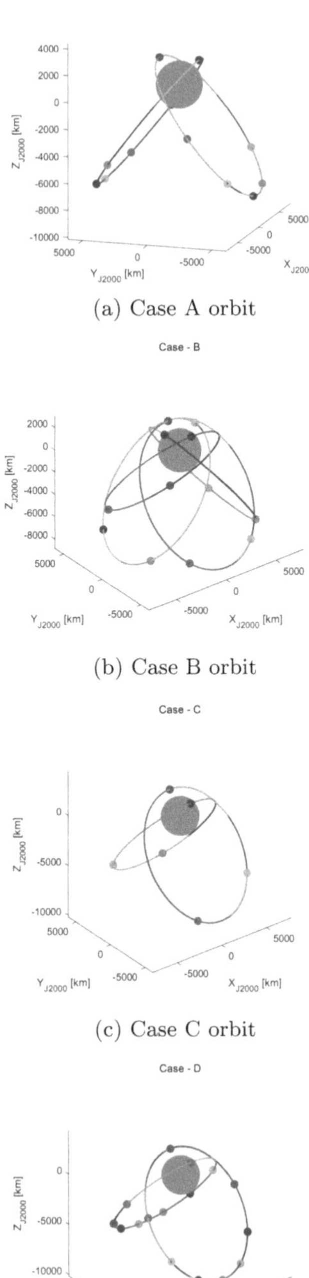

(a) Case A orbit

(b) Case B orbit

(c) Case C orbit

(d) Case D orbit

Fig. 2. Orbit configurations for all scenarios

Table 3. Summary of simulation results for performance metrics of the four configuration schemes.

Evaluation Layer	Performance Metric	Configuration A (12-sat)	Configuration B (12-sat)	Configuration C (6-sat)	Configuration D (16-sat)
Qualification Threshold	Nav Service Availability (Mean)	100.00%	100.00%	88.27%	100.00%
(Basic Availability)	Comm Service Availability (Mean)	100.00%	83.69%	76.10%	100.00%
Reliability Threshold	N-1 Nav Service Availability (Mean)	100.00%	100.00%	24.99%	100.00%
(N-1 Fault Tolerance)	N-1 Comm Service Availability (Mean)	88.27%	76.10%	62.11%	98.98%
Performance Optimization	98% GDOP	6.519	129.342	231.230	3.192
(Performance Comparison)	Daily Data Volume (GB)	4139.9	4241.4	8254.7	2321.9

geometric configuration, capable of providing better positioning accuracy. At the same time, the daily data volume results indicate that, under the adopted scaling model and the same total mass constraint, the large-platform configuration (Configuration C) achieves the highest daily data volume (8254.7 GB/day). Meanwhile, Configurations A, B, and D all exceed the > 500 GB/day reference value, highlighting a throughputcoverage/robustness trade-off under a fixed total mass constraint. It is worth noting that Configuration A achieves a more ideal balance between navigation accuracy and communication bandwidth, ensuring positioning accuracy while maintaining high data transmission capability; Configuration D, however, trades some communication capability for extreme PNT accuracy and reliability, with its positioning performance and fault tolerance superior to other configurations, but its overall communication capacity is reduced. Although Configuration C achieves a higher daily data volume in this model, its smaller constellation size leads to insufficient navigation availability and markedly poorer fault tolerance.

In summary, the simulation results clearly reveal the performance differences of different architectures under unified constraints. The large-platform scheme excels in single-satellite performance but has shortcomings in service coverage and fault tolerance, making it difficult to meet the continuity and reliability requirements of critical missions. The miniaturized constellations, through their advantage in numbers and multi-plane distribution, perform more robustly in service availability, robustness, and data transmission capability, making them particularly suitable for supporting long-term missions in key areas such as the lunar south pole. These results not only validate the rationality of the hierarchical threshold-based evaluation framework but also provide a scientific decision-making basis for the initial construction of future lunar communication and navigation constellations.

5 Conclusion

This paper proposes a systematic evaluation framework for the large-satellite platform and all-miniaturized constellation paths for lunar communication and navigation constellations. The framework, by disaggregating design constraints and performance metrics, conducts a hierarchical threshold-based evaluation under a unified total mass constraint, sequentially screening from basic service availability and reliability to performance optimization, which ensures the fairness and scientific rigor of the inter-scheme comparison.

Simulation results show that under identical resource constraints, the large-satellite platform scheme, while exhibiting superior single-satellite performance, has obvious deficiencies in service coverage and fault tolerance, rendering it incapable of meeting the continuity and reliability requirements of critical missions. In contrast, the all-miniaturized constellation, through its advantage in numbers and multi-plane distribution, delivers more robust performance in navigation service availability, system robustness, and communication link capacity, thereby better supporting long-term exploration and development activities in key lunar regions such as the lunar south pole.

The research findings not only validate the rationality of the hierarchical evaluation framework but also provide a quantitative decision-making basis for the initial phase of lunar communication and navigation constellation construction. Meanwhile, this study adopts a simplified engineering scaling model to estimate data rates in the communication performance evaluation; consequently, the specific data rate requirements are not used as hard constraints in this stage of the trade-off analysis. In the future, more precise link budget models can be introduced to enhance the engineering realism of the evaluation and verify compliance with absolute rate standards. In the PNT performance evaluation, this paper focuses on analyzing the GDOP metric; in the future, detailed analysis combining the user equivalent range error model can be conducted to more comprehensively characterize the navigation service quality.

Overall, this study provides a systematic evaluation tool and scientific decision-making basis for the architecture selection of lunar communication and navigation constellations. Future work can be further extended to the comprehensive evaluation of hybrid orbit schemes, exploration of approaches to achieve global coverage, and the integration of advanced payloads and novel communication technologies to facilitate the evolution of lunar communication and navigation infrastructure to a higher level.

Acknowledgments. This paper was supported by the Pre-research Project on Civil Aerospace Technologies of China (No. D040102).

References

1. Ge, P., Zhang, T.X., Kang, Y., Chen, P.: Progress and prospects of deep space exploration in 2021. Aerosp. China, 9–19 (2022). (in Chinese)
2. Cislunar Technology Interagency Working Group: National Cislunar Science & Technology Strategy. Executive Office of the President of the United States, Washington, DC (2022)
3. Pei, Z.Y., Liu, J.Z., Wang, Q., et al.: Overview of lunar exploration and International Lunar Research Station. Chin. Sci. Bull. **65**, 2577–2586 (2020). (in Chinese)
4. Clinton, C.: Artemis partnerships are key to sustainable lunar presence. in: 2022 Aerospace States Association (ASA) Annual Meeting and 3rd State Aerospace Policy Summit (2022)
5. Reibald, G.: Towards a Moon Village Generation (2022)
6. Zemba, M., Vaden, K., Reinhart, R., Gramling, C., Heckler, G.: NASA's lunar communications and navigation architecture. NASA (2023)
7. Hamera, K., Mosher, T., Gefreh, M., Paul, R., Slavkin, L., Trojan, J.: An evolvable lunar communication and navigation constellation concept. In: 2008 IEEE Aerospace Conference, pp. 1–20. IEEE (2008)
8. Bhamidipati, S., Mina, T., Sanchez, A., Gao, G.: Satellite constellation design for a lunar navigation and communication system. Navigation **70**(4) (2023)
9. Chen, S.Y., Ni, Y.S., Peng, J.: Orbit design method for near-lunar space constellation. Chin. Space Sci. Technol. **44**, 15–29 (2024). (in Chinese)
10. Israel, D.J., Gramling, C.J.: LunaNet interoperability specification document (2023)
11. Gramling, C., et al.: Assessing utility of different orbits for a lunar PNT constellation. In: Institute of Navigation-Joint Navigation Conference (2024)

FashionAtlas: Enhancing Semantics and Control in Multimodal Fashion Image Editing

Enzhen Gu, Jinpei Wang, and Yingjie Shi(✉)

Beijing Institute of Fashion Technology, Beijing, China
shiyingjie1983@163.com

Abstract. In recent years, with the rapid advancement of diffusion-based image generation and virtual try-on technologies, novel research methodologies integrating multimodal inputs such as text and images have emerged. These approaches have become a significant direction in fashion image editing. However, most existing datasets only provide images with basic attribute annotations, lacking systematic support for explicit structural constraints such as sketches and structure maps. This makes it difficult to ensure structural consistency and controllability during the editing and generation processes. Simultaneously, existing textual descriptions often remain confined to superficial semantics like color and category, lacking multidimensional annotation information regarding material properties and design styles. This limits the model's ability to understand and generalize complex instructions and authentic fashion contexts. To address this, we propose constructing a novel benchmark dataset: FashionAtlas. This dataset provides more refined sketches as structural constraints to enhance the controllability of the generated results. Simultaneously, we introduce more detailed and layered prompts generated by large language models (LLMs), integrating structured clothing attribute ontologies with specialized terminology systems. This enhances the model's comprehension of fashion semantics and styling logic, thereby better supporting complex editing and generation requirements. Experimental results demonstrate that FashionAtlas outperforms traditional image-annotation-only baseline dataset in terms of generation accuracy, semantic consistency, detail fidelity, and user controllability. This benchmark dataset aims to fill the current gap in combining structured constraints with fine-grained semantic prompts, providing a new research standard for multimodal control editing and in-context generation tasks in the fashion domain.

Keywords: Multimodal dataset · Image editing · Fashion

1 Introduction

Denoising diffusion models [12] have emerged as one of the most mainstream technologies in image generation and editing tasks [34]. By progressively adding

J. Zhan et al. (Eds.): Bench 2025, LNCS 16471, pp. 82–96, 2026.
https://doi.org/10.1007/978-981-95-9694-2_7

noise to data and learning the reverse denoising process, these models can reconstruct realistic images from pure noise. They support various generation paradigms ranging from unconditional generation to conditional generation based on diverse inputs such as text and images, significantly enhancing the flexibility and quality of image editing. As model capabilities continue to improve, image editing has increasingly evolved toward multimodal approaches [14]. Recent research in diffusion-based image editing has shown a clear trend toward integrating multiple conditioning signals. An expanding body of work attempts to combine text, sketches, depth maps, segmentation maps, and other modalities, enabling users to control editing results in more natural and intuitive ways [5,15,20,23,24,37,40]. Statistical analysis of recent literature reveals that while the majority of diffusion-based editing research focuses on semantic-level modifications, there is growing attention toward style editing and structural editing tasks. This diversification of editing modalities reflects the increasing demand for more sophisticated control mechanisms that go beyond simple textual descriptions.

In most image editing tasks, text or semantic guidance can effectively convey the high-level intentions of the users. However, in fields such as fashion image editing that require precise control of the structure, these methods often perform poorly. These methods are unable to achieve precise operations on the contours of clothing, detailed structures, texture variations, or adjustments to fit. Consequently, more fine-grained and structured editing modalities have become increasingly important to meet the demands of specialized application domains. Fashion-related engineering problems constitute a highly diverse and complex research ecosystem, encompassing fundamental image techniques, design tasks, and extending to trend forecasting, garment retrieval and recommendation, as well as fashion analysis. These areas form a complete research pipeline [34]. In these image editing related tasks, design and image-based synthesis tasks such as virtual try-on, garment editing, and style manipulation exhibit particularly strong dependencies on image structural information. Garment silhouettes, wrinkles, and texture orientations determine whether the resulting edited images can provide stable outputs that meet user editing requirements, thereby supporting subsequent technical applications.

Despite the existence of some related work in fashion editing, most existing datasets face significant limitations. For instance, in the virtual try-on domain, representative datasets such as VITON-HD [7] and DressCode [28] provide substantial paired images of garments and human bodies for researchers. However, these datasets remain relatively limited in modality diversity, primarily offering only human body photographs and corresponding garment images. Moreover, keypoint detection accuracy remains suboptimal, particularly in recognizing facial details and finger joints. This implies that in image editing tasks such as virtual try-on, human pose information still contains biases, potentially leading to unnatural generation results regarding garment-body alignment, hand movements, or facial occlusions. Additionally, these datasets lack multimodal information such as sketches and textual descriptions, as well as fine-grained annotations of garment details and structural information, such as wrinkle directions, texture flows, and fabric layering, which limits the precision and naturalness of high-quality virtual try-on applications. To address these challenges, we propose FashionAtlas, a multimodal fashion dataset with comprehensive editing capabilities. Based on the VITON-HD dataset, we construct 13,679 paired samples containing 123,111 annotation entries. Each sample pair provides eight fully aligned modalities. FashionAtlas provides explicit structural constraints through dual sketches combined with pose information, helping models better understand garment texture, wrinkles, and shapes, thereby achieving more natural and controllable fashion image generation and editing.

2 Related Work

Fashion Datasets. The performance and innovation in fashion image editing and generation tasks depend heavily on dataset quality and diversity. Existing fashion datasets such as DeepFashion [26], FashionAI [41], VITON-HD [7], and Fashionpedia [16] have established solid foundations for research in garment classification, outfit coordination, and virtual try-on. As illustrated in Fig. 1, the VITON-HD dataset is a high-resolution (1024×768) dataset specifically designed for virtual garment try-on. It comprises 13,679 image pairs of frontal-view female models and corresponding top garments. This dataset has been widely adopted as a benchmark for virtual try-on tasks in the field of image editing. Moreover, existing datasets such as Fashion-Gen [31] and DeepFashion-MultiModal [18] add the corresponding textual descriptions and other modalities. Fashion-Gen present a large-scale fashion dataset consisting of 293,008 high-resolution images (1360×1360) paired with stylist–provided item descriptions, along with baseline results for high-resolution and text-conditioned image generation. The DeepFashion-MultiModal dataset contains 44,096 high-resolution human images with rich annotations. However, it does not fully cover several modalities required for fashion image editing. In summary, these datasets reflect common issues related to multimodal alignment and structured semantic representation in existing fashion datasets.

In authentic fashion creation and editing scenarios, designers rely on multi-source information to collaboratively express design intentions. They use sketches to depict silhouettes, fabric textures to showcase material qualities, textual descriptions to convey style imagery, and reference images to demonstrate overall outfit aesthetic. To enable AI models to possess similar human perception and generation capabilities, it is essential to establish a multimodal dataset that integrates visual, textual, structural, and design language elements.

Multimodal Image Editing for Fashion. With the continuous development of diffusion models in the field of image generation, fashion image editing has gradually evolved from single-modal input to multi-modal fusion. Researchers have begun to explore how to achieve more refined and controllable image editing while ensuring the consistency of clothing structure and the authenticity

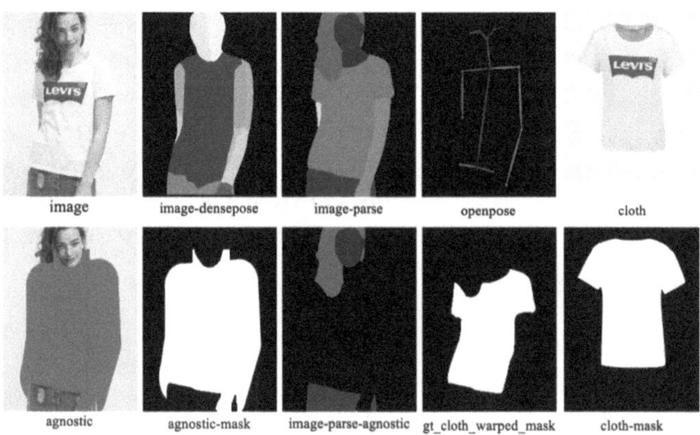

Fig. 1. The overview of VITON-HD dataset.

of details. Several works have explored local control through sketch information for fine-grained fashion editing. F Girella proposed LOTS of Fashion [9], which achieves fine-grained generation through local sketch-text pairs. It adopts modular paired representation to independently encode each sketch with its corresponding text and implements cross-modal fusion. Meanwhile, it constructs the Sketchy dataset, providing local sketch-text pairs for each garment. Multimodal Garment Designer (MGD) [2] similarly proposes a multimodal conditional generation framework, extending the Dress Code and VITON-HD high-resolution fashion datasets to generate multimodal versions containing both text and sketches. Di Cheng et al. proposed ControlEdit [6], a method that performs multi-level control in image generation through sketch–text pairs, reformulating garment image editing as a multimodality-guided local inpainting task for clothing images.

Apart from the framework of the reference sketch, other related multimodal image editing frameworks are also gradually emerging, such as DPDEdit [35]. By introducing Grounded-SAM to precisely locate the editing area of clothing and designing texture injection and refinement mechanisms, it enables further fashion image editing. Fashion-RAG [32] proposes a retrieval-enhanced generation method specifically for fashion image editing. By integrating user textual descriptions with multiple clothing images retrieved from an external database, it utilizes text inversion technology to map visual features into the CLIP text space, thereby guiding the Stable Diffusion model to achieve more refined and personalized clothing image generation. IPAdapter [39] introduces a lightweight adapter that injects image conditions into the denoising process. However, as multimodal research continues to grow, existing fashion datasets still suffer from the following common limitations:

- They lack rich structural constraints, making models prone to generating try-on results with deformations, unnatural silhouettes, or loss of wrinkle details.

- Most fashion related image editing datasets only provide coarse attributes (category, color). They lack structured fashion semantics such as garment length, collar style, silhouette, and wearing scenarios, which limits the reasoning capabilities of generative models.
- Designers typically go through stages from sketch design to pattern design to fabric selection to final presentation, yet existing datasets only provide final RGB images. This mismatch limits the model's understanding of iterative design editing workflows.

3 Dataset Construction

FashionAtlas is constructed based on the VITON-HD dataset, comprising 13,679 paired samples with 123,111 annotation entries. Building upon the original structural information, we expand to eight comprehensive modalities: text descriptions, garment sketch, full-body sketch, pose keypoints, garment image, sewing pattern, texture annotation, and mask. As illustrated in Fig. 2, our construction dataset addresses three issues: (1) it reduces the gap between real clothing images and structured fashion semantics; (2) the modal attributes are consistent with the designer's workflow from sketches to patterns, enabling the same dataset to undergo image editing in each process; (3) it supports various multimodal editing tasks beyond single-purpose applications.

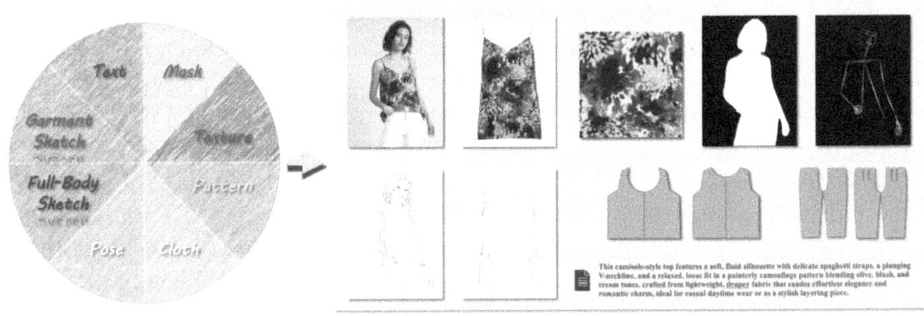

Fig. 2. FashionAtlas dataset construction, showing the systematic organization of eight aligned modalities from source images.

Data Structure. We begin with the VITON-HD dataset as our foundation, which provides high-quality fashion images with diverse coverage of garment categories, styles, and wearing contexts. After collecting the source images, we systematically partition the data according to different downstream tasks to generate corresponding modalities. Figure 3 presents an overview of the comprehensive annotations. The construction process proceeds through parallel streams: (1) structural extraction generating dual sketches and enhanced pose keypoints; (2)

visual property extraction capturing sewing patterns and textures; (3) semantic annotation producing LLM-generated descriptions; (4) sewing pattern modality generation providing designer-oriented structural representations. All modalities are strictly aligned at the sample level, ensuring consistency across different annotation types. Table 1 compares several commonly used fashion image datasets in terms of their modality annotations. Generally speaking, FashionAtlas provides more comprehensive modality coverage, offering a stronger reference foundation for multimodal image editing tasks (Table 1).

Table 1. Comparison of modality annotations in fashion datasets.

Dataset	Text	Garment Sketch	Full-body Sketch	Pose	Pattern	Texture	Mask
VITON-HD [7]	✗	✗	✗	✓	✗	✗	✓
Dress Code [28]	✗	✗	✗	✓	✗	✗	✓
DeepFashion2 [8]	✓	✗	✗	✗	✗	✗	✓
Fashion-200K [10]	✓	✗	✗	✗	✗	✗	✗
Fashion-Gen [31]	✓	✗	✗	✗	✗	✗	✗
PolyvoreOutfits [11]	✓	✗	✗	✗	✗	✗	✗
FashionIQ [36]	✓	✗	✗	✗	✗	✗	✗
Sketchy [9]	✓	✓	✗	✗	✗	✗	✓
FashionAtlas (ours)	✓	✓	✓	✓	✓	✓	✓

Textual Annotation. To establish a comprehensive textual annotation system, we draw inspiration from the Fashion Semantic Space (FSS) proposed by Yihui Ma [27], which is designed to provide a quantitative description of fashion styles. FSS is a two-dimensional image-scale semantic space that contains hundreds of vocabulary terms commonly used by consumers on shopping platforms to describe garments. Based on FSS, we integrate everyday outfit styles with runway fashion and reorganize keywords in the fashion semantic space into three distinct structural categories, as illustrated in Fig. 3, This forms the overall framework of our text-modality generation pipeline. Leveraging recent open-source vision–language models, we extract fashion semantics into three hierarchical structures: (1) *Physical Attributes* encompass directly observable garment characteristics organized into primary attributes (model gender, garment length, sleeve type, collar type, category), design details (closure methods, knitting techniques, pleats, waist designs), and decorative details (sewing patterns, materials, ornamental elements); (2) *Fashion Semantic Dimensions* capture abstract style concepts including modern aesthetics, classic elegance, formal sophistication, casual comfort, vintage charm, and avant-garde innovation, enabling models to understand high-level design intentions; (3) *Contextual Information* provides scenario-based guidance including occasion suitability, seasonal appropriateness, and styling recommendations.

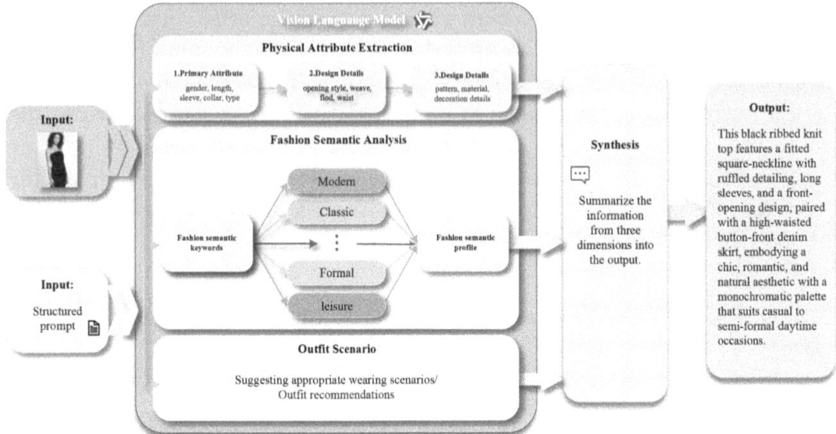

Fig. 3. An overview of the textual annotation framework, illustrating three structured semantic categories for fashion description.

To improve the efficiency of annotation generation, we proposed a semi-automated framework in which the reference image and predefined prompts are fed into our three-level structure and processed by the latest open-source Qwen3-VL [1] model for inference. To ensure the accuracy and stability of the outputs, the model temperature is set to 0.1 [22]. The results demonstrate that, while precisely capturing garment attributes, the model also produces local detail descriptions that are consistent with human expression, and additionally provides suggestions for outfit coordination and usage scenarios.

Sketch Extraction. Textual descriptions exhibit inherent modal limitations when conveying garment information. While language effectively communicates semantic attributes such as style, color schemes, and textures, it demonstrates relatively weak capacity in describing spatial geometric features like silhouette contours and structural proportions. This expressive gap constrains users' precise control over generation results, making it difficult to achieve deep customization beyond the style level. Meanwhile, Designers typically require both presentation fashion illustrations (full-body) and technical flats (garment-only) to assist in design development, yet many existing datasets overlook this crucial aspect of the fashion industry workflow. To address this gap, we generate two types of sketches that provide essential structural constraints for fashion editing tasks. By comparing the reconstruction quality of different variational autoencoder architectures, we selected the latest open-source model Flux-Kontext [3], which is a diffusion transformer architecture [30] based on flow-matching [25] denoising. In addition, given the inherent ability of LoRA [13,29] to guide Diffusion models for style transfer, as shown in the Fig. 4, we applied LoRA fine-tuning on top of the original architecture, where the backbone model parameters were frozen and low-rank adaptation modules were inserted into the attention layers, enabling the model to generate sketches that are clearer and more structurally accurate. These sketches preserve essential garment details while effectively removing unnecessary background noise.

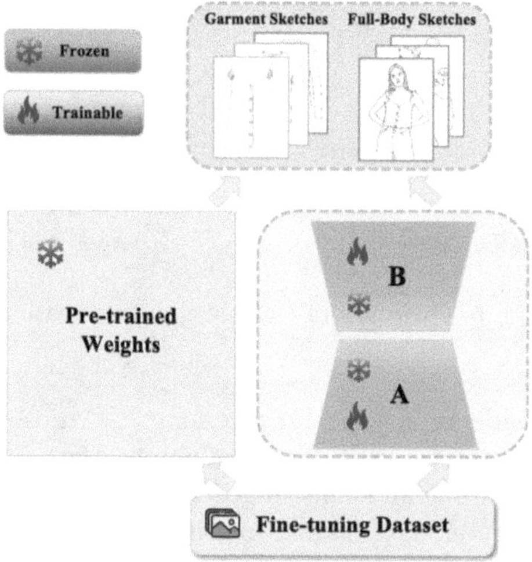

Fig. 4. LoRA is applied on pretrained weights to inject a sketch-related dataset, producing sketch modality information with more details.

Our dual sketch generation produces: (1) *Garment Sketches (Technical Flats)* that isolate individual garments, clearly depicting silhouettes, necklines, sleeve constructions, closure details, and design elements, providing fine-grained structural constraints for editing specific garment pieces while preserving characteristic features; (2) *Full-Body Sketches (fashion illustrations)* that capture complete outfit compositions including body proportions, garment-body relationships, and spatial arrangements between different clothing items, proving essential for maintaining consistency in complete outfit editing scenarios.

Figure 5 illustrates our dual sketch generation results. Both garment sketches and full-body sketches maintain high structural accuracy while preserving essential design details such as silhouettes, necklines, etc.

Pose Extraction. Precise pose information is especially critical in fashion editing, particularly for hand regions. Hands frequently occlude garments through interactions such as grasping edges, pocketing, or gesturing. Inaccurate hand positions easily cause sleeve misalignment, finger occlusion, or structural deformation in subsequent virtual try-on or other fashion image editing applications. Therefore, accurate hand keypoints enable models to better understand occlusion relationships and maintain natural garment structures, resulting in more realistic generated images regarding action and wearing states.

We utilize YOLOv11 [19] for human presence detection and bounding box localization, performing anatomical skeletal analysis within detected regions. We

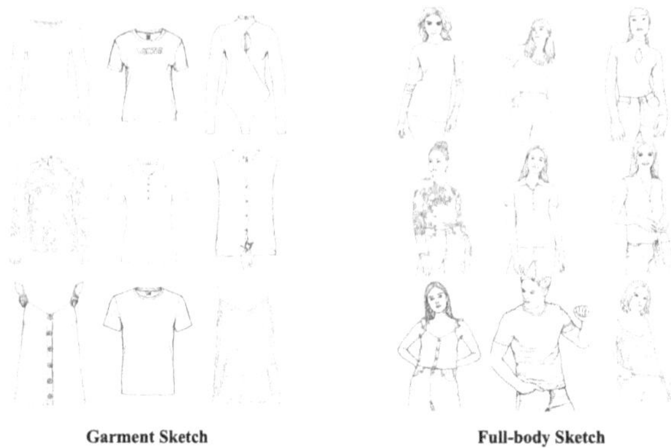

Fig. 5. Overview of Dual-Sketch Information

employ a hybrid confidence approach combining RTMPose [17], MMPose [33], and DWPose [38] to extract precise hand keypoints. Each hand is detected with 21 keypoints covering all joints and finger articulations, including fingertips, knuckles, and palm centers. As shown in Fig. 6, our enhanced pose detection captures both full-body skeletal structure and detailed hand articulations.

In addition to image editing tasks such as virtual try-on, these pose maps further support 3D rendering in tools like Blender, enabling physics-based garment simulation and animation. The enhanced hand keypoint accuracy significantly reduces artifacts in hand-garment interaction regions, which is a challenge in existing virtual try-on related fashion image editing datasets.

Extracting Textures. Relying solely on RGB information and textual prompts is relatively limited for capturing fabric characteristics. Texture information provide explicit surface detail information at the garment level, bridging the gap between semantic prompts and actual visual texture presentation. We apply the same LoRA fine-tuning technique used for sketch generation to extract texture information from each garment, successfully capturing intricate surface details including fabric textures, decorative patterns, and material characteristics while maintaining structural integrity.

As shown in Fig. 7, textures are accurately extracted from garments, preserving essential surface details and enabling realistic garment rendering.

Pattern Generation. We additionally generate an independent sewing pattern modality to address the most critical missing component in existing datasets: garment structural shape information. In practice, fashion designers modify garments by first adjusting structural elements—garment length, silhouette, opening positions, sleeve styles, hem shapes—then importing these sewing patterns into 3D tools like Blender or Maya for fabric draping simulation. This step is essential, as garment sewing patterns determine subsequent wrinkles, draping quality, fit characteristics, and ultimately whether the garment appears realistic and natural when worn.

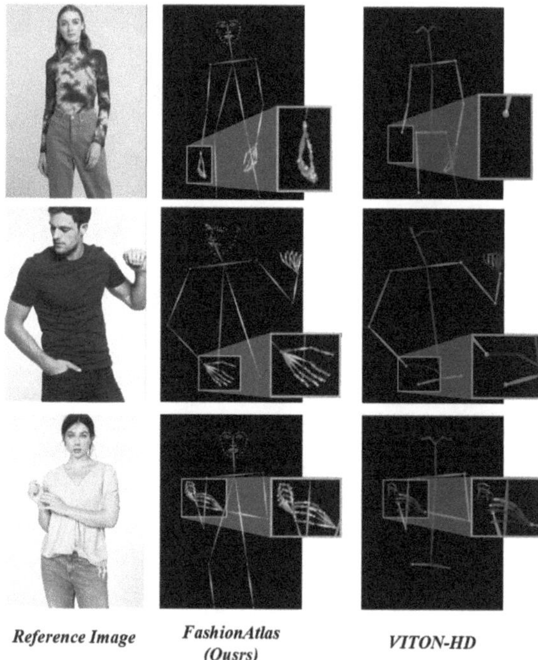

Fig. 6. Comparison between our human pose maps and those from VITON-HD under the same reference image.

Current mainstream fashion datasets offer at most human pose or segmentation maps, insufficient for models to truly understand garment "shape" or "how it falls on the body." Our sewing pattern modality directly reveals garment structural outlines, enabling subsequent editing tasks, such as shortening sleeves, adjusting widths, or changing hem shapes, to become more controllable, predictable, and physically plausible. In essence, the sewing pattern modality addresses a gap in structural information in fashion datasets, bringing models closer to real designer workflows and establishing a more reliable foundation for structure-based editing tasks.

Figure 8 demonstrates our independent pattern generation results. We use the ChatGarment [4] pipeline to take images as input and generate JSON files along with the corresponding two-dimensional sewing pattern information. The generated JSON files can then be decoded into 2D sewing patterns using GarmentCode [21] and subsequently draped onto the human body. These structural representations capture garment silhouettes, construction lines, and key design elements that designers use for technical specifications and 3D modeling workflows [4,34]. Meanwhile, sewing patterns play a fundamental role in controlling garment fit and provide essential guidance for the large-scale production of standardized clothing.

Fig. 7. Texture extraction examples showing the progression from original garment images to extracted texture that preserve surface details, fabric texture, and decorative elements essential for realistic garment rendering.

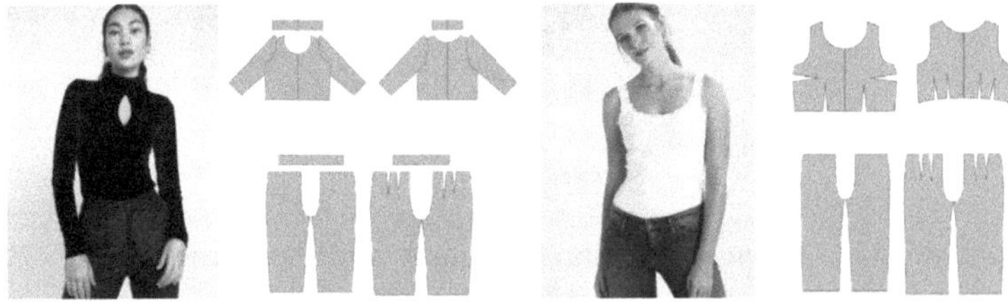

Fig. 8. As shown in the figure, with the 2D garment sewing patterns, designers can modify the pattern information of the upper and lower garments before proceeding to subsequent three-dimensional draping simulations.

Quality Assurance. The final FashionAtlas dataset comprises 13,679 paired samples with complete eight-modality annotations. In addition, text descriptions generated by large language models are reviewed by fashion domain experts to ensure semantic accuracy. The structural integrity of the dual sketches is verified against the original images to guarantee faithful representation of garment shapes. Pose annotations pay particular attention to hand regions to prevent missing or occluded hands from affecting accurate modeling. Texture extraction also follows the original garment patterns to preserve surface details. Taken together, these steps ensure that FashionAtlas provides reliable, high-quality annotations suitable for developing and evaluating multimodal fashion editing methods.

4 Dataset Statistics and Qualitative Analysis

Semantic Consistency. Our LLM-generated textual descriptions significantly enhance semantic consistency between input prompts and generated images.

Models trained with our fine-grained annotations demonstrate superior understanding of complex fashion terminology and can accurately interpret multi-attribute editing instructions. Our qualitative observations indicate that adopting detailed annotations leads to improved fidelity in texture, sketch, and pose modalities, enhancing the visual realism of generated garments.

Human Evaluation. To comprehensively assess the quality and effectiveness of images generated using FashionAtlas, we conducted extensive human evaluation studies. We compare the images provided in FashionAtlas with those from existing datasets, including DeepFashion-MultiModal, VITON-HD, and VITON-HD Multimodal. These images were presented to 120 participants recruited from fashion design students, professional stylists, and general consumers to ensure diverse perspectives.

Participants were asked to evaluate the generated images across four key dimensions: (1) **Realism**, assessing whether the garments appear natural and photographically realistic; (2) **Structural Accuracy**, evaluating how well the generated images preserve garment silhouettes, proportions, and design details; (3) **Semantic Alignment**, measuring consistency between the input descriptions and the visual attributes of generated garments; (4) **Fashion Aesthetics**, judging the overall styling, color coordination, and fashion appropriateness. Participants were allowed to select multiple images that met specified criteria for each evaluation dimension.

5 Conclusion

FashionAtlas is the first comprehensive multimodal fashion dataset specifically designed for controllable image editing, conditioned by diverse inputs including text, dual sketches, pose keypoints, sewing patterns, and textures. The novel annotation framework, constructed through semi-automatic pipelines combining vision-language models, enables systematic evaluation and benchmarking of controllable fashion image generation under complex, multi-condition settings.

Acknowledgments. This work was financially supported by the Key Project for Quality Improvement of Graduate Students at Beijing Institute of Fashion Technology (NHFZ20250441), the Teaching Reform Project of Beijing Institute of Fashion Technology (ZDJG-2508), the Open Project of Hubei Engineering Research Center for Textile and Garment Intelligentization (2023HBITF01), the National Natural Science Foundation of China (62062058), and the Scientific Research Project of Beijing Municipal Education Commission (KM202210012002).

References

1. Bai, S., Cai, Y., Chen, R., et al.: Qwen3-VL technical report (2025). https://arxiv.org/abs/2511.21631

2. Baldrati, A., Morelli, D., Cartella, G., Cornia, M., Bertini, M., Cucchiara, R.: Multimodal garment designer: human-centric latent diffusion models for fashion image editing. In: Proceedings of the IEEE/CVF International Conference on Computer Vision, pp. 23393–23402 (2023)
3. Batifol, S., et al.: FLUX. 1 Kontext: flow matching for in-context image generation and editing in latent space. arXiv e-prints, arXiv–2506 (2025)
4. Bian, S., et al.: ChatGarment: garment estimation, generation and editing via large language models. In: Proceedings of the Computer Vision and Pattern Recognition Conference, pp. 2924–2934 (2025)
5. Brooks, T., Holynski, A., Efros, A.A.: InstructPix2Pix: learning to follow image editing instructions. In: Proceedings of the IEEE/CVF Conference on Computer Vision and Pattern Recognition, pp. 18392–18402 (2023)
6. Cheng, D., Shi, Y., Sun, S., Zhang, J., Wang, W., Liu, Y.: ControlEdit: a Multi-Modal local clothing image editing method. arXiv preprint arXiv:2409.14720 (2024)
7. Choi, S., Park, S., Lee, M., Choo, J.: VITON-HD: high-resolution virtual try-on via misalignment-aware normalization. In: Proceedings of the IEEE/CVF Conference on Computer Vision and Pattern Recognition, pp. 14131–14140 (2021)
8. Ge, Y., Zhang, R., Wang, X., Tang, X., Luo, P.: DeepFashion2: a versatile benchmark for detection, pose estimation, segmentation and re-identification of clothing images. In: Proceedings of the IEEE/CVF Conference on Computer Vision and Pattern Recognition, pp. 5337–5345 (2019)
9. Girella, F., Talon, D., Liu, Z., Ruan, Z., Wang, Y., Cristani, M.: Lots of fashion! Multi-conditioning for image generation via sketch-text pairing. In: Proceedings of the IEEE/CVF International Conference on Computer Vision, pp. 19711–19720 (2025)
10. Han, X., et al.: Automatic spatially-aware fashion concept discovery. In: Proceedings of the IEEE International Conference on Computer Vision, pp. 1463–1471 (2017)
11. Han, X., Wu, Z., Jiang, Y.G., Davis, L.S.: Learning fashion compatibility with bidirectional LSTMS. In: Proceedings of the 25th ACM International Conference on Multimedia, pp. 1078–1086 (2017)
12. Ho, J., Jain, A., Abbeel, P.: Denoising diffusion probabilistic models. In: Advances in Neural Information Processing Systems, vol. 33, pp. 6840–6851 (2020)
13. Hu, E.J., et al.: LoRA: low-rank adaptation of large language models. In: ICLR, vol. 1, no. 2, p. 3 (2022)
14. Huang, Y., et al.: Diffusion model-based image editing: a survey. IEEE Trans. Pattern Anal. Mach. Intell. (2025)
15. Huang, Y., et al.: SmartEdit: exploring complex instruction-based image editing with multimodal large language models. In: Proceedings of the IEEE/CVF Conference on Computer Vision and Pattern Recognition, pp. 8362–8371 (2024)
16. Jia, M., et al.: Fashionpedia: ontology, segmentation, and an attribute localization dataset. In: European Conference on Computer Vision, pp. 316–332. Springer (2020)
17. Jiang, T., et al.: RTMPose: real-time multi-person pose estimation based on MMPose. arXiv preprint arXiv:2303.07399 (2023)
18. Jiang, Y., Yang, S., Qiu, H., Wu, W., Loy, C.C., Liu, Z.: Text2Human: text-driven controllable human image generation. ACM Trans. Graph. (TOG) **41**(4), 1–11 (2022)
19. Khanam, R., Hussain, M.: YOLOv11: an overview of the key architectural enhancements. arXiv preprint arXiv:2410.17725 (2024)

20. Kim, K., Park, S., Lee, J., Choo, J.: Reference-based image composition with sketch via structure-aware diffusion model. arXiv preprint arXiv:2304.09748 (2023)
21. Korosteleva, M., Sorkine-Hornung, O.: GarmentCode: programming parametric sewing patterns. ACM Trans. Graph. (TOG) **42**(6), 1–15 (2023)
22. Li, L., Sleem, L., Nichil, G., State, R., et al.: Exploring the impact of temperature on large language models: hot or cold? Procedia Comput. Sci. **264**, 242–251 (2025)
23. Li, M., et al.: ControlNet++: improving conditional controls with efficient consistency feedback: project page: liming-ai. github. io/controlnet_plus_plus. In: European Conference on Computer Vision, pp. 129–147. Springer (2024)
24. Li, S., Singh, H., Grover, A.: InstructAny2Pix: flexible visual editing via multimodal instruction following. arXiv preprint arXiv:2312.06738 (2023)
25. Lipman, Y., Chen, R.T., Ben-Hamu, H., Nickel, M., Le, M.: Flow matching for generative modeling. arXiv preprint arXiv:2210.02747 (2022)
26. Liu, Z., Luo, P., Qiu, S., Wang, X., Tang, X.: DeepFashion: powering robust clothes recognition and retrieval with rich annotations. In: Proceedings of the IEEE Conference on Computer Vision and Pattern Recognition, pp. 1096–1104 (2016)
27. Ma, Y., Jia, J., Zhou, S., Fu, J., Liu, Y., Tong, Z.: Towards better understanding the clothing fashion styles: a multimodal deep learning approach. In: Proceedings of the AAAI Conference on Artificial Intelligence, vol. 31 (2017)
28. Morelli, D., Fincato, M., Cornia, M., Landi, F., Cesari, F., Cucchiara, R.: Dress code: high-resolution multi-category virtual try-on. In: Proceedings of the IEEE/CVF Conference on Computer Vision and Pattern Recognition, pp. 2231–2235 (2022)
29. Ouyang, Z., Li, Z., Hou, Q.: K-LoRA: unlocking training-free fusion of any subject and style LoRAs. arXiv preprint arXiv:2502.18461 (2025)
30. Peebles, W., Xie, S.: Scalable diffusion models with transformers. In: Proceedings of the IEEE/CVF International Conference on Computer Vision, pp. 4195–4205 (2023)
31. Rostamzadeh, N., et al.: Fashion-GEN: the generative fashion dataset and challenge. arXiv preprint arXiv:1806.08317 (2018)
32. Sanguigni, F., Morelli, D., Cornia, M., Cucchiara, R.: Fashion-RAG: multimodal fashion image editing via retrieval-augmented generation. arXiv preprint arXiv:2504.14011 (2025)
33. Sengupta, A., Jin, F., Zhang, R., Cao, S.: mm-Pose: real-time human skeletal posture estimation using mmWave radars and CNNs. IEEE Sens. J. **20**(17), 10032–10044 (2020)
34. Shi, W., Wong, W., Zou, X.: Generative ai in fashion: overview. ACM Trans. Intell. Syst. Technol. **16**(4), 1–73 (2025)
35. Wang, X., Cheng, Z.Q., Wang, J., Peng, X.: DPDEdit: detail-preserved diffusion models for multimodal fashion image editing. arXiv preprint arXiv:2409.01086 (2024)
36. Wu, H., et al.: Fashion IQ: a new dataset towards retrieving images by natural language feedback. In: Proceedings of the IEEE/CVF Conference on Computer Vision and Pattern Recognition, pp. 11307–11317 (2021)
37. Xie, S., Zhang, Z., Lin, Z., Hinz, T., Zhang, K.: SmartBrush: text and shape guided object inpainting with diffusion model. In: Proceedings of the IEEE/CVF Conference on Computer Vision and Pattern Recognition, pp. 22428–22437 (2023)
38. Yang, Z., Zeng, A., Yuan, C., Li, Y.: Effective whole-body pose estimation with two-stages distillation. In: Proceedings of the IEEE/CVF International Conference on Computer Vision, pp. 4210–4220 (2023)

39. Ye, H., Zhang, J., Liu, S., Han, X., Yang, W.: IP-adapter: text compatible image prompt adapter for text-to-image diffusion models. arXiv preprint arXiv:2308.06721 (2023)
40. Zhang, L., Rao, A., Agrawala, M.: Adding conditional control to text-to-image diffusion models. In: Proceedings of the IEEE/CVF International Conference on Computer Vision, pp. 3836–3847 (2023)
41. Zou, X., Kong, X., Wong, W., Wang, C., Liu, Y., Cao, Y.: FashionAI: a hierarchical dataset for fashion understanding. In: Proceedings of the IEEE/CVF Conference on Computer Vision and Pattern Recognition Workshops, pp. 0–0 (2019)

Review of LLM Jailbreaks: White-Box and Black-Box Perspectives on Attacks, Defenses, and Critical Metrics

Shuyuan Liu[1], Jiawei Chen[1,2], and Zhaoxia Yin[1](✉)

[1] East China Normal University, Shanghai, China
zxyin@cee.ecnu.edu.cn
[2] Zhongguancun Academy, Beijing, China

Abstract. With the rapid advancement of technology, large language models (LLMs) have become key content generators that shape social discourse and exert far-reaching influence. However, the ability of these models to produce potentially harmful or inappropriate content poses a significant threat to the health and harmony of the online environment. In response, researchers have actively worked to guide models in generating content that aligns with universally accepted societal values, aiming to curb the spread of malicious information. Despite these efforts, the issue of "jailbreak" attacks remains a critical challenge. This not only tests the technological boundaries of LLMs but also raises significant concerns regarding the ethical application and social responsibility of such models. This paper explores the diversity of jailbreak attacks and the complexity of defense algorithms from both white-box and black-box perspectives. Additionally, key evaluation metrics such as attack success rate, robustness, efficiency, and portability are discussed to provide a comprehensive framework for assessing the effectiveness of offensive and defensive strategies. In conclusion, this paper offers a holistic view of LLM jailbreak attacks and defenses, underscoring the importance of vigilance and proactive exploration of effective defense strategies as LLMs continue to be widely deployed.

Keywords: Jailbreak Attacks · LLM Safety Alignment · Large language model · Defense

1 Introduction

In recent years, Large Language Models (LLMs) have brought about disruptive changes in academic research and industrial practice with their outstanding text generation and generalization capabilities, and have rapidly become the core infrastructure in the field of artificial intelligence. However, behind the powerful capabilities of the model, complex and severe security challenges are increasingly prominent - especially the vulnerability of its built-in value alignment mechanism in the face of adversarial attacks. Specifically, attackers can use carefully designed "Jailbreaking" attack strategies to systematically bypass the model's preset ethical constraints and security boundaries by taking advantage of the model's overgeneralization of fuzzy semantics and context depen-

J. Zhan et al. (Eds.): Bench 2025, LNCS 16471, pp. 97–113, 2026.
https://doi.org/10.1007/978-981-95-9694-2_8

dence, thereby triggering security risks such as the generation of harmful content and privacy leakage.

In terms of attack strategy research, the current focus is on how to induce LLMS to output harmful content [24,25,47]. Zou et al. [47] innovatively proposed an adversarial jailbreak attack algorithm. By adding specific adversarial suffixes to malicious questions, even language models that have achieved value alignment can be effectively induced to generate inappropriate or harmful content. Liu et al. [25] introduced the AutoDAN framework, which employs a complex hierarchical genetic algorithm to automatically generate jailbreak prompts that are difficult to detect. These prompts enable LLMS to evade the original value alignment mechanism when facing malicious input and generate corresponding responses accordingly.

With the increasing attention paid to the value security of LLMs, especially how to ensure that LLM outputs are not affected by harmful information has become a research focus, researchers have begun to actively explore various defense strategies [1,2,31,44]. Alon et al. [1] adopted a mechanism based on confusion filtering to detect and curb jailbreak attacks, aiming to reduce the generation of harmful content; Zhang et al. [43] protected LLMS from jailbreak attacks by setting the target priority prompted by the system. Although these studies [4,21] have explored the relevant fields from different perspectives, most of them have only focused on a specific subset at the technical level. Dong et al. [7] provided a comprehensive overview of the research on the value security of LLMS, covering aspects such as LLM attacks, defenses, and evaluations. However, this review lacks a more comprehensive and unified perspective on the various dimensions of LLM value security, especially the discussion on the security classification of open-source and closed-source LLMS, as well as the update summary of the latest attack and defense technologies.

In view of this, this paper aims to provide a comprehensive review of LLM jailbreak attacks, defense strategies, evaluation datasets, and evaluation metrics, as shown in Fig. 1 and 2. It is expected that through this comprehensive and systematic research, a solid theoretical foundation will be provided for subsequent studies, and the continuous development of the LLM value security field will be promoted. The contributions of this article are as follows:

The Research Perspective is Comprehensive and Systematic. This paper breaks through the limitations of a single research perspective and, starting from the two different yet complementary perspectives of black box and white box, conducts an in-depth analysis of the attack methods and corresponding defense technology routes faced by the values of large models.

The Research Results are Cutting-Edge and Practical. This article provides a comprehensive and detailed summary of the recently published classic and high-quality research techniques on large model attack and defense.

2 Jailbreak

From the perspective of formulaic definition, a jailbreak attack can be formally described as follows: Given a target system (large language model LLM) S, whose

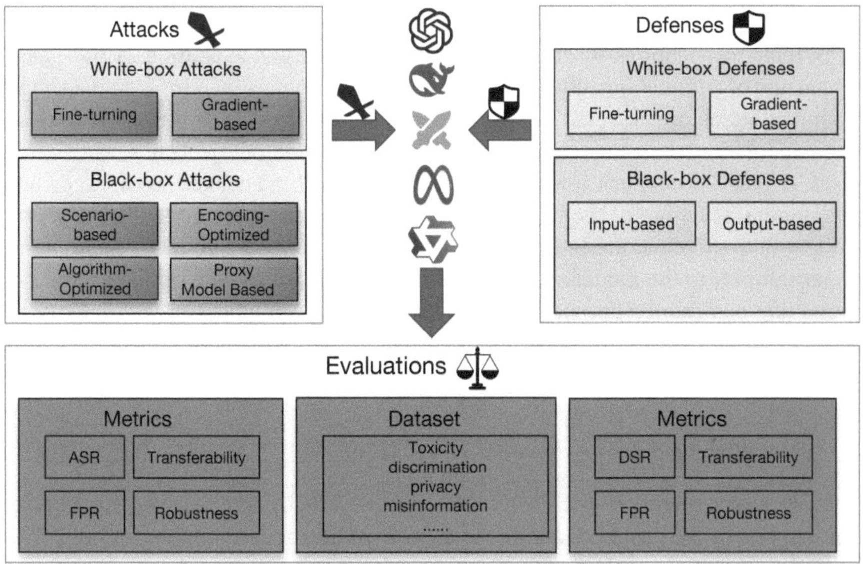

Fig. 1. System Framework for LLM Jailbreak Attacks, Defenses, and Evaluations.

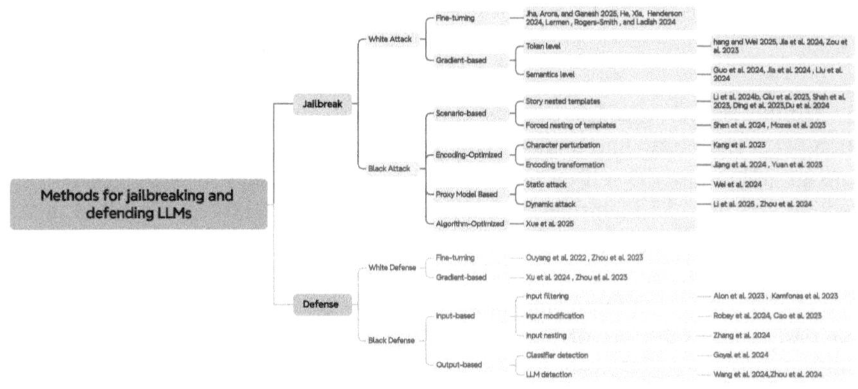

Fig. 2. Overview of Attack and Defense Methods for Large Language Models.

preset security policy set is S, the attacker triggers the system output y' by inputting x', such that y' does not belong to S and y' satisfies the attack target T. The specific formulaic expression is as follows:

$$y' \notin \mathrm{S} \quad \text{and} \quad y' \in \mathrm{T} \tag{1}$$

Here, T represents the set of attack targets (such as inducing the model to output the steps for making bombs, leaking user passwords, etc.).

LLMs are classified into open-source models and closed-source models based on their openness. Correspondingly, jailbreak attacks targeting these models can also be divided into two major categories: white-box attacks and black-box attacks. White-box attacks refer to situations where attackers have a deep understanding of the internal mechanisms of a model, including its architecture, parameters, and training data, etc. In this kind of attack, the attacker can use the detailed information of the model to design specific inputs to induce the model to generate incorrect outputs or leak sensitive information. A black-box attack refers to a situation where the attacker has no knowledge of the internal structure of the model and can only infer its working mode based on its input and output behaviors. In this type of attack, the attacker submits a large number of input samples to the model and observes its output patterns, attempting to find input patterns that can induce the model to produce incorrect outputs. In Sect. 2.1, we will outline white-box attack methods, and in Sect. 2.2, we will outline black-box attack methods.

2.1 White-Box Attack

White-box attack methods specifically refer to those attack strategies that require a deep understanding of the internal working mechanism of the model, as shown in Fig. 3. Such methods can be further subdivided into two major categories: fine-tuning-based methods and gradient-based methods. The former misleads the model output by adjusting the model parameters or introducing specific training data, while the latter carefully constructs the attack input by using the gradient information of the model to achieve the purpose of deceiving the model.

Fine-Tuning-Based Attacks. Studies show that fine-tuning can eliminate RLHF protection [41]. Therefore, fine-tuning techniques have gradually emerged as an effective means to undermine the self-protection mechanisms of LLMS, thereby giving rise to potentially harmful LLM instances. Specifically, this attack strategy involves meticulous adjustments to model parameters or the ingenious introduction of specific training data, aiming to induce the model to make misleading predictions or responses in specific situations. The successful implementation of this method highly depends on the meticulous design and selection of fine-tuning datasets, which can ensure that the model exhibits the erroneous behavior patterns expected by attackers when faced with specific inputs. By this means, attackers can effectively exploit the inherent learning mechanism of the model to mislead its output, thereby achieving the preset attack goals. In related research, Piyush Jha et al. [14] used reinforcement learning (RL) loops to fine-tune the attacker LLM. He et al. [13] delved deeply into why benign fine-tuning could unintentionally lead to jailbreaking. Simon Lermen et al. [18] adopted quantized low-rank adaptive (LoRA) as an effective fine-tuning method and successfully untrained the safe training of Llama 2-Chat models and Mixtral indication models of 7B, 13B, and 70B sizes. These studies not only reveal the security challenges currently faced by large language models, but also provide important reference bases for future defense strategies.

Gradient-Based Attacks. Gradient-based attacks are mainly divided into two categories: Token-level attacks and Semantics attacks. Token-level attack: This type of method mainly optimizes the general trigger tokens [15,47], which are usually used as additional prefixes or suffixes to the original instructions to enforce specific instructions. It is worth noting that these trigger tags do not guarantee compliance with formal natural language rules, so in many cases they may be meaningless strings. In addition, Zhang et al. [42] proposed the momentum-accelerated GCG (MAC) attack, which integrates momentum terms into gradient heuristics to enhance and stabilize the random search for markers in adversarial prompts. Semantics attack: Given that meaningless triggers are easily recognized by detection systems [47], the Semantics attack method is dedicated to automatically finding natural language templates similar to heuristic methods. For instance, AutoDan [25] have utilized genetic algorithms based on large language models to optimize artificially designed adversarial examples. Guo et al. [11] adopted the energy-based Langevin Dynamic Constraint Decoding (COLD) and introduced the Cold-Attack framework to automate the search for adversarial LLM attacks under various control requirements, such as fluency, concealment, emotion, and left-right coherence. This method aims to generate more natural and hard-to-detect attack statements, thereby enhancing the concealment and success rate of attacks.

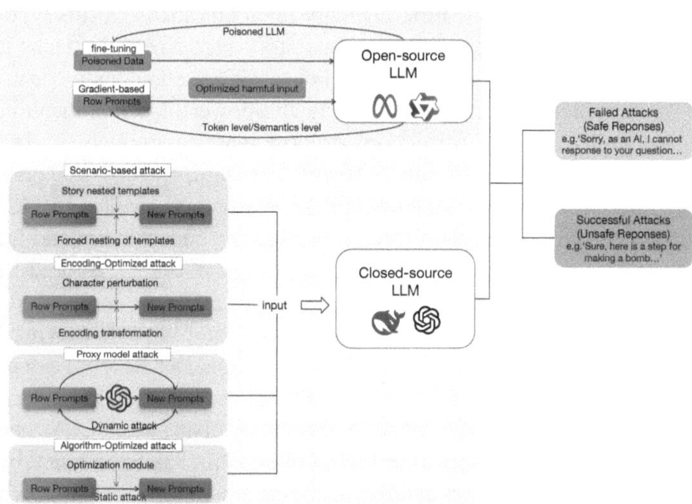

Fig. 3. LLM jailbreak attack system framework

2.2 Black Box Attack

The methods of black-box attacks can be classified into the following four categories: Scenario-based attacks: This type of attack method mainly focuses on exploiting vulnerabilities in specific application scenarios or environments for attacks. Attackers analyze the usage scenarios of the target system and construct attack payloads that fit those scenarios to achieve effective attacks on the system. Coding-based attacks: In such attacks, attackers focus on the coding implementation details of the target system, especially potential coding vulnerabilities or errors. Through carefully crafted input data, attackers can trigger these vulnerabilities, thereby executing malicious code or obtaining sensitive information. Proxy LLM-based attacks: This type of attack method utilizes the capabilities of large language models to generate or optimize attack prompts. Attackers may use LLMS to generate deceptive text input to bypass the security protection measures of the target system, or take advantage of the reasoning ability of LLMS to guess the vulnerabilities of the system and carry out targeted attacks. Attacks based on optimization algorithms: This type of attack refers to the situation where attackers iteratively generate the optimal attack input through mathematical optimization algorithms to bypass system defenses or induce the system to produce incorrect outputs. The core logic is to transform the attack process into an optimization problem and maximize the attack effect by constantly adjusting the input features.

Scenario-Based Attacks. Scenario-based attacks, as a highly targeted black-box attack method, its core strategy lies in exploiting the specific application scenarios or potential environmental vulnerabilities in which the target system is located to carry out attacks. Recent studies have demonstrated the diversity and complexity of this type of attack. Here, it is mainly divided into two categories: story-based nested attacks and forced nested attacks. Story-based nested attacks: Li et al. [22] meticulously constructed various scene or character Settings by leveraging the powerful personification capabilities and high compliance with instructions of large language models. In these specific scenarios, LLMS are induced to output harmful content, thereby demonstrating the potential risks of scenario-based attacks. This attack method enables LLMS to unconsciously output harmful responses, further revealing the concealment and harmfulness of scenario-based attacks. In addition, a series of studies have explored the specific implementation methods of scenario-based attacks in different application scenarios. These scenarios include but are not limited to translation [30], role-playing [32], code completion and table filling [6], as well as other fictional or deceptive scenarios [8]. Attack based on forced nesting: Its core concept lies in exploiting the potential imbalance between security mechanisms and effective mechanisms when LLMS output decisions. When the security mechanisms of LLMS are insufficient to completely curb their effective mechanisms, there is a possibility of outputting harmful content. To carry out such an attack, an effective approach is to use strong and clear instructions to prioritize task completion over security constraints. For instance, some methods guide LLMS to ignore their built-in security or defense mechanisms by providing explicit instructions [33]. In this way, when processing input, LLMS may be more inclined to complete tasks rather than strictly adhere to security rules, thus providing opportunities for attackers. Another strategy is to include in the prompt an encouragement for the LLM to give a hint of a successful "prison break" when answering, such as using positive words like "Sure" [27]. This method aims to take advantage of LLMS 'tendency towards positive responses to increase the probability of them outputting harmful content.

Attacks Based on Coding. The core of coding-based attacks lies in employing strategies to obscure or disguise the true intention of the original input, thereby evading system security protections. These attacks can be broadly categorized into two main types:

character perturbation and encoding transformation. Character Perturbation: Character perturbation involves making subtle modifications to the original input at the character level to conceal malicious intent. One common technique is splitting the original input into multiple segments. Through this fragmentation processing, malicious content is ingeniously scattered among multiple seemingly harmless fragments. For example, researchers [17] have adopted this method, effectively increasing the difficulty for detection systems to identify the hidden threats. This approach not only enhances the concealment of the attack but also adds complexity to defensive measures, as the fragments individually appear benign and may not trigger security alerts. Encoding transformation: Encoding transformation, on the other hand, focuses on converting the original input into different encoding formats to blur the attacker's intentions and bypass content-based filtering defenses. An attacker might, for instance, transform the original input into ASCII code, Morse code, or other encoding schemes [39]. This transformation makes it challenging for security systems to recognize and block malicious content, as the encoded input no longer resembles its original, potentially harmful form. Jiang et al. [16] further advanced this strategy by identifying words in a given prompt that might trigger a large language model's (LLM) rejection mechanism. They then used ASCII art to visually encode these triggering words, creating a set of invisible prompts. These carefully designed hidden prompts are sent to the victim's LLM, inducing it to engage in unsafe behavior—a tactic known as a "prison break attack."

Attacks Based on Proxy LLM. Attacks based on proxy LLMS can be divided into two major categories: dynamic attacks and static attacks. Static attack: Static attacks mainly rely on context examples that have been successfully jailbroken to induce LLMS to output harmful content. For instance, Wei Z et al. [35] collected a series of harmful prompts and their corresponding harmful answers, and used these as examples of context attacks. When these harmful contexts are input into the LLM along with specific prompts, they work together to make it easier for the LLM to generate illegal output, thereby achieving jailbreaking. Dynamic attack: In contrast, dynamic attack is more flexible and diverse. Zhou et al. [46] leveraged the capabilities of LLMS to adjust prompts and enhance attack capabilities through dynamic adversarial games to generate deceptive and misleading text inputs. To achieve scalability and universality, Li et al. [20] meticulously trained the attack model to automatically generate covert jailbreak prompts. This type of attack not only increases the difficulty of detection but also can more effectively bypass the existing security protection measures, posing a greater threat to system security.

Attacks Based on Optimization Algorithms. Xue et al. [38] mainly utilized the anchoring effect in psychology to design attack strategies and proposed a dual intention escape (DIE) jailbreak attack framework to generate more covert and toxic cues to deceive LLMS into output harmful content.

3 Defense

Llm-based defense algorithms are also divided into white box defense and black box defense from the perspective of open source and closed source, as shown in Fig. 4.

Section 3.1 describes the white-box defense mechanism, and Sect. 3.2 describes the black-box defense method.

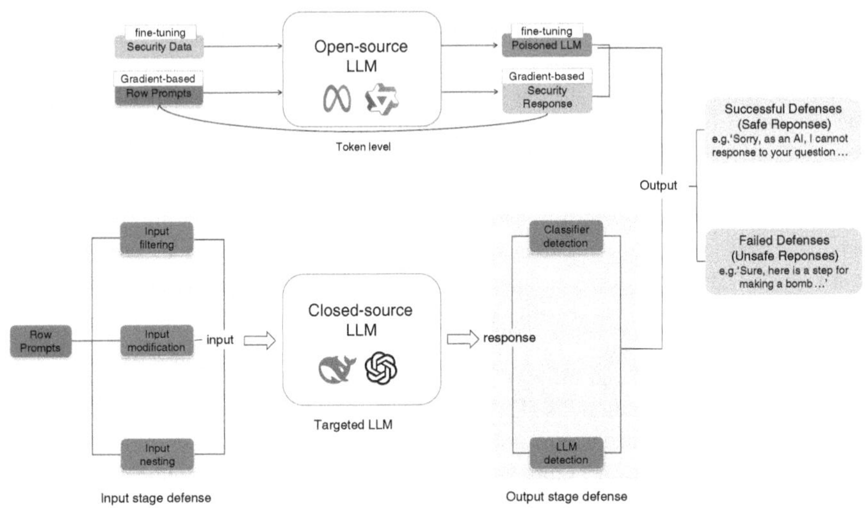

Fig. 4. LLM defense system framework.

3.1 White Box Defense

White box defense and white box attack algorithms are classified in the same way, including: fine-tuning based approach and gradient-based approach.

Fine Tuning-Based Defenses. The heart of the defense mechanism lies in ensuring that the output of the LLM is consistent with our intended goals, such as security, which is usually achieved through alignment algorithms. Alignment algorithms cover a variety of approaches, among which supervised fine-tuning (SFT) refers to fine-tuning LLM by supervised learning of presentation data in immediate response (input-output). In the process, LLM minimizes experience loss with high-quality presentation data, ensuring that the output of the model is both practical and safe [45]. Another approach is to use reinforcement learning combined with human feedback (RLHF), which uses human feedback and preferences to improve LLM performance [29].

Gradient-Based Defense. Similar to the jailbreak attack algorithm, the strategy of optimizing universal trigger tokens is also used to guide large language models (LLMS) to produce secure outputs. Zhou et al. [45] propose an approach that targets open source LLM by adding an adversarial suffix to its input prompt. This suffix is carefully designed through gradient descent algorithms to make the output content of LLM more secure. Xu et al. [37] proposed a security-aware decoding strategy for LLMS to generate responses that are useful and harmless to user queries. With this technique, it is possible to ensure that the model can produce a response that meets safety standards in the face of potential risks.

3.2 Black-Box Defense

The methods of black box attack can be divided into the following two categories: input-phase based defense and output-phase based defense. These two defense methods aim at the malicious operations that attackers may carry out in the input and output of the model respectively, and provide a comprehensive strategy for the security protection of NLP system.

Input Filter-Based Defenses. The defense strategy based on input phase can be further refined into the following three methods: input filtering, input modification, and input nesting. Input filtering: It mainly checks the prompt input into the large language model (LLM) through specific rules to identify and block the input with offensive characteristics. For example, to identify and defend against attacks that may lead to decreased language fluency, PPL (Perplexity) filters can be used [1]. This filter uses the confusion measure to identify and filter out overly complex inputs, thereby effectively improving the defense capability of the model. Input modification: This method mainly works by slightly changing those prompts that have adversarial attack characteristics to destroy their attack effect, while ensuring that the output effect of harmless prompts is not affected. For example, Robey et al. [31] used character-level perturbation techniques to neutralize perturbation-sensitive methods by randomly substituting, swapping, or inserting multiple tokens. Another approach, Cao et al. [2], is to destroy the structure of harmful hints by randomly deleting markers, so as to achieve effective defense. Input nesting: This approach is to add system prompts on the basis of the original prompts to standardize and alert the LLM to fully consider the security mechanism when output. For example, Zhang et al. [43] protected LLMS from jailbreaking attacks by setting the target priority prompted by the system. The experimental results show that the introduction of target priority can significantly reduce the ASR of jailbreak attacks without affecting the overall performance of the model, thus improving the security of the model.

Output Filter-Based Defenses. The defense strategy for the output stage has a clear goal, that is, to detect and filter the harmfulness of the output content generated by the model. This strategy can be further subdivided into two main methods: classifier-based detection and LLM-based detection. Classifier-based detection: Binary classifiers, such as support vector machines (SVM) or random forests, are often used to identify and filter malicious content. This method has been widely used in earlier studies [3,28,36,40]. For example, Goyal et al. [10] trained a set of classifiers that detect both input and output content, designed to monitor a user's interaction with an LLM application and flag the content of a particular behavior or conversation topic. Llm-based detection: can be classified into static defense and dynamic defense. Static defense methods directly detect output content by introducing additional LLM. For example, Wang et al. [34] proposed an approach in which they design a back-translation model that incorporates the initial response to backguess the original prompt that might have caused that response. If the guessed prompt is rejected for reverse translation by the target LLM, then the original prompt is considered harmful. In contrast, the dynamic defense approach utilizes the LLM to analyze why an attack succeeds or fails, and based on that analysis, iterate and optimize the original prompt to reduce its potential aggressiveness until a successful defense is achieved. Zhou et al. [46] introduced the concept of contextual adversarial games, an approach that enables LLMs to dynamically enhance their own security through an iterative adversarial process between attack agent and defense agent without fine-tuning, in order to respond more effectively to various attacks.

4 Evaluation

Evaluation metrics are critical to the above attack and defense methods. The evaluation data set is outlined in Sect. 4.1 and the evaluation metrics are outlined in Sect. 4.2.

4.1 DataSets

The dataset includes various topics related to harmful content, such as toxicity, discrimination, privacy, and misinformation. The toxicity dataset covers offensive language, hacking, and criminal topics [9,47]. The discrimination dataset addresses prejudice against marginalized groups, including gender, race, age, and health [12]. The privacy dataset focuses on protecting personal information and property [19], while the misinformation dataset evaluates whether the LLM generates incorrect or misleading information [5,23]. These diverse topics provide a comprehensive basis for assessing the effectiveness of attack and defense methods across different dimensions (Table 1).

Table 1. Characteristics of Datasets for LLM Safety Evaluation.

Dataset	Size	Topic			
		Toxicity	Discrimination	Privacy	Error message
RTPrompts [9]	100K	✓			
ToxiGen [12]	137405	✓	✓		
Truthful-QA [23]	817				✓
AdvBench [47]	1K				
SafetyBench [43]	2K	✓	✓	✓	
JailBreakV [26]	28K	✓	✓	✓	✓

4.2 Evaluation Metrics

In the evaluation of attack and defense algorithms for LLM jailbreak scenarios, the metrics can be categorized separately for attacks and defenses, including their definitions, roles, and importance.

Attack Evaluation Metrics

ASR (Attack Success Rate)

- Definition: The ratio of successful attacks to the total number of attack attempts.
- Role: Measures the effectiveness of the attack in compromising or manipulating the model.
- Importance: A high ASR indicates a potent attack method that can significantly impact model security. It is crucial for understanding the vulnerability of LLMs to specific attack strategies.

Efficiency

- Definition: The time and computational resources required to execute the attack algorithm.
- Role: Evaluates how quickly and with what resources an attack can be launched.
- Importance: Efficient attacks can be executed more frequently and with less detection, increasing their potential threat. It also helps in assessing the practicality of implementing such attacks in real-world scenarios.

Transferability

- Definition: The ability of an attack developed for one model to be effective on other LLMs.
- Role: Assesses the generalizability of attack strategies across different models or architectures.
- Importance: High transferability means that an attack discovered on one model could potentially compromise many others, highlighting a broader security concern.

False Positive Rate (FPR)

- Definition: In the context of attacks, it might refer to the rate at which non-targeted or benign outputs are incorrectly considered successful attacks.
- Role: Helps in understanding the precision of the attack method.
- Importance: A low FPR indicates that the attack is precise and mainly affects the intended targets, reducing unintended consequences.

Defense Evaluation Metrics

DSR (Defense Success Rate)

- Definition: The ratio of successfully mitigated attacks to the total number of attack attempts.
- Role: Measures the effectiveness of the defense method in protecting the model from attacks.
- Importance: A high DSR indicates a robust defense strategy that can effectively safeguard LLMs against various attack vectors.

Robustness

- Definition: The ability of the model to maintain its performance and accuracy under adversarial conditions or perturbations.
- Role: Evaluates the resilience of the defense mechanism against different types of attacks.
- Importance: Robust defenses are essential for ensuring the reliability and safety of LLMs in real-world applications where they may encounter malicious inputs.

Transferability

- Definition: The ability of a defense strategy to protect against attacks that were not specifically targeted or considered during its development.
- Role: Assesses the adaptability and comprehensiveness of the defense mechanism.
- Importance: High transferability in defenses means they can protect against a wide range of attacks, including emerging threats, providing a more secure environment for LLMs.

FPR (False Positive Rate)

- Definition: The rate at which benign content is incorrectly flagged as harmful by the defense mechanism.
- Role: Measures the tendency of the defense to over-block or misclassify non-harmful inputs.
- Importance: A low FPR is crucial for maintaining the usability and user experience of LLMs, as excessive false positives can lead to legitimate content being blocked, reducing the model's utility.

Efficiency

- Definition: The computational cost and time required to implement and run the defense strategy.
- Role: Evaluates the practicality and scalability of the defense mechanism.
- Importance: Efficient defenses are necessary for real-time applications where quick response times are critical. They also help in reducing the overall computational burden, making it feasible to deploy defenses in resource-constrained environments.

These metrics provide a comprehensive framework for evaluating the performance and reliability of both attack and defense strategies in the context of LLM security, helping researchers and practitioners to develop more secure and robust language models.

5 Challenges and Future Works

5.1 Complexity of Attack and Defense Strategies

As LLMs become more sophisticated, so do the strategies employed to attack and defend them. This increasing complexity makes it challenging to design evaluation metrics that can comprehensively capture all aspects of an attack or defense. The dynamic nature of attacks and defenses, requires evaluation frameworks to be adaptable and updatable. Future research should focus on developing more comprehensive evaluation frameworks that can capture the multifaceted nature of LLM jailbreak attacks and defenses. These frameworks should be adaptable to new attack and defense techniques.

5.2 Balancing Multiple Metrics

Evaluating attack and defense algorithms involves multiple metrics, such as ASR, DSR, robustness, efficiency, transferability, and FPR. Balancing these metrics to provide a holistic view of an algorithm's performance is challenging. Different applications may prioritize different metrics, making it difficult to establish a one-size-fits-all evaluation standard.

5.3 Data Scarcity and Quality

High-quality datasets for evaluating jailbreak attacks and defenses are scarce. Existing datasets may not cover a wide range of attack scenarios or may contain biases that affect evaluation results. The lack of standardized datasets makes it difficult to compare the performance of different algorithms objectively.

6 Conclusion

This paper analyzes the complexity of jailbreak attacks, defense and evaluation indicators for LLMs. It compares attack and defense algorithms from both white-box and black-box perspectives. In the white-box context, we explore how attackers exploit in-depth knowledge of LLM internals to launch precise jailbreak attacks, manipulating the model or stealing sensitive information. White-box defenses focus on strengthening internal security mechanisms to resist potential attacks. From the black-box perspective, we analyze how attackers detect harmful responses using nested methods, without internal knowledge of the model. Black-box defenses aim to detect harmful output content. To ensure the effectiveness of these strategies, we introduce key evaluation indicators, including attack success rate, robustness, and transferability. Overall, this paper offers a comprehensive understanding of jailbreak attacks and LLM defenses by combining white-box and black-box approaches, emphasizing the need for vigilance as LLMs gain widespread use.

Acknowledgments. This work is supported by the Project of the National Natural Science Foundation of China No. 62472177.

References

1. Alon, G., Kamfonas, M.: Detecting language model attacks with perplexity (2023). https://arxiv.org/abs/2308.14132
2. Cao, B., Cao, Y., Lin, L., Chen, J.: Defending against alignment-breaking attacks via robustly aligned LLM (2023)
3. Cheng, J., Danescu-Niculescu-Mizil, C., Leskovec, J.: Antisocial behavior in online discussion communities. Proc. Int. AAAI Conf. Web Soc. Media **9**(1), 61–70 (2021). https://doi.org/10.1609/icwsm.v9i1.14583. https://ojs.aaai.org/index.php/ICWSM/article/view/14583
4. Chu, J., Liu, Y., Yang, Z., Shen, X., Backes, M., Zhang, Y.: Jailbreakradar: comprehensive assessment of jailbreak attacks against LLMs. arXiv preprint arXiv:2402.05668 (2024)
5. Cui, S., et al.: FFT: towards harmlessness evaluation and analysis for LLMs with factuality, fairness, toxicity. CoRR abs/2311.18580 (2023). https://doi.org/10.48550/ARXIV.2311.18580
6. Ding, P., et al.: A wolf in sheep's clothing: generalized nested jailbreak prompts can fool large language models easily (2023)
7. Dong, Z., Zhou, Z., Yang, C., Shao, J., Qiao, Y.: Attacks, defenses and evaluations for LLM conversation safety: a survey. In: Duh, K., Gomez, H., Bethard, S. (eds.) Proceedings of the 2024 Conference of the North American Chapter of the Association for Computational Linguistics: Human Language Technologies (Volume 1: Long Papers), pp. 6734–6747. Association for Computational Linguistics, Mexico City, Mexico (2024). https://doi.org/10.18653/v1/2024.naacl-long.375. https://aclanthology.org/2024.naacl-long.375/
8. Du, Y., Zhao, S., Ma, M., Chen, Y., Qin, B.: Analyzing the inherent response tendency of LLMs: real-world instructions-driven jailbreak (2024). https://arxiv.org/abs/2312.04127
9. Gehman, S., Gururangan, S., Sap, M., Choi, Y., Smith, N.A.: RealToxicityPrompts: evaluating neural toxic degeneration in language models. In: Cohn, T., He, Y., Liu, Y. (eds.) Findings of the Association for Computational Linguistics: EMNLP 2020, pp. 3356–3369. Association for Computational Linguistics, Online (2020). https://doi.org/10.18653/v1/2020.findings-emnlp.301. https://aclanthology.org/2020.findings-emnlp.301/
10. Goyal, S., et al.: LLMGuard: guarding against unsafe LLM behavior. In: Proceedings of the Thirty-Eighth AAAI Conference on Artificial Intelligence and Thirty-Sixth Conference on Innovative Applications of Artificial Intelligence and Fourteenth Symposium on Educational Advances in Artificial Intelligence, AAAI'24/IAAI'24/EAAI'24. AAAI Press (2024). https://doi.org/10.1609/aaai.v38i21.30566
11. Guo, X., Yu, F., Zhang, H., Qin, L., Hu, B.: Cold-attack: jailbreaking LLMs with stealthiness and controllability. In: Proceedings of the 41st International Conference on Machine Learning, ICML 2024. JMLR.org (2024)
12. Hartvigsen, T., Gabriel, S., Palangi, H., Sap, M., Ray, D., Kamar, E.: ToxiGen: a large-scale machine-generated dataset for adversarial and implicit hate speech detection. In: Muresan, S., Nakov, P., Villavicencio, A. (eds.) Proceedings of the 60th Annual Meeting of the Association for Computational Linguistics (Volume 1: Long Papers), pp. 3309–3326. Association for Computational Linguistics, Dublin, Ireland, May 2022. https://doi.org/10.18653/v1/2022.acl-long.234. https://aclanthology.org/2022.acl-long.234/
13. He, L., Xia, M., Henderson, P.: What is in your safe data? Identifying benign data that breaks safety (2024). https://arxiv.org/abs/2404.01099
14. Jha, P., Arora, A., Ganesh, V.: LLM stinger: Jailbreaking LLMs using RL fine-tuned LLMs (student abstract). In: Proceedings of the AAAI Conference on Artificial Intelligence, vol. 39, pp. 29393–29395 (2025)
15. Jia, X., et al.: Improved techniques for optimization-based jailbreaking on large language models (2024). https://arxiv.org/abs/2405.21018

16. Jiang, F., et al.: ArtPrompt: ASCII art-based jailbreak attacks against aligned LLMs. In: Ku, L.W., Martins, A., Srikumar, V. (eds.) Proceedings of the 62nd Annual Meeting of the Association for Computational Linguistics (Volume 1: Long Papers), pp. 15157–15173. Association for Computational Linguistics, Bangkok, Thailand, August 2024. https://doi.org/10.18653/v1/2024.acl-long.809. https://aclanthology.org/2024.acl-long.809/
17. Kang, D., Li, X., Stoica, I., Guestrin, C., Zaharia, M., Hashimoto, T.: Exploiting programmatic behavior of LLMs: dual-use through standard security attacks (2023). https://arxiv.org/abs/2302.05733
18. Lermen, S., Rogers-Smith, C., Ladish, J.: Lora fine-tuning efficiently undoes safety training in llama 2-chat 70B (2024). https://arxiv.org/abs/2310.20624
19. Li, H., et al.: PrivLM-bench: a multi-level privacy evaluation benchmark for language models. In: Ku, L.W., Martins, A., Srikumar, V. (eds.) Proceedings of the 62nd Annual Meeting of the Association for Computational Linguistics (Volume 1: Long Papers), pp. 54–73. Association for Computational Linguistics, Bangkok, Thailand (2024). https://doi.org/10.18653/v1/2024.acl-long.4. https://aclanthology.org/2024.acl-long.4/
20. Li, H., Ye, J., Wu, J., Yan, T., Wang, C., Li, Z.: JailPO: a novel black-box jailbreak framework via preference optimization against aligned LLMs. In: Proceedings of the AAAI Conference on Artificial Intelligence, vol. 39, pp. 27419–27427 (2025)
21. Li, T., et al.: Revisiting jailbreaking for large language models: a representation engineering perspective. In: Proceedings of the 31st International Conference on Computational Linguistics, pp. 3158–3178 (2025)
22. Li, X., Zhou, Z., Zhu, J., Yao, J., Liu, T., Han, B.: DeepInception: hypnotize large language model to be jailbreaker (2024). https://arxiv.org/abs/2311.03191
23. Lin, S., Hilton, J., Evans, O.: TruthfulQA: measuring how models mimic human falsehoods. In: Muresan, S., Nakov, P., Villavicencio, A. (eds.) Proceedings of the 60th Annual Meeting of the Association for Computational Linguistics (Volume 1: Long Papers), pp. 3214–3252. Association for Computational Linguistics, Dublin, Ireland, May 2022. https://doi.org/10.18653/v1/2022.acl-long.229. https://aclanthology.org/2022.acl-long.229/
24. Liu, S., Chen, J., Ruan, S., Su, H., Yin, Z.: Exploring the robustness of decision-level through adversarial attacks on LLM-based embodied models. In: Proceedings of the 32nd ACM International Conference on Multimedia, pp. 8120–8128 (2024)
25. Liu, X., Xu, N., Chen, M., Xiao, C.: AutoDAN: generating stealthy jailbreak prompts on aligned large language models. In: The Twelfth International Conference on Learning Representations (2024). https://openreview.net/forum?id=7Jwpw4qKkb
26. Luo, W., Ma, S., Liu, X., Guo, X., Xiao, C.: JailBreakV-28K: a benchmark for assessing the robustness of multimodal large language models against jailbreak attacks (2024)
27. Mozes, M., He, X., Kleinberg, B., Griffin, L.D.: Use of LLMs for illicit purposes: threats, prevention measures, and vulnerabilities (2023). https://arxiv.org/abs/2308.12833
28. Nobata, C., Tetreault, J., Thomas, A., Mehdad, Y., Chang, Y.: Abusive language detection in online user content. In: Proceedings of the 25th International Conference on World Wide Web, WWW 2016, pp. 145–153. International World Wide Web Conferences Steering Committee, Republic and Canton of Geneva, CHE (2016). https://doi.org/10.1145/2872427.2883062
29. Ouyang, L., et al.: Training language models to follow instructions with human feedback. In: Proceedings of the 36th International Conference on Neural Information Processing Systems, NIPS 2022. Curran Associates Inc., Red Hook, NY, USA (2022)
30. Qiu, H., Zhang, S., Li, A., He, H., Lan, Z.: Latent jailbreak: a benchmark for evaluating text safety and output robustness of large language models (2023). https://arxiv.org/abs/2307.08487
31. Robey, A., Wong, E., Hassani, H., Pappas, G.J.: SmoothLLM: defending large language models against jailbreaking attacks (2024). https://arxiv.org/abs/2310.03684

32. Shah, R., Feuillade-Montixi, Q., Pour, S., Tagade, A., Casper, S., Rando, J.: Scalable and transferable black-box jailbreaks for language models via persona modulation (2023). https://arxiv.org/abs/2311.03348
33. Shen, X., Chen, Z., Backes, M., Shen, Y., Zhang, Y.: "Do anything now": characterizing and evaluating in-the-wild jailbreak prompts on large language models (2024). https://arxiv.org/abs/2308.03825
34. Wang, Y., Shi, Z., Bai, A., Hsieh, C.J.: Defending LLMs against jailbreaking attacks via backtranslation. In: Ku, L.W., Martins, A., Srikumar, V. (eds.) Findings of the Association for Computational Linguistics: ACL 2024, pp. 16031–16046. Association for Computational Linguistics, Bangkok, Thailand (2024). https://doi.org/10.18653/v1/2024.findings-acl.948. https://aclanthology.org/2024.findings-acl.948/
35. Wei, Z., Wang, Y., Li, A., Mo, Y., Wang, Y.: Jailbreak and guard aligned language models with only few in-context demonstrations (2024). https://arxiv.org/abs/2310.06387
36. Wulczyn, E., Thain, N., Dixon, L.: Ex machina: personal attacks seen at scale. In: Proceedings of the 26th International Conference on World Wide Web, WWW 2017, pp. 1391–1399. International World Wide Web Conferences Steering Committee, Republic and Canton of Geneva, CHE (2017). https://doi.org/10.1145/3038912.3052591
37. Xu, Z., Jiang, F., Niu, L., Jia, J., Lin, B.Y., Poovendran, R.: SafeDecoding: defending against jailbreak attacks via safety-aware decoding. In: Ku, L.W., Martins, A., Srikumar, V. (eds.) Proceedings of the 62nd Annual Meeting of the Association for Computational Linguistics (Volume 1: Long Papers), pp. 5587–5605. Association for Computational Linguistics, Bangkok, Thailand (2024). https://doi.org/10.18653/v1/2024.acl-long.303. https://aclanthology.org/2024.acl-long.303/
38. Xue, Y., et al.: Dual intention escape: Penetrating and toxic jailbreak attack against large language models. In: Proceedings of the ACM on Web Conference 2025, WWW 2025, pp. 863–871. Association for Computing Machinery, New York, NY, USA (2025). https://doi.org/10.1145/3696410.3714654
39. Yuan, Y., et al.: GPT-4 is too smart to be safe: stealthy chat with LLMs via cipher (2023)
40. Zellers, R., et al.: Defending Against Neural Fake News. Curran Associates Inc., Red Hook, NY, USA (2019)
41. Zhan, Q., Fang, R., Bindu, R., Gupta, A., Hashimoto, T., Kang, D.: Removing RLHF protections in GPT-4 via fine-tuning. In: Duh, K., Gomez, H., Bethard, S. (eds.) Proceedings of the 2024 Conference of the North American Chapter of the Association for Computational Linguistics: Human Language Technologies (Volume 2: Short Papers), pp. 681–687. Association for Computational Linguistics, Mexico City, Mexico (2024). https://doi.org/10.18653/v1/2024.naacl-short.59. https://aclanthology.org/2024.naacl-short.59/
42. Zhang, Y., Wei, Z.: Boosting jailbreak attack with momentum. In: ICASSP 2025 - 2025 IEEE International Conference on Acoustics, Speech and Signal Processing (ICASSP), pp. 1–5 (2025). https://doi.org/10.1109/ICASSP49660.2025.10888812
43. Zhang, Z., Yang, J., Ke, P., Mi, F., Wang, H., Huang, M.: Defending large language models against jailbreaking attacks through goal prioritization. In: Ku, L.W., Martins, A., Srikumar, V. (eds.) Proceedings of the 62nd Annual Meeting of the Association for Computational Linguistics (Volume 1: Long Papers), pp. 8865–8887. Association for Computational Linguistics, Bangkok, Thailand (2024). https://doi.org/10.18653/v1/2024.acl-long.481. https://aclanthology.org/2024.acl-long.481/
44. Zhou, A., Li, B., Wang, H.: Robust prompt optimization for defending language models against jailbreaking attacks (2024)
45. Zhou, C., et al.: Lima: less is more for alignment. In: Proceedings of the 37th International Conference on Neural Information Processing Systems, NIPS 2023. Curran Associates Inc., Red Hook, NY, USA (2023)

46. Zhou, Y., et al.: Defending jailbreak prompts via in-context adversarial game. In: Al-Onaizan, Y., Bansal, M., Chen, Y.N. (eds.) Proceedings of the 2024 Conference on Empirical Methods in Natural Language Processing, pp. 20084–20105. Association for Computational Linguistics, Miami, Florida, USA (2024). https://doi.org/10.18653/v1/2024.emnlp-main.1121. https://aclanthology.org/2024.emnlp-main.1121/
47. Zou, A., Wang, Z., Carlini, N., Nasr, M., Kolter, J.Z., Fredrikson, M.: Universal and transferable adversarial attacks on aligned language models (2023). https://arxiv.org/abs/2307.15043

Research on the Effectiveness Evaluation System of Lunar-Based Near-Earth Asteroid Monitoring Systems

Zhiliu Lu[1], Maodeng Li[1,2](✉), Zhenyu Hu[1], Shuangliang Liu[1], and Wangwang Liu[1]

[1] Deep Space Exploration Lab, Hefei, China
[2] Beijing Institute of Control Engineering, Beijing, China
mdengli@foxmail.com

Abstract. The threat of near-Earth asteroid (NEA) impacts is a major catastrophic risk facing humanity, and the construction of an efficient monitoring system is a key prerequisite for implementing planetary defense. Currently, the world relies on ground-based optical telescopes and radar systems for NEA monitoring. However, traditional ground-based monitoring systems are severely restricted by the Sun-Earth geometric relationship, with large observation blind spots in the direction of the Sun. Asteroids approaching Earth from the solar background direction are difficult to detect in a timely manner, making it impossible to achieve all-weather, full-coverage threat early warning.

Leveraging the unique spatial location and environmental advantages of the Moon, the lunar-based monitoring system can effectively compensate for the shortcomings of ground-based systems and significantly improve the detection probability and monitoring efficiency of NEAs. Addressing the key scientific issue of evaluating the effectiveness of the lunar-based monitoring system, this study analyzes the core factors influencing the effectiveness of the lunar-based NEA monitoring system based on research on the layout scheme of lunar-based NEA monitoring and initially establishes an effectiveness evaluation index system for the lunar-based NEA monitoring system. The research results not only provide a solid theoretical basis and technical support for the scheme design optimization, parameter configuration selection, and performance prediction evaluation of the lunar-based monitoring system but also lay a methodological foundation for the subsequent engineering implementation and effect evaluation of lunar-based monitoring missions. This is of great theoretical value and engineering application prospects for the future construction of an integrated space-Earth-Moon asteroid monitoring and early warning system and the improvement of humanity's planetary defense capabilities.

Keywords: Near-Earth Asteroid (NEA) · Lunar-Based Monitoring · Effectiveness Evaluation · Planetary Defense · Monitoring System

J. Zhan et al. (Eds.): Bench 2025, LNCS 16471, pp. 114–123, 2026.
https://doi.org/10.1007/978-981-95-9694-2_9

1 Overview of Near-Earth Asteroids

Asteroids are celestial bodies that orbit the Sun, have significantly smaller volume and mass than planets and dwarf planets, and do not release gas or dust. In the solar system, except for planets, comets, natural satellites, and dwarf planets, all other celestial bodies orbiting the Sun can be identified as asteroids. Among the 1.3 million confirmed asteroids in the solar system, approximately 92% are concentrated in the asteroid belt between the orbits of Mars and Jupiter, known as main-belt asteroids. The total mass of all main-belt asteroids is about 3.0×10^{21} kg, which is approximately 4% of the Moon's mass. The remaining asteroids are distributed near Earth's orbit (near-Earth asteroids), on Jupiter's orbit (Jupiter Trojans), between the orbits of Saturn and Uranus (Centaurs), and beyond Neptune's orbit (trans-Neptunian objects, Kuiper Belt objects). The diameter of asteroids ranges from 0.010 to 1000 km. Based on material composition, common types of asteroids include Type S, Type C, Type M, and Type E.

Astronomically, an asteroid with a minimum distance to the Sun of less than 1.3 AU is defined as a near-Earth asteroid. As of December 10, 2025, humans have discovered 40,226 near-Earth asteroids. According to their spatial orbital distribution, they can be categorized into: Apollo, Amor, Aten, and Atira types (see Table 1).

As of December 10, 2025, among the cataloged NEAs, 11,503 have a size of more than 140 m, and 876 have a size of more than 1 km. Among the NEAs with a diameter greater than 140 m, the number of threatening asteroids with a minimum orbital distance to Earth of less than 0.05 AU has reached 2,473. Such asteroids have a low probability of impacting Earth but pose extremely high risks. In addition, many asteroids with tens of meters can cause major disasters if they impact densely populated areas, which must be given priority attention.

Table 1. Classification of Near-Earth Asteroids

Type	Definition	Meaning	Quantity	Proportion
Apollo-type	$a > 1.0$ AU; $q < 1.017$ AU	Orbits intersect Earth's, semi-major axis > 1.0 AU	22830	56.7%
Amor-type	$a > 1.0$ AU; 1.017 AU $< q <$ 1.3 AU	Orbits outside Earth's, inside Mars'	14103	35.1%
Aten-type	$a < 1.0$ AU; $Q > 0.983$ AU	Semi-major axis < 1.0 AU, partial orbit intersects Earth's	3254	8.1%
Atira-type	$a < 1.0$ AU; $Q < 0.983$ AU	Orbits completely inside Earth's	39	0.1%

Note: a = orbital semi-major axis; q = perihelion; Q = aphelion

2 Existing Monitoring Capabilities, Shortcomings, and Advantages of Lunar-Based Monitoring

According to statistics on discovered NEAs by the Center for Near Earth Object Studies (CNEOS) established by NASA (as of November 30, 2025, Fig. 1), the

NEAs newly discovered in the past two decades are mainly detected by several ground-based NEA monitoring systems such as LINEAR, Catalina, Pan-STARRS, and ATLAS, with contributions also from space-based NEA monitoring facilities represented by NEOWISE.

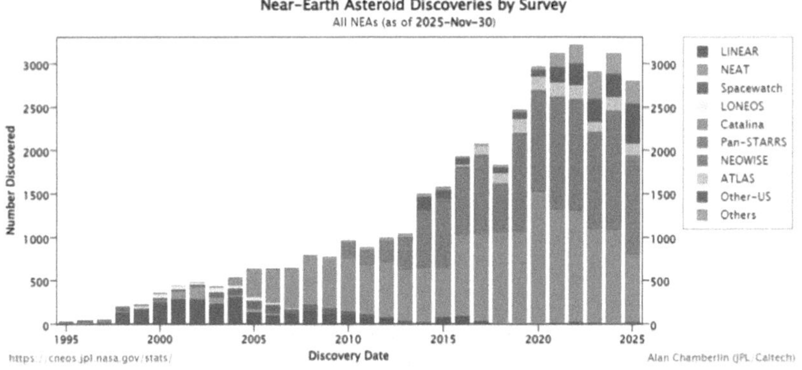

Fig. 1. Near-Earth Asteroid Discoveries by Survey [1].

Ground-based monitoring systems have the advantages of mature technology, low construction costs, and convenient scale expansion. However, they still have the following problems: 1. Short effective observation time and short continuous observation time per station: Ground-based optical telescopes can only work at night and are easily affected by weather, moonlight, etc., resulting in short effective observation time (less than 1/3 of the year), which affects the efficiency of sky survey observations. In addition, due to Earth's rotation, the observation arcs are discontinuous, and the observation time per station is short, making it impossible to continuously track targets for a long time, which affects the efficiency of tracking observations. 2. Observation blind spots in the direction of the Sun: Due to atmospheric scattering, the light on Earth during the day is strong, and asteroid signals are submerged in background noise. Therefore, ground-based optical telescopes have observation blind spots in the direction of the Sun. If an NEA approaches Earth from the direction of the Sun, ground-based telescopes cannot provide early warning in advance. 3. Limited ground-based observation methods: Asteroid observations include visible light, infrared, and radar methods. Among them, optical and infrared are passive observation methods that detect asteroids by receiving their reflected and radiated signals, which can be used for sky survey searches over a wide range of celestial regions with a long detection distance. Radar is an active observation method used for tracking known asteroids. By transmitting signals and receiving echoes reflected by asteroids, it conducts detailed detection of the asteroid's orbit, shape, structure, and material composition. Radar is used to detect known asteroids flying by Earth. The combination of infrared and optical band observations can obtain the albedo and relatively accurate size of asteroids, which is of great significance for accurately estimating the impact energy of asteroids. Due to atmospheric absorption of infrared rays, ground-based observations suffer significant infrared signal loss and are not suitable for ground-based infrared sky surveys. In contrast, space-based and lunar-based observations are not affected by the atmosphere and are very suitable for infrared observations. 4. Unbalanced geographical distribution: Affected by factors such as global economic development imbalances and land-sea distribution, the ground-based telescope observation network is unevenly distributed between the northern and southern hemispheres and the eastern and western hemispheres. Most observation equipment is concentrated in the northern and western hemispheres, while there is a lack of observation equipment in the southern and eastern hemispheres. If an asteroid approaches Earth from the southern hemisphere, it is difficult to detect in advance. 5. Potential impact from many human space activities near Earth in the future: With the construction of low-Earth orbit constellations, a large number of satellites will be launched into near-Earth orbits, which may have a significant impact on ground-based optical observations by leaving trajectories with long tails in telescope images, thereby affecting the detection efficiency of NEAs. In addition, the increasing frequency of human space activities has generated an enormous number of space objects and space debris in near-Earth orbits, which may interfere with asteroid observations.

Lunar-based and space-based monitoring can effectively compensate for the disadvantages of ground-based monitoring, with the following advantages: 1. Long effective observation time and long continuous observation time per station: There is no atmosphere on the Moon. With sufficient energy, sky survey observations can be conducted continuously without being affected by day and night. The slow rotation of the Moon allows for long-term continuous tracking observations of specific targets. In this regard, space-based observations have greater advantages. By selecting a reasonable orbit, energy and field of view issues can be ensured, enabling continuous sky survey observations and long-term continuous tracking observations of specific targets. 2. Improved coverage of ground-based blind spots: Without atmospheric scattering on the Moon and in orbit, observations of celestial regions near the Sun can be carried out, thereby forming a beneficial supplement to the observation blind spots of ground-based optical systems, improving the monitoring capability of NEAs approaching Earth from the direction of the Sun, and providing support for the formation of a comprehensive monitoring system. 3. Improved observation methods to obtain detailed characteristic information of asteroids: Infrared telescopes can be deployed on the Moon and in orbit to obtain information such as the size, albedo, and thermophysics of asteroids, providing rich data for asteroid defense, resource exploration, and scientific research. 4. Compensation for the lack of observation equipment in the southern hemisphere: Deploying telescopes at the lunar south pole can make up for the current lack of observation equipment in the southern hemisphere of Earth. If another set of telescopes is deployed at the lunar north pole, it will have the capability to observe celestial regions in both the northern and southern hemispheres. Telescopes deployed in orbit have an almost full-sky field of view, only needing to avoid certain celestial regions in the direction of the Sun. The lack of observation equipment in the southern hemisphere of Earth can also be compensated through observation pointing planning. 5. Minimal impact from human space activities: The Moon is far from near-Earth space and is not affected by giant constellations and human space activities. By selecting a reasonable orbital layout, the impact of giant constellations can be avoided, resulting in minimal impact from human space activities.

Based on the above analysis, the deployment of a lunar-based NEA monitoring system can effectively improve the effectiveness of NEA monitoring and provide more space and opportunities for NEA defense in terms of time and space. To support the demonstration and design of the lunar-based NEA monitoring system, it is necessary to analyze and construct an effective evaluation system for the lunar-based NEA monitoring system.

3 Performance Evaluation Factors of Lunar-Based Near-Earth Asteroid Monitoring Equipment

Like existing NEA monitoring systems, the proposed lunar-based NEA monitoring system also uses optical telescopes for NEA monitoring. The performance of optical telescopes can be analyzed through an accurate telescope parameter design model, which is based on key design parameters such as aperture, focal ratio, wavelength band, and single exposure time. The specific analysis process is as follows:

First, according to the signal-to-noise ratio (SNR) formula:

$$\mathrm{SNR}_{\mathrm{limit}} = \frac{N_{\mathrm{obj\_limit}}}{\sqrt{N_{\mathrm{obj\_limit}} + N_{\mathrm{sky}} + N_{\mathrm{camera}}}} \tag{1}$$

where N_{sky} is the sky background flux, N_{camera} is the detector noise (usually a constant), and $N_{\mathrm{obj\_limit}}$ is the target flux. Before calculating $N_{\mathrm{obj\_limit}}$, it is necessary to first determine the number of photons that the telescope can receive from Vega (the zero point of magnitude) in the observation band:

$$N_0 = N_{\mathrm{total}} \cdot \left(\pi \cdot \left(\frac{D \cdot 10^{-1}}{2}\right)^2\right) \cdot \mathrm{exptime} \tag{2}$$

where N_{total} is the total number of photons from Vega in the observation band, D is the telescope aperture (unit: mm), and exptime is the single image exposure time (unit: s). Subsequently, the real solution of the target flux $N_{\mathrm{obj\_limit}}$ corresponding to the limiting magnitude is derived:

$$N_{\mathrm{obj\_limit}} = \frac{1}{2}\left(\mathrm{SNR}_{\mathrm{limit}}^2 + \sqrt{\mathrm{SNR}_{\mathrm{limit}}^4 + 4 \cdot \mathrm{SNR}_{\mathrm{limit}}^2 \cdot (N_{\mathrm{sky}} + N_{\mathrm{camera}})}\right) \tag{3}$$

In the above formula, the calculation formula for N_{sky} is:

$$N_{\mathrm{sky}} = \mathrm{obj\_pixel} \cdot N_0 \times 10^{-0.4 \cdot m_{\mathrm{sky}}} \cdot \eta \cdot \mathrm{Pixel\_Scale}^2 \tag{4}$$

where obj_pixel is the number of pixels occupied by the target, m_{sky} is the sky background brightness in the observation band, η is the optical system efficiency, and Pixel_Scale is the angular range of the celestial region corresponding to each pixel (unit: arcseconds), calculated as follows:

$$\mathrm{PixelScale} = \frac{\mathrm{Camera\_PixelSize}}{f \times 10^{-3}} \times 0.206265 \tag{5}$$

Finally, according to the flux-magnitude formula, the observable limiting magnitude of the telescope can be calculated:

$$m_{\mathrm{limit}} = -2.5 \log_{10} \frac{N_{\mathrm{obj\_limit}}}{N_0} \tag{6}$$

The limiting magnitude is a core indicator for measuring the observation capability of an optical telescope, defining the brightness level of the dimmest celestial body that the telescope can detect.

Since NEAs are distributed near the ecliptic plane, telescopes used for NEA monitoring are affected by zodiacal light during observations. According to observation data from the WFC3 camera of the Hubble Space Telescope, zodiacal light is the brightest within the range of ecliptic latitude $\beta = 30^\circ$ and ecliptic longitude $\lambda = 45^\circ$, with an average V-band sky background flux of approximately 22.1 mag/arcsec^2; in the space with $|\lambda| > 45^\circ$ and $|\beta| < 15^\circ$, the average V-band sky background flux is approximately 22.6 mag/arcsec^2 [3]. Therefore, 22.6 mag/arcsec^2 is used as the calculation basis for the detection background brightness in the design of telescopes for NEA monitoring. Combined with the conditions of a minimum signal-to-noise ratio $\mathrm{SNR}_{\mathrm{limit}} = 3$ and a single image exposure time of 10 s, the limiting magnitudes of optical telescopes with apertures of 1 m, 2 m, 3 m, and 5 m are calculated using the model, resulting in V-band magnitudes of 23.0, 24.5, 25.4, and 26.5, respectively. If the single image exposure time of a 2 m aperture telescope is increased to 20 s, the observation limiting magnitude of the telescope will reach 25.5 mag.

The basic condition for an NEA to be detected by a monitoring telescope is whether its apparent magnitude at the time of monitoring is less than the limiting magnitude of the monitoring telescope. The apparent magnitude of an NEA is a function of multiple parameters coupling, related to the asteroid's size, albedo, three-dimensional shape, distance from the observation platform, and solar phase angle.

Currently, the widely used NEA photometry prediction model is the H-G magnitude model proposed by Bowell et al. in 1989 [2]. This method considers single and multiple scattering on the asteroid's surface and changes in the observation phase distance and is one of the calculation methods for ephemerides provided by the Minor Planet Center (MPC). The formula for calculating the apparent magnitude of an asteroid using this method is:

$$V_{\mathrm{mag}} = H(\alpha) + 5 \times \log_{10}(d_{\mathrm{OA}} \cdot d_{\mathrm{SA}}) \tag{7}$$

where V_{mag} is the apparent magnitude at the observer's position, d_{OA} is the distance between the observation equipment and the asteroid, d_{SA} is the distance between the Sun and the asteroid (both units are AU), and $H(\alpha)$ is the reduced magnitude of the asteroid, calculated as follows:

$$H(\alpha) = H - 2.5\log_{10}\left[(1-G)\Phi_1(\alpha) + G\Phi_2(\alpha)\right] \tag{8}$$

In the formula, G is the slope parameter used to describe the shape of the phase curve, which has a clear positive correlation with albedo. For NEAs with an albedo less than 0.1, $G \approx 0.04$; for the average albedo of NEAs (0.147), $G \approx 0.15$ [2]. H represents the absolute magnitude of the asteroid, whose physical meaning is the magnitude of the asteroid at a phase angle of 0° and a distance of 1 AU from both the Sun and the observer, which can indicate the asteroid's own light-reflecting ability; the two parameters are mainly obtained through asteroid photometry fitting models. $\Phi_1(\alpha)$ and $\Phi_2(\alpha)$ are functions that manage the physical models of single and multiple scattering of asteroids, respectively, defined as follows:

$$\Phi_i(\alpha) = W\left(1 - \frac{C_i \sin\alpha}{0.119 + 1.341\sin\alpha - 0.754\sin^2\alpha}\right) + (1-W)\exp\left[-A_i\left(\tan\frac{\alpha}{2}\right)^{B_i}\right], \quad i = 1, 2 \tag{9}$$

In the above formula, $W = \exp\left[-90.56\tan^2\left(\frac{\alpha}{2}\right)\right]$, $\Phi_1(\alpha)$ corresponds to parameters $A_1 = 3.332$, $B_1 = 0.631$, $C_1 = 0.986$, and $\Phi_2(\alpha)$ corresponds to parameters $A_2 = 1.862$, $B_2 = 1.218$, $C_2 = 0.238$.

Based on the above model, combined with the formula for calculating the radius of NEAs provided on the official website of CNEOS [1]:

$$D = 10^{(3.1236 - 0.5\log_{10} a - 0.2H)} \tag{10}$$

the minimum diameter of NEAs that can be monitored by the telescope for NEA monitoring at a certain distance from Earth can be calculated. Taking the 2 m aperture telescope mentioned earlier as an example, if the maximum monitoring distance is set to 0.25 AU, the minimum diameter of asteroids that can be monitored by the telescope is 50 m.

The design of NEA monitoring facilities involves numerous factors and parameters, but the equipment performance can be evaluated through two parameters: the minimum diameter of detectable asteroids and the maximum monitoring distance.

4 Effectiveness Evaluation Factors of Lunar-Based Near-Earth Asteroid Monitoring System

For the lunar-based NEA monitoring system, the performance of the monitoring telescope only specifies the boundaries of the monitoring system in terms of monitoring distance and detectable asteroid size. The number of NEAs that the monitoring system can detect within these boundaries is closely related to the sky survey strategy and layout position of the monitoring telescope.

A statistical analysis was conducted on NEAs in the MPC database that can enter the range of 0.25 AU around Earth during 2030–2031. Among more than 40,000 NEAs, only 1,413 meet the requirements during this period. Telescopes for NEA monitoring were deployed at the lunar south pole, lunar north pole, Earth-Moon Lagrangian points L4/5 in the Earth-Moon space, and Earth's sun-synchronous orbit. The relative positions of the telescopes at each location or orbit with 1,413 NEAs, the apparent magnitude relative to the station, the topocentric ecliptic coordinates, the solar angular distance, the Earth angular distance, and the real-time distance from the NEAs to Earth were calculated for the period 2030–2031. The coordinate distribution of these NEAs in the heliocentric ecliptic coordinate system shows obvious clustering, i.e., dense near the ecliptic plane and sparse in celestial regions with higher ecliptic latitudes. However, as NEAs gradually approach Earth, their ecliptic latitudes usually increase due to changes in relative positions, and the topocentric ecliptic coordinates of the detectable samples at various times are very scattered. The commonly used block periodic full-sky search in astronomical observations will waste a lot of observation resources on celestial regions where NEAs of key concern are not located. At the same time, the advantageous celestial regions with high all-sky monitoring efficiency of the sun-synchronous orbit, Earth-Moon L4, Earth-Moon L5, lunar north pole, and lunar south pole are mutually complementary: the sun-synchronous orbit platform can efficiently cover the celestial region opposite to the Sun; Earth-Moon L4 and L5 have minimal occlusion near the ecliptic; the lunar north pole can continuously monitor the northern half of the celestial sphere above the ecliptic for a long time, and the lunar south pole can continuously monitor the southern half of the celestial sphere below the ecliptic for a long time. Combined with the fact that the average motion speed of NEAs with an absolute magnitude < 25.0 mag in the sky background given by the MPC database does not exceed 3.2 degrees/day, 20 minutes of stellar staring observation can meet the continuous time requirement for orbit determination, and the NEA will not move out of the field of view.

In summary, based on the actual spatial distribution of NEAs and the observation condition advantages of each observation platform, the following monitoring sky survey strategy scheme is designed: 1) Observation samples: All NEA samples within the real-time range of 0.25 AU around Earth with an apparent magnitude < 25.5 mag, solar angular distance $> 20°$, Earth angular distance $> 10°$, and lunar angular distance $> 5°$ (not considered for lunar-based equipment). 2) Equipment observation mode: Adopt the stellar staring mode and perform continuous exposure monitoring with the moving target in the field of view as the center. Each field of view celestial region is continuously tracked and monitored for 20 minutes (including pointing adjustment and image readout time, ensuring a continuous monitoring time of more than 15 minutes) with a single exposure of 20 s. 3) Monitoring platform allocation: According to the real-time topocentric ecliptic latitude of NEAs, the eligible NEAs to be observed are divided into three categories: NEAs with ecliptic latitudes between $-12°$ and $+12°$ are tracked and observed by monitoring equipment at Earth-Moon

L4 and L5; NEAs with ecliptic latitudes between +12° and +90° are tracked and observed by monitoring equipment at the lunar north pole; NEAs with ecliptic latitudes between −90° and −12° are tracked and observed by monitoring equipment at the lunar south pole; the sun-synchronous orbit platform equipment performs reciprocating scanning of all celestial regions with ecliptic latitudes from −90° to 90° to improve the re-inspection rate.

By analyzing whether the real-time ecliptic coordinates (time resolution of 1 hour) of all NEAs that can enter the range of 0.25 AU of Earth's orbit within 2030–2031 relative to each observation platform are located in the real-time pointing celestial region of the telescope, the number of NEAs that can be monitored by different monitoring points in a year is obtained, as shown in Table 2.

Table 2. Number of NEAs Monitored by Different Monitoring Positions

Monitoring Facility Location	Number of Monitored NEAs
Lunar South Pole	570
Lunar North Pole	617
Earth-Moon L4 Point	280
Earth-Moon L5 Point	264
Sun-Synchronous Orbit	241

Different monitoring points are combined to form five monitoring layout schemes. The specific composition and monitoring effects of each scheme are as follows (see Table 3): 1. Lunar South Pole + Earth-Moon L4 Point: A total of 713 NEAs can be monitored throughout the year, including 280 monitored by 1 telescope in the L4 orbit and 570 monitored by 4 telescopes at the lunar south pole. After deduplication statistics, the detection rate of NEAs with a diameter of more than 50 m within 0.25 AU is 50.46%. 2. Lunar South Pole + Earth-Moon L4/L5 Points: A total of 830 NEAs can be monitored throughout the year, including 280 monitored by 1 telescope in the L4 orbit, 264 monitored by 1 telescope in the L5 orbit, and 570 monitored by 4 telescopes at the lunar south pole. After deduplication statistics, the detection rate of NEAs with a diameter of more than 50 m within 0.25 AU is 58.74%. 3. Lunar South/North Poles + Earth-Moon L4 Point: A total of 1,010 NEAs can be monitored throughout the year, including 280 monitored by 1 telescope in the L4 orbit, 570 monitored by 4 telescopes at the lunar south pole, and 617 monitored by 4 telescopes at the lunar north pole. The detection rate of NEAs with a diameter of more than 50 m within 0.25 AU is 71.48%. 4. Lunar South/North Poles + Earth-Moon L4/L5 Points: A total of 1,095 NEAs can be monitored throughout the year, including 280 monitored by 1 telescope in the L4 orbit, 264 monitored by 1 telescope in the L5 orbit, 570 monitored by 4 telescopes at the lunar south pole, and 617 monitored by 4 telescopes at the lunar north pole. The detection rate of NEAs with a diameter of more than 50 m within 0.25 AU is 77.49%. 5. All above +

Sun-Synchronous Orbit: A total of 1,117 NEAs can be monitored throughout the year, including 280 monitored by 1 telescope in the L4 orbit, 264 monitored by 1 telescope in the L5 orbit, 570 monitored by 4 telescopes at the lunar south pole, 617 monitored by 4 telescopes at the lunar north pole, and 241 monitored by 1 telescope in the SSO orbit. The detection rate of NEAs with a diameter of more than 50 m within 0.25 AU is 79.05%.

Table 3. Evaluation Results of Monitoring Effectiveness of Candidate Layouts

No.	Monitoring Facility Locations	Number of Monitored NEAs	Total System Monitoring Quantity	Coverage Rate
1	Lunar South Pole + Earth-Moon L4 Point	570 + 280	713	50.46%
2	Lunar South Pole + Earth-Moon L4/L5 Points	570 + 280 + 264	830	58.74%
3	Lunar South/North Poles + Earth-Moon L4 Point	570 + 617 + 280	1010	71.48%
4	Lunar South/North Poles + Earth-Moon L4/L5 Points	570 + 617 + 280 + 264	1095	77.49%
5	All above + Sun-Synchronous Orbit	570 + 617 + 280 + 264 + 241	1117	79.05%

The detection rate of NEAs above a certain diameter within a certain time and space range can intuitively reflect the monitoring effect of different schemes of the lunar-based NEA monitoring system, making it suitable as a core factor for evaluating the effectiveness of the lunar-based NEA monitoring system.

5 Conclusions

In the research on the parameter design analysis of lunar-based NEA monitoring facilities and the layout scheme of the monitoring system, an effectiveness evaluation system for the lunar-based NEA monitoring system based on three dimensions—monitoring range, monitoring target size, and monitoring target coverage rate—is initially established. This provides a theoretical basis and technical support for the scheme design optimization, parameter configuration selection, and performance prediction evaluation of the lunar-based monitoring system and lays a methodological foundation for the subsequent engineering implementation and effect evaluation of lunar-based monitoring missions. It is of great theoretical value and engineering application prospects for the future construction of an integrated space-Earth-Moon asteroid monitoring and early warning system and the improvement of humanity's planetary defense capabilities.

References

1. Center for near earth object studies. https://cneos.jpl.nasa.gov/
2. Buchheim, R.K.: Methods and lessons learned determining the H-G parameters of asteroid phase curves. In: The Society for Astronomical Sciences 29th Annual Symposium on Telescope Science, Big Bear Lake, CA, pp. 101–115 (2010)
3. Marinelli, M., Green, J.: WFC3 instrument handbook for cycle 33 v. 17. (2024). https://hst-docs.stsci.edu/wfc3ihb

Leveraging Network and Content Features for Open Source Software Value Assessment

Wenlong Dai[1(✉)], Shuang Wu[1], Wei Wang[1,2], and Jianzhong Li[2]

[1] East China Normal University, Shanghai, China
51265903033@stu.ecnu.edu.cn, wwang@dase.ecnu.edu.cn
[2] Singularity Intelligence Research Institute, Palo Alto, China

Abstract. As open source software (OSS) gains prominence in the tech ecosystem, assessing its value and that of commercial OSS companies is vital for innovation and industry growth. Despite its importance, accurately evaluating OSS remains complex. This study employs an asset pricing comparison method from finance, analyzing the value indicators of similar projects to approximate the value of target projects. Key factors representing OSS value include development activity, quality, and potential influence, represented by collaborative network features and repository text features.

Keywords: Open Source Software · Asset Pricing · Machine Learning

1 Introduction

With the in-depth development of the information technology era, Open Source Software (OSS) has increasingly occupied a pivotal position in the global software ecosystem [1,2]. OSS, with its characteristics of easy accessibility and modifiability, has lowered the barriers to software development, fostered cross-border innovation and technology sharing, and emerged as a significant driving force for global technological innovation [3]. However, with the surge in the number of open-source projects, accurately assessing the value of OSS and the Commercial Open Source Software Companies (COSS Companies) behind them to guide investment, development, and policy formulation has become a complex and pressing issue. Traditional value assessment methods predominantly focus on financial and market performance but fail to fully capture intrinsic attributes such as OSS community activity, contributor behavior, and documentation quality [4,5]. Despite the increasingly widespread application of text processing technologies like Natural Language Processing (NLP) in the field of software engineering [6], existing research rarely combines the principles of the Comparative Approach in finance with NLP techniques to construct a comprehensive assessment model.

J. Zhan et al. (Eds.): Bench 2025, LNCS 16471, pp. 124–141, 2026.
https://doi.org/10.1007/978-981-95-9694-2_10

Current research on OSS value assessment suffers from three major limitations: First, the assessment dimensions are singular, often emphasizing community activity or technical characteristics while neglecting the interactive effects of multiple factors. Second, the application of text processing technologies is confined to code comment analysis and requirement extraction, lacking in-depth mining of large-scale documentation and community discussions [12–20]. Third, value assessment models for COSS Companies are not yet mature, with existing research heavily relying on financial data and market performance while overlooking the dynamics of open-source communities and their unique value creation mechanisms [8–11]. Additionally, both domestic and international research exhibit systemic deficiencies: international studies, although proposing various assessment models, mostly focus on specific projects or limited indicators [21]; domestic research, in particular, lacks a systematic assessment of the business model value of OSS [22].

This study proposes an OSS value assessment model that integrates the Comparative Approach with text processing technologies. Its core contributions include: constructing a comprehensive dataset for COSS Companies that encompasses investment information, GitHub activity data, and README documentation; developing a novel assessment model that predicts OSS value by analyzing the community influence and documentation quality of similar projects; validating the model's effectiveness through empirical analysis to provide theoretical and practical tools for investment decisions; and ultimately creating a user-oriented value assessment tool to enhance the model's accessibility and practicality.

The organizational structure of this paper is as follows: Sect. 2 reviews key concepts related to OSS and COSS Companies and elaborates on assessment methods for collaborative network characteristics and repository text features. Section 3 details the dataset construction, the application of web crawler technology, and the data governance framework. Section 4 integrates the Dynamic OpenRank metric with BERT text features to construct a model for predicting community activity and influence. Section 5 validates the advantages of the new model in predicting OSS value through empirical analysis involving multiple model comparisons.

2 Background Knowledge and Theoretical Foundations

2.1 Open Source Software (OSS) and Commercial Open Source Software Companies (COSS Companies)

OSS refers to software whose source code can be used, viewed, modified, and shared by the public. Compared with proprietary software, OSS emphasizes the concepts of open collaboration and knowledge sharing [23]. The main characteristics of OSS include transparency, accessibility, and a community-driven development model. These features not only facilitate rapid technological innovation and iteration but also reduce the costs associated with software development and maintenance [10].

The emergence of COSS Companies represents an innovation in traditional software development and sales models. As the status of OSS continues to rise within the global technology ecosystem, an increasing number of commercial companies have started to build their business models based on open-source projects. COSS Companies employ a variety of business models, including but not limited to providing paid support and consulting services, selling open-source licenses, developing proprietary extensions for OSS, and adopting an open-source-based Software as a Service (SaaS) model [11].

2.2 Work Related to OSS Value Evaluation

When conducting asset, project, or enterprise valuation, traditional valuation models primarily include the Comparative Approach, the Cost Approach, and the Income Approach. These methods are widely applied in commercial and financial analysis, each having its specific applicable scenarios, advantages, and disadvantages.

The Comparative Approach, also known as the Market Approach, mainly estimates the value of the target asset by comparing it with similar assets with known prices. In practice, this requires a sufficient number of similar cases as references and an active and transparent market to obtain such information. The Comparative Approach is particularly commonly used in real estate appraisal and the second-hand market [24,25]. The Cost Approach evaluates value based on the cost required to replace or reconstruct the target asset. It takes into account all the costs necessary to acquire the same functions and utilities, including materials, labor, and overhead expenses. The Cost Approach is suitable for the valuation of unique assets, such as buildings with special purposes [26,27].

The Income Approach estimates value based on the net income generated by the asset in the future. It determines the asset's value by discounting the future income stream to its present value. This method is applicable to assets that can generate predictable cash flows, such as investment properties and enterprises [28,29].

In the valuation of open-source projects, the applicability of the Cost Approach and the Income Approach is limited. The Cost Approach finds it difficult to accurately assess the indirect benefits and community value brought about by open-source projects. The Income Approach, on the other hand, faces the challenge of being unable to predict the future direct income of open-source projects, especially for those projects that mainly rely on community contributions and non-direct business models.

In contrast, the Comparative Approach appears more suitable for open-source project valuation due to its flexibility and adaptability. By comparing the performance of similar open-source projects or COSS Companies in certain dimensions (such as community activity and project influence), the value of the target open-source project can be estimated. However, this requires a reasonable evaluation framework and accurate comparative dimensions to ensure the validity and accuracy of the assessment.

2.3 The Characteristics of OSS Communities and Their Influence, Along with the OpenRank Metric

The success of OSS projects largely hinges on the communities behind them. Community members contribute by reporting bugs, submitting code, writing documentation, and participating in discussions, which not only enhances the software's quality and security but also accelerates the development of new features [30]. An active community often indicates that the project can continuously attract and retain contributors, serving as a crucial metric for measuring the influence of OSS [31].

The influence of OSS is also reflected in its ability to drive the formulation of technical standards, facilitate the sharing of best practices within the industry, and exert a long-term impact on the global software development paradigm [32]. By analyzing community activity, the diversity of contributors, as well as the project's acceptance and usage scope, one can comprehensively evaluate the influence and value of OSS [7].

OpenRank is a quantitative metric aiming to comprehensively evaluate the influence and community activity of OSS projects [33].

The OpenRank algorithm is a variant of the PageRank algorithm, specifically tailored for nodes such as collaborative units in open-source projects (e.g., Issues and Pull Requests) and developers. Similar to the PageRank algorithm, OpenRank employs an algorithm to determine the centrality of issues/pull requests and developers as indicators of contribution value. However, unlike PageRank, when calculating the centrality of each node, the OpenRank algorithm takes into account not only the structure of the collaborative network but also the intrinsic value of the nodes themselves. By considering both collaborative behaviors in open-source projects and contributions from participants, the OpenRank algorithm provides an effective tool for quantifying and assessing the value of collaboration and contributions within open-source communities.

2.4 Natural Language Processing (NLP)

Natural Language Processing (NLP) is a branch of computer science and artificial intelligence. NLP integrates theories and methods from multiple disciplines, focusing on enabling computers to understand and process human language.

The core tasks of NLP include language understanding (extracting meaning from text) and language generation (producing natural language responses). With the development of deep learning and big data technologies, NLP has made significant progress, and its application scope has expanded from text classification and sentiment analysis to multiple fields such as machine translation, automatic summarization, and question-answering systems [36].

Deep learning has brought revolutionary changes to the development of NLP. In particular, pretrained language models, such as BERT (Bidirectional Encoder Representations from Transformers) and GPT (Generative Pretrained Transformer), can capture rich language patterns and knowledge by pretraining on large-scale text data. Subsequently, fine-tuning them on specific tasks has substantially improved the performance of NLP tasks [37,38].

In addition to BERT and GPT, other models like XLNet, RoBERTa, and ELECTRA have also demonstrated their superiority in multiple NLP fields, including text classification, sentiment analysis, question-answering systems, and natural language inference [39–41]. These models have further pushed the boundaries of NLP technology, making it more efficient and accurate to extract useful information from complex texts.

As the "face" of open-source projects, the README file provides users and developers with key information such as project overviews, installation guides, usage instructions, and contribution guidelines. By applying deep learning models such as BERT, researchers can automatically identify information gaps, potential ambiguities, and areas for improvement in README files, thereby guiding developers to optimize the documentation content [42].

Through in-depth analysis of README files and other documents, NLP can not only enhance the quality of software documentation but also promote the healthy development of open-source communities, increasing user engagement and the influence of projects.

3 Construction of a Benchmark Dataset to Support the Task of Evaluating the Commercial Value of OSS

This section focuses on constructing a benchmark dataset to support the task of evaluating the commercial value of OSS. The crux of this task lies in gaining an in-depth understanding of the behaviors within the open-source community, commercial operations, as well as the sources, collection methods, and strategies of their textual data, and subsequently assessing their commercial value through these data. In light of this, the data of concern in this study encompasses commercial data of OSS, collaborative network data, and repository text data.

3.1 Sources of Foundational Data

For basic investment data of COSS companies, data collection mainly relies on the regularly updated datasets from COSS.community. However, this website has an anti-crawling mechanism. To address this issue, during the data collection process, this study adopted a method that combines screen recording software, action assistant software for screenshot capture, and Optical Character Recognition (OCR) technology. Subsequently, manual proofreading was conducted to ensure data accuracy [43].

The collection of OSS behavioral data relies on GHArchive [50], REST API [44], and the Open-Digger project.

GitHub's REST API offers an intuitive and powerful way to access almost all types of public data on GitHub. By constructing precise API requests, researchers can obtain the README files of specific open-source projects and other relevant project information in a targeted manner, providing a data foundation for analyzing project documentation using NLP techniques [45].

Additionally, in Sect. 2, this paper introduced OpenRank, a network structural characteristic metric. This section will introduce a variant of OpenRank.

OpenRank is a Markov process algorithm similar to PageRank. Its iterative calculation formula for all nodes v_i is as follows:

$$v_i = (1 - a_i) \sum_{j=1}^{|V|} \frac{w_{ji}}{d_{o_j}} v_j + a_i v_0$$

Among them, v_0 represents the initial value of the node, a_i indicates the degree to which the node relies on its initial value, d_{oj} denotes the weighted out-degree of node j, and w_{ji} is the weight of the edge from node j to node i.

However, in real - life scenarios, the transition probabilities within different OSS community networks vary. Setting them to the same coefficient is an intuitive but not sufficiently meticulous approach.

Therefore, this study improves the OpenRank algorithm by allowing the damping coefficients (d_{oj}) of different types of OSS network sub - graphs to be set to different values. This study names this algorithm Dynamic OpenRank.

3.2 Data Model and Feature Specification

For the model construction of commercial, collaborative network, and repository text data of OSS, this study presents a data model in Fig. 1 that revolves around the collaborative networks, commercial relationships, and textual relationships among COSS companies, their core open-source organizations, and projects.

In this model, investors invest in COSS companies. These COSS companies possess one or more core OSS organizations. Each OSS organization encompasses multiple OSS projects. Each OSS project has collaborative relationships with other OSS projects, forming a complex collaborative network. Additionally, each OSS repository has repository text information (usually in the form of a README file).

3.3 Construction of Benchmark Dataset

The data collection process is divided into the following steps:

1. Collect basic COSS investment data.
2. Utilize two authoritative commercial data platforms, Wind and Crunchbase, to deeply obtain specific commercial data of open-source companies, such as financial data, market performance, and investment status.
3. Based on the commercial data obtained in the first two steps, further precisely identify relevant GitHub organizations and projects through GitHub's REST API.

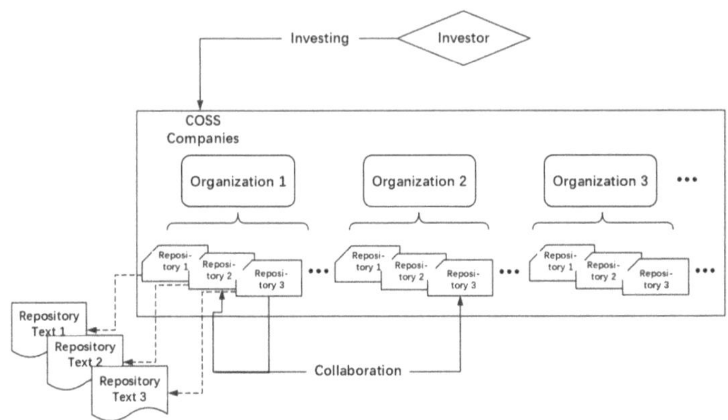

Fig. 1. COSS Companies, Collaborative Network and Repository Text Model

4. Comprehensively collect behavioral data of the target OSS organizations and projects through GHArchive, GitHub's REST API, and the processed Open-Digger data.
5. Specifically obtain the README text information of the target organizations and projects using GitHub's REST API.

4 Modeling Core Characteristics of Collaborative Networks and Repository Text

This section is dedicated to developing and evaluating a model that integrates the collaborative network characteristics and repository text features of OSS to more accurately model and predict the community activity and influence of OSS.

4.1 Feature Selection and Description

The overall construction process is illustrated in Fig. 2. The model development in this study relies on a comprehensive understanding and analysis of collaborative network metrics and repository textual features (e.g., README files) in OSS. Specifically, we employ the BERT model to conduct deep semantic analysis of README files, enabling the extraction of key information that summarizes repository textual characteristics from their content.

Following the procedure outlined in Fig. 2, a list containing seven attributes will be generated. All collected data then undergo the following sequential operations:

1. Standardization/normalization;
2. Principal Component Analysis (PCA);
3. Dimensionality reduction via Kernel Principal Component Analysis (KPCA).

The final dataset comprises 26 attributes representing the significant components extracted through KPCA applied to all non-textual features described above.

The modeling process for textual data proceeds as follows: First, the content of repository README files is converted into token vectors using BERT's tokenizer. For COSS companies, token vectors from all repositories under their ownership are aggregated into a unified list. Two distinct processing approaches are then considered for this vector list:

1. Aggregation: This method ensures effective model training when employing smaller-scale models;
2. Dynamic Padding: This approach guarantees comprehensive model training for larger-scale architectures by addressing variable sequence lengths.

When constructing the supply chain valuation model for OSS, feature selection with strong predictive power is of critical importance. Based on exploratory data analysis and prior hypotheses, we carefully selected four novel features:

- Total number of participants in COSS organizations at funding time
- Aggregate Star counts across all projects within COSS organizations at funding time
- Sum of Dynamic OpenRank scores at funding time
- Processed result list from README file analysis

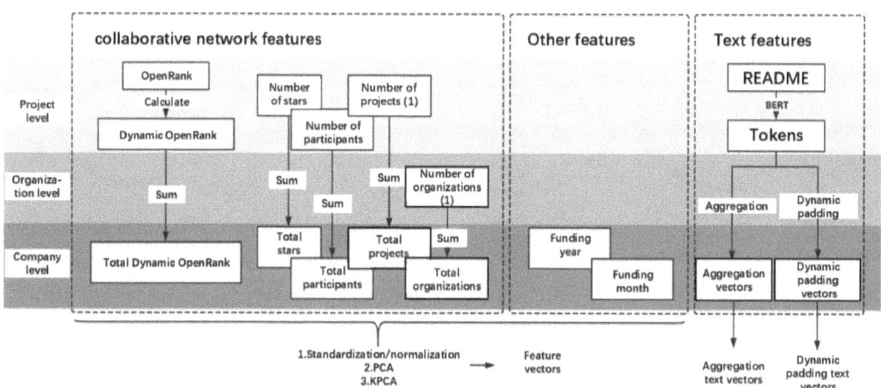

Fig. 2. Construction Process of a Data Model Integrating Collaborative Network Features and Repository Textual Features

4.2 Core Feature Modeling for Data

This study proposes a unified data processing framework that initiates with a normality test on the dataset to determine the appropriate analytical approach. Specifically, if the data conform to a normal distribution, multi-factor analysis techniques are employed; conversely, for non-normally distributed data, the Kruskal-Wallis test, permutation test, and feature importance metrics from random forests are utilized to evaluate the influence of each feature. Features demonstrating low influence are deemed insignificant and subsequently removed from the dataset.

Following this, principal component analysis (PCA) is applied to low-dimensional linear data to reduce dimensionality while extracting major sources of variation. For high-dimensional nonlinear data, kernel principal component analysis (KPCA) is implemented through nonlinear mapping of the remain-

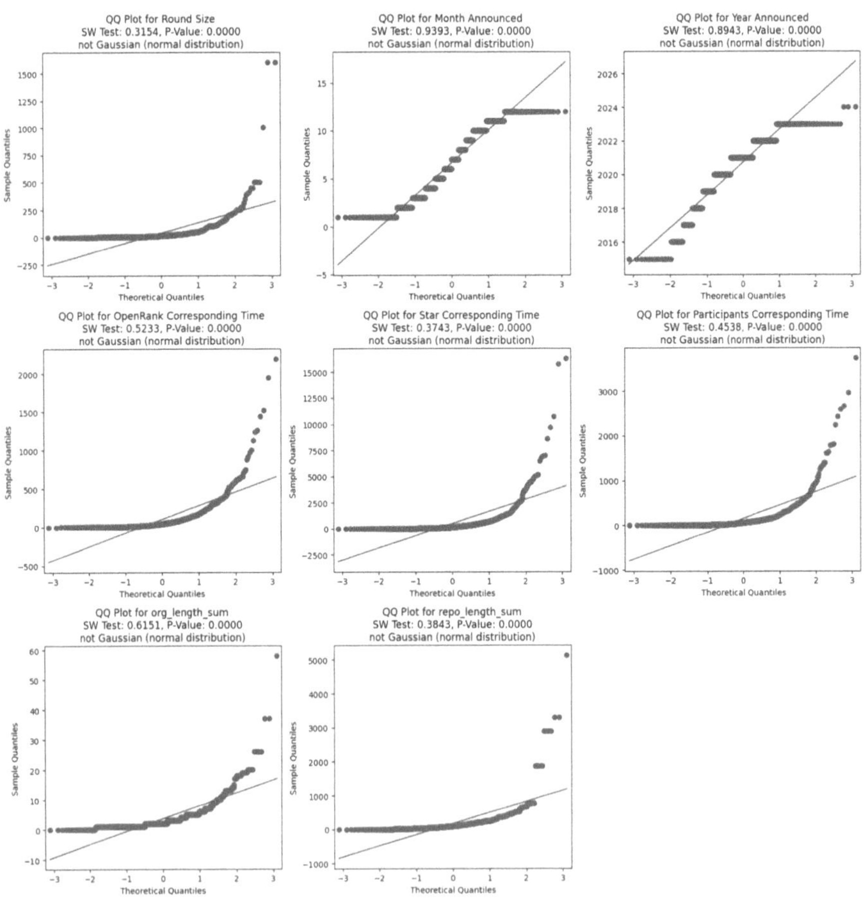

Fig. 3. QQ Plots for Each Data Attribute

ing principal features, thereby revealing the underlying data structure. Feature extraction is terminated when cumulative importance reaches a predefined threshold (typically 90%), at which point the remaining components are discarded. The application of KPCA constitutes the core innovation of this research, as it not only enables integrated analysis of complex OSS project data but also uncovers interactive relationships and potential causal mechanisms between high-dimensional nonlinear features and low-dimensional linear ones.

4.3 Modeling Results and Analysis

The results of the normality test are shown in Fig. 3. For all variables, the data points deviate from the straight line to some extent, indicating that the data do not follow a normal distribution. In particular, this deviation is more pronounced at both ends, suggesting the presence of extreme values. Moreover, their Quantile-Quantile (QQ) plots also reveal that the data points exhibit a non-linear shift to the right, implying skewness in the high-value region.

After applying logarithmic transformation, square root transformation, and Box-Cox transformation to the data, it was found that none of the transformed results conformed to a normal distribution. Consequently, this finding necessitates the adoption of non-parametric tests for subsequent data analysis in this study.

As shown in Table 1, "Funding year", "Participants", "Organizations", and "Repositories" are significant features influencing the dependent variable.

In particular, "Organizations" and "Repositories" exhibit highly significant differences in the Kruskal-Wallis test and also demonstrate relatively high values

Table 1. Statistical Results of Kruskal-Wallis Test, Permutation Test, and Random Forest Feature Importance

Feature	**Kruskal-WallisStatistic**	**P-Value**
Funding Month	17.19	0.102
Funding Year	39.38	9.84e-06
OpenRank	1018.86	0.332
Star	559.16	0.256
Participants	407.68	0.003
Organizations	92.91	1.09e-10
Repositories	406.12	6.59e-14

Permutation Test:	**Importance ± Std**
Funding Year	3.80%±1.40%
OpenRank	3.10%±1.00%
Repositories	3.10%±0.60%
Organizations	1.10%±0.30%

Feature Importance from Random Forest	
OpenRank	20.85%
Repositories	19.27%
Star	19.14%
Funding Year	11.99%
Participants	11.35%
Funding Month	10.86%
Organizations	6.54%

in feature importance scores, suggesting a strong potential association between these features and the dependent variable.

Furthermore, although "OpenRank" and "Star" do not show statistically significant differences in the Kruskal-Wallis test, they rank relatively high in the random forest feature importance scores, likely due to their favorable predictive performance within the random forest model.

On the other hand, "Funding month" reveals no significant differences in the Kruskal-Wallis test and also scores relatively low in feature importance, indicating its potentially limited influence on the dependent variable.

5 A DCNN-ETNN-Based Valuation Method for Open Source Software

This section introduces the development process of a deep learning-based OSS valuation method and explores six different algorithm designs. These algorithms are designed to comprehensively leverage the collaborative network characteristics and repository text features of OSS, so as to provide an in-depth evaluation of software value.

Ultimately, this section presents a deep neural network model (DCNN-ETNN) that combines a deep convolutional neural network with an enhanced Transformer layer. This method outperforms other models on the dataset formed in Sect. 3. Based on this model, this study constructs an OSS valuation method.

5.1 Valuation Methods

For regression tasks, there are several commonly used algorithms. In this paper, six algorithms are constructed for comparison and overview, namely linear regression, random forest, XGBoost, a basic neural network, a deep neural network with an added Transformer layer, and a self-developed complex Multi-neural network (incorporating a self-built Transformer layer) optimized according to the data format.

The linear regression algorithm does not utilize text BERT data. This approach is beneficial for evaluating the contribution of other features to software valuation when complex text information is not taken into account.

Random forest, XGBoost, and the basic neural network employ aggregated text BERT data. In contrast, the last two methods utilize dynamically padded text BERT data.

This design is based on the following considerations. When the network structure is relatively simple, processing a large volume of high-dimensional text data may lead to suboptimal training results. On the other hand, when the model structure is complex, adopting dynamic padding can optimize the computational efficiency of the model without sacrificing the richness of text information.

5.2 Technical Challenges

In the realm of OSS valuation, the core issue can be distilled into how to effectively integrate and analyze multi-source heterogeneous data from OSS projects to accurately predict their value.

With respect to non-textual features, this study confronts the following four challenges:

- KPCA involves non-linear mapping, and the valuation model needs to be capable of identifying and exploiting these non-linear relationships.
- Features after dimensionality reduction through KPCA may no longer conform to a normal distribution, which undermines the effectiveness of traditional statistical models.
- The data exhibits non - convex characteristics, posing a challenge to the search for a globally optimal valuation model.
- Despite dimensionality reduction via KPCA, the data still resides in a high - dimensional space. The model is required to effectively utilize these high - dimensional features while steering clear of the "curse of dimensionality".

When it comes to the fusion of textual and non - textual features, this study encounters the following challenges:

- The collaborative relationships among open - source projects form a complex network structure. The model is required to analyze this network structure and extract valuable features.
- OSS projects are characterized by high - dimensional features and a large volume of data. The model needs to effectively handle high - dimensional data while maintaining its generalization ability.

5.3 DCNN-ETNN Model

The core concept of this method lies in comprehensively leveraging the collaborative network metrics of OSS and the repository text features extracted from README files. By utilizing a deep learning model, it can not only capture the quantitative information of traditional metrics but also delve into the complex semantic information embedded in the text data. Consequently, this enables a comprehensive evaluation of the value of OSS.

This method captures the deep-level features of collaborative network metrics, including indicators such as Dynamic OpenRank, through a deep convolutional neural network. Simultaneously, it employs the BERT model to comprehend and analyze the repository text data in README files. By utilizing techniques such as Bayesian optimization [46], K - fold cross - validation [35], and the Adam optimizer [47], the model parameters are meticulously tuned to achieve optimal performance.

The model structure is illustrated in Fig. 4.

The DCNN-ETNN model combines a deep convolutional neural network (DCNN) with an enhanced Transformer layer (ETNN). Unlike traditional Transformer models, ETNN incorporates several structural enhancements aimed at improving performance in specific tasks, such as long-sequence processing and parallel computation efficiency. These enhancements may include additional layers, more sophisticated attention mechanisms, or extra processing modules tailored for the task of open-source software value assessment. By integrating these improvements, ETNN offers a more powerful and adaptable solution compared to its traditional counterparts, making it particularly well-suited for capturing the complex dynamics within open-source software communities.

In terms of the evaluation methods, this study employs Mean Squared Error (MSE) [34,48] and Coefficient of Determination (R-squared) [49].

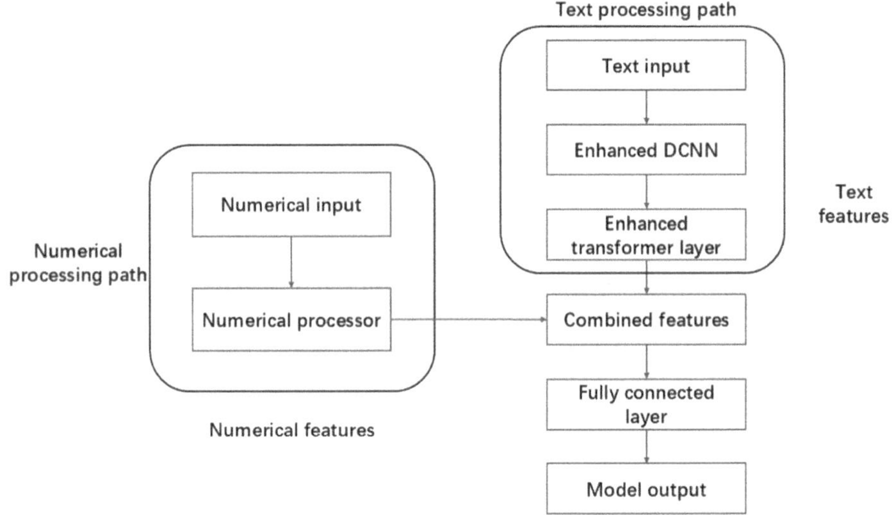

Fig. 4. Structure of DCNN-ETNN Model

5.4 Comparison of Methods: Experimental Results of Each Approach

When conducting model evaluation, in addition to employing standard evaluation metrics such as MSE and R-squared, this study also adopts baseline comparison as a crucial approach to measure model performance. The baseline model utilizes an extremely simple prediction strategy: for any given input, it always predicts the mean of the training samples of the target variable. This method disregards any information from the input features and merely uses the average value of the target variable as the benchmark for all predictions.

The experimental results are presented in Table 2. All the models outperform the baseline model to a certain extent. In particular, the XGBoost model, the

Table 2. Comparison of Model Performances (Raw Values)

Model	MSE	R^2
Baseline	1361.43	−59.18%
Regression	980.89	−14.68%
Random Forest	766.33	10.40%
XGBoost	735.37	14.02%
Simple Neural Network	827.30	3.27%
Neural Network with Transformer	758.37	11.33%
DCNN-Enhanced Transformer	577.97	32.42%

Table 3. Comparison between Prediction Results of Different Algorithms and Actual Target Results (Partial Rows)

COSS(Time)	Actual	Reg	RF	XGB	NN	NNw/T	DCNN-T
Webiny(2019-10)	0.347	21.19	13.21	13.21	14.37	18.36	13.12
Rasa(2019-04)	13.00	23.99	18.79	18.79	25.46	54.46	13.21
ToolJet(2023-01)	4.600	10.29	25.53	7.62	24.75	12.93	7.29
ZEDEDA(2019-02)	15.90	18.40	18.54	18.54	21.04	21.80	18.09
Orkes(2022-02)	9.300	12.08	17.52	17.52	11.09	22.30	18.02
Recurve(2022-08)	18.00	54.19	24.05	25.03	0.62	24.06	18.01
Tecton(2020-04)	20.00	29.15	14.70	15.36	24.25	21.99	19.97
env0(2020-07)	3.500	23.18	16.66	16.66	14.46	12.41	17.19
TileDB(2019-02)	3.000	22.91	19.03	19.03	15.51	26.32	19.57
Sysdig(2016-04)	15.00	24.27	16.08	16.08	15.74	19.49	16.63
Sysdig(2017-10)	25.0	33.28	17.73	17.73	13.47	17.86	23.17
Sanity(2019-09)	2.4	44.76	20.71	20.71	26.02	18.50	4.33

deep neural network with added Transformer layers, and the model combining DCNN with a deep neural network enhanced by Transformer layers all demonstrate favorable performance. This indicates that these models exhibit good capabilities in explaining data variation. For reference, this study has extracted a portion of the data and a comparison of prediction results from different models as examples in Table 3.

Here, "Reg" represents the Regression model; "RF" denotes the Random Forest; "XGB" signifies the XGBoost method; "NN" stands for the basic Neural Network; "NNw/T" indicates the Neural Network with added Transformer layers; and "DCNN-T" refers to the Deep Neural Network that combines a Deep Convolutional Neural Network with enhanced Transformer layers.

6 Conclusion

This study focuses on the issue of value assessment within OSS communities and proposes an innovative evaluation model. By integrating the Comparative Approach and text processing techniques, it aims to offer new theoretical and practical tools for investment decision-making in the realm of OSS.

To begin with, this paper delves deeply into the core concepts of OSS and COSS companies. Subsequently, it constructs a benchmark dataset to support the task of evaluating the commercial value of OSS. Following that, this paper presents the DCNN-ETNN model and validates its effectiveness through multiple evaluation methods.

This research provides a more precise evaluation tool, which assists investors and enterprises in better identifying promising open-source projects for investment and thereby reducing investment risks.

The leaders of OSS projects can leverage the evaluation model offered by this study to monitor and assess the health status of their projects. This enables them to identify potential issues during project development and formulate strategies accordingly to optimize community management and project promotion, ultimately enhancing the project's influence and value.

References

1. Wang, X., Dong, C., Zeng, W., Xu, Z., Zhang, J.: Survey of data value evaluation methods based on open source scientific and technological information. In: International Conference of Pioneering Computer Scientists, Engineers and Educators, pp. 172–185. Springer, Singapore (2019). https://doi.org/10.1007/978-981-15-0118-0_14
2. Tassone, J., Xu, S., Wang, C., Chen, J., Du, W.: Quality assessment of open source software: a review. In: 2018 IEEE/ACIS 17th International Conference on Computer and Information Science (ICIS), pp. 411–416. IEEE (2018)
3. Stamelos, I., Gonzalez-Barahona, J.M., Varlamis, I., Anagnostopoulos, D. (eds.): Open Source Systems: Enterprise Software and Solutions: 14th IFIP WG 2.13 International Conference, OSS 2018, Athens, Greece, June 8-10, 2018, Proceedings, vol. 525. Springer, Cham (2018). https://doi.org/10.1007/978-3-319-92375-8
4. Adewumi, A., Misra, S., Omoregbe, N., Sanz, L.F.: FOSSES: framework for open-source software evaluation and selection. Softw. Pract. Exp. **49**(5), 780–812 (2019)
5. Zhao, Y., Liang, R., Chen, X., Zou, J.: Evaluation indicators for open-source software: a review. Cybersecurity **4**(1), 20 (2021)
6. Madaehoh, A., Senivongse, T.: OSS-AQM: An open-source software quality model for automated quality measurement. In: 2022 International Conference on Data and Software Engineering (ICoDSE), pp. 126–131. IEEE (2022)
7. Hars, A., Ou, S.: Working for free? Motivations for participating in open-source projects. Int. J. Electron. Commer. **6**(3), 25–39 (2002)
8. Akatsu, S., Fujita, Y., Kato, T., Tsuda, K.: Structured analysis of the evaluation process for adopting open-source software. Procedia Comput. Sci. **126**, 1578–1586 (2018)

9. Wasserman, A.I.: Software engineering issues for mobile application development. In: Proceedings of the FSE/SDP Workshop on Future of Software Engineering Research, pp. 397–400 (2010)
10. Fitzgerald, B.: The transformation of open source software. MIS Q., 587–598 (2006)
11. Riehle, D.: The commercial open source business model. In: SIGeBIZ Track of the Americas Conference on Information Systems, pp. 18–30 (2009)
12. Panichella, S., Di Sorbo, A., Guzman, E., Visaggio, C.A., Canfora, G., Gall, H.C.: How can i improve my app? classifying user reviews for software maintenance and evolution. In: 2015 IEEE International Conference on Software Maintenance and Evolution (ICSME), pp. 281–290. IEEE (2015)
13. Guzman, E., Bruegge, B.: Towards emotional awareness in software development teams. In: Proceedings of the 2013 9th Joint Meeting on Foundations of Software Engineering, pp. 671–674 (2013)
14. Bird, S., Klein, E., Loper, E.: Natural Language Processing with Python: Analyzing Text with the Natural Language Toolkit. O'Reilly Media, Inc. (2009)
15. Alqaimi, A., Thongtanunam, P., Treude, C.: Automatically generating documentation for lambda expressions in Java. In: 2019 IEEE/ACM 16th International Conference on Mining Software Repositories (MSR), pp. 310–320. IEEE (2019)
16. Klein, D., Manning, C.D.: Accurate unlexicalized parsing. In: Proceedings of the 41st Annual Meeting of the Association for Computational Linguistics, pp. 423–430 (2003)
17. Bacchelli, A., Bird, C.: Expectations, outcomes, and challenges of modern code review. In: 2013 35th International Conference on Software Engineering (ICSE), pp. 712–721 (2013)
18. Lam, A.N., Nguyen, A.T., Nguyen, H.A., Nguyen, T.N.: Combining deep learning with information retrieval to localize buggy files for bug reports (n). In: 2015 30th IEEE/ACM International Conference on Automated Software Engineering (ASE), pp. 476–481. IEEE (2015)
19. Lamkanfi, A., Demeyer, S., Giger, E., Goethals, B.: Predicting the severity of a reported bug. In: 2010 7th IEEE Working Conference on Mining Software Repositories, MSR 2010, pp. 1–10. IEEE (2010)
20. Novielli, N., Calefato, F., Lanubile, F.: A gold standard for emotion annotation in stack overflow. In: Proceedings of the 15th International Conference on Mining Software Repositories, pp. 14–17 (2018)
21. Gezici, B., Özdemir, N., Yılmaz, N., Coşkun, E., Tarhan, A., Chouseinoglou, O.: Quality and success in open source software: a systematic mapping. In: 2019 45th Euromicro Conference on Software Engineering and Advanced Applications (SEAA), pp. 363–370. IEEE (2019)
22. Rashid, M., Clarke, P.M., O'Connor, R.V.: A systematic examination of knowledge loss in open source software projects. Int. J. Inf. Manage. **46**, 104–123 (2019)
23. Raymond, E.S.: The Cathedral and the Bazaar. In: The Cathedral and the Bazaar: Musings on Linux and Open Source by an Accidental Revolutionary, pp. 27–78. O'Reilly & Associates Inc., Cambridge (1999)
24. Institute, A.: The Appraisal of Real Estate, 13th edn. [S.l.]: Appraisal Institute (2008)
25. Pritchard, A.: Comparative method in software valuation. J. Softw. Value Manage. **1**(1), 34–45 (2017)
26. Riggs, J., West, T.: Financial Management for the Construction Industry. [S.l.]: William Morrow (1986)
27. Hitchner, J.R.: Financial Valuation, +Website: Applications and Models. Wiley (2017)

28. Brealey, R.A., Myers, S.C., Allen, F., Krishnan, V.S.: Corporate Finance, 8th edn. McGraw-Hill/Irwin, Boston (2006)
29. Damodaran, A.: Investment Valuation: Tools and Techniques for Determining the Value of Any Asset, vol. 666. Wiley (2012)
30. Crowston, K., Wei, K., Howison, J., Wiggins, A.: Free/Libre open-source software development: what we know and what we do not know. ACM Comput. Surv. (CSUR) **44**(2), 1–35 (2008)
31. Stewart, K.J., Ammeter, A.P., Maruping, L.M.: Impacts of license choice and organizational sponsorship on user interest and development activity in open source software projects. Inf. Syst. Res. **17**(2), 126–144 (2006)
32. Mockus, A., Fielding, R.T., Herbsleb, J.D.: Two case studies of open source software development: Apache and Mozilla. ACM Trans. Softw. Eng. Methodol. (TOSEM) **11**(3), 309–346 (2002)
33. Zhao, S., et al.: OpenRank leaderboard: motivating open source collaborations through social network evaluation in Alibaba. In: Proceedings of the 46th International Conference on Software Engineering: Software Engineering in Practice, pp. 346–357 (2024)
34. James, G., Witten, D., Hastie, T.: An Introduction to Statistical Learning, Vol 112. Springer, Heidelberg (2013)
35. Kohavi, R., Others: A study of cross-validation and bootstrap for accuracy estimation and model selection. In: IJCAI, vol. 14, pp. 1137–1145 (1995)
36. Jurafsky, D., Martin, J.H.: Speech and Language Processing: An Introduction to Natural Language Processing, Computational Linguistics, and Speech Recognition. [No Springer LNCS - like book format details provided, assumed as a book]
37. Devlin, J., Chang, M.-W., Lee, K., Toutanova, K.B.: BERT: pretraining of deep bidirectional transformers for language understanding. arXiv preprint arXiv:1810.04805 (2018)
38. Radford, A., Narasimhan, K., Salimans, T., Sutskever, I.: Improving language understanding by generative pretraining (2018)
39. Yang, Z., Dai, Z., Yang, Y., Carbonell, J., Salakhutdinov, R., Le, Q.V.: XLNet: generalized autoregressive pretraining for language understanding. In: Advances in Neural Information Processing Systems, vol. 32 (2019)
40. Liu, Y., et al.: RobertA: a robustly optimized BERT pretraining approach. arXiv preprint arXiv:1907.11692 (2019)
41. Clark, K., Luong, M.-T., Le, Q.V., Manning, C.D.: Electra: pretraining text encoders as discriminators rather than generators. arXiv preprint arXiv:2003.10555 (2020)
42. Tan, X., Zhou, M., Fitzgerald, B.: Scaling open source communities: an empirical study of the Linux kernel. In: Proceedings of the ACM/IEEE 42nd International Conference on Software Engineering, pp. 1222–1234 (2020)
43. Bird, S.: NLTK: the natural language toolkit. In: Proceedings of the COLING/ACL 2006 Interactive Presentation Sessions, pp. 69–72 (2006)
44. Kalliamvakou, E., Gousios, G., Blincoe, K., Singer, L., German, D.M., Damian, D.: The promises and perils of mining github. In: Proceedings of the 11th Working Conference on Mining Software Repositories, pp. 92–101 (2014)
45. Prana, G.A.A., Treude, C., Thung, F., Atapattu, T., Lo, D.: Categorizing the content of github readme files. Empir. Softw. Eng. **24**(3), 1296–1327 (2019)
46. Snoek, J., Larochelle, H., Adams, R.P.: Practical Bayesian optimization of machine learning algorithms. In: Advances in Neural Information Processing Systems, vol. 25 (2012)

47. Kingma, D.P., Ba, J.: Adam: a method for stochastic optimization. arXiv preprint arXiv:1412.6980 (2014)
48. Hyndman, R.J., Koehler, A.B.: Another look at measures of forecast accuracy. Int. J. Forecast. **22**(4), 679–688 (2006)
49. Theil, H.: Economic forecasts and policy (1961)
50. Gousios, G.: The GHTorent dataset and tool suite. In: 2013 10th Working Conference on Mining Software Repositories (MSR), pp. 233–236 (2013)

Compiler Tuning Method Based on Program Feature Extraction and Model Prediction

Chenghua Xu[1,2(✉)], Jingwei Sun[1], Mengna Sai[2], Dian Chen[2], Guangzhong Sun[1], and Weiwu Hu[2,3]

[1] School of Computer Science and Technology, University of Science and Technology of China, Hefei, China
{sunjw,gzsun}@ustc.edu.cn

[2] Loongson Technology Corporation Limited, Beijing, China
chxu@mail.ustc.edu.cn, {saimengna,xuchenghua,hww}@loongson.cn

[3] Institute of Computing Technology, Chinese Academy of Sciences, Beijing, China

Abstract. The optimization of compiler options has become increasingly crucial for improving the performance of programs. This paper proposes a compiler option optimization method based on feature extraction and model prediction, aiming to guide the optimal selection of compiler options by predicting the programs' speedup. In this study, we utilized various program feature extraction methods, including traditional approaches, BERT-based methods, and large language model-based techniques, to extract program features. An experimental design was used to build a quantitative model of the relationship between compiler options and program's speedups. Using the extracted program features and experimental data, we trained a regression model to predict programs' speedup. Furthermore, a genetic algorithm was applied to optimize the selection of compiler options, with the aim of achieving optimal programs' performance. Experimental results demonstrate that this method effectively optimizes compiler options, significantly improving programs' runtime efficiency. This research offers a new perspective on the automated optimization of compiler options and establishes a foundation for future research.

Keywords: Program Feature · Model Prediction · Compiler Tuning

1 Introduction

As a critical bridge connecting program source code with hardware, compilers play an indispensable role in program performance optimization. However, modern compilers offer numerous compiler options (e.g., optimization levels, instruction selection, parallelization options), and different combinations of these options can significantly impact program execution performance. Modern compilers typically provide two hundred to three hundred optimization options, making it challenging to find an optimal set of configurations within such a large

J. Zhan et al. (Eds.): Bench 2025, LNCS 16471, pp. 142–161, 2026.
https://doi.org/10.1007/978-981-95-9694-2_11

search space. To address this issue, researchers have explored various compiler tuning methods and techniques. In the field of compiler option tuning, performance improvements are primarily achieved through the following approaches: a) Rule-based expert systems that match predefined optimization strategy templates to specific scenarios [22]; b) Machine learning-driven methods that train models on the historical compilation data to predict optimal parameter combinations [9,14,17]; c) Multi-objective optimization algorithms (e.g., genetic algorithms, Bayesian optimization) for efficient parameter search within the configuration space [1,16]; d) Heuristic search techniques that dynamically adjust configurations based on performance feedback [15].

Moreover, the diversity of program types further complicates compiler tuning. For instance, programs whose core algorithms are dominated by loops require loop-related optimization options, while those with control-flow-heavy code necessitate control-flow optimization options. Previously, compiler tuning has rarely leveraged such program-specific information to select beneficial optimization strategies.

To address this challenge, researchers have begun investigating machine learning-based methods to optimize compiler options. Machine learning techniques can extract patterns from program features and execution data, construct predictive models, and thereby guide compiler option selection. However, program feature extraction remains a persistent challenge in this field. Traditional feature extraction methods typically rely on program structural information (e.g., loop hierarchy, conditional branches), which often fails to capture deep semantic information in the code. In recent years, deep learning-based natural language processing techniques (e.g., BERT-series models) have demonstrated significant potential in code analysis. These models, through their semantic understanding of code, can extract richer and higher-level features of programs. For example, models like CodeBERT and GraphBERT are specifically designed for code analysis tasks, effectively capturing semantic relationships within program code. With advancements in large model technology, large models have achieved remarkable performance in core tasks such as code generation, code reasoning, and code repair. However, research on feature extraction using BERT-series models or large models is still in its early stages.

In the prediction of program speedup, regression models are a commonly used approach. By establishing numerical relationships between compiler options and program performance, regression models can predict the impact of different option combinations on program performance. However, the combinatorial space of compiler options is typically vast, posing challenges for efficiently searching for optimal configurations. Genetic algorithms, as a global optimization method, demonstrated strong search capabilities and can approximate optimal solutions in complex search spaces, making them widely applied in compiler option optimization problems.

This study evaluates the advantages and disadvantages of transitioning from traditional program feature extraction methods to model-based program feature extraction approaches. Through experimental design, we build quantitative models linking compiler options to program's speedups and employ regression models to predict acceleration ratios. Simultaneously, genetic algorithms are utilized to optimize compiler option selection, aiming to achieve the best possible speedup. The goal of this research is to provide a novel approach for automating compiler option optimization, reducing the time and cost of manual tuning while improving program execution efficiency.

Our work makes the following major contributions:

- We evaluated a series of program feature extraction methods, ranging from traditional extraction approaches to modern large model-based methods.
- We constructed a prediction model that uses the model's predictions combined with genetic algorithms to determine the optimal program speedup.
- We tested widely used benchmarks (Polybench and Cbench), during the initialization phase of compiler tuning, the candidate options selected by our method outperform those generated by genetic algorithms, Opentuner, and BOCA.

2 Background and Related Work

2.1 Problem Definition

This paper investigates a classical compiler optimization problem: the selection of compiler passes without considering their execution order. The problem is formulated as choosing a subset of optimization options, where each option is represented by a binary switch. Consider a system with n binary switches, each representing a compiler optimization options. For instance, in GCC-14, the number of such switches is 276. Let:

- $x_i \in \{0, 1\}$ denotes the state of the ith option, where:
  - $x_i = 1$ indicates the option is active (on),
  - $x_i = 0$ indicates the option is inactive (off).
- v_i represents the variable controlled by the ith switch, which is function of switch states ($v_i = g_i(\mathbf{x})$), Such as the program's execute time.

The goal is to select a subset of options (i.e., determine $\mathbf{x} = (x_1, x_2, \ldots, x_n)$) that optimizes a given objective function $f(\mathbf{x}, \mathbf{v})$, where:

$$f : \{0, 1\}^n \times \mathbb{R}^n \rightarrow \mathbb{R}$$

The optimization problem can be formulated as:

$$\text{Find } \mathbf{x}^* \in \{0, 1\}^n \text{ such that } \mathbf{x}^* = \arg\min_{\mathbf{x}} f(\mathbf{x}, \mathbf{v})$$

This optimization problem presents significant computational challenges in the domain of compiler tuning. The objective function f typically exhibits:

- Non-convexity: Contains multiple local minima where algorithms can become trapped.
- Nonlinearity: Lacks simple proportional relationships between inputs and outputs.
- Discontinuity: Abrupt changes occur when options are enabled or disabled.

These properties, combined with the exponential search space of size 2^n (e.g., $>10^{83}$ configurations for GCC-14's 276 options), render traditional optimization methods ineffective. Consequently, we employ heuristic approaches, such as genetic algorithms or simulated annealing that can navigate this complex landscape without requiring gradient information or convexity assumptions.

2.2 Motivation

The evolution of CPU architectures from x86's out-of-order execution to ARM's energy-efficient pipelines has created a performance optimization conundrum for compiler developers. Traditional one-size-fits-all optimization strategies fail to address three critical challenges in modern heterogeneous computing landscapes:

- **Architecture-Specific Bottlenecks**: Different instruction sets (e.g., SIMD extensions like AVX2 vs. NEON) exhibit divergent efficiency characteristics for identical code patterns.
- **Compiler Heuristic Limitations**: Static analysis-based optimization selection struggles with unpredictable hardware behaviors like branch prediction penalties or cache hierarchies.
- **Trade-Off Complexity**: The Pareto frontier between performance and power consumption becomes architecture-dependent.

These observations motivate our research into *adaptive compiler tuning*, where optimization decisions are dynamically determined by both static code characteristics and runtime hardware feedback. The subsequent sections will detail our machine learning-based approach to bridge this architectural heterogeneity gap.

2.3 Related Work

Compiler optimization techniques have evolved significantly, with various approaches proposed to enhance performance. Fursin et al. [7] adopted a community-driven methodology by creating a platform to aggregate performance tuning data, enabling collaborative contributions for future optimization efforts. Wu et al. [20] introduced an automated tuning framework to address the expanding parameter space in high-performance computing (HPC). Their approach utilizes Bayesian optimization to explore compiler configurations, specifically for LLVM Clang/Polly loop optimizations using the PolyBench benchmark suite for benchmarking. By integrating four machine learning models (RF, ET, GBRT, and GP), their framework demonstrated superior performance over manual compilation, particularly for large-scale datasets.

To mitigate the time overhead of iterative tuning, Zhao et al. [21] proposed a configurable parallel tuning framework. This solution leverages high-performance computing resources to accelerate the optimization process while maintaining effectiveness. Jain et al. [11] developed a reinforcement learning-based loop optimization technique, utilizing IR2Vec [18] for feature representation and a simplified loop dependence graph (RDG) derived from strongly connected components (SCC).

Further advancing automation, Seeker et al. [15] introduced Heurkea, a framework designed to automatically uncover compiler heuristics with minimal human intervention. Applied to 8,000 functions in LLVM optimization passes (approximately 2% of available functions), Heurkea achieved a 19.5% reduction in binary size compared to the -Oz baseline, using only a single heuristic and random search. The framework was validated using the NAS and PolyBench benchmark suites. Pan et al. [12] proposes a novel compiler auto-tuning method that leverages the synergistic relationships between inter-procedural optimization passes to effectively reduce the search space, achieving performance optimization across multiple benchmark datasets. Evaluated on ten benchmark datasets including MiBench, CBench, NPB, and CHStone, the results demonstrate that compared to Oz, their method achieves an average reduction of 7.5% in intermediate representation (IR) instruction count.

3 Approach

Modern compilers typically provide 200–300 optimization options, making compiler tuning exceptionally time-consuming within this enormous search space. The structural diversity of programs, which varies in terms of control flow complexity, data locality, and parallelization patterns, poses additional challenges. This diversity makes it difficult to reuse optimization configurations across different applications.

The core challenges in modern compiler tuning primarily stem from two aspects: combinatorial explosion in the optimization space and the heterogeneous nature of program characteristics. Within this vast configuration space, traditional exhaustive search methods struggle to find optimal solutions under constrained time budgets. More critically, programs exhibit significant structural variations, while scientific computing applications are particularly sensitive to loop optimizations, transaction processing systems depend more heavily on inter-procedural optimizations. This heterogeneity in program features makes monolithic optimization approaches difficult to generalize across diverse workloads.

This forces developers to repeatedly perform time-consuming parameter searches for each target program. Currently, there is an urgent need for intelligent prediction models based on program feature analysis, which can dynamically establish mappings between optimization options and program-specific characteristics.

3.1 Approach Overview

The workflow proposed in this paper is illustrated in Fig. 1. It involves obtaining the features of the test program, compiling the program with different optimization options, and running it to obtain the speedup ratios under different options. The program features, optimization options, and corresponding speedup ratios are then used for model training. Once the model is obtained, when encountering a new test program, the program's features and options are input to predict the speedup ratio, which is used for candidate evaluation in the genetic algorithm.

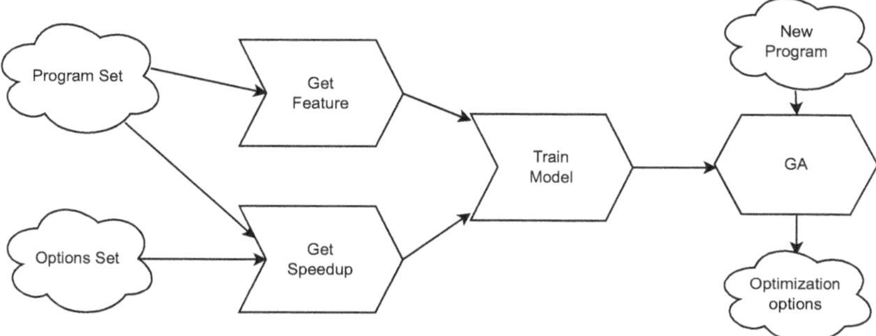

Fig. 1. Overview of the WorkFlow

Our approach aims to establish the performance relationships between various programs under different compilation optimization options, thereby enabling the training of a predictive model. Once the model is trained, we employ a genetic algorithm to search for optimization options that yield high speedup ratios, thereby accelerating the tuning process. Specifically, our method consists of five steps:

- **Program Collection**: We collect a diverse set of over 6,000 programs, including benchmarks such as CoreMark, MiBench, ExeBench [2], compiler test suites, and programming competition problems.
- **Compiler Option Selection and Performance Modeling**: We select a wide range of compiler optimization options and evaluate the performance of each program under these options to build a mapping between the optimization flags and the resulting speedup ratios.
- **Program Feature Extraction**: We extract both syntactic and semantic features from the source code or intermediate representations (IRs) of the programs, which serve as input features for model training.
- **Model Training**: Using the extracted program features as input and the observed speedup ratios with options as labels, we train a machine learning model to predict the performance impact of different optimization options for unseen programs.

- **Compiler Tuning**: Finally, we combine model predictions with a genetic algorithm to efficiently search the vast optimization space and identify a set of optimization options that maximize performance improvement.

3.2 Program Features

Program feature extraction or code representation involves transforming source code into structured mathematical representations, such as vectors and graphs, which capture syntactic, semantic, and structural patterns. This enables machine learning models to analyze, understand, and manipulate software. The key concepts and techniques are presented in Table 1.

Table 1. Code Analysis Features and Applications

Feature	Description	Applications
Natural Code Sequence (NCS)	Raw tokenized code (e.g., keywords, identifiers). Simple but loses structural context.	Basic Code Similarity, Clone Detection
Abstract Syntax Tree (AST)	Hierarchical tree of code syntax (nodes = constructs, edges = relationships).	Syntax-aware Analysis, Code Summarization
Control Flow Graph (CFG)	Directed graph of execution paths (nodes = basic blocks, edges = control transfers).	Vulnerability Detection, Program Analysis
Data Flow Graph (DFG)	Tracks variable dependencies/transformations across CFG paths.	Bug Detection, Optimization
Program Dependence Graph (PDG)	Combines CFG + DFG to capture control/data dependencies in one unified graph.	Program Slicing, Security Analysis

Due to the lack of systematic research and comparison on various feature extraction approaches, representative methods were selected for further analysis. **Perf:** The Perf tool, integrated into the Linux kernel, serves as a powerful performance analysis utility for extracting comprehensive program characteristics. As a lightweight profiling interface, Perf enables researchers to: (1) monitor hardware performance counters, (2) trace software events, and (3) analyze call graphs with minimal overhead. Its key capabilities include precise measurement of CPU cycles, cache references or misses, branch predictions, and context switches through simple command-line interfaces. The tool's statistical sampling approach (using perf_events subsystem) provides low-intrusion profiling suitable for production environments. This information can be used to characterize the program [13].

Processors typically have 100–200 performance events, but only 1–4 events can be captured at a time (the exact number varies across processors; however, this is the case for most). Referencing the paper by [13], and based on our understanding, we have selected the 20 events that best characterize program behavior.

This paper selects 20 events, including cycle count, instruction count, branch count, branch mispredictions, cache misses, instruction types (integer, floating-point, scalar, vector), load store instruction count, arithmetic operation count, and TLB misses, to characterize program behavior. In principle, if a program has a high number of integer instructions but a low number of floating-point instructions, the optimization options will tend to favor integer-related optimizations while avoiding floating-point-related ones, thereby pruning the search space. Similar logic applies to other characteristics.

The perf feature is a dynamic characteristic, while the other methods are static features. As previously described, dynamic features influence the selection of compiler options. This paragraph explains how the static features affect option selection. Generally, static features analyze program composition. For instance, if a program contains a for loop, compiler options related to loop optimizations are favored.

MILEPOST-GCC: is the first practical open-source adaptive production compiler (also usable for research). It aims to automate performance tuning for arbitrary architectures using iterative feedback-driven compilation, machine learning (ML), and collective optimization. By correlating program features with optimization strategies during empirical iterative compilation, it predicts effective optimizations for unseen programs based on prior learning, extracting static structural features (e.g., number of basic blocks, CFG edges, operation types) via static analysis [6].

IR2Vec: is a distributed embedding framework based on LLVM Intermediate Representation (IR) that efficiently extracts cross-language, cross-platform program features. By integrating symbolic encoding and flow-aware encoding, it generates generalized embeddings for tasks like heterogeneous computing optimization and thread scheduling. Key innovations include its non-sequential graph-based approach, architecture independence, low data dependency, and exceptional Out-of-vacabulary(OOV) handling, achieving state-of-the-art results in device mapping and thread coarsening while enabling efficient inference [18].

CodeBERT: is a Transformer-based pretrained model jointly developed by Microsoft Research Asia, Harbin Institute of Technology, and Sun Yat-sen University. It unifies representation learning for programming languages (PL) and natural language (NL). Its primary objective is to enhance performance in code comprehension, generation, and cross-modal tasks by learning cross-modal code representations through large-scale pretraining on NL-PL pairs. It excels in capturing bidirectional code context and cross-modal relationships. Validated applications include improved code search accuracy and documentation generation. Its architecture supports fine-tuning for diverse code-related tasks. [5].

CodeT5+-770M: is an open-source large language model proposed by Salesforce, built upon an encoder-decoder architecture to enhance performance in code understanding and generation tasks. Through a phased hybrid pre-training approach, it demonstrates significant advantages in both unimodal (code-only) and bimodal (code-text pair) tasks. The foundation of CodeT5+ lies in the Transformer architecture, integrating unimodal and bimodal pre-training objectives. Excels in diverse tasks (e.g., code generation, mathematical programming, code retrieval) through hybrid pre-training, outperforming larger closed models [19].

GraphCodeBERT: is a pre-trained model using data-flow graphs (DFG) to capture program logic. It extracts variable-level dependencies via three steps: syntax parsing, variable extraction, and edge construction. Key features include triple-modal input (text/code/variables), position-aware variable encoding, and lightweight DFG structure. It outperforms AST-based methods in code-related tasks despite the static analysis limitations [8].

Qwen2.5-Coder: is the latest series of Code-Specific Qwen large language models (formerly known as CodeQwen). It extracts program features via deep semantic encoding, tokenizing code into syntax units mapped to vectors. It captures cross-file dependencies and processes long contexts using positional encoding. Key features include support for 92 languages, multi-task capabilities (generation, completion, repair, reasoning), cost-effectiveness, and flexible deployment (edge-to-cloud) [10].

It should be noted that BERT-based feature extraction tools (e.g., CodeBERT, CodeT5p, GraphCodeBERT) all impose an input token limit of 512 tokens. When inputs exceed this threshold, average pooling is performed. In contrast, Qwen2.5-Coder-3b supports up to 32K tokens. Other non-BERT architecture tools exhibit no inherent limitation. We compared Qwen2.5-coder1.5b, 3b, and 7b, and the results showed that the performance of the three model scales was quite similar. This is not difficult to explain because we only used qwen's tokenizer to represent program features, which is independent of the model parameters.

This paper employs seven distinct program feature extraction methods, with the following dimensionalities: perf (20), milepost (116), ir2vec (300), CodeBERT (768), CodeT5+ (1024), GraphCodeBERT (768), and QWen2.5-Coder-3B (2048). Among these, perf is a dynamic feature, while the others are static features. Both static and dynamic features can effectively characterize program behavior, as discussed earlier. While both static and dynamic features can characterize program behavior, different methods may depict them with variations. This paper conducts a comparative analysis of these approaches.

3.3 Building Predict Model

Having collected the programs and their behavioral features, we trained the model using a Keras multilayer architecture. It is a deep neural network regression model implemented using Keras and TensorFlow. We collected 6,000+ programs to test the speedup ratios across different compiler options. Using the execution time under the O2 option as the baseline, we selects several compiler options to build the programs, and measure their execution times to calculate the speedup ratio. The program features, compiler options, and corresponding speedup ratio will form a single data point for model training. During inference, the trained model, given a program's features and a set of compiler options, will predict the speedup ratio.

As show in Algorithm 1, it takes an input with a specified dimensionality and progressively transforms it through multiple layers to produce a single output value. Three dense (fully connected) layers with 1024, 1024, and 512 neurons respectively, followed by a final dense layer with 256 neurons. Each hidden layer uses LeakyReLU activation with negative slope. Batch normalization after each activation layer to stabilize and accelerate training. Dropout (20% rate) after each batch normalization layer for regularization to prevent overfitting.

Algorithm 1. Compiler Parameter Optimization Model

```
1: function CREATE_MODEL(input_dim)
2:                                                        ▷ Define model architecture
3:     inputs ← INPUT(shape=(input_dim,))                 ▷ Input layer
4:     x ← DENSE(1024)(inputs)                            ▷ First dense layer
5:     x ← LEAKYRELU(x)                                   ▷ Activation
6:     x ← BATCHNORMALIZATION(x)
7:     x ← DROPOUT(0.2)(x)
8:     x ← DENSE(1024)(x)                                 ▷ Second dense layer
9:     x ← LEAKYRELU(x)
10:    x ← BATCHNORMALIZATION(x)
11:    x ← DROPOUT(0.2)(x)
12:    x ← DENSE(512)(x)                                  ▷ Third dense layer
13:    x ← LEAKYRELU(x)
14:    x ← DENSE(256)(x)                                  ▷ Final dense layer
15:    x ← LEAKYRELU(x)
16:    outputs ← DENSE(1, activation='linear')(x)         ▷ Regression output
17:    model ← MODEL(inputs, outputs)
18:    model.compile(optimizer = Adam(learning_rate = 0.001), loss =' mse')
19:    return model
20: end function
21: function TRAIN(model, X_train, y_train, X_val, y_val, epochs, batch_size)
22:                                                       ▷ Model training
23:    model.fit(X_train, y_train,
24:        validation_data=(X_val, y_val),
25:        epochs=epochs,
26:        batch_size=batch_size,
27:        callbacks=[early_stop])                        ▷ Early Stop
28: end function
29: function PREDICT(model, X_test)
30:                                                       ▷ Model prediction
31:    return model.predict(X_test)
32: end function
```

3.4 Compiler Tuning

In this study, we propose a hybrid optimization framework that integrates machine learning model predictions with a genetic algorithm (GA), aiming to efficiently explore the vast configuration space and identify the optimal combination of parameters. The specific implementation involves the following steps:
Model Training with Historical Program Features: First, a predictive model is trained using features extracted from historical programs. This model serves as the foundation for subsequent performance predictions.
Feature Extraction and Performance Prediction for New Programs: When a new program is introduced, its features along with a set of specified optimization options are extracted and fed into the trained model. The model then predicts the speedup ratio (i.e., the performance improvement) that would result from applying those optimization options to the program.
Initialization of the Genetic Algorithm: Based on the trained model, the GA begins by randomly generating an initial population consisting of 512 candidate optimization configurations. This population serves as the starting point for the evolutionary search process.
Evolutionary Optimization via Selection, Crossover, and Mutation: The GA iteratively evolves the population over 300 generations through the operations of selection, crossover, and mutation. A mutation rate of 0.18 is employed to maintain population diversity and prevent premature convergence to suboptimal solutions. In each generation, the model predicts the performance gain (i.e., speedup ratio) for each candidate configuration, and the GA aims to maximize this value as its optimization objective.
Synergy Between Machine Learning and Global Search: This approach effectively combines the machine learning model's ability to generalize patterns from program features with the global search capabilities of the genetic algorithm. As a result, the method enables efficient discovery of high-performance optimization configurations that might be difficult to identify through traditional search strategies.

This hybrid approach not only leverages the predictive power of machine learning to reduce the computational burden of exhaustive search but also ensures robustness and adaptability through the evolutionary mechanisms of genetic algorithms. It represents a promising direction in the domain of automated program optimization and performance tuning.

4 Evaluation

4.1 Compilers and Programs

In our experiments, we employ GCC (version 14.2.0) as the target compiler. While our proposed method is theoretically general and applicable to other mainstream compilers such as LLVM, Intel Compiler (ICC) and AMD Optimizing Compiler (AOCC), we focus exclusively on GCC for experimental validation. This selection was made due to the significant time overhead associated with exhaustive testing across multiple compilers under diverse optimization settings. By concentrating on a single compiler, we efficiently demonstrate the effectiveness of our approach while maintaining broad applicability.

PolyBench, is a benchmark suite specifically designed to evaluate the performance of polyhedral model optimizations in compiler implementations. The suite comprises programs featuring nested loops and computationally intensive numerical operations, which are representative of scientific and engineering applications. PolyBench serves as a valuable tool for analyzing loop transformations and data locality optimizations within controlled experimental conditions, offering critical insights into the optimization of computational kernels.

CBench, is a comprehensive repository of open-source programs designed for compiler research and automated tuning. It encompasses a diverse set of real-world applications and computational kernels spanning multiple domains, including signal processing and numerical methods. The broad spectrum of workloads in CBench ensures that our evaluation captures a wide range of computational patterns, making it a robust benchmark for assessing the adaptability and performance enhancements introduced by compiler optimizations in diverse real-world scenarios.

To avoid confusion, the PolynBech and CBench mentioned in this section are used to verify the effectiveness of the model, while the aforementioned 6,000+ programs from previous chapters are intended for model training.

4.2 Compared Approaches

We compare our method to several state-of-the-art methods:

- **GA (Genetic Algorithm-based Optimization)**: A classic evolutionary approach that applies genetic operators (selection, crossover, mutation) to generate optimal compiler flags. GA excels in exploring large search spaces, GA tuning represents a classic approach to automatic compiler optimization [4].
- **OpenTuner**: is an open-source framework for automating program tuning using smart search algorithms to optimize compiler parameters and performance-critical code. OpenTuner integrates GA, hill climbing algorithms, and multi-armed bandits [1].
- **BOCA**: is the first Bayesian optimization based approach for compiler autotuning. The goal is to tune compiler's optimization flags as efficiently as possible in order to achieve the required runtime performance of the compiled programs. The author further proposes a searching strategy in BOCA to improve the efficiency of Bayesian optimization that can strike a balance between exploitation and exploration [3].

4.3 Implementations and Configurations

We implemented the method mentioned in the paper using TensorFlow/Keras-2.15.0 and Python-3.10.0. The parameters of the genetic algorithm were set as follows: population size 512, iterations 300, and mutation probability 0.18. Our study is conducted on a workstation with 256- core AMD EPYC Processor, 1.5T memory, and Ubuntu 22.04.5 LTS operating system. The performance test data was collected from several personal computers, each equipped with a 4/8-core CPU and 16/32 GB of RAM.

4.4 Measurement

The execution time of the test program was measured using Python's time function, which offers microsecond-level precision. To account for measurement variability and performance fluctuations, each test was repeated three times, and the average execution time was recorded.

5 Results and Analysis

5.1 Model Evaluation

We evaluate models of various program feature extraction methods by analyzing loss and val_loss curves. As illustrated in the Fig. 2, despite the convergence of the training loss curve, the validation loss fails to converge for models trained on randomly generated program features. This indicates that such features cannot be effectively utilized for model training and indirectly demonstrates the superior efficacy of alternative features. Furthermore, the loss curves reveal the following performance hierarchy: graphcodebert > qwencoder3b > codebert > codet5p > perf > milepost > ir2vec.

Residual analysis is a diagnostic technique used to evaluate the validity of a model by examining the residuals, which are the differences between observed values and the model's predicted values. If the residuals are normally distributed, it indicates that the model has captured the primary patterns in the data without introducing systematic bias. Below we evaluate from the perspective of residual analysis. As shown in the Fig. 3, for features of randomly generated, the residuals do not follow a normal distribution. Based on residual plots: feature codebert > graphcodebert > codet5p > qwencoder3b > perf > milepost > ir2vec.

Regression analysis is a fundamental statistical method used to model the relationship between dependent and independent variables. To assess the performance of regression models, several key metrics are employed: Mean Absolute Error (MAE), Mean Squared Error (MSE), Root Mean Squared Error (RMSE), and the R-squared (R^2) score. These metrics provide insights into the accuracy and predictive power of the model.

1. Mean Absolute Error (MAE)

The Mean Absolute Error measures the average magnitude of errors in a set of predictions, without considering their direction. It is calculated as:

$$[\text{MAE} = \frac{1}{n}\sum_{i=1}^{n} |y_i - \hat{y}_i|]$$

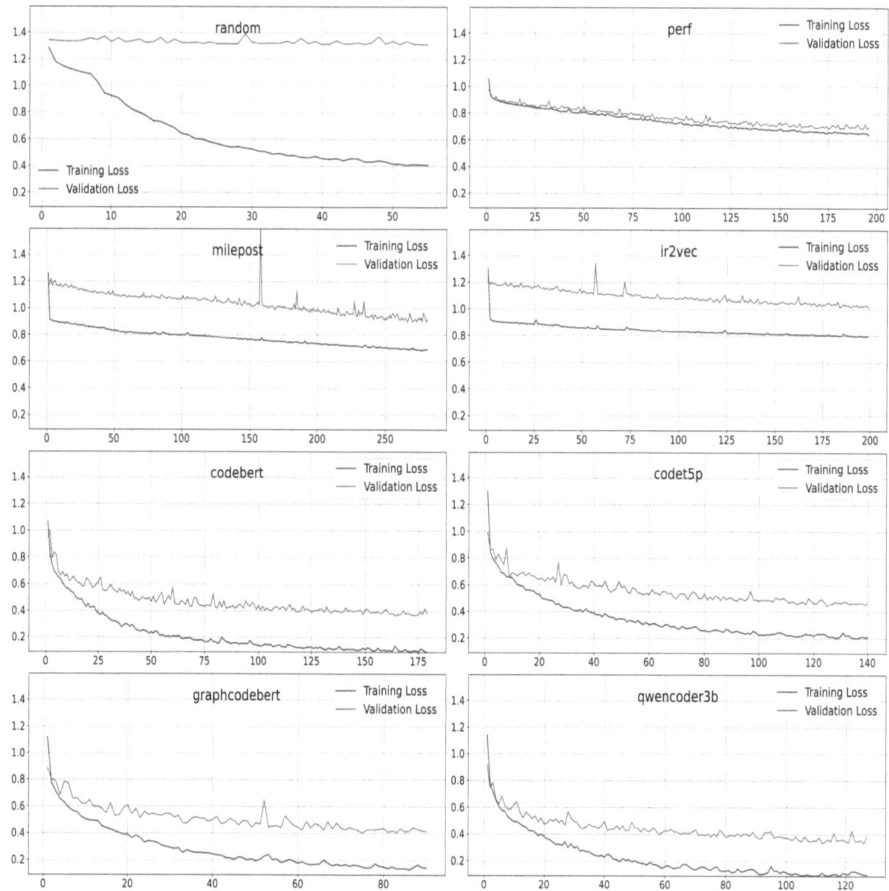

Fig. 2. Loss vs Val_loss of 8 Different Models

where (y_i) is the actual value, ($\hat{y}_i$) is the predicted value, and (n) is the number of observations. MAE is robust to outliers and provides an interpretable measure of error in the same units as the dependent variable.

2. Mean Squared Error (MSE)

The Mean Squared Error quantifies the average of the squares of the errors that is, the average squared difference between the estimated values and the actual value. The formula is:

$$[\mathrm{MSE} = \frac{1}{n}\sum_{i=1}^{n}(y_i - \hat{y}_i)^2]$$

MSE penalizes larger errors more heavily due to the squaring operation, making it sensitive to outliers. It is commonly used in optimization problems where minimizing the error is critical.

3. Root Mean Squared Error (RMSE)

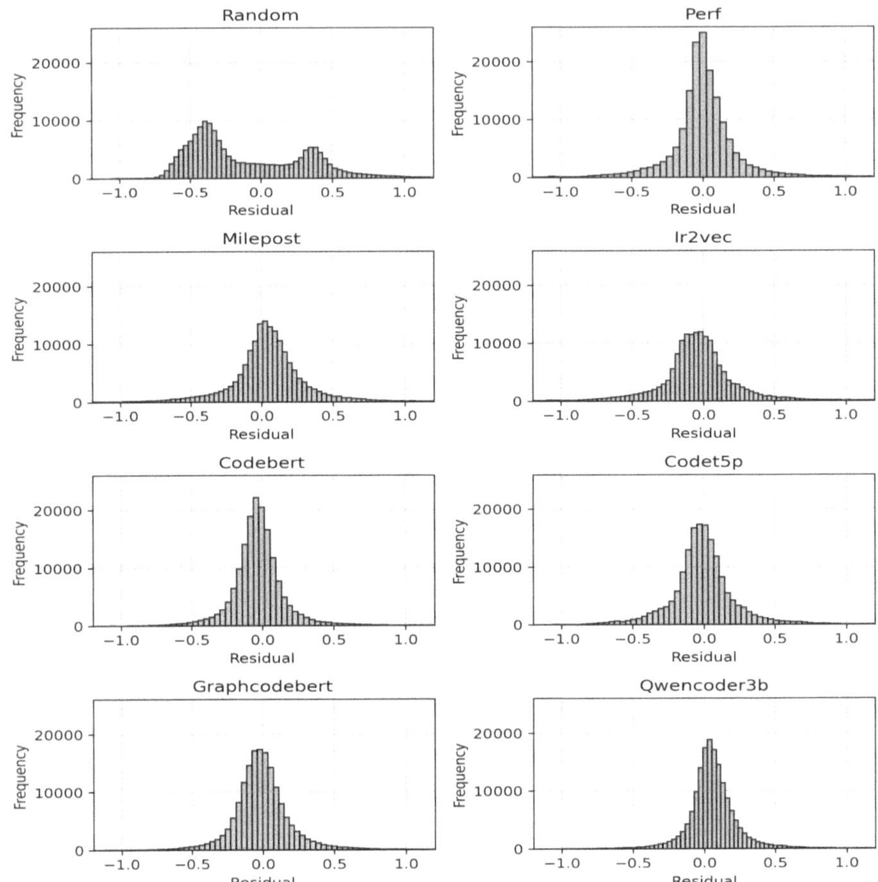

Fig. 3. Residual Analysis of 8 Different Models

The Root Mean Squared Error is the square root of the MSE, bringing the error metric back to the original scale of the dependent variable:

$$[\text{RMSE} = \sqrt{\text{MSE}}]$$

RMSE is particularly useful when interpretability is important, as it provides the average error magnitude in the same units as the dependent variable. It is widely used in fields like meteorology and economics.

4. R-squared (R^2) Score

The R-squared score measures the proportion of the variance in the dependent variable that is predictable from the independent variables. It is calculated as:

$$[R^2 = 1 - \frac{\sum_{i=1}^{n}(y_i - \hat{y}i)^2}{\sum i = 1^n (y_i - \bar{y})^2}]$$

where ($\bar{y}$) is the mean of the actual values. R^2 ranges from 0 to 1, with higher values indicating a better fit. A value of 1 means the model explains all the variability of the response data around its mean.

We evaluate the model performance based on MAE, MSE, RMSE, and R^2 score. As shown in the Table 2, the ranking is: qwencoder3b > codebert > graphcodebert > codet5p > perf > milepost > ir2vec.

Table 2. The evaluation metrics for various program features

Feature	Data	MAE	MSE	RMSE	R^2score	Data	MAE	MSE	RMSE	R^2score
random	train	0.4202	0.4332	0.6582	0.6222	test	0.4642	1.3101	1.1446	−0.0096
perf	train	0.2200	0.6000	0.7746	0.4875	test	0.2233	0.6846	0.8274	0.4293
milepost	train	0.2636	0.6557	0.8097	0.4135	test	0.2771	0.8975	0.9474	0.3669
ir2vec	train	0.2747	0.7727	0.8790	0.3089	test	0.2851	1.0135	1.0067	0.2851
codebert	train	0.1399	0.0790	0.2811	0.9311	test	0.1664	0.3617	0.6015	0.7212
codet5p	train	0.1817	0.1789	0.4230	0.8440	test	0.2018	0.4421	0.6649	0.6593
graphbert	train	0.1599	0.1028	0.3206	0.9103	test	0.1812	0.4016	0.6337	0.6905
qwen3b	train	0.1407	0.0747	0.2732	0.9355	test	0.1630	0.3339	0.5779	0.7330

The overall time consumption of the workflow is roughly as follows: feature extraction is time-consuming, with significant variations across different methods, ranging from approximately 0.5 to 50 h. Model training times are similar across different methods, taking approximately 1.0 h, while genetic algorithm search times are also comparable, approximately 0.1 h. To compare the time consumption of various program feature extraction methods, 100 programs were randomly selected, and their extraction times were tested on the same hardware platform. The execution times for the evaluated methods are as follows: perf (2,811 s), ir2vec (1,207 s), milepost (501 s), qwencoder3b (162 s), codet5p (70 s), graphcodebert (24 s), and codebert (23 s).

5.2 Tuning Results

This paper combines model prediction with a genetic algorithm. Specifically, the conventional genetic algorithm requires evaluating the quality of candidates, which often incurs significant execution costs in compiler tuning. This work employs a trained model to predict speedup ratios for evaluating candidate quality. We set the initial population size to 512, a mutation factor of 0.18, and performed 300 iterations, ultimately selecting the top 10 candidates from the pool for actual program execution evaluation.

The tuning method used in this paper is based solely on prediction and does not involve actual execution during iterative optimization. Therefore, when comparing with existing techniques, we selected randomly generated initial configurations as the baseline. Specifically, for comparison with GA, we used the results from the first generation with a population size of 10. In comparison with OpenTuner, which adapts its initial values based on the selected algorithm, we used the first 10 iterations as the basis for comparison. In the case of BOCA, which starts with four randomly chosen initial values and then performs iterative tuning, we standardized the evaluation by collecting a total of 10 results specifically, the initial 4 random samples plus 6 additional iterations. The test results on PolyBench and Cbench are shown in Fig. 4, with compiler -O2 as the baseline. The figure presents bar charts comparing OpenTuner, GA, and BOCA methods, using the average speedup of benchmark programs across different program feature models. Figure 5 shows the proportion of programs (relative to -O2) that achieved positive speedup for OpenTuner, the GA, and BOCA across different program feature models.

From the Fig. 4 and 5, we can observe that the ranking of feature effectiveness, based on the performance improvement ratios in the PolyBench and CBench benchmarks, is as follows: codet5p > milepost > perf > qwencoder3b > graphcodebert > codebert > ir2vec. This order is notably different from the previous ranking derived from model-centric evaluation metrics, which was: qwencoder3b > codebert > graphcodebert > codet5p > perf > milepost > ir2vec.

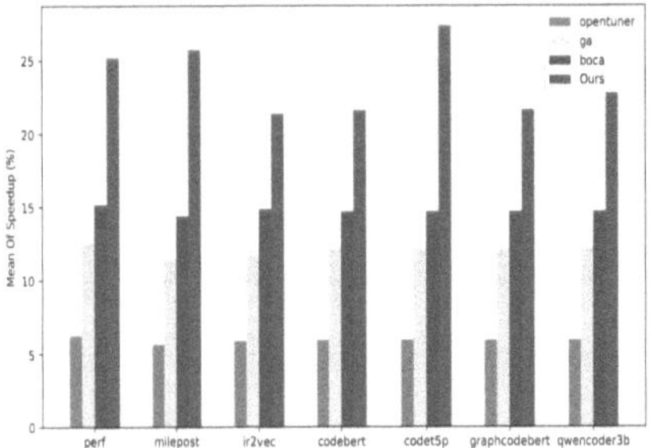

Fig. 4. Speedup ratios

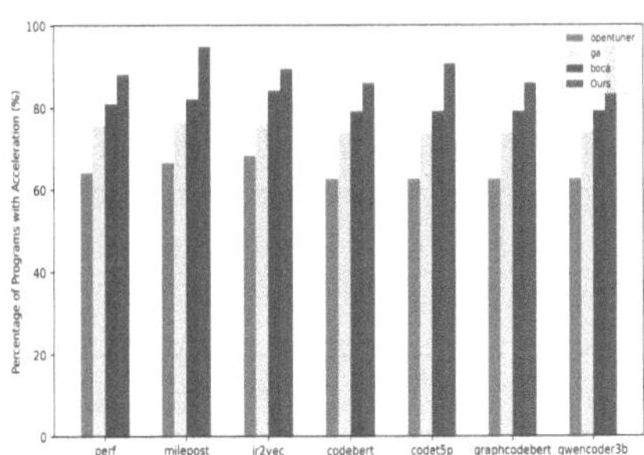

Fig. 5. Performance improvement rates

Intuitively, a model that performs better on training data should also perform better in downstream prediction and search tasks. However, our experimental results contradict this expectation, reminding us that model selection must be evaluated based on its actual performance in downstream tasks rather than merely its training data accuracy. This counterintuitive finding is particularly insightful, and we are delighted to share these results with the compiler tuning community.

To facilitate a more intuitive presentation of the experimental results, we visualize both the model's characteristic metrics (model loss, kurtosis of the residual distribution, and R^2 score) and its downstream task performance (compiler tuning results, including average speedup ratio and the rate of positive improvements) using radar charts and heatmaps. To ensure dimensionless comparison, the data were normalized to the range of 5 to 10.

Visual inspection of Figs. 6 and 7 reveals that although CodeBERT exhibits stronger model performance metrics (e.g., loss, R^2 score), its actual effectiveness in the downstream compiler tuning task is comparatively poor. Conversely, MILEPOST demonstrates moderate model metrics but achieves significantly better results in the downstream compiler tuning task. Overall, among the seven evaluated features, CodeT5p demonstrates the most balanced performance across both model metrics and downstream compiler tuning effectiveness.

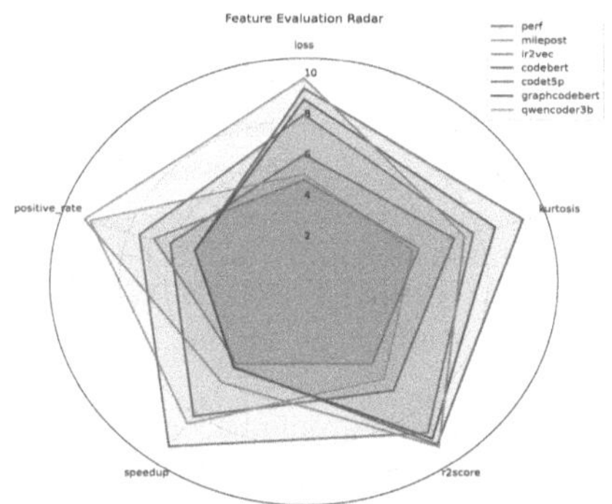

Fig. 6. Radar chart of model metrics and performance improvement

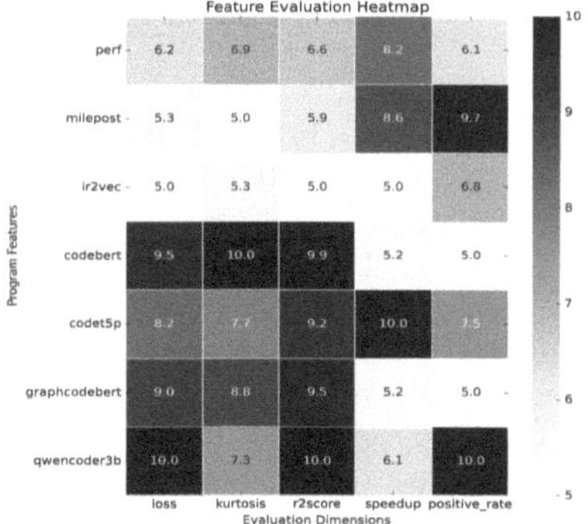

Fig. 7. Heatmap of model metrics and performance improvement

6 Conclusion and Future Work

This paper collected a large set of programs and tested their speedup ratios under various compiler optimization options. Features were extracted from these programs using seven distinct methods, and models were trained by correlating feature data with speedup results. The trained models were then integrated with a genetic algorithm to predict speedup ratios for new test programs. Compared to the baseline genetic algorithm initial stage, this approach achieved approximately 15% performance improvement on widely adopted benchmarks (PolyBench and CBench).

Limited by time and resources, this study employs only the Qwen-2.5-Coder-3B model to collect program features. Future work will utilize larger models and advanced versions of Qwen-3-Coder or other LLMs to evaluate the accuracy of the trained models and the speedup ratio on downstream tasks.

Acknowledgments. This work was supported by the Industry-University-Research Cooperation Project of the Ministry of Education of China (No. 230906392304024).

References

1. Ansel, J., et al.: OpenTuner: an extensible framework for program autotuning. In: International Conference on Parallel Architectures and Compilation, PACT '14, Edmonton, AB, Canada, 24–27 August 2014, pp. 303–316 (2014). https://doi.org/10.1145/2628071.2628092
2. Armengol-Estapé, J., Woodruff, J., Brauckmann, A., Magalhães, J.W.d.S., O'Boyle, M.F.P.: ExeBench: an ML-scale dataset of executable C functions. In: Proceedings of the 6th ACM SIGPLAN International Symposium on Machine Programming, MAPS '22, June 2022, pp. 50–59. ACM (2022). https://doi.org/10.1145/3520312.3534867
3. Chen, J., Xu, N., Chen, P., Zhang, H.: Efficient compiler autotuning via Bayesian optimization. In: 2021 IEEE/ACM 43rd International Conference on Software Engineering (ICSE), May 2021 (2021). https://doi.org/10.1109/icse43902.2021.00110
4. Cooper, K.D., Schielke, P.J., Subramanian, D.: Optimizing for reduced code space using genetic algorithms. In: Proceedings of the ACM SIGPLAN 1999 Workshop on Languages, Compilers, and Tools for Embedded Systems, LCTES99, May 1999. ACM (1999). https://doi.org/10.1145/314403.314414
5. Feng, Z., et al.: CodeBERT: a pre-trained model for programming and natural languages. In: Findings of the Association for Computational Linguistics, EMNLP 2020. Association for Computational Linguistics (2020). https://doi.org/10.18653/v1/2020.findings-emnlp.139
6. Fursin, G., et al.: Milepost GCC: machine learning enabled self-tuning compiler. Int. J. Parallel Prog. **39**, 296–327 (2011)
7. Fursin, G., Lokhmotov, A., Savenko, D., Upton, E.: A collective knowledge workflow for collaborative research into multi-objective autotuning and machine learning techniques. CoRR (2018). http://arxiv.org/abs/1801.08024v1
8. Guo, D., et al.: GraphcodeBERT: pre-training code representations with data flow (2021). https://doi.org/10.48550/arXiv.2009.08366, https://arxiv.org/abs/2009.08366
9. Hakimi, Y., Baghdadi, R., Challal, Y.: A hybrid machine learning model for code optimization. Int. J. Parallel Prog. **51**(6), 309–331 (2023)
10. Hui, B., et al.: Qwen2.5-Coder Technical Report (2024)
11. Jain, S., VenkataKeerthy, S., Aggarwal, R., Dangeti, T.K., Das, D., Upadrasta, R.: Reinforcement learning assisted loop distribution for locality and vectorization. In: 2022 IEEE/ACM Eighth Workshop on the LLVM Compiler Infrastructure in HPC (LLVM-HPC), November 2022. IEEE (2022). https://doi.org/10.1109/llvm-hpc56686.2022.00006
12. Pan, H., Wei, Y., Xing, M., Wu, Y., Zhao, C.: Towards efficient compiler auto-tuning: leveraging synergistic search spaces. In: Proceedings of the 23rd ACM/IEEE International Symposium on Code Generation and Optimization, CGO '25, March 2025, pp. 614–627. ACM (2025). https://doi.org/10.1145/3696443.3708961
13. Panda, R., Song, S., Dean, J., John, L.K.: Wait of a decade: did spec CPU 2017 broaden the performance horizon? In: 2018 IEEE International Symposium on High Performance Computer Architecture (HPCA), February 2018. IEEE (2018). https://doi.org/10.1109/hpca.2018.00032

14. Anirudh. S., Kavitha C.R.: Enhancing GCC compiler optimization through natural language processing-driven automation. In: 2024 5th International Conference on Data Intelligence and Cognitive Informatics (ICDICI), November 2024, pp. 494–499. IEEE (2024). https://doi.org/10.1109/icdici62993.2024.10810996
15. Seeker, V., Cummins, C., Cole, M., Franke, B., Hazelwood, K., Leather, H.: Revealing compiler heuristics through automated discovery and optimization. In: 2024 IEEE/ACM International Symposium on Code Generation and Optimization (CGO), March 2024. IEEE (2024). https://doi.org/10.1109/cgo57630.2024.10444847
16. Shao, A.: Efficient compiler option tuning: exploiting objective interdependencies for enhanced performance. In: 2024 7th International Conference on Advanced Algorithms and Control Engineering (ICAACE), March 2024, pp. 1524–1527. IEEE (2024). https://doi.org/10.1109/icaace61206.2024.10548334
17. Shi, Z., Gao, J., Guan, X.: Machine learning-driven GCC loop unrolling optimization: compiler performance enhancement strategy based on XGBoost. J. Circ. Syst. Comput.**34**(01) (2024). https://doi.org/10.1142/s0218126625500355
18. VenkataKeerthy, S., Aggarwal, R., Jain, S., Desarkar, M.S., Upadrasta, R., Srikant, Y.N.: IR2Vec: LLVM IR based scalable program embeddings. ACM Trans. Archit. Code Optim. **17**(4) (2020). https://doi.org/10.1145/3418463
19. Wang, Y., Le, H., Gotmare, A., Bui, N., Li, J., Hoi, S.: CodeT5+: open code large language models for code understanding and generation. In: Proceedings of the 2023 Conference on Empirical Methods in Natural Language Processing. Association for Computational Linguistics (2023). https://doi.org/10.18653/v1/2023.emnlp-main.68
20. Wu, X., et al.: Autotuning PolyBench benchmarks with LLVM Clang/Polly loop optimization pragmas using Bayesian optimization. Concurrency Comput. Pract. Exp. **34**(20) (2021). https://doi.org/10.1002/cpe.6683
21. Zhao, J., Zhu, Q., Wu, W., Wei, H.: A configurable parallel iterative tuning framework. In: 2021 14th International Conference on Advanced Computer Theory and Engineering (ICACTE), September 2021. IEEE (2011). https://doi.org/10.1109/icacte53799.2021.00015
22. Zhu, M., Hao, D.: Compiler auto-tuning via critical flag selection. In: 2023 38th IEEE/ACM International Conference on Automated Software Engineering (ASE), September 2023, pp. 1000–1011. IEEE (2023). https://doi.org/10.1109/ase56229.2023.00209

Multidimensional Identification and Complex System Transmission Pathway Analysis of Scale-up Risks for Sustainable Aviation Fuel (SAF) in China

Zhujun Liu, Jianxiong Chen, and Lin Zou(✉)

Civil Aviation Flight University of China, Beijing, China
zoulin@cafuc.edu.cn

Abstract. Driven by carbon neutrality goals of the aviation industry, the large-scale application of Sustainable Aviation Fuel (SAF) confronts multidimensional systemic risks. However, the interaction mechanisms and transmission paths of its non-technical risks remain inadequately explored. This study employs the PESTEL model to identify and integrate risks into three systemic categories: institutional, supply-side, and demand-side. By applying complex systems theory, it constructs causal loop diagrams to unveil three core feedback mechanisms governing risk interactions. The research further identifies critical leverage points and proposes cross-domain intervention strategies to disrupt negative feedback loops. From the perspective of China's SAF scale development, this paper provides a systematic framework for risk management in the aviation industry's low-carbon transformation, offering theoretical and practical guidance for optimizing risk mitigation pathways.

Keywords: Sustainable Aviation Fuel (SAF) · scale-up risks · PESTEL integration · causal loop diagram · leverage points

1 Introduction

Sustainable Aviation Fuel (SAF) is recognized as a critical technological pathway for achieving aviation sector decarbonization under global carbon neutrality goals [2]. However, its large-scale deployment in China faces complex systemic barriers beyond technical challenges, including policy inconsistencies, economic constraints, and social acceptance issues [11]. Current SAF production costs remain 2–5 times higher than conventional jet fuel, creating fundamental economic headwinds that impede market competitiveness [8].

Existing research predominantly examines isolated risk factors, overlooking the dynamic interactions and transmission mechanisms that characterize complex energy transitions [10]. For instance, China's position as the world's largest waste cooking oil exporter creates international feedstock competition

J. Zhan et al. (Eds.): Bench 2025, LNCS 16471, pp. 162–175, 2026.
https://doi.org/10.1007/978-981-95-9694-2_12

as domestic SAF capacity expands, generating cross-border market distortions that undermine domestic supply security [9]. This study addresses this critical gap by integrating PESTEL analysis with complex systems theory to develop a comprehensive risk assessment framework. The research identifies synergistic risk clusters and their transmission pathways through causal loop analysis, providing actionable insights for breaking systemic barriers to SAF scale-up while maintaining methodological rigor.

2 PESTEL Analysis and Risk Identification

The PESTEL framework systematically examines six macro-environmental dimensions (Political, Economic, Social, Technological, Environmental, Legal) influencing SAF development. This study advances beyond conventional PESTEL application by integrating these dimensions into three functional risk categories based on their primary loci of impact within the SAF value chain, enabling more targeted intervention strategies.

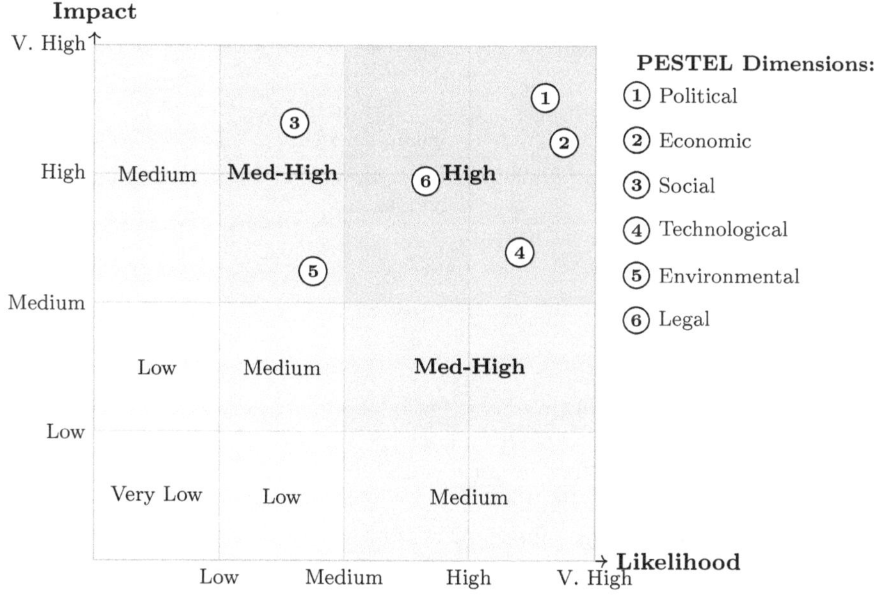

Fig. 1. Systematic PESTEL Risk Assessment Matrix for SAF Scale-up

Figure 1 presents the integrated risk assessment, revealing distinct clustering patterns that inform subsequent systemic analysis and intervention strategies. The matrix positions Political and Economic risks in the critical zone, highlighting their interconnected nature and systemic impact on SAF deployment timelines.

2.1 Political Factors

China's "Dual Carbon" strategy positions SAF as essential for aviation decarbonization, with the 14th Five-Year Plan targeting carbon-neutral growth by 2035. Despite comprehensive policy direction (Table 1), implementation gaps persist between national ambitions and local execution. Inconsistent policy signals and unpredictable subsidy mechanisms create investor hesitancy, slowing industry maturation compared to international counterparts with binding mandates and stable fiscal support [12]. The absence of legislatively-enforced blending targets undermines long-term investment planning, perpetuating the pilot project phase without achieving commercial scale.

Table 1. Key SAF Development Policies in China

Time	Policy Name	Key SAF Content
2021.10	Carbon Peaking Action Plan	Promote SAF as alternative fuel, improve fuel efficiency
2022.1	Civil Aviation Green Plan	Target 50,000 tons cumulative SAF by 2025
2023.7	Sustainability Requirements	Establish domestic certification standards framework
2023.10	Green Aviation Outline	Support multiple technology pathways including SAF
2024.10	Renewable Energy Guidance	Pilot bio-jet fuel applications in selected regions

2.2 Economic Factors

SAF production costs of 2–5 times conventional jet fuel present the primary economic barrier, with feedstock costs comprising approximately 60% of total production expenses [6]. With fuel comprising 25–40% of airline operating expenses, this cost premium severely limits voluntary adoption absent regulatory mandates. Current carbon pricing mechanisms fail to adequately value SAF's emission reductions, creating a fundamental market failure where environmental benefits remain unpriced [3]. Limited production scale prevents cost reductions through economies of scale, trapping the industry in a high-cost equilibrium that requires strategic intervention to escape [5].

2.3 Social Factors

Public acceptance exhibits a pronounced "green premium gap"–strong environmental support in principle but limited willingness to pay 10–30% ticket premiums in practice [7]. Consumer awareness remains low regarding SAF technical details and lifecycle emission benefits, with fewer than 20% of travelers familiar with SAF concepts. Airlines demonstrate systematic reluctance to absorb cost premiums without regulatory mandates or demonstrated consumer demand, creating market stagnation where limited procurement prevents scale economies.

2.4 Technological Factors

Technology concentration in HEFA processes (86.8% of planned capacity) creates systemic vulnerability to feedstock constraints and import dependencies for critical catalysts and processing equipment [8]. Domestic certification systems remain underdeveloped, forcing reliance on international standards that may not align with domestic priorities and create additional compliance costs. Limited R&D investment in second-generation technologies (PtL, cellulose) constrains long-term innovation and diversification potential [1], while the emerging threat of hydrogen aviation introduces additional technological uncertainty that impacts investment time horizons [2].

2.5 Environmental Factors

Feedstock sustainability presents dual challenges: resource intensity constraints (particularly water consumption exceeding local quotas in some regions) and emissions accounting inconsistencies across certification schemes. Some projects achieve only 50–60% lifecycle emissions reductions, below the 65% threshold required by international standards, potentially excluding them from carbon markets and international recognition. Export-oriented feedstock flows, particularly for used cooking oil, complicate domestic supply security while creating sustainability auditing complexities across jurisdictions with varying standards [9].

2.6 Legal Factors

Regulatory misalignment between evolving domestic frameworks and international standards creates layered compliance burdens that increase transaction costs by 10–15%. The EU's ReFuelEU regulations and Carbon Border Adjustment Mechanism impose additional certification requirements that domestic producers must navigate, while domestic legal frameworks remain underdeveloped in critical areas such as carbon accounting and sustainability verification [3]. This legal uncertainty increases investment risks and creates non-tariff barriers to international market access, particularly for export-oriented aviation sectors facing carbon competitiveness pressures.

3 Risk Transmission Pathway Analysis

3.1 Risk Classification and Systemic Integration

Building on the PESTEL multidimensional analysis, this study synthesizes the identified risk factors into three systemic risk categories based on their functional roles within the SAF ecosystem. This classification moves beyond descriptive taxonomy to reveal the fundamental mechanisms through which risks manifest and interact.

Institutional/Governance Risks. Institutional risks emerge from the interplay of political and legal dimensions, creating systemic barriers through policy instability and regulatory fragmentation:

- **Political Factors:** Policy target uncertainty and subsidy instability create an unpredictable investment environment, undermining long-term capital commitment.
- **Legal Factors:** Inconsistent standards and regulatory gaps between domestic and international frameworks generate compliance complexities and market fragmentation [3].

The convergence of political uncertainty and legal inconsistencies forms a self-reinforcing institutional risk cluster that permeates the entire SAF value chain.

Supply-Side Risks. Supply-side risks originate from the nexus of economic and technological challenges that constrain production capacity and efficiency:

- **Economic Factors:** High production costs (2–5× conventional jet fuel) and low carbon pricing eliminate economic incentives for SAF production [4].
- **Technological Factors:** Insufficient technology readiness levels (TRL) and over-reliance on single pathways (HEFA) limit production scalability and resilience [8].

This economic-technological risk complex creates a fundamental barrier to achieving the production scale necessary for market transformation.

Demand-Side Risks. Demand-side risks arise from the intersection of social and economic factors that suppress market uptake:

- **Social Factors:** Low public acceptance and limited willingness to pay for green premiums constrain voluntary demand creation.
- **Economic Factors:** High ticket price sensitivity among consumers and airlines creates resistance to cost pass-through mechanisms [5].

The social-economic risk combination establishes a persistent demand gap that undermines the business case for SAF production [6].

Table 2 demonstrates the systematic integration of PESTEL dimensions into three functional risk categories. This classification reveals that:

Cross-dimensional synergy is evident in each risk category, where factors from different PESTEL dimensions interact to create compounded challenges.

Table 2. Systematic Integration of PESTEL Dimensions into Three Risk Categories

PESTEL Dimensions	Key Risk Factors	Risk Category
Political + Legal	– Policy target uncertainty – Subsidy instability – Inconsistent standards – Regulatory gaps	Institutional/Governance Risks
Economic + Technological	– High production costs – Low carbon price signals – Technology readiness gaps – Single-pathway dependence	Supply-side Risks
Social + Economic	– Low public acceptance – Limited willingness to pay – High price sensitivity – Cost pass-through resistance	Demand-side Risks

For instance, political uncertainty (Political) amplifies regulatory gaps (Legal) in the institutional risk cluster.

Economic factors bifurcate naturally between supply-side (production economics) and demand-side (consumption economics), reflecting their distinct roles in the value chain.

Environmental considerations, while crucial for SAF sustainability, primarily manifest through their influence on supply-side technological options and regulatory requirements, rather than constituting an independent risk category.

This integrated classification provides the foundation for analyzing risk transmission pathways that cut across traditional disciplinary boundaries, offering a more holistic understanding of SAF scale-up challenges.

3.2 Risk Transmission Pathway Analysis and Systemic Dynamics

Building on the integrated risk classification framework, this section traces how risks propagate across institutional, supply-side, and demand-side boundaries. The transmission pathways reveal the dynamic interactions that transform isolated challenges into systemic barriers, providing the foundation for targeted intervention strategies.

Cross-Category Risk Transmission Pathways. Five characteristic transmission pathways emerge from the analysis, each demonstrating how risks cascade across the SAF ecosystem:

Pathway 1: Institutional to Supply-side Transmission

Policy Instability → Investment Hesitation → Capacity Constraints → Cost Escalation → Demand Contraction

This pathway originates in the institutional domain, where political uncertainty (Policy target ambiguity) and legal gaps (Regulatory inconsistency) create investment hesitation [12]. This transmits to the supply-side through reduced capital allocation, constraining production capacity and driving cost escalation, ultimately suppressing demand [5].

Pathway 2: Supply-side Self-reinforcement

Feedstock Competition → Price Volatility → Cost Instability → Profit Compression → Capital Withdrawal

Emerging from supply-side economic and technological factors, this pathway demonstrates internal supply-chain vulnerabilities [6]. Competition for limited feedstocks creates price volatility that erodes profitability, triggering capital flight that further constrains supply capacity.

Pathway 3: Technological-Institutional Lock-in

Technology Dependence → Import Restrictions → Upgrade Barriers → Substitution Threats → Demand Collapse

This pathway reveals the dangerous interplay between supply-side technological limitations and institutional barriers [8]. Dependence on specific technology pathways creates vulnerability to import restrictions, while institutional shortcomings in standards and certification hinder technological upgrading, exposing the sector to substitution threats [2].

Pathway 4: Institutional-Demand Transmission

Certification Gaps → Compliance Costs → Export Barriers → Carbon Tariff Pressure → Margin Compression

Originating in institutional legal deficiencies, this pathway shows how certification inconsistencies generate compliance costs that transmit to demand-side challenges through export barriers and carbon tariff exposure, compressing operator margins [3].

Pathway 5: Demand-Side Reinforcement

Low Public Acceptance → Procurement Stagnation → Scale Inefficiency → Persistent High Costs → Demand Vicious Cycle

This demand-side pathway demonstrates how social acceptance barriers interact with economic sensitivities to create a self-reinforcing cycle where low demand prevents scale economies, perpetuating high costs that further suppress demand [7].

Systemic Integration Through Causal Loops. Figure 2 integrates the five transmission pathways into three core feedback loops that capture the systemic dynamics of SAF scale-up challenges:

Reinforcing Loop R1 (Policy-Investment Trap) demonstrates how institutional risks transmit to supply-side constraints. Policy uncertainty undermines investment confidence, constraining capacity expansion and driving cost escalation, which further discourages investment–creating a self-perpetuating institutional-supply barrier.

Reinforcing Loop R2 (Cost-Demand Deadlock) reveals the supply-demand interaction where high costs suppress market uptake, preventing the scale economies needed to reduce those same costs [5]. This loop explains the persistence of the SAF cost premium despite technological improvements.

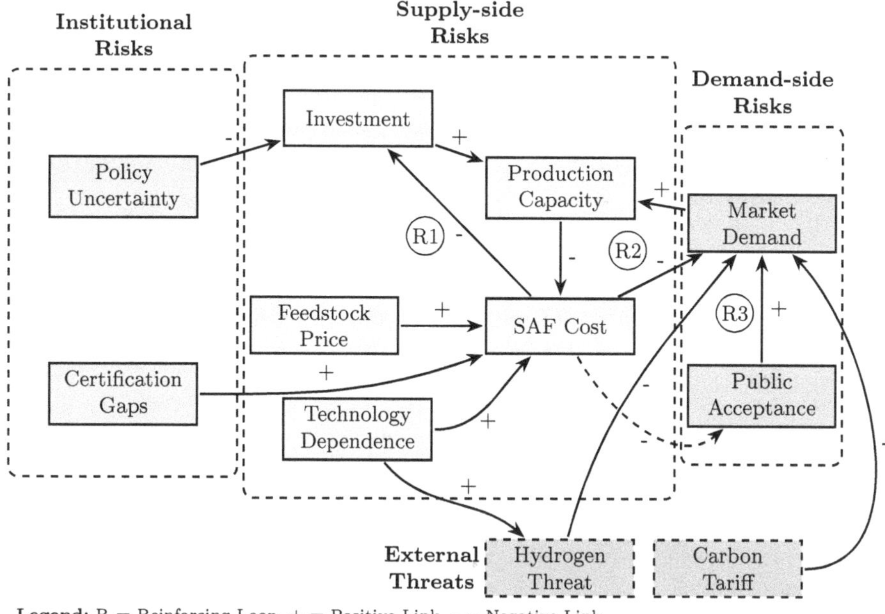

Fig. 2. Systemic Causal Loop Diagram of SAF Risk Transmission Pathways

Reinforcing Loop R3 (Acceptance-Cost Barrier) captures the demand-side reinforcement where low public acceptance limits market growth, maintaining high costs that further validate public resistance to price premiums.

The diagram further illustrates how cross-category risk transmission occurs:

- **Institutional to Supply-side:** Certification gaps and policy uncertainty directly increase production costs
- **Supply-side to Demand-side:** Cost pressures and technology limitations suppress market acceptance
- **Cross-category Amplification:** External threats like hydrogen substitution and carbon tariffs exploit vulnerabilities across all risk categories [2]

This systemic perspective reveals that effective intervention requires breaking multiple feedback loops simultaneously, as solutions targeting single pathways may be neutralized by countervailing pressures from other system components.

3.3 Leverage Point Identification and Systemic Intervention Strategies

Building on the systemic risk transmission analysis, this section identifies critical leverage points and proposes targeted intervention strategies. The approach recognizes that effective SAF scale-up requires coordinated actions across institutional, supply-side, and demand-side domains to break the identified feedback loops.

Institutional-Governance Leverage Points Leverage Point 1: Policy Credibility and Stability
Target: Breaking R1 Policy-Investment Trap (Pathway 1)

- **Legislative SAF Mandates:** Establish legally-binding SAF blending targets (e.g., 10% by 2030) to provide long-term market certainty and de-risk private investment decisions.
- **Multi-year Fiscal Frameworks:** Implement predictable subsidy mechanisms with 5–10 year budget allocations, moving away from annual discretionary funding that creates investment uncertainty [12].
- **Policy Consistency Mechanisms:** Create cross-ministerial coordination bodies to ensure alignment between energy, transportation, and environmental policies, reducing regulatory fragmentation [9].

Leverage Point 2: Regulatory Harmonization
Target: Mitigating Pathway 4 (Certification-Compliance Costs)

- **Domestic-International Standard Alignment:** Accelerate mutual recognition of China's CSCA certification with international schemes (RSB, ISCC) to reduce duplicate compliance burdens.
- **Technology-Neutral Certification:** Develop certification frameworks that accommodate emerging pathways (PtL, FT) beyond traditional HEFA processes [8].
- **Streamlined Approval Processes:** Establish fast-track regulatory pathways for SAF projects meeting sustainability criteria [3].

Supply-Side Transformation Leverage Points Leverage Point 3: Cost Reduction through Scale and Innovation
Target: Breaking R2 Cost-Demand Deadlock (Pathways 2 & 5)

- **Production Tax Credits:** Implement technology-neutral production incentives that directly address the 2–5× cost premium relative to conventional jet fuel [4].
- **Infrastructure Co-investment:** Public-private partnerships for biorefineries and logistics infrastructure to reduce capital barriers and achieve scale economies [6].
- **R&D Concentration:** Targeted research funding for second-generation technologies (PtL, cellulose) with highest cost-reduction potential [1].

Leverage Point 4: Feedstock Security and Diversification
Target: Disrupting Pathway 2 (Feedstock Competition)

- **Strategic Feedstock Allocation:** Implement waste oil export quotas to prioritize domestic SAF production and stabilize input prices [9].
- **Multi-feedstock Development:** Support non-food feedstocks (agricultural residues, municipal waste) to reduce competition with food and biodiesel sectors.

- **Supply Chain Integration:** Create information platforms connecting feedstock suppliers, processors, and airlines to optimize logistics and reduce volatility [6].

Demand-Side Activation Leverage Points Leverage Point 5: Mandatory Demand Creation
Target: Breaking R3 Acceptance-Cost Barrier (Pathway 5)

- **Airline Procurement Mandates:** Require progressive SAF blending ratios for domestic carriers, starting with 1% in 2025 and escalating to 10% by 2035.
- **Corporate Offtake Agreements:** Facilitate long-term purchase commitments from corporate travel programs to provide demand certainty for producers.
- **Public Sector Leadership:** Mandate SAF use for government and military aviation to demonstrate commitment and build initial market scale [12].

Leverage Point 6: Consumer Engagement and Willingness to Pay
Target: Enhancing Pathway 5 Effectiveness

- **Transparent Environmental Accounting:** Develop clear carbon footprint labeling for flights to enable informed consumer choices and premium justification.
- **Frequent Flyer Incentives:** Integrate SAF contributions into airline loyalty programs to encourage voluntary participation.
- **Corporate Sustainability Linkage:** Align SAF procurement with corporate ESG reporting frameworks to drive business demand.

Cross-Cutting Systemic Interventions Leverage Point 7: Carbon Market Integration
Target: Addressing Multiple Pathways Simultaneously

- **Aviation Sector Inclusion:** Incorporate aviation into national carbon markets to create economic value for SAF emissions reductions [3].
- **Carbon Credit Multipliers:** Design preferential treatment for SAF-derived carbon credits to enhance project economics [5].
- **International Offset Recognition:** Ensure Chinese SAF projects qualify under CORSIA to access global carbon finance.

Leverage Point 8: Technology Portfolio Management
Target: Mitigating Pathway 3 (Technology Lock-in)

- **Strategic Technology Mapping:** Maintain diversified SAF technology portfolio to avoid over-reliance on single pathways [8].
- **Hydrogen Transition Planning:** Develop integrated strategy that positions SAF as bridge technology while preparing for potential hydrogen aviation transition [2].
- **International Collaboration:** Participate in global SAF R&D initiatives to access emerging technologies and best practices [11] (Table 3).

Table 3. Systemic Intervention Framework for SAF Scale-up

Risk Category	Leverage Point	Priority Interventions
Institutional	Policy Credibility	Legally-binding mandates, Multi-year subsidies, Cross-ministerial coordination
Institutional	Regulatory Harmonization	International standard alignment, Technology-neutral certification, Fast-track approvals
Supply-side	Cost Reduction	Production tax credits, Infrastructure co-investment, Targeted R&D funding
Supply-side	Feedstock Security	Export quotas, Multi-feedstock development, Supply chain integration
Demand-side	Mandatory Procurement	Airline blending mandates, Corporate offtake agreements, Public sector leadership
Demand-side	Consumer Engagement	Carbon labeling, Loyalty program integration, ESG framework alignment
Cross-cutting	Carbon Markets	Aviation sector inclusion, Credit multipliers, International recognition
Cross-cutting	Technology Management	Portfolio diversification, Hydrogen transition planning, Global collaboration

Implementation Sequencing and Synergies. The proposed intervention framework requires strategic sequencing to maximize synergistic effects:
Short-term (2025–2027): Focus on institutional foundations and demand activation through immediate policy certainty and procurement mandates to break the R1 and R3 feedback loops.
Medium-term (2028–2030): Scale supply-side interventions as production capacity responds to stable demand signals, addressing the R2 cost-demand deadlock through economies of scale [5].
Long-term (2031–2035): Fully integrate carbon markets and technology innovation systems to create self-sustaining market dynamics independent of direct subsidies [3].

This systemic intervention approach recognizes that SAF scale-up success depends on coordinated action across all three risk domains, with interventions carefully sequenced to create positive reinforcement rather than working at cross-purposes.

4 Conclusion

This study has systematically deconstructed the complex challenges facing sustainable aviation fuel scale-up in China through an integrated analytical framework that progresses from multidimensional risk identification to systemic intervention design. The research demonstrates that SAF scale-up represents not merely a technological or economic challenge, but a complex systemic transition requiring coordinated governance across institutional, supply-side, and demand-side domains.

4.1 Theoretical and Methodological Contributions

This study makes three primary contributions to the literature on sustainable energy transitions:

Integrated Risk Assessment Framework: By synthesizing PESTEL dimensions into three functional risk categories–institutional (political-legal), supply-side (economic-technological), and demand-side (social-economic)–this research moves beyond descriptive taxonomies to reveal the fundamental mechanisms through which risks manifest and interact within the SAF ecosystem.

System Dynamics Application: The identification of three core feedback loops–the policy-investment trap (R1), cost-demand deadlock (R2), and acceptance-cost barrier (R3)–provides a dynamic systems perspective that explains why isolated interventions have historically failed to achieve scale-up breakthroughs.

Cross-Category Transmission Analysis: The five risk transmission pathways demonstrate how challenges propagate across institutional, supply-side, and demand-side boundaries, creating systemic barriers that cannot be addressed through single-domain solutions.

4.2 Policy Implications and Practical Applications

The systemic analysis yields several critical policy insights:

Sequenced Intervention Strategy: Successful SAF scale-up requires carefully sequenced interventions, beginning with institutional stabilization to break the policy-investment trap, followed by supply-side transformation to achieve cost competitiveness, and culminating in demand-side activation to create self-sustaining market dynamics [5].

Leverage Point Prioritization: Policy interventions should target key leverage points where multiple risk pathways converge, particularly:

- Institutional stabilization through legally-binding mandates and multi-year fiscal frameworks
- Cost reduction through production incentives and infrastructure co-investment [4]
- Demand activation through procurement mandates and carbon market integration [3]

Cross-Ministerial Coordination: The interconnected nature of SAF challenges necessitates coordinated governance mechanisms that bridge traditional ministerial silos, particularly between energy, transportation, environment, and finance sectors [9].

4.3 Limitations and Future Research Directions

While this study provides a comprehensive systemic analysis, several limitations suggest promising directions for future research:

Quantitative Modeling: The qualitative systems analysis presented here could be extended through quantitative system dynamics modeling to simulate intervention impacts and identify optimal policy mixes under different scenarios.
Regional Specificity: Future research could adapt the framework to account for regional variations within China's diverse economic and resource contexts, particularly comparing coastal industrial bases with inland agricultural regions.
International Comparative Analysis: Comparative studies examining how different national approaches to SAF scale-up navigate similar systemic challenges could yield valuable insights for policy learning and adaptation [11].
Technology Transition Pathways: As hydrogen and electric aviation technologies advance, research is needed on optimal transition pathways that balance near-term SAF deployment with long-term technology neutrality [2].

4.4 Concluding Remarks

The successful scale-up of sustainable aviation fuel in China represents a critical test case for the nation's ability to navigate complex energy transitions while maintaining economic competitiveness [9]. This research demonstrates that achieving aviation decarbonization requires moving beyond technical fixes and isolated policy measures to embrace a systemic perspective that recognizes the interconnected nature of institutional, economic, technological, and social challenges.

The integrated framework developed in this study–progressing from PESTEL risk identification through systemic classification, transmission pathway analysis, and leverage point intervention–provides both a diagnostic tool for understanding current impediments and a strategic roadmap for coordinated action. By addressing the root causes of systemic inertia rather than their surface manifestations, China can transform SAF scale-up from a persistent challenge into a demonstration of its capacity for integrated, sustainable innovation.

Future research should build upon this foundation to develop more precise quantitative models, regional adaptation strategies, and international comparative analyses that further refine our understanding of complex energy transition dynamics. Through continued systematic investigation and evidence-based policy design, the vision of sustainable aviation can progress from aspiration to reality.

References

1. Amhamed, A.I., Assaf, A.H.A., Le Page, L.M., Alrebei, O.F.: Alternative sustainable aviation fuel and energy (SAFE)- a review with selected simulation cases of study **11**, 3317–3344. https://doi.org/10.1016/j.egyr.2024.03.002, https://www.sciencedirect.com/science/article/pii/S2352484724001471
2. Bardon, P., Massol, O.: Decarbonizing aviation with sustainable aviation fuels: Myths and realities of the roadmaps to net zero by 2050 **211**, 115279. https://doi.org/10.1016/j.rser.2024.115279, https://www.sciencedirect.com/science/article/pii/S1364032124010050

3. Chen, D., Yin, J., Xu, F., Huang, C., Li, Z.: A market-based framework for CO2 emissions reduction in China's civil aviation industry **143**, 150–158. https://doi.org/10.1016/j.tranpol.2023.09.018, https://www.sciencedirect.com/science/article/pii/S0967070X23002561
4. Cui, Q., Chen, B.: Cost-benefit analysis of using sustainable aviation fuels in South America **435**, 140556. https://doi.org/10.1016/j.jclepro.2024.140556, https://www.sciencedirect.com/science/article/pii/S0959652624000039
5. Dray, L., et al.: Cost and emissions pathways towards net-zero climate impacts in aviation **12**(10), 956–962. https://doi.org/10.1038/s41558-022-01485-4, https://www.nature.com/articles/s41558-022-01485-4
6. Ebrahimi, S., Haji Esmaeili, S.A., Sobhani, A., Szmerekovsky, J.: Renewable jet fuel supply chain network design: application of direct monetary incentives **310**, 118569. https://doi.org/10.1016/j.apenergy.2022.118569, https://www.sciencedirect.com/science/article/pii/S030626192200054X
7. Gössling, S.: Risks, resilience, and pathways to sustainable aviation: a COVID-19 perspective **89**, 101933. https://doi.org/10.1016/j.jairtraman.2020.101933, https://www.sciencedirect.com/science/article/pii/S0969699720305160
8. Lau, J.I.C., et al.: Emerging technologies, policies and challenges toward implementing sustainable aviation fuel (SAF) **186**, 107277. https://doi.org/10.1016/j.biombioe.2024.107277, https://www.sciencedirect.com/science/article/pii/S0961953424002307
9. Ng, K.S., Farooq, D., Yang, A.: Global biorenewable development strategies for sustainable aviation fuel production **150**, 111502. https://doi.org/10.1016/j.rser.2021.111502, https://www.sciencedirect.com/science/article/pii/S1364032121007814
10. Pearson, R., Bardsley, D.K.: Applying complex adaptive systems and risk society theory to understand energy transitions **42**, 74–87. https://doi.org/10.1016/j.eist.2021.11.006, https://www.sciencedirect.com/science/article/pii/S2210422421001209
11. Watson, M.J., et al.: Sustainable aviation fuel technologies, costs, emissions, policies, and markets: A critical review **449**, 141472. https://doi.org/10.1016/j.jclepro.2024.141472, https://www.sciencedirect.com/science/article/pii/S095965262400920X
12. Winchester, N., McConnachie, D., Wollersheim, C., Waitz, I.A.: Economic and emissions impacts of renewable fuel goals for aviation in the US **58**, 116–128. https://doi.org/10.1016/j.tra.2013.10.001, https://www.sciencedirect.com/science/article/pii/S096585641300181X

An Empirical Analysis of Contribution Evaluation in Open Source Courses Using OpenRank

Wentong Dai[1], Jie Wang[1], Wenrui Huang[1], Shengyu Zha[2], Xiaoya Xia[1], Fanyu Han[1], Yanbin Zhang[1], and Wei Wang[1](✉)

[1] East China Normal University, Shanghai, China
51265903033@stu.ecnu.edu.cn, wwang@dase.ecnu.edu.cn
[2] Tongji University, Shanghai, China

Abstract. This paper presents an OpenRank-based approach for evaluating contributions in open source projects, addressing the challenge of quantifying student participation. Using the "Open Source Software Design and Development" course as a case study, the method evaluates student contributions across key open source practices, including discussions, problem-solving, and coding. Built on developer collaboration networks, the OpenRank algorithm provides a comprehensive assessment of student performance. Experimental results indicate that OpenRank aligns with traditional grading methods while offering a more holistic evaluation of contributions. By integrating OpenRank with conventional grading systems, this approach delivers a more scientific and thorough assessment of student contributions and skills in open source projects.

Keywords: Design studies · Open Source · Evaluation

1 Introduction

With the rapid advancement of technology and the increasing demand for software development talent, open source software development has emerged as a vital component of modern software engineering education [1]. Open source projects not only encourage developers to collaborate and leverage diverse resources and expertise but have also demonstrated the ability to sustain long-term developer engagement. By fostering a culture of innovation, collaboration, and transparency, open source development plays a pivotal role in preparing students to meet the dynamic demands of the software industry.

Over the past two decades, colleges and universities worldwide have actively explored practical approaches to integrating open source education into their curricula. Recognized as a critical avenue for cultivating skilled software engineers, open source education equips students with real-world experience while simultaneously advancing the software industry. However, despite significant efforts, there remain substantial challenges in cultivating open source talent. A primary

J. Zhan et al. (Eds.): Bench 2025, LNCS 16471, pp. 176–191, 2026.
https://doi.org/10.1007/978-981-95-9694-2_13

obstacle lies in the lack of effective methods for systematically and accurately evaluating students' contributions to open source projects. Traditional grading systems often fail to capture the complexity and diversity of student engagement in open source practices, particularly in collaborative and distributed development environments.

Our research specifically addresses this pressing issue by focusing on the effective evaluation of students' contributions within the context of practical open source education. Using the "Open Source Software Design and Development" course as a case study, we explore the application of innovative teaching methods designed to enhance students' open source software development skills. This includes hands-on training in open source project practices, fostering team collaboration, improving problem-solving abilities, and strengthening communication skills. As part of this effort, we propose an OpenRank-based evaluation framework, which leverages the principles of developer collaboration networks to quantitatively and qualitatively assess contributions in open source repositories. By incorporating metrics such as code contributions, issue resolution, and collaborative discussions, the OpenRank approach provides a more comprehensive and objective evaluation mechanism, addressing the shortcomings of traditional assessment methods.

Our main contributions are as follows:

1. Innovative Integration of Open Source Practices into Software Engineering Education. We have successfully integrated open source principles and practices into soft-ware engineering education by designing and implementing the "Open Source Software Design and Development" course. This course emphasizes open learning, real-world project practices, and collaboration on open-source platforms. By conducting all teaching, learning, and project activities within open-source environments, we provide students with an authentic experience that mirrors real-world software development workflows. This approach enhances students' technical proficiency, collaborative abilities, and problem-solving skills, preparing them to meet the demands of the software industry.
2. Development of an OpenRank-Based Evaluation Framework. We propose a novel evaluation framework based on the OpenRank algorithm, which leverages collaborative network analysis to quantify contributions in open-source repositories. This model evaluates students' involvement in various dimensions, such as coding, issue resolution, and collaborative discussions, providing a comprehensive assessment of their contributions. Unlike traditional evaluation methods, which often fail to capture the complexity of open-source practices, our framework offers a more objective, nuanced, and data-driven approach to measuring individual contributions in distributed development environments.
3. Validation of the Evaluation Model through Empirical Analysis. To verify the effectiveness of the OpenRank-based evaluation model, we conducted empirical studies within the context of the "Open Source Software Design and Development" course. By comparing the results of our model with tradi-

tional grading approaches, we demonstrate that OpenRank not only aligns with established evaluation methods but also delivers a more holistic and precise assessment of students' contributions. This validation highlights the practicality and reliability of the model in educational settings, addressing a critical gap in the evaluation of open-source talent.

2 Related Work

2.1 Open Source Software and Education

Open source software has been widely recognized as an ideal platform for education, as it fosters collaboration among developers and encourages the sharing of resources and expertise to address challenges in innovative ways [6]. Over the years, schools and universities have increasingly incorporated open source software into their curricula, acknowledging its significant role in training future software professionals and advancing the software industry. By engaging students in real-world, open source development environments, educators provide them with opportunities to gain hands-on experience in collaborative software engineering practices.

The use of open source software in education has been shown to increase student interest in software development and promote long-term involvement in the field [1]. However, challenges remain when integrating open source into educational contexts. Inexperienced student developers often struggle to adhere to established design principles, submit poorly organized pull requests, or fail to follow project contribution guidelines. Such mistakes are common in student contributions, as highlighted in prior research [8]. These challenges underline the need for better guidance and structured frameworks to help students effectively contribute to open source projects.

Despite these difficulties, participation in large-scale open source projects offers significant benefits for students. It provides them with valuable experience in software engineering practices, strengthens their technical and collaborative skills, and enhances their sense of professionalism [9]. Moreover, research into student motivations for participating in open source projects reveals that engagement in these activities not only improves their technical expertise but also fosters social skills and teamwork, both of which are critical for their future careers [6]. By contributing to open source projects, students gain practical experience in software development while building a foundation of skills that are highly sought after in the software industry.

2.2 Evaluation of Open Source Contributions

The evaluation of contributions to open source projects has been a critical focus of research in recent years. Early studies primarily concentrated on measuring project code workload [2,3]. For instance, Gousios et al. proposed a linear model to evaluate developer contributions by analyzing multiple trajectories of development and social activities[4]. However, the limitations of linear models have been increasingly evident. Xia X further examined contributions by mining repository activities and argued that linear models fail to capture the influence of social factors within open source software communities [5]. In addition, Tsay et al. provided strong evidence that social factors, such as communication during pull request reviews, significantly impact maintainer assessments of developer contributions [11]. These findings highlight the importance of considering both technical and social dimensions when evaluating open source contributions.

More recent studies have explored network-based methods for assessing developer contributions. Joblin et al. [12] and Cheng et al. [13] proposed approaches that leverage developer networks and user activities to classify contributors, although these methods primarily focus on categorizing developers rather than quantifying their individual contributions. Building upon this body of research, this study introduces a collaboration network-based approach to comprehensively assess developer contributions and their value within open source communities.

One of the key inspirations for this study comes from PageRank [14], a widely used algorithm that calculates the importance of web pages based on link relevance. Over the years, PageRank and its derivative algorithms have been applied in various fields, including document relevance ranking, user value assessment, and recommendation systems. For example, Li et al. [15] proposed ArticleRank, a ranking algorithm that measures the influence of journal papers by considering the categories of cited papers, thus refining ranking results among papers with similar citation frequencies. Similarly, Li et al. [16] introduced MovieRank, a ranking algorithm based on complex network theory, which takes into account the roles and identities of movie participants to evaluate their impact on movie rankings.

This study adopts a similar network-based approach inspired by PageRank to evaluate open source contributions. By leveraging collaboration network theory, our method goes beyond traditional models to incorporate both technical contributions and social interactions. This comprehensive framework addresses the limitations of prior evaluation methods and provides a more nuanced understanding of developers' roles and value within open source communities.

3 Course Design

3.1 Course Overview

Our research centers on the course "Open Source Software Design and Development", which is designed to cultivate students' professional skills and knowledge in software engineering through active participation in and contributions to open source software projects. The course curriculum is structured into three major sections: understanding open source, contributing to open source, and developing open source. This structure emphasizes the seamless integration of theoretical knowledge with practical application, ensuring an open and collaborative learning process. The detailed course content is summarized in Table 1.

A key feature of the course is its emphasis on an open learning environment. Leveraging e-textbooks, interactive teaching methods, and hands-on activities, the course caters to the diverse learning needs of students. All course resources, including learning materials, assignments, and discussions, are hosted in an open repository on GitHub. This ensures that students can freely access, use, and share materials while fostering a culture of transparency and collaboration. By conducting all course activities within an open-source framework, the course enables students to experience the principles and practices of open source software development firsthand.

Table 1. Open source modules overview

Module	Content Overview
S1 Embracing Open Source	This module provides a foundational understanding of open source by exploring its history and evolution, as well as its role in the global software ecosystem. Key topics include: –The origins and history of open source. – An introduction to open source projects and their significance. –Exploring the open source world through multidisciplinary perspectives. – The relationship between software, the software industry, and the commercialization of open source software. – The development of the global open source ecosystem. – Applications of open source in software engineering and data science. This module aims to help students appreciate the scope and impact of open source in both technical and industrial contexts.
S2 Contributing to Open Source	This module focuses on equipping students with the knowledge and tools necessary to actively contribute to open source projects. Students will learn about: – The complete process of open source collaboration and engineering workflows. – Personal development tools and practices for effective open source contributions. – The features and design thinking behind Git and version control systems. –Contribution strategies and community management within open source projects. – Team collaboration in open source development environments. – DevOps practices in open source software engineering. By the end of this module, students will have a practical understanding of how to participate in and contribute to open source projects effectively.
S3 Developing Open Source	The focus of this module is on advanced topics in open source governance, community operations, and professional development. Key areas include: – Fundamentals of enterprise open source governance. – Open source intellectual property rights and legal considerations. – Building secure and reliable open source systems. – Analyzing open source communities using digital tools and metrics. – Becoming an effective committer and maintaining open source projects. – Learning from the open source journey of Apache and its governance model. – Developer relations and operations within open source ecosystems. – Career opportunities and development pathways in the open source field. This module prepares students to not only develop open source software but also contribute to sustainable open source ecosystems and build successful careers in open source communities.

3.2 Practical Assignments

The course is heavily focused on practical, project-based learning, where students engage in hands-on assignments using real-world open source projects. These assignments are designed to mirror the processes and workflows of professional open source software development. The key tasks include project selection, task assignment, issue discussion, and code submission. To ensure that projects are suitable for educational purposes, instructors and teaching assistants carefully curate and select open source projects for students to work on.

Throughout the project lifecycle, students are guided to follow industry-standard practices:

- Task Management and Collaboration: Students use GitHub Issues to allocate tasks, discuss technical challenges, and track progress collaboratively.
- Version Control and Code Development: Students write code locally, manage branches, and handle version control using Git. This includes creating branches, submitting code changes, and merging pull requests into the main branch.
- Transparency and Community Practices: All activities, including discussions, code reviews, and submissions, are conducted openly within the course repository to simulate real-world open source community workflows.

These assignments provide students with valuable experience in software development while immersing them in the operational dynamics of open source communities. By participating in these projects, students gain a practical understanding of open source collaboration culture, project management methodologies, and community-driven development processes.

3.3 Educational Objectives and Outcomes

The open-source project tasks are designed not only to strengthen students' technical competencies but also to foster essential soft skills. Specifically, the course aims to achieve the following objectives:

- Teamwork and Collaboration: Through collaborative projects, students develop the ability to work effectively as part of a team, divide responsibilities, and communicate clearly.
- Problem-Solving Skills: By tackling real-world issues in open source projects, students enhance their analytical and problem-solving abilities.
- Communication Skills: Engaging in technical discussions and providing feedback during code reviews helps students improve their written and verbal communication skills.

Professional Development: Exposure to open source community practices prepares students for future careers in software development, equipping them with both technical expertise and an appreciation for transparency, openness, and global collaboration.

By combining theoretical instruction with practical, hands-on assignments, the course bridges the gap between academia and industry. Students leave the course with not only a deeper understanding of open source software development but also with the skills and mindset required to thrive in professional software engineering roles.

3.4 Course Evaluation

The evaluation system for the course is designed with inspiration drawn from the principles of the Apache Way, ensuring fairness, transparency, and alignment with open source community values. The evaluation framework is built on three core principles:

1. Open Communication Principle

   In the open source ecosystem, communication that is not recorded or made publicly accessible is considered non-existent. Following this principle, all discussions, collaborations, and contributions in the course must occur within the GitHub repository to ensure transparency and accountability.

   Documentation and Transparency: All communication threads and collaborative activities are required to be clearly documented, timestamped, and traceable within the repository. This ensures that every interaction, whether through comments, issue discussions, or pull request reviews, can be fairly evaluated.

   Evaluation Metrics: The quality and consistency of communication are assessed, emphasizing meaningful contributions to discussions, clarity of problem articulation, and responsiveness to feedback. This approach fosters a culture of open and constructive communication while simulating real-world open source community practices.
2. Contribution Measurement Principle

   This principle ensures that contributions are evaluated objectively, focusing on the quality, relevance, and impact of the work rather than the contributor's background or experience. The evaluation emphasizes long-term, meaningful involvement in open source projects.

   Assessing Contribution Impact: Contributions are assessed based on their significance to the project, with greater weight assigned to impactful tasks such as critical bug fixes, major code improvements, or implementing new features. For example, resolving a critical issue or submitting a substantial pull request (PR) will receive high-er scores compared to minor contributions.

Diverse Contribution Types: Contributions are not limited to code. Active participation in discussions, proposing valuable ideas, reviewing code, resolving issues, and other non-code contributions are also considered. This holistic approach aligns with the inclusive nature of open source communities, recognizing the value of diverse contributions.

Quantitative and Qualitative Metrics: Metrics such as the number of issues re-solved, pull requests merged, and discussions initiated or participated in are used alongside qualitative evaluations of their relevance and depth.

3. Community Priority Principle

In the open source world, a project's long-term sustainability and active community engagement are critical factors. This principle prioritizes contributions to projects with established, vibrant, and active communities over projects that may have initial technical appeal but lack sustained maintenance or support.

Collaborative Relationships as a Metric: Rather than solely evaluating individual contributions, the evaluation system emphasizes collaboration and teamwork. Students are assessed on their ability to work effectively within a group and con collectively to the success of a project. For instance, a group that successfully completes a complex open-source project through effective collaboration, task distribution, and mutual support will receive higher evaluations.

Social and Technical Interactions: The system also measures the degree of intera-tion among students, such as the frequency and quality of code reviews, constructive feedback, and collaborative problem-solving. This reflects the importance of teamwork and fostering a community-oriented mindset in open source development.

Community Engagement: Contributions to projects with mature, long-active communities are highly encouraged, as they provide a more realistic and challenging environment for students. Engaging with such projects enables students to experience the dynamics of established open source communities, including navigating their workflows and adhering to their standards.

4. Educational Value of the Evaluation System

This evaluation framework not only assesses students' technical contributions but also instills values essential for success in open source development: transparency, collaboration, and community-oriented thinking. By aligning the evaluation with open source principles, the course prepares students for future participation in professional open source projects and equips them with the skills to thrive in collaborative, global software development environments.

Skill Development: The system ensures that students develop both technical skills (e.g., coding, debugging, version control) and soft skills (e.g., communication, team-work, adaptability).

Real-World Simulation: The focus on collaboration, transparency, and community engagement mirrors real-world open source practices, bridging the gap between academic learning and industry requirements.

Fair and Inclusive Assessment: By prioritizing measurable, objective criteria such as contribution quality and collaboration, the framework provides a fair and inclusive evaluation mechanism that values diverse contributions.

4 OpenRank Algorithm

The OpenRank algorithm [17] is a variant and extension of the PageRank algorithm, designed to apply PageRank principles to heterogeneous information networks while also extending its applicability to high-dimensional nodes. Like PageRank and HITS, OpenRank determines the centrality of a node based on the centrality of other nodes pointing to it. Specifically, the higher the centrality of the nodes pointing to a given node, the higher the centrality of that node itself. However, unlike PageRank, OpenRank incorporates not only the structural relationships within the collaborative network but also the intrinsic value of each node.

In the context of open source collaboration, OpenRank evaluates the centrality of developer nodes by considering their interactions with PR (Pull Request) and Issue nodes. For example, the centrality of a developer is influenced by the centrality of the PRs and Issues they participate in, with higher centrality PRs or Issues contributing more significantly to the developer's centrality. This approach enables a more comprehensive and nuanced evaluation of collaborative contributions within open source ecosystems.

4.1 Network Model

The OpenRank algorithm is specifically tailored to model collaborative interactions in open source projects, focusing on key elements such as Issues and Pull Requests. The foundational collaborative network model, illustrated in Fig. 1, represents developers collaborating around Issue and PR nodes within a GitHub repository. These interactions encompass a variety of behaviors, including submitting, discussing, reviewing, and resolving Issues or PRs.

By incorporating these diverse collaborative behaviors, the network model captures the intricate relationships between developers and their contributions, providing a comprehensive framework for analyzing open source collaboration dynamics. OpenRank leverages this model to quantify the influence and value of both developers and their contributions, offering a robust approach to understanding the roles and interactions within open source communities.

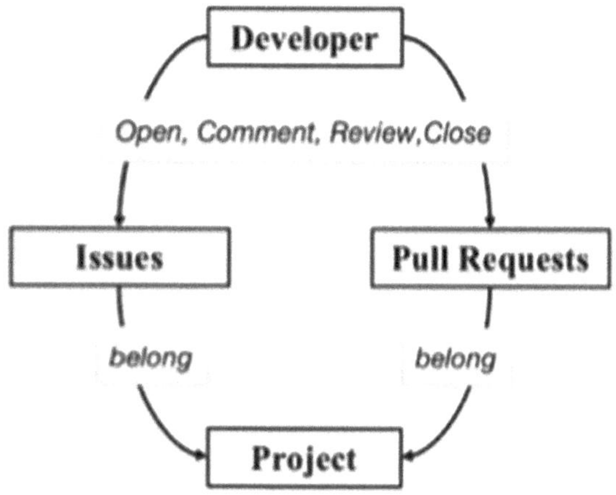

Fig. 1. The Basic Collaborative Network Model

4.2 OpenRank Algorithm

In the OpenRank algorithm, the OpenRank value of each node v_i in each iteration is represented by the following formula:

$$v_i = (1 - a_i) \sum_{j=1}^{|V|} \frac{w_{ji}}{d_{oj}} v_j + a_i v_0$$

where v_0 represents the initial value of the node, ai indicates the node's dependence on its initial value, d_{oj} is the weighted out-degree of node j, and w_{ji} is the weight of the edge from node j to node i. If we organize the normalized weights w_{ji}/d_{oj} into a matrix S and a_i as diagonal values into a matrix A, according to the convergence proof, the OpenRank values of all nodes will converge to a vector, as shown below:

$$\begin{aligned} v &= \lim_{k \to \infty} v^{(k)} \\ &= \lim_{k \to \infty} \left[\text{ASv}^{(k-1)} + (E - A)\, v^{(0)} \right] \\ &= limk \to \infty \left[(AS)\, kv\,(0) + t = 0k - 1\,(AS)\, t\,(E - A)\, v\,(0) \right] \\ &= (E - AS)^{-1} (E - A)\, v^{(0)} \end{aligned}$$

Developers and Issue/PR nodes are connected through different types of collaborative behavior edges, including opening, commenting, reviewing, and closing. Since these behaviors represent different efforts from developers, they should be weighted differently, i.e.:

$$w_{ij} = \sum_{k=0}^{n} w_{ijk} c_k$$

where c_k represents the weight proportion of the k-th type of edge.

4.3 Selection of Initial Node Values

In real-world graph networks, nodes generally have some prior information or features that can be reflected as the node's initial value. The OpenRank algorithm considers the initial values of each type of node when calculating centrality. Since OpenRank is calculated based on monthly data, if a node participated in the calculation last month and has already obtained a centrality value, its initial value will be inherited from last month. If a node does not have a centrality value, its initial value will be set to 1. For Issue/PR nodes, the initial value is increased based on developers' likes. If a PR node is merged within the month, its initial value is additionally increased by 50.

4.4 Dependence on Initial Values

When determining the centrality of different types of nodes within the network, both the intrinsic value of the node (representing its inherent features) and the value derived from interactions with other nodes (i.e., network value transfer) are taken into account. It is crucial to establish the extent to which a node's centrality depends on its own intrinsic attributes versus the influence of the network structure.

5 Experiment

The experimental process is structured into three key stages: data collection, model construction, and result analysis.

5.1 Data Collection

The data used in this experiment was obtained from the "Open Source Design and Development" course conducted during the Spring 2023 semester. To ensure detailed and accurate records of student activity, the OpenDigger tool was utilized to collect GitHub log data for 85 students over the period from March to May. The collected data included various types of activities, such as Issue Comments, Issue Opens, Issue Closes, PR Reviews, PR Opens, PR Closes, and PR Merges. Based on this dataset, a collaboration network was constructed to analyze student interactions and contributions.

5.2 Network Construction

Using the log data, node information for developers, Issues, and PRs, along with their corresponding collaborative relationships, was extracted. The total number of each type of node over the three-month course duration is summarized in Table 2. This network serves as the foundation for analyzing the collaborative behaviors and interactions within the GitHub repository.

As the course progressed, the number of active developers in the course repository steadily increased. This growth exceeded the number of enrolled students

Table 2. Statistics on the number of network node types

Month	User	Issue	PR
2023-03	75	34	2
2023-04	94	58	42
2023-05	117	54	124

due to participation from teaching assistants and external contributors. Additionally, the primary collaboration units in the repository shifted over time. Early in the course, Issues were the most commonly used unit, reflecting a focus on theoretical discussions. However, as the course transitioned to more practical content, Pull Requests (PRs) became the dominant collaboration unit.

To analyze these interactions, we constructed a collaboration network comprising four types of nodes, including Repository nodes. Figure 2 illustrates the collaboration network of the course repository in May 2023. In the figure, blue nodes represent repositories, red nodes correspond to developers, while green and yellow nodes represent Issues and Pull Requests (PRs), respectively.

Fig. 2. Open Source Course Collaboration Network – May 2023

5.3 Results

We applied the OpenRank algorithm to evaluate student contributions by calculating their scores for the period from March to May 2023. To assess the alignment between OpenRank scores and traditional teacher assessments, Pearson and Spearman correlation analyses were performed. These analyses compared OpenRank scores with teacher-assigned grades, including regular scores, midterm and final assignment scores, and overall grades, as summarized in Table 3.

The results revealed correlation coefficients ranging from 0.25 to 0.53 for Pearson and 0.28 to 0.60 for Spearman, indicating a moderate to strong relationship between OpenRank scores and teacher-assigned grades. All correlation tests yielded p-values below 0.01, confirming the statistical significance of the findings.

The moderate correlations suggest that OpenRank complements traditional grading methods by providing a more comprehensive evaluation of diverse contributions in open-source projects. For instance, a student named Surefour, despite receiving the lowest overall course grade, achieved an OpenRank score of 5.12. This score high-lights their significant engagement in the course repository through valuable code contributions and active participation in discussions, demonstrating the algorithm's ability to capture contributions that may not be fully reflected in conventional grading systems.

On the other hand, RTEnzyme, despite achieving a lower OpenRank score of 2.99, received a high overall grade but demonstrated limited activity in the repository. This contrast underscores OpenRank's ability to evaluate collaborative contributions and communication skills that may be overlooked by traditional grading methods.

OpenRank's comprehensive assessment incorporates various elements, including code submissions, pull requests, Issue discussions, and documentation contributions, providing a more detailed and well-rounded reflection of students' practical skills and involvement. By integrating OpenRank with traditional grading systems, educators can offer more nuanced feedback, helping students identify areas for improvement and fostering their holistic development. This combined approach enables a fairer and more thorough evaluation of students' abilities, emphasizing both individual effort and practical contributions.

Table 3. CORRELATION ANALYSIS RESULTS BETWEEN OPENRANK AND STUDENT SCORES

Student Scores	Pearson Correlation Coefficient	Pearson p-value	Spearman Correlation Coefficient	Spearman p-value
Regular Score	0.54	1.11×10^{-7}	0.60	1.07×10^{-9}
Mid-term Assignment	0.25	1.95×10^{-2}	0.28	9.79×10^{-3}
Final Assignment	0.31	4.19×10^{-3}	0.33	1.93×10^{-3}
Total Score	0.53	1.57×10^{-7}	0.58	8.19×10^{-9}

6 Threats to Validity

While this research has demonstrated the effectiveness of the OpenRank metric in evaluating students' contributions to open-source projects, several limitations remain. First, the sample size is relatively small, and the diversity of student backgrounds and course content is limited, which may restrict the generalizability of the findings. Second, the study primarily focuses on students' contributions and performance during the course, without examining the long-term impact of OpenRank on their learning trajectories or career development. Third, the qualitative analysis of students' actual learning processes—such as the specifics of their collaboration, problem-solving strategies, and motivational factors—lacks sufficient depth and granularity.

Future research should address these limitations by expanding the study to include a larger and more diverse range of courses, participants, and educational settings to validate the broader applicability of the findings. Moreover, tracking students' performance and career outcomes post-course could provide valuable insights into the long-term effects of OpenRank on their learning development, employability, and professional growth.

To further enhance the analysis, future studies could incorporate mixed-method approaches, such as in-depth interviews, surveys, and behavioral observations, to explore the underlying mechanisms behind OpenRank scores. This would allow for a more nuanced understanding of how OpenRank reflects collaboration dynamics, individual contributions, and learning outcomes. Additionally, analyzing factors such as team dynamics, communication styles, and the role of mentorship within the repository could provide deeper insights into how OpenRank fosters practical skills and collaborative learning. By addressing these aspects, future research could not only refine the metric but also contribute to the development of more comprehensive evaluation frameworks for open-source education.

7 Conclusion

Our study designed and implemented the "Open Source Software Design and Development" course, emphasizing the themes of open learning processes and project-based practice. To evaluate students' contributions to open-source projects, we proposed the OpenRank indicator, which leverages collaborative network centrality. By constructing a collaborative activity network based on students' data from the course repository, we calculated their OpenRank scores and assessed their contributions to open-source projects.

The results demonstrate that students' OpenRank scores align closely with teachers' evaluation results, indicating the effectiveness of OpenRank in capturing students' daily learning behaviors and achievements. Unlike traditional evaluations that primarily rely on homework grades, OpenRank provides a more comprehensive reflection of students' contributions and abilities in key areas such as problem discussion, teamwork, and task allocation.

By integrating OpenRank with traditional evaluation methods, educators can achieve a more holistic and equitable assessment of students' overall abilities and practical contributions. This approach not only ensures fairness but also fosters the development of essential skills such as teamwork, collaborative problem-solving, and practical application of knowledge. Ultimately, the combination of

OpenRank and traditional assessments offers a more nuanced framework for cultivating students' practical competencies and preparing them for real-world collaborative environments.

References

1. Ellis, H.J.C., Hislop, G.W., Jackson, S., Postner, L.: Team project experiences in humanitarian free and open source software (HFOSS). ACM Trans. Comput. Educ. (TOCE) **15**(4), 1–23 (2015)
2. Kan, S.H.: Metrics and Models in Software Quality Engineering. Addison-Wesley Professional (2003)
3. Walston, C.E., Felix, C.P.: A method of programming measurement and estimation. IBM Syst. J. **16**(1), 54–73 (1977)
4. Gousios, G., Kalliamvakou, E., Spinellis, D.: Measuring developer contribution from software repository data. In Proceedings of the 2008 International Working Conference on Mining Software Repositories, pp. 129–132 (2008)
5. Xia, X., Weng, Z., Wang, W., Zhao, S.: Exploring activity and contributors on GitHub: who, what, when, and where. In: 2022 29th Asia-Pacific Software Engineering Conference (APSEC), pp. 11–20. IEEE (2022)
6. Pinto, G., Ferreira, C., Souza, C., Steinmacher, I., Meirelles, P.: Training software engineers using open-source software: the students' perspective. In: 2019 IEEE/ACM 41st International Conference on Software Engineering: Software Engineering Education and Training (ICSE-SEET), pp. 147–157. IEEE (2019)
7. Silva, J., Wiese, I., German, D.M., Treude, C., Gerosa, M.A., Steinmacher, I.: A theory of the engagement in open source projects via summer of code programs. In: Proceedings of the 28th ACM Joint Meeting on European Software Engineering Conference and Symposium on the Foundations of Software Engineering, pp. 421–431 (2020)
8. Hu, Z., Song, Y., Gehringer, E.F.: Open-source software in class: students' common mistakes. In: Proceedings of the 40th International Conference on Software Engineering: Software Engineering Education and Training, pp. 40–48 (2018)
9. Holmes, R., Allen, M., Craig, M.: Dimensions of experientialism for software engineering education. In: Proceedings of the 40th International Conference on Software Engineering: Software Engineering Education and Training, pp. 31–39 (2018)
10. DeKoenigsberg, G.: How successful open source projects work, and how and why to introduce students to the open source world. In: 2008 21st Conference on Software Engineering Education and Training, pp. 274–276. IEEE (2008)
11. Tsay, J., Dabbish, L., Herbsleb, J.: Influence of social and technical factors for evaluating contribution in GitHub. In: Proceedings of the 36th International Conference on Software Engineering, pp. 356–366 (2014)
12. Joblin, M., Apel, S., Hunsen, C., Mauerer, W.: Classifying developers into core and peripheral: an empirical study on count and network metrics. In: 2017 IEEE/ACM 39th International Conference on Software Engineering (ICSE), pp. 164–174. IEEE (2017)
13. Cheng, J., Guo, J.L.C.: Activity-based analysis of open source software contributors: roles and dynamics. In: 2019 IEEE/ACM 12th International Workshop on Cooperative and Human Aspects of Software Engineering (CHASE), pp. 11–18. IEEE (2019)

14. Page, L., Brin, S., Motwani, R., Winograd, T.: The PageRank citation ranking: bring order to the web. In: Proceedings of the 7th International World Wide Web Conference (1998)
15. Li, J., Willett, P.: ArticleRank: a PageRank-based alternative to numbers of citations for analysing citation networks. In: ASLIB Proceedings, vol. 61, no. 6, pp. 605–618. Emerald Group Publishing Limited (2009)
16. Li, Y., Li, C., Chen, W.: Research on influence ranking of Chinese movie heterogeneous network based on PageRank algorithm. In: 15th International Conference on Web Information Systems and Applications, WISA 2018, Taiyuan, China, 14–15 September 2018, Proceedings 15, pp. 344–356. Springer, Cham (2018). https://doi.org/10.1007/978-3-030-02934-0_32
17. Zhao, S.Y., et al.: OpenRank leaderboard: motivating open source collaborations through social network evaluation in Alibaba. In: Proceedings of the 46th International Conference on Software Engineering: Software Engineering in Practice, pp. 346–357 (2024)

Relationship Evaluation for Developer Recommendation in Open Source Communities

Xuanhao Zhao, Xin Liu(✉), and Xuesong Lu(✉)

East China Normal University, Shanghai, China
xhzhao@stu.ecnu.edu.cn, {xliu,xslu}@dase.ecnu.edu.cn

Abstract. In the process of open source software development, teamwork has become a mainstream trend. However, developers generally tend to communicate with acquaintances, and it is difficult to find high-quality unfamiliar developers, which brings a series of negative effects. To some extent, developers' development efficiency and enthusiasm are negatively affected, and open source projects are easy to fall into the "homogenization trap", and even die early. At the same time, the open source community faces the risk of isolation and rigidity. Therefore, developer recommendation is an important task for improving the efficiency of developers, promoting the rapid iteration of technology, and continuing to inject vitality into the open source community. To this end, we design an LLM-and-Edge enhanced HGT model (LEHGT), and investigate the developer recommendation task on the datasets constructed from the GitHub community. The core idea is to evaluate the relationships between developers and repositories in text and use the evaluation feature to enhance the HGT-based recommender. Experimental results show that the proposed model performs significantly better than comparative methods.

Keywords: Developer Recommendation · Relationship Evaluation · Large Language Models

1 Introduction

In the field of open source software, teamwork development has become a mainstream trend [25]. Since 2008, GitHub has provided a code collaboration platform for developers worldwide. Currently, GitHub is the largest open source platform in the world, and by 2023, has more than 100 million developers. Developers can easily create repositories to enable collaborative development. However, they mostly rely on direct search to discover repositories of interest, as the platform lacks an efficient repository recommendation mechanism [28]. At the same time, there is no efficient way for stranger developers to communicate with each other, so that most developers form small circles. It is difficult for them to break through the circles and select new appropriate teammates [4].

J. Zhan et al. (Eds.): Bench 2025, LNCS 16471, pp. 192–208, 2026.
https://doi.org/10.1007/978-981-95-9694-2_14

As such, developer communities on GitHub often evolve into a core-periphery structure, in which peripheral contributors are sparsely connected and easily isolated from other subgroups [22]. This structural pattern implies that the lack of interaction with unfamiliar developers accelerates community fragmentation. To address the issue, developer recommendation has been studied, which can enhance collaboration between stranger developers and promote rapid iterative development [7,29,30].

Existing developer recommendation methods mostly leverage the topological structure of the GitHub social graph, which is formed by relationships such as collaboration between developers and creation or forking between developers and repositories. However, pure topology-based methods ignore the rich semantics in such relationships and may prevent the models from learning more distinctive representations of developers, which eventually affects the accuracy of developer recommendation. For instance, developers that have the same number of neighbors in the GitHub social graph may be embedded in similar representations, although their relationships against the neighbors can be quite different. To this end, we propose to evaluate the relationships between neighbor developers and repositories by describing them in text and model the textual feature to enhance the structural modeling. The core idea that, since each edge in the GitHub social graph represents a semantic relationship between the nodes, we evaluate the relationship in explicit text using large language models, and embed the evaluation text to obtain edge features. Then, together with the node feature embeddings, we use them as the input of the downstream recommender. The process can guide the recommender to learn more accurate relationships between developers and repositories, thereby improving the performance of developer recommendation. We use Heterogeneous Graph Transformer (HGT) [11] as the backbone of the recommender and refer to our proposed method as LLM-and-Edge enhanced HGT (LEHGT). Experimental results show that LEHGT greatly outperforms comparative methods in recommending potential developers for collaboration.

To summarize, our contribution in this paper is as follows:

- We use large language models to evaluate the relationships between developers and repositories and use the evaluations to enhance developer recommendation. LLM is used to perform multi-dimensional evaluation of edges on heterogeneous graphs, and generate feature embeddings for both nodes and edges to enhance semantic features.
- We extend the HGT-based recommender into LEHGT by adding an information transmission path starting from the edge to the target node, which aims to incorporate the edge features into the self-attention, messaging and feature aggregation steps of the network architecture. The extension can effectively enhance the node representation learning of the model.
- We construct the GitSAED dataset from the GitSED dataset for the recommendation task, which extracts the key APIs as the semantic features of developers and repositories, and constructs heterogeneous graphs based on the collaborations and contributions to the repositories of the developers.

Experimental results show that LEHGT greatly improves the comparative methods by a large margin.

2 Related Work

2.1 Studies on GitHub Social Graphs

As the most popular open source platform, the social graph on GitHub has been studied to solve different problems. Moradi-Jamei et al. [22] find that GitHub communities are composed of multiple small-scale blocks with strong connectivity. Wachs et al. [32] point out that cooperation is highly concentrated in a few core areas, and the vast majority of developers are in the periphery. Jo et al. [13] further conduct k-core analysis to show that contributors in the core layer of the graphs are more likely to participate in the long-term. At the same time, user behavioral data accumulated by the platform, such as pull requests, starring, development activities, etc., support multi-dimensional research. For instance, Batoun et al. [3] find that "reaction" in pull requests reduces communication costs, which supplements text comments and enhances community atmosphere in collaboration. Koch et al. [16] analyze the starring behavior to explore its effectiveness as an indicator to measure the popularity and importance of projects. Le et al. [18] quantify team collaboration activities and interaction patterns based on developers' interaction data.

These structural features and behavioral data form the basis of GitHub developer recommendation research, which should not only capture developer association by using network topology, but also combine with developer behaviors to mine potentials of collaboration. At present, using the behavior data for GitHub developer recommendation has become a research hotspot. For example, Fan et al. [7] propose a GNN-based framework to simultaneously capture user-item and user-user interactions to optimize recommendation. Based on the Stargazers dataset, Thakrar et al. [30] use GNNs to classify communities and predict potential collaborations. Sun et al. [29] combine social and development activities, learn developer embeddings through GNNs to infer technical expertise, and support team formation and recommendation. Differently from above studies, we further investigate the effect of relationship evaluation using LLMs in developer recommendation.

2.2 Link Prediction on Graphs

Developer recommendation in GitHub social graphs is essentially a problem of predicting potential collaborative links between developers in graphs, i.e., link prediction on graphs. Link prediction has been widely investigated in recommendation systems [6,8,17,27] and social network analysis [1,12,21]. The former focuses on predicting potential user-item connection and the latter focuses on interring potential user-user relationship.

In recommendation systems, GNNs can make full use of graph structures to improve recommendation quality. Elmahdy et al. [6] propose a new matrix completion method, which uses the hierarchical graph structure as side information to enhance the completion performance. Safae et al. [27] model the recommendation task as link prediction on a bipartite graph, which effectively captures high-order structural information. Lakshmi et al. [17] use graph structure information to infer potential connections for recommendation.

In social network analysis, GNNs are combined with structural information to improve link prediction accuracy. Ayoub et al. [1] combine betweenness centrality with GNNs to capture both local and global structures. Lv et al. [21] propose path-aware Siamese GNNs to predict potential connections using path information of node pairs. For dynamic social networks, Huang et al. [12] learn node representations and capture time evolution and causal dependency through GCNs for link prediction.

3 The GitSAED Dataset

To facilitate the research in the current work, we construct a dataset from the GitSED dataset[1], namely, GitHub Socially and API Enhanced Dataset (GitSAED). GitSAED enriches the semantic information of the developers and repositories in GitSED with API expertise. In particular, GitSAED contains APIs of two mainstream programming languages, Python and JavaScript, used by the developers, and a total of 27,291 valid repositories and 71,065 valid developers. The construction process of GitSAED is shown in Fig. 1.

3.1 Raw Data Collection

The GitSED dataset can fully demonstrate the cooperative relationships among developers on GitHub [2,24]. We sort the code contribution behaviors in descending order based on the time when a developer first contributes to a repository. For the projects using Python as the main language, we select the first 200,000 records, which include 25,910 repositories and 67,043 developers. For the projects using JavaScript as the main language, we select the first 100,000 records, which contain 23,453 repositories and 54,205 developers.

3.2 API Extraction for Repositories and Developers

We extract the APIs of developers and repositories to represent their expertise. We first remove repositories without code files, which results in 15,812 valid repositories of Python projects and 11,479 valid repositories for JavaScript projects. We extract APIs from the code files in each repository. Subsequently, inspired by the process of constructing repository features in TOSE dataset [20], we use the key APIs of each repository to represent its expertise. In particular,

[1] https://zenodo.org/records/5021329.

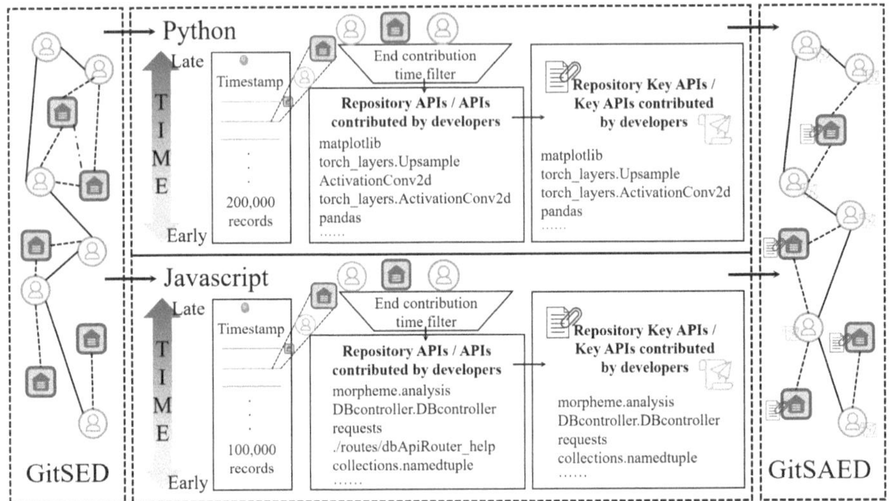

Fig. 1. The construction of GitSAED.

we embed all APIs into vectors using API embedding model [5] and calculate the average API embedding of each repository. The key APIs of a repository are the 5 APIs that are the closest to the average API in the embedding space.

For the developers, we remove developers who do not contribute code files, which results in 43,685 developers for the Python projects and 27,380 developers for the JavaScript projects. We extract the APIs in the code files contributed by the developers and extract the 5 key APIs of each developer using the method similar to that of extracting the key APIs of each repository.

Ultimately, on the two datasets, the feature description of the repository is the key APIs of the repository, and the feature description of the developer is the key APIs used by the developer in the repository. In the dataset where Python is the main language, each developer contributes to 1.18 repositories on average. In the dataset where JavaScript is the main language, each developer contributes to 0.76 repositories on average.

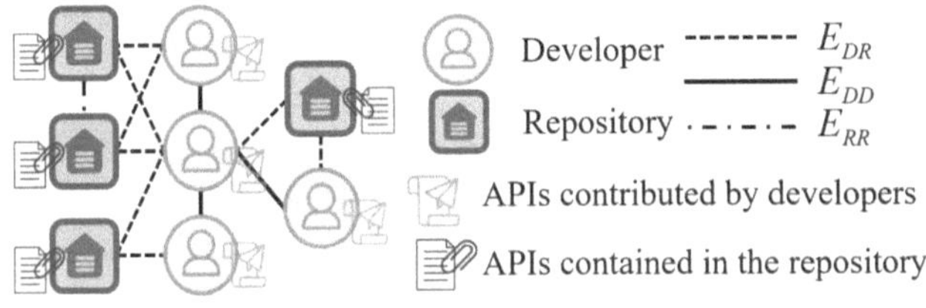

Fig. 2. Schematic diagram of the heterogeneous graphs.

3.3 Heterogeneous Graph Construction

As shown in Fig. 2, we construct heterogeneous graphs based on the GitSAED dataset. There are two types of nodes and three types of edges. The nodes are repositories and developers, where the key APIs are the node features. The edges include E_{DD}, E_{DR} and E_{RR}. E_{DD} indicates the edges that connect two developers contributing to the same repository. E_{DR} indicates the edges that connect a developer and a repository contributed to by the developer. E_{RR} indicates the edges that connect two repositories contributed to by the same pair of developers. In GitSAED, the heterogeneous graph for the Python projects has 99,186 E_{DD} edges, 51,403 E_{DR} edges and 5,577 E_{RR} edges. The heterogeneous graph for the JavaScript projects has 39,100 E_{DD} edges, 33,138 E_{DR} edges and 5,014 E_{RR}s edges. Table 1 reports the summary statistics of the heterogeneous graphs.

Table 1. The summary statistics.

language		Python	JavaScript
Number of nodes	Repository	15812	11479
	Developer	43685	27380
Number of edges	E_{DR}	51403	33138
	E_{DD}	99186	39100
	E_{RR}	5577	5014

4 The LEHGT Method

In this section, we describe the proposed LLM-and-Edge enhanced HGT (LEHGT) in detail. The overview is shown in Fig. 3, which contains three main steps: 1) evaluating the relationships between nodes using an LLM; 2) embedding the node and edge features using an LLM; 3) Training the edge-enhanced heterogeneous graph transformer as the recommender.

4.1 Relationship Evaluation Using an LLM

Relationships between developers are key features to enable accurate recommendation. To make the implicit relationships represented by the edges explicit, we leverage the outstanding reasoning and context understanding capability of large language models [19] and prompt an LLM to generate evaluation text for each edge of the constructed heterogeneous graphs.

Inspired by [10], unlike the common "yes/no" response, we adopt an "open and elicitation" questioning strategy. In particular, we prompt the LLM to evaluate each edge of the heterogeneous graphs in different dimensions, which represents an explicit evaluation of the relationship between the corresponding nodes and eventually facilitates developer recommendation.

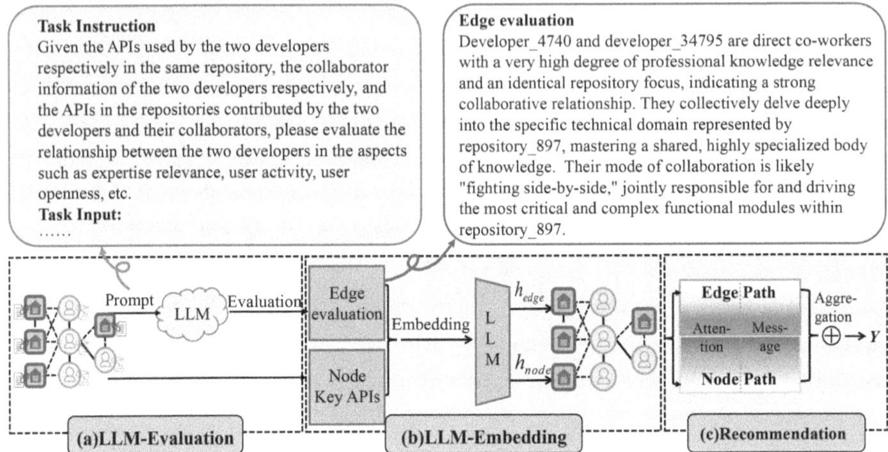

Fig. 3. The Overview of LEHGT.

We design three prompt templates for E_{DD}, E_{DR} and E_{RR}, respectively. Each template contains task instruction, task input and task output. As an example in Fig. 4, for each edge in E_{DD}, we instruct the LLM to evaluate the relationship between the two developers in multiple aspects, including expertise relevance, user activity, user openness, etc. The LLM gives the evaluation based on *the APIs used by the two developers in the same repository, the collaborator information of the two developers, and the APIs in the repositories created by the developers and their collaborators*, which are given in the task input. Eventually, the LLM gives the evaluation of the relationship between the two developers in the task output.

Similarly, for each edge in E_{DR} connecting a developer and a repository, we provide in the task input *the APIs of the repository and APIs of other repositories contributed by the developer.* Then we guide the LLM to evaluate the relationship between the developer and the repository in the aspects including expertise relevance, repository domain relevance, user openness, etc.

For each edge in E_{RR}, we provide in the task input *the APIs of the two repositories, respectively, and the APIs of other repositories contributed by the developers who contribute to both repositories.* The latter represents the tie strength between the two repositories implicitly from the other repositories contributed by the same group of developers. Then we guide the LLM to evaluate the relationship between the two repositories in the aspects such as expertise relevance, repository domain relevance, etc.

The specific task instruction and input are customized and adjusted according to edge types and programming languages (i.e., Python or JavaScript).

Task Instruction:
Given the APIs used by the two developers respectively in the same repository, the collaborator information of the two developers respectively, and the APIs in the repositories contributed by the two developers and their collaborators, please evaluate the relationship between the two developers in the aspects such as expertise relevance, user activity, user openness, etc.

Task Input:
"Developer_A" and "Developer_B" have contributed to "Repository_A".
- The APIs used by "Developer_A" are: {"sklearn.metrics", "numpy", "pandas"}
- The APIs used by "Developer_B" are: {"json", "csv", "time"}

"Developer_A" has a collaborator "Developer_C".
"Developer_C" has contributed to "Repository_B" and "Repository_C".
- The APIs of "Repository_B" are: {"pathlib","sys","shutil.copyfile"}
- The APIs of "Repository_C" are: {"matplotlib", "sklearn", "tqdm"}

"Developer_B" has a collaborator "Developer_D".
"Developer_D" has contributed to "Repository_D".
...
Please evaluate the relationship between "Developer_A" and "Developer_B" in the aspects such as expertise relevance, user activity, user openness, etc.

Task Output: The relationship between Developer_A and Developer_B is primarily based on their collaboration on Repository_A. However, due to low expertise relevance, similar but limited user activity, and a weak network connection, their relationship is not strong. They likely interact only within the context of Repository_A without significant overlap in skills or broader collaboration networks.

Fig. 4. An example of evaluating the relationship between two developers using an LLM.

4.2 Generating Node and Edge Embeddings Using an LLM

LLMs have strong computing capabilities and extremely rich knowledge reserves. During the training process, they absorb a vast amount of text, and their weights are encoded with rich factual knowledge [26]. Therefore, compared to traditional embedding Models, using an LLM to generate the embeddings of nodes and edges can better convey the features of text information and enhance the overall semantic features of the heterogeneous graphs. Specifically, we generate the feature embeddings of the edges and nodes in the heterogeneous graphs, respectively, using an LLM, which are subsequently fed into the downstream recommender. The process can be formulated as:

$$h_e = LLM(s^e), \tag{1}$$

$$h_n = LLM(s^n), \tag{2}$$

where h_e is the feature embedding of an edge, h_n is the feature embedding of a node, s^e is the evaluation text of the edge, and s^n is the API text of the node.

4.3 Training the Recommender Using HGT

To train the recommender, we incorporate the embedding h_e of each edge into HGT [11]. This means that the HGT model is added with a new information transmission path starting from an edge to the target node, in addition to the original information transmission path starting from the source node to the target node. This new path is used to enhance the delivery of side information on the edge. For ease of presentation, we refer to as **the source node path** the information transfer path starting from the source node to the target node, and refer to as the **the edge path** the information transfer path starting from the edge to the target node.

Following the architecture of HGT, our proposed LEHGT model has three main components: LLM-and-edge enhanced heterogeneous mutual attention, LLM-and-edge enhanced heterogeneous message passing and LLM-and-edge enhanced target node aggregation. Specifically, LEHGT adds edge features to the node features for mutual attention learning in HGT. In the messaging phase, we further strengthen the information transfer from the edge to the target node. In the aggregation phase, we first calculate the features updated by all neighbor nodes of the target node on the two paths, and then concatenate them to obtain the edge-enhanced feature. Finally, we aggregate all edge-enhanced neighbor node information to the target node t, and transform the aggregated feature into type-specific output, which are then used for link prediction.

Heterogeneous Graph Abstraction. We can represent a heterogeneous graph as $G = (V, E, P, R)$, where V represents nodes, E represents edges, P represents node types, and R represents edge types. There is a mapping from nodes to node types $\tau(v) : V \to P$, a mapping from edges to edge types $\Phi(e) : E \to R$. In this paper, for an edge $e = (s, t)$ connecting a source node s to a target node t, the meta-relation is expressed as $< \tau(s), \Phi(e), \tau(t) >$.

LLM-and-Edge Enhanced Heterogeneous Mutual Attention. Based on HGT, in order to fully utilize the features of edges, we also incorporate edge features into the operation of the multi-head attention mechanism. In particular, for each edge $e = (s, t)$, we follow HGT and calculate $Attention_n(s, e, t)$ using the method in HGT based on the source node path and in addition calculate $Attention_e(s, e, t)$ based on the edge path, which can be calculated as:

$$Attention_n(s, e, t) = \left(K(s) W_{\Phi(e)}^{ATTN} Q(t)^T\right) \cdot \frac{\mu}{\sqrt{d}}. \tag{3}$$

$$Attention_e(s, e, t) = \left(KE(e) W_{\Phi(e)}^{ATTE} Q(t)^T\right) \cdot \frac{\mu}{\sqrt{d}}. \tag{4}$$

In the formula, $K(s)$ is the key vector of the source node, $Q(t)$ is the query vector of the target node, $KE(e)$ is the key vector of the edge, $W_{\Phi(e)}^{ATTN}$ is a matrix based on different edge types on the source node path, which enables the model to capture different semantic associations between pairs of the same node type, $W_{\Phi(e)}^{ATTE}$ is the matrix of the edge path based on different edge types, which can enhance the semantic association between the edge and the target node, $\mu$is a prior tensor, which serves as an adaptive scaling factor of the attention mechanism, and d is the embedding size.

LLM-and-Edge Enhanced Heterogeneous Message Passing. We transfer the edge feature from the edge to the associated target node, so as to enhance the relationship information in the graph learning. For a pair of nodes (s,t), in addition to calculating the $Message_n(s,e,t)$ on the source node path, we also calculate the $Message_e(s,e,t)$ on the edge path.

$$Message_n(s,e,t) = V(s)W_{\Phi(e)}^{MSGN}. \tag{5}$$

$$Message_e(s,e,t) = VE(e)W_{\Phi(e)}^{MSGE}. \tag{6}$$

In the formula, $V(s)$ is the value vector of the source node, $VE(e)$ is the value vector of the edge. Meanwhile, $W_{\Phi(e)}^{MSGN}$ is used to integrate edge dependencies on the path of the source node, $W_{\Phi(e)}^{MSGE}$ is used to integrate edge dependencies on the path of the edge.

LLM-and-Edge Enhanced Target Node Aggregation. At this stage, we aggregate the information from the source node to the target node based on the two paths, and then concatenate the features on the two paths to obtain the edge-enhanced latent vector $\underset{s\in N(t)}{\tilde{h}_s}[t]$, which can be formulated as:

$$\underset{s\in N(t)}{\tilde{h}_s}[t] = Concat\text{-}linear\left(CAT[\underset{s\in N(t)}{h\text{-}\tilde{node}_s}[t], \underset{s\in N(t)}{h\text{-}\tilde{edge}_s}[t]]\right). \tag{7}$$

In the formula, we define $CAT[A,B]$ as the concatenation of matrix A and matrix B. $\underset{s\in N(t)}{h\text{-}\tilde{node}_s}[t]$ is the vector updated by each neighbor node of the target node on the source node path, $\underset{s\in N(t)}{h\text{-}\tilde{edge}_s}[t]$ is the vector updated by each neighbor node of the target node on the edge path.

We stack the above layers twice to construct LEHGT, and use the final output for predicting developer recommendation, using the binary cross-entropy loss. Given a pair of developers (s,t), the formulas are as follows:

$$\hat{y_e} = \sigma(z_s \cdot z_t), \tag{8}$$

$$z_s, z_e, z_t = LEHGT(h_n(s), h_e(e), h_n(t)).$$

$$L(y_e, \hat{y_e}) = -y_e \cdot \log(\hat{y_e}) - (1-y_e) \cdot \log(1-\hat{y_e}), \tag{9}$$

where y_e is the true label of the existence of collaboration between two developers, and $\hat{y_e}$ is the probability of the existence of collaboration between two developers predicted by LEHGT. In addition, σ is the sigmoid function, z_s is the embedding of the source node after passing through LEHGT, z_e is the embedding of the edge after passing through LEHGT, z_t is the embedding of the target node after passing through LEHGT, $h_n(s)$ is the feature embedding of the source node, $h_e(e)$ is the feature embedding of the edge, $h_n(t)$ is the feature embedding of the target node.

5 Performance Evaluation

All experiments are conducted on a server equipped with CentOS 9.0 and a NVIDIA A800 80GB GPU. We particuarly demonstrate the effectiveness of LEHGT by addressing the following three research questions:

- **RQ1:** How does LEHGT perform compared to the baseline model for developer recommendation?
- **RQ2:** How much do the various components of LEHGT contribute to its performance?
- **RQ3** How do LEHGT's hyperparameters affect the recommendation performance?

5.1 Data Splitting

To prevent information leakage, we split the GitSAED dataset based on the timestamp of developerrepository contribution records, whcih can simulate the chronological nature of real-world developer behaviors on GitHub, thereby ensuring the validity of the model's predictive performance. The first 60% of contributions are used as the training set, and the remaining 40% are randomly divided into validation and testing sets, yielding an 6:2:2 split. We mask an edge in E_{DR} if the developer contributes to the repository after the timestamp. We mask an edge in E_{DD} if two developers contribute to the same repository after the timestamp. Similarly, we mask an edge in E_{RR} if two repositories are linked by the same pair developers whose contribution occurs after the timestamp. We use the matched developer-developer pairs who have collaborated before the timestamp as the training objectives. For each matched pair, we conduct three unmatched pairs by randomly selecting a developer who has never collaborated with the developer.

5.2 Evaluation Metrics and Baseline Methods

To evaluate the performance of LEHGT and the baseline methods, we adopt three widely used metrics: accuracy (**Acc**), precision (**Pre**), and F1-score (**F1**). We compare LEHGT with eight baseline methods, which can be categorized into three groups: graph neural network (GNN) group, link prediction (LP) group, and developer recommendation (DR) group. For the GNN group, we implement four representative models, SAGE [9], GCN [15], GAT [31], and GIN [33]. For the LP group, we reproduce PaGNN [34] and LHGNN [23] to predict links among developers. For the DR group, we reproduce ELPA [30] and GraphRec [7] to learn developer embeddings for recommendation. Since all baseline models are graph-based, we initialize node features with embeddings obtained from LLMs and use them as input to the models. For all baseline methods, we use the implementations with their recommended hyperparameter settings in their papers to ensure fair comparison.

5.3 Hyperparameters

For the LLM selection, we adopt deepseek-llm-7b-base[2] to evaluate the relationships of the edges and Qwen3-Embedding-8B[3] to obtain embeddings of the edges and nodes, respectively, without performing fine-tuning on either model. All methods are trained for 200 epochs, with early stopping applied using a patience of 30. Each method is trained four times using different random seeds, and the average performance on the testing data is reported. For the Python dataset, we set number of layer to 2, the number of heads to 4, the hidden state size of nodes and edges to 256, the dropout rate to 0.3, the learning rate to 5e−3 and weight decay to 2e−5. In JavaScript dataset, the number of head is 2, and other settings are the same as those for the Python dataset. The Adam optimizer [14] is used for both datasets.

5.4 RQ1: LEHGT Vs. the Baseline Models

We compare the performance of LEHGT with the baseline models in developer recommendation. Table 2 presents the performance comparison between LEHGT and baseline models.

Table 2. LEHGT Vs. Baseline Methods.

Groups	Methods	Python			JavaScript		
		Acc	Pre	F1	Acc	Pre	F1
GNN	SAGE [9]	56.67	60.74	54.25	61.43	58.87	63.59
	GCN [15]	58.78	63.22	61.64	63.99	61.86	62.50
	GAT [31]	55.44	59.75	52.76	59.79	59.16	59.58
	GIN [33]	61.53	62.93	64.08	62.63	61.98	63.61
LP	PaGNN [34]	65.18	61.32	62.58	61.61	64.37	64.43
	LHCNN [23]	62.88	63.00	63.69	<u>67.94</u>	65.32	67.26
DR	ELPA [30]	59.20	60.03	59.94	60.81	61.29	61.38
	GraphRec [7]	<u>65.53</u>	<u>63.34</u>	<u>65.14</u>	67.46	<u>66.63</u>	<u>67.71</u>
Ours	LEHGT	**68.92** (↑ 3.39)	**68.73** (↑ 5.39)	**68.75** (↑ 3.61)	**68.41** (↑ 0.47)	**69.02** (↑ 2.39)	**71.04** (↑ 3.33)

We observe that LEHGT significantly outperforms all the baseline models in all evaluation metrics. In particular, the recommendation precision of LEHGT on the Python dataset improves against the second best model, GraphRec, by more than 5 points, which fully proves the effectiveness of evaluating the relationships between developers and using the evaluated results for developer recommendation. The performance improvement of LEHGT on the JavaScript dataset is

[2] https://huggingface.co/deepseek-ai/deepseek-llm-7b-base.
[3] https://huggingface.co/Qwen/Qwen3-Embedding-8B.

slightly smaller than that on the Python dataset, where the recommendation F1 socre of LEHGT can still improve against the second best model, GraphRec, by more than 3 points. Compared to the Python dataset, the JavaScript dataset has a smaller heterogeneous graph with fewer edges and repositories contributed by developers, which means that less evaluation information can be provided for developer recommendation. This indicates by contradiction that relationship evaluation is important for developer recommendation, where more edge information can improve the accuracy of recommendation.

5.5 RQ2: Ablation Study of LEHGT

To verify the effectiveness of each step in LEHGT, we compare LEHGT with two ablation models by controlling the existence and composition of edge features. Firstly, after calculating the embeddings of nodes by the LLM, we adhere to the original HGT model, that is, using an HGT model without edge enhancement during link prediction. We refer to the model as w/o Edge-Enh. Secondly, we do not use the LLM to embed the nodes and edges, and adopt the general API embedding model [5] to output the feature embeddings of nodes and edges, which are then used as input to the recommender. We refer to the model as w/o LLM-Emb.

Table 3. LEHGT Vs. Ablation Methods

Methods	Python			JavaScript		
	Acc	Pre	F1	Acc	Pre	F1
w/o Edge-Enh	65.08	64.74	66.21	66.00	67.97	69.86
w/o LLM-Emb	66.25	67.34	66.97	67.40	68.15	68.75
LEHGT	**68.92**	**68.73**	**68.75**	**68.41**	**69.02**	**71.04**

Table 3 presents the results of the two ablation experiments. We observe that the performance of the two ablation models decreases to different degrees, which fully demonstrates the effectiveness of using LLMs to generate evaluation and embed edges and nodes in LEHGT. On the whole, the performance degradation of the ablation model without edge enhancement (w/o Edge-Enh) is more significant, which proves the importance of edge information for developer recommendation. Compared between the two datasets, the performance of the two ablation models on the Python dataset decreases more than that on the JavaScript dataset, indicating that the LEHGT model can achieve more significant improvements when more relationships are evaluated and integrated.

5.6 RQ3: Hyperparameter Tuning

We tune two important hyperparameters. The first is the ratio k of the negative samples to the positive samples. The second is the number of attention heads n_h. We vary the k in $\{1,3,5\}$ and n_h in $\{2,4,8\}$, respectively.

Table 4. The performance of LEHGT under different hyperparameters

Hyperparameters	Value	Python			JavaScript		
		Acc	Pre	F1	Acc	Pre	F1
k	1	67.35	67.23	67.51	65.34	65.68	65.09
	3	**68.92**	**68.73**	**68.75**	**68.41**	**69.02**	**71.04**
	5	68.32	68.35	68.29	68.08	68.01	68.81
n_h	2	64.81	65.34	65.06	**68.41**	**69.02**	**71.04**
	4	**68.92**	**68.73**	**68.75**	67.98	68.57	69.03
	8	67.02	67.45	67.70	67.65	67.09	68.16

Table 4 shows the results. Regarding the negative sampling ratio k, we observe that $k = 3$ achieves the best performance. A smaller k (e.g., 1) reduces the diversity of negative samples, which may limit the model's ability to distinguish between positive and negative samples. Conversely, a larger k (e.g., 5) may introduce redundant or noisy samples, which may increase difficulty of model optimization. Therefore, a moderate sampling ratio maintains informative contrast while avoiding excessive noise, enabling the model to capture relational semantics among developers and improving recommendation accuracy.

Then, we observe that the optimal number of attention heads varies across datasets, with $n_h = 4$ achieving the best performance on the Python dataset and $n_h = 2$ on the JavaScript dataset. This suggests that attention heads contribute differently depending on language-specific graph complexity. Interestingly, the model performance declines when using a larger number of heads (e.g., $n_h = 8$). This is likely because excessive heads lead to over-fragmented feature subspaces and increase optimization difficulty, resulting in diluted attention and reduced generalization. Therefore, rather than "more heads yielding better representation", our finding highlights the importance of language-adaptive head configurations to effectively capture API expertise and edge semantics.

6 Conclusion and Future Work

In this paper, we study the problem of recommending potential collaborators to developers based on relationship evaluation between developers and repositories. We construct the GitSAED dataset based on the GitSED dataset by extracting the key APIs of developers and repositories and constructing the heterogeneous graphs based on the collaboration and contribution to the repositories of the developers. We propose the LEHGT method by extending HGT, which uses an LLM to generate the evaluation of edges and feature embeddings for nodes and edges, and incorporates the edge information to enhance the recommender. We conduct extensive experiments to verify the effectiveness of the proposed method.

Our results are of great value to the open source community. At the project level, the model recommends potential collaborators to the developers of the project, which could accelerate the project development, improve the quality of the project code, and promote the sharing of knowledge. From the perspective of developers themselves, the model recommends potential partners to newbies who have just entered the industry, which could reduce the barriers for them to enter the industry. Recommending potential collaborators to freelance developers who are actively online can provide valuable networking and professional development opportunities. From the perspective of the open source community, the model recommends potential collaborators to developers, promotes the connection between developers, prevents the community from becoming rigid or isolated, and maintains the vitality and innovation of the open source community as a whole.

The current study uses APIs as features for relationship evaluation. Future studies can incorporate dynamic interaction data from interactions between developers for comprehensive consideration.

Acknowledgment. This work is supported by the grant from the National Natural Science Foundation of China (Grant Nos. 62277017 and 62137001).

References

1. Ayoub, J., Lotfi, D., Hammouch, A.: Link prediction using betweenness centrality and graph neural networks. Soc. Netw. Anal. Min. **13**(1), 5 (2022)
2. Batista, N.A., Brandão, M.A., Alves, G.B., da Silva, A.P.C., Moro, M.M.: Collaboration strength metrics and analyses on GitHub. In: Proceedings of the International Conference on Web Intelligence, pp. 170–178 (2017)
3. Batoun, M.A., Yung, K.L., Tian, Y., Sayagh, M.: An empirical study on GitHub pull requests' reactions. ACM Trans. Softw. Eng. Methodol. **32**(6), 1–35 (2023)
4. Constantino, K., Souza, M., Zhou, S., Figueiredo, E., Kästner, C.: Perceptions of open-source software developers on collaborations: an interview and survey study. J. Softw. Evol. Process **35**(5), e2393 (2023)
5. Dey, T., Karnauch, A., Mockus, A.: Representation of developer expertise in open source software. In: 2021 IEEE/ACM 43rd International Conference on Software Engineering (ICSE), pp. 995–1007 (2021)
6. Elmahdy, A., Ahn, J., Suh, C., Mohajer, S.: Matrix completion with hierarchical graph side information. Adv. Neural. Inf. Process. Syst. **33**, 9061–9074 (2020)
7. Fan, W., et al.: Graph neural networks for social recommendation. In: The World Wide Web Conference, pp. 417–426 (2019)
8. Gao, C., et al.: A survey of graph neural networks for recommender systems: challenges, methods, and directions. ACM Trans. Recommender Syst. **1**(1), 1–51 (2023)
9. Hamilton, W., Ying, Z., Leskovec, J.: Inductive representation learning on large graphs. Adv. Neural Inf. Process. Syst. **30** (2017)
10. He, X., Bresson, X., Laurent, T., Perold, A., LeCun, Y., Hooi, B.: Harnessing explanations: LLM-to-LM interpreter for enhanced text-attributed graph representation learning. arXiv preprint arXiv:2305.19523 (2023)
11. Hu, Z., Dong, Y., Wang, K., Sun, Y.: Heterogeneous graph transformer. In: Proceedings of the Web Conference 2020, pp. 2704–2710 (2020)

12. Huang, X., Li, J., Yuan, Y.: Link prediction in dynamic social networks combining entropy, causality, and a graph convolutional network model. Entropy **26**(6), 477 (2024)
13. Jo, S., Kwon, G.: The impact of collaboration patterns and network centrality on long-term contribution in GitHub project. Appl. Sci. **15**(1), 352 (2025)
14. Kingma, D.P., Ba, J.: Adam: a method for stochastic optimization. arXiv preprint arXiv:1412.6980 (2014)
15. Kipf, T.N., Welling, M.: Semi-supervised classification with graph convolutional networks. CoRR abs/1609.02907 (2016). http://arxiv.org/abs/1609.02907
16. Koch, S., Klein, D., Johns, M.: The fault in our stars: an analysis of GitHub stars as an importance metric for web source code. In: Workshop on Measurements, Attacks, and Defenses for the Web (MADWeb). vol. 2024 (2024)
17. Lakshmi, T.J., Bhavani, S.D.: Link prediction approach to recommender systems. Computing **106**(7), 2157–2183 (2024)
18. Le, Q., Phan, K., Hui, B., Putri, A.: Using GitHub analytics to assess the quality of collaboration in software engineering teams. In: 2024 IEEE Frontiers in Education Conference (FIE), pp. 1–9. IEEE (2024)
19. Levy, M., Jacoby, A., Goldberg, Y.: Same task, more tokens: the impact of input length on the reasoning performance of large language models (2024). https://arxiv.org/abs/2402.14848
20. Liu, X., Wang, Y., Dong, Q., Lu, X.: Job title prediction as a dual task of expertise prediction in open source software. In: Bifet, A., Krilavičius, T., Miliou, I., Nowaczyk, S. (eds.) Machine Learning and Knowledge Discovery in Databases, Applied Data Science Track. LNCS, pp. 381–396. Springer, Cham (2024). https://doi.org/10.1007/978-3-031-70381-2_24
21. Lv, J., Li, Z., Chen, H., Li, T.: Path-aware Siamese graph neural network for link prediction. In: Sheng, Q.Z., et al. (eds.) International Conference on Advanced Data Mining and Applications, pp. 263–274. Springer, Singapore (2024). https://doi.org/10.1007/978-981-96-0821-8_18
22. Moradi-Jamei, B., Kramer, B.L., Calderón, J.B.S., Korkmaz, G.: Community formation and detection on GitHub collaboration networks. In: Proceedings of the 2021 IEEE/ACM International Conference on Advances in Social Networks Analysis and Mining, pp. 244–251 (2021)
23. Nguyen, T.K., Liu, Z., Fang, Y.: Link prediction on latent heterogeneous graphs (2023). https://arxiv.org/abs/2302.10432
24. Oliveira, G.P., Batista, N.A., Brandão, M.A., Moro, M.M.: Tie strength in GitHub heterogeneous networks. In: Proceedings of the 24th Brazilian Symposium on Multimedia and the Web, pp. 363–370 (2018)
25. Pal, S., Nair, A., Zuo, Z.: Collaborative dynamics in open source software development: unveiling the influence of team interaction and the role of project manager. J. Oper. Manag. **70**(7), 1076–1099 (2024). Publisher Copyright: 2024 The Author(s). Journal of Operations Management published by Wiley Periodicals LLC on behalf of Association for Supply Chain Management Inc. https://doi.org/10.1002/joom.1324
26. Roberts, A., Raffel, C., Shazeer, N.: How much knowledge can you pack into the parameters of a language model? CoRR abs/2002.08910 (2020). https://arxiv.org/abs/2002.08910
27. Safae, H., Mohamed, L., Chehri, A., Yasser, E.M.E.A., Saadane, R.: Link prediction using graph neural networks for recommendation systems. Procedia Comput. Sci. **225**, 4284–4294 (2023)

28. Sun, X., Xu, W., Xia, X., Chen, X., Li, B.: Personalized project recommendation on GitHub. Sci. China Inf. Sci. **61**(5), 050106 (2018)
29. Sun, Y., et al.: Automatically deriving developers' technical expertise from the GitHub social network. In: Proceedings of the 39th IEEE/ACM International Conference on Automated Software Engineering, pp. 2462–2463 (2024)
30. Thakrar, K., Chauhan, A.: GitHub stargazers | building graph-and edge-level prediction algorithms for developer social networks. arXiv preprint arXiv:2502.00058 (2025)
31. Veličković, P., Cucurull, G., Casanova, A., Romero, A., Liò, P., Bengio, Y.: Graph attention networks (2018). https://arxiv.org/abs/1710.10903
32. Wachs, J., Nitecki, M., Schueller, W., Polleres, A.: The geography of open source software: evidence from GitHub. Technol. Forecast. Soc. Chang. **176**, 121478 (2022)
33. Xu, K., Hu, W., Leskovec, J., Jegelka, S.: How powerful are graph neural networks? (2019). https://arxiv.org/abs/1810.00826
34. Yang, S., et al.: Inductive link prediction with interactive structure learning on attributed graph. In: Joint European Conference on Machine Learning and Knowledge Discovery in Databases, pp. 383–398. Springer, Cham (2021). https://doi.org/10.1007/978-3-030-86520-7_24

Current Status and Future Trends of Evaluation Methods for Artificial Intelligence Chips

Xiaotong Yu(✉), Yi Zhang, and Chengcheng Fu

Aerospace Science and Industry Defense Technology Research and Test Center, China Innovation Center for Component Application Verification Technology, Shanghai, China
iamfcc@buaa.edu.cn

Abstract. As specialized chips designed to accelerate artificial intelligence (AI) algorithms, with core capability in enabling large-scale parallel computing, AI chips have been widely adopted in diverse fields, including smart home appliances, robotics, mobile terminals, and automotive manufacturing. This extensive application has further drawn industry attention to verifying whether their computing performance meets the demands of practical scenarios. However, existing AI chip evaluation systems still lack systematic integration, and conventional quality assurance methodologies cannot fully address the uniqueness of AI chips. As an emerging and indispensable process, AI chip evaluation plays a pivotal role in guiding the selection and practical deployment of AI chips. This work systematically sorts out the current status, inherent characteristics, and relevant standards of domestic and international existing AI chip evaluation systems. Furthermore, it puts forward targeted suggestions for future research directions of AI chip evaluation methods, aiming to provide a reference for optimizing AI chip evaluation systems and promoting the healthy development of the AI chip industry.

Keywords: Artificial intelligence chip · Chip selection · Evaluation standard · Evaluation metrics · Benchmark

1 Introduction

In recent years, artificial intelligence (AI) technology has advanced rapidly in both industrial and academic domains. Innovative application scenarios that integrate AI with intelligent drones, intelligent vehicles, and other fields have emerged consecutively. However, to promote their respective products, various manufacturers have developed corresponding strategies, while all algorithm, software, and hardware vendors have launched proprietary products supporting AI training and inference [1]. Notably, to enhance product promotion, manufacturers have established a multitude of evaluation benchmarks that are only applicable to their specific products. Meanwhile, the challenges in mutual recognition of

J. Zhan et al. (Eds.): Bench 2025, LNCS 16471, pp. 209–220, 2026.
https://doi.org/10.1007/978-981-95-9694-2_15

AI test benchmarks, coupled with their limited practical implementation, have impeded the development of AI products throughout the industrial chain [2].

In the computer field, the most extensive and successful application of benchmark testing lies in performance testing, which primarily measures key metrics such as response time, transmission rate, and throughput. Beyond performance evaluation, benchmark testing can also be applied to function verification, operability assessment, and the validation of applicability for data processing development. Specifically, in the field of computing product testing, benchmark testing is utilized to evaluate the performance of both hardware and software systems. By executing one or more sets of standard test programs, it generates comparable and quantifiable indicator data, which further serves as a critical basis for product selection and quality optimization.

How to design a multi-dimensional benchmarking scheme for mainstream industrial AI chips based on real-world application scenarios, generate an overall performance score for each AI chip, thereby evaluating the performance of different AI chips across diverse scenarios, and further provide targeted product selection recommendations for end-users, has emerged as an urgent issue to be addressed in the field [18].

2 Fundamentals and Core Attributes of AI Chips

2.1 Concept and Current Development Status of AI Chips

AI chips are integrated circuits specifically designed or optimized to efficiently execute the core computational tasks of artificial intelligence algorithms, serving as the fundamental hardware underpinning the development of intelligent technologies. The computational power of AI chips stems from their large-scale parallel architecture, constructed via the integration of massive numbers of transistors. Consequently, AI chips significantly outperform CPUs in both throughput and energy efficiency, delivering orders-of-magnitude performance improvements in practical applications [3]. According to a Next Move Strategy Consulting research report, the global AI chip market is expected to grow from approximately 52.9 billion in 2024 to over 295.5 billion by 2030, reflecting a compound annual growth rate (CAGR) of 33.2

The global AI chip industry is flourishing. Driven by factors such as cost, differentiated competition, innovation, and supply chain diversification, a growing number of manufacturers have begun designing self-developed AI chips. Companies like NVIDIA, Google, and Intel have all launched dedicated AI chips [4], which are widely deployed in fields such as cloud computing, edge computing, autonomous driving, and fifth-generation mobile communications (5G).

In recent years, against the backdrop of the United States continuously strengthening export controls on high-end chips, AI chip industry in China has gradually transitioned from keeping pace with international technological advancements to running shoulder-to-shoulder with global leaders, driven by both policy support and market demand. Currently, leading domestic companies have established multiple differentiated technology pathways: Huawei

Ascend 910 chip integrates more than 20 billion transistors and delivers performance comparable to mainstream international chips when handling complex AI tasks; Baidu Kunlun Core focuses on large-scale model cluster optimization and has achieved deployment on a scale of ten thousand cards in areas such as internet search and multimodal processing; Cambricon Siyuan 370, utilizing Chiplet technology, delivers 256 TOPS of computing power and is dedicated to general-purpose intelligent computing scenarios; Horizon Robotics' Journey series chips focus on in-vehicle edge computing and hold a leading position in the smart driving market due to their low-latency characteristics. Overall, despite facing technical constraints such as advanced process technologies, AI chip industry in China has initially built a competitive ecosystem across multiple technological pathways.

2.2 Deployment Locations and Functional Classification of AI Chips

Based on application scenarios and performance requirements, AI chips are deployed across three tiers: cloud, edge, and endpoint. According to actual task demands, they can be categorized as training or inference chips. Cloud chips serve as the computational core and are deployed in large server clusters to focus on high-throughput, massively parallel AI model training and complex inference tasks. Examples include high-end chips like the NVIDIA H100, which provide the computational foundation for large language models, such as ChatGPT, and cloud computing. Edge chips are located near the network edge or at the beginning of a scenario and handle real-time inference and data processing tasks. Chips such as Huawei Ascend series and Cambricon Shenwei are widely used in this area. Terminal chips are embedded in smartphones, smart home devices, and wearables. They focus on localized, low-power, instant inference. Qualcomm Snapdragon series chips are an example of this type of chip. They enable functions like image enhancement and voice interaction while safeguarding user data privacy. The "cloud-edge-terminal" collaborative deployment architecture uses specialized chips at each tier to efficiently meet diverse application demands regarding computational scale, response speed, and energy efficiency.

2.3 Architecture of AI Chips

From a technical architecture perspective, AI chips fall into three main categories: Graphics Processing Units (GPU), Field-Programmable Gate Arrays (FPGA), and Application-Specific Integrated Circuits (ASIC) [5,6]. GPUs, represented by NVIDIA's products, have become the mainstream choice for AI training and inference due to their powerful parallel computing capabilities and mature software ecosystem, though they consume relatively high power. FPGAs offer hardware programmability, enabling the dynamic reconfiguration of logic units based on specific algorithms. They excel in scenarios requiring low latency and high flexibility, such as edge computing and communication acceleration. FPGAs achieve a good balance between performance and power efficiency. Major manufacturers include Xilinx and Altera, as well as domestic companies such as

Fudan Microelectronics. ASICs are customized for specific applications, achieving extreme performance and energy efficiency by hardening the hardware logic for the intended tasks. Despite their lack of flexibility and high development costs, their advantages in terms of high computational density, cost control, and algorithm compatibility are increasingly valued by manufacturers and users. Examples include Google's TPU, Broadcom's XPU, and various NPUs.

Beyond mainstream architectures, heterogeneous computing has become an important trend in AI chip development. The core concept of heterogeneous computing involves integrating different types of processors, such as CPUs, GPUs, FPGAs, and ASICs, into a single system. These processors collaborate by leveraging their respective strengths to achieve optimal performance and efficiency. The "CPU + GPU" combination is currently the dominant form of heterogeneous computing in AI and is widely used for high-performance computing and AI training tasks [7].

3 Evaluation Benchmarks for AI Chips

3.1 MLPerf

Originating in 2018, MLPerf is a platform that provides universal evaluation benchmarks for the performance of AI learning hardware and software, as well as strategies for improvement. Built on the Fathom project [8] from Harvard University and the DAWNBench project [9] from Stanford University, MLPerf draws on the former's adoption of a variety of AI tasks in the evaluation process to ensure sufficient representativeness, and the latter's use of comparative evaluation metrics to ensure fairness. Owing to its detailed task classification and simple metrics, numerous vendors have submitted the test results of their products based on its benchmarks. By August 2025, MLPerf has released five rounds of training test results.

The latest version of MLPerf is the MLPerf Training v5.0 benchmark, which is used to measure the speed at which a platform trains a model to a predefined quality value. It covers the following areas: large language models (LLMs) pretraining, LLM fine-tuning, text-to-image generation, recommendation systems, graph neural networks, natural language processing, and object detection, etc. In August 2025, MLPerf released the MLPerf Storage v2.0 storage performance benchmark. Designed to evaluate data-intensive applications under real-world AI workloads, this benchmark not only emphasizes traditional performance indicators such as throughput bandwidth and IO throughput but also focuses on typical scenarios including large-scale concurrency, massive data processing, large-scale training, and checkpoint saving and restoration.

3.2 AI-Benchmark

First released by ETH Zurich in 2018, AI-Benchmark [10] is specifically designed to evaluate the performance of AI chips in mobile devices (such as smartphones) when running deep learning models. AI-Benchmark conducts tests based on the Android Neural Network API and also supports customized programs from chip manufacturers. It enables compatibility with chips of different vendors by integrating various TensorFlow Lite Delegates. By August 2025, AI-Benchmark has launched Version 6.0, which is developed for next-generation AI accelerators. This version introduces a host of new tests and workloads, including those based on the Transformer architecture, LLM, and even supports running the stable diffusion network directly on devices.

3.3 AI-Matrix

Launched by Alibaba in 2018, AI Matrix [11] is an AI benchmarking platform aimed at measuring the performance of AI hardware platforms and software frameworks, identifying various factors that affect AI hardware performance, and helping users optimize hardware design. AI Matrix enables performance evaluation at different granularity levels, including basic matrix multiplication tests, tests for common operation layers of convolutional neural networks and recurrent neural networks, tests for commonly used network models, and tests based on operation feature synthesis.

3.4 AImark

Released by Ludashi in 2018, AImark [12] is an AI performance evaluation tool designed for mobile devices. In terms of hardware assessment, it targets the module responsible for AI computing within the SoC of the device. Between 2017 and 2018, smartphone chips began to integrate dedicated AI processing units on a large scale. However, traditional CPU/GPU tests failed to accurately measure this newly added dedicated AI computing power. The evaluation method of AImark can be summarized as quantitative scoring based on end-to-end inference tasks, where an overall AImark score is used to represent the comprehensive speed of a chip when running these mainstream AI models. Up to now, the latest version of AImark is 4.9, which supports the latest chips such as Qualcomm Snapdragon 7 Gen 3.

3.5 Mobile AI Benchmark

Mobile AI Benchmark is a mobile AI performance benchmarking tool released by Xiaomi Group in 2018. Its evaluation method leverages mobile inference frameworks and interfaces to allocate the inference computing tasks of each model to different hardware backends, followed by repeated inference computations for multiple times. This tool supports a variety of deep learning frameworks and covers different types of hardware devices, including CPU, GPU, DSP, and NPU to evaluate the performance of models on different hardware.

3.6 AIIA DNN Benchmark

Released by the China AI Industry Development Alliance (AIIA) in 2019, the AIIA DNN Benchmark [13] is a benchmarking method for edge-side AI chips, which reflects the performance indicators of AI processors or accelerators. This method is capable of distinguishing the performance comparison results between integer-type and floating-point-type models. Up to now, the latest version of the AIIA DNN Benchmark is v0.6.

3.7 AIPerf

To address the gap in the field of AI computing power evaluation for large-model computing systems, Tsinghua University and Peng Cheng Laboratory jointly developed and launched the AI computing power benchmark program ALPerf Benchmark (AIPerf) in 2020 [14]. Up to August 2025, AIPerf consists of three ranking lists: AIPerf evaluates the training performance of intelligent computing capabilities using classical convolutional models; AIPerf-LLM assesses the training performance of intelligent computing capabilities with LLMs; AIPerf-Inference measures the inference performance of intelligent computing capabilities. Users can optimize system performance by adjusting various parameters of each application. In addition, they can use a customized inference engine to fully utilize the functions of the underlying hardware.

3.8 AI-Rank

To establish multi-dimensional evaluation indicators for assessing the comprehensive performance of tested systems, the Zhongguancun Institute of Artificial Intelligence proposed AI-Rank [15] in 2020, which is an open-source benchmarking system oriented to the AI industry. AI-Rank covers three evaluation directions, including hardware infrastructure, general algorithm capabilities, and vertical industry scenarios. For the evaluation of hardware infrastructure, under given software environments and AI tasks, multi-dimensional indicator tests are conducted on different types of hardware such as edge devices and mobile devices, etc. to assess the performance of various hardware (Table 1).

4 Evaluation and Testing Standards for AI Chips

Multiple AI chip evaluation and testing standards have been released domestically. The China electronics standardization institute has issued T/ CESA 1121–2020 AI chips-test metrics and test method of deep learning chips for terminal side, T/ CESA 1120–2020 AI chips-test metrics and test method of deep learning chips for edge side, T/ CESA 1119-2020 AI chips-test metrics and test method of deep learning chips for cloud side. These three standards respectively specify the technical requirements, testing methods, and testing indicators for deeping chips on the terminal side, edge side and cloud side. The China Academy of information and communications technology has released YD/T 3944-2021 evaluation

Table 1. Comparison of AI Benchmarks.

Benchmark	Year	Coverage Scope	Evaluation Method	Evaluation Metrics
MLPerf	2018	Image classification, medical image segmentation, object detection, et al.	Training: Divided into closed-model division and open-model division. Inference: Use the load generator tool to simulate the real behavior of the tested inference system through four scenarios to evaluate system performance.	Training: Clock time taken to train a model on the dataset to reach the quality target, including total time for model construction, data preprocessing, training, and quality testing. Inference: Metrics include latency and throughput, etc.
AI-Benchmark	2018	Object recognition, object classification, face recognition, et al.	Run a series of standardized neural network models locally on the device, and tests their execution speed and accuracy.	Inferences per second or processing time, comprehensive score.
AI Matrix	2018	Operator level: common operators; Macro-benchmark: models covering computer vision, et al.; Micro-benchmark: focus on operations such as matrix multiplication and tensor operations.	Micro benchmark, Layer based-benchmarks, macro benchmarks, synthetic benchmarks.	Time consumption, energy consumption, hardware utilization, etc.
AImark	2018	Covers AI modules of mainstream mobile SoC. Test scenarios include: image tasks; text tasks; real-time applications.	Image recognition, portrait segmentation, image super-resolution, natural language processing, et al.	Quantitative values combining speed and accuracy; inference speed; accuracy; energy efficiency ratio; compatibility.
Mobile AI Benchmark	2018	Natural language processing, multimodality, trust and security.	Runs multiple neural network models on the device, and records inference latency and power consumption of each hardware unit.	Latency, throughput, energy efficiency; finally summarized into a weighted comprehensive score.
AIIA DNN Benchmark	2019	Image classification, object detection, semantic segmentation, super-resolution.	Adopt end-to-end real inference task testing (balancing performance and accuracy).	Throughput, latency, algorithm accuracy, power consumption (including metrics such as Top-1, Top-5, mAP, mIoU, PSNR).
AIPerf	2020	Question answering, visual question answering (VQA), image recognition, text-to-image generation, text-to-video generation.	Based on Microsoft NNI open-source framework, with automated machine learning as the workload; use network morphism for network structure search and tree-structured Parzen estimator for hyperparameter search to find neural network structures or hyperparameters with higher accuracy.	Operations per second (OPS) as the main metric to quantify AI performance.
AI-Rank	2020	Computer vision, natural language processing, intelligent recommendation.	Use a consistent framework and model; specifies the same model structure, dataset, and accuracy requirements for testing.	Throughput, latency; Energy efficiency metrics: Performance-power ratio; Cost metrics: Performance/price.

method for artificial intelligence chip benchmark, which specifies the benchmark testing schemes, testing scenarios, evaluation methods, and measurement indicators for AI chips. Comparatively, international standards like ITU-T F.748.11-2020 align closely with this performance-focused benchmarking approach, while emerging frameworks such as ISO/IEC TS 25058:2024 advocate for a more comprehensive evaluation paradigm. This broader perspective encompasses not only performance metrics but also critical dimensions including functional suitability, security, reliability, and ethical risk mitigation, thereby presenting a complementary and evolutionary pathway for future standard development (Tables 2, 3 and 4).

5 Existing Problems and Future Research Directions

The core differences between AI chip performance benchmark and traditional CPU/GPU benchmark are mainly reflected in the following three aspects: (1) Hardware implementation schemes for AI computing capabilities are highly diverse, leading to a lack of universal evaluation methodologies that can cover all application scenarios; (2) The performance of AI computing capabilities exhibits a strong coupling relationship with software systems, including key components such as algorithm design, dataset characteristics, data preprocessing procedures, and model optimization strategies; (3) The industry has not yet established a universally recognized and unified evaluation index system for AI computing capabilities. Against this backdrop, the following five directions should be prioritized when designing AI chip evaluation schemes:

5.1 Differential Comparison of Hardware Unit Performance

Currently, there are significant differences in hardware architectures and types of acceleration units adopted by chip manufacturers. In addition to traditional CPU and GPU, dedicated units for enhancing AI computing power also include NPU (Neural Processing Units), APU (AI Processing Units), DSP (Digital Signal Processors), etc. Manufacturers usually provide exclusive calling interfaces for different hardware units. Therefore, the evaluation scheme needs to design separate test scenarios for various hardware units of the chip, and clarify the performance advantages and application scopes of different hardware units through multi-dimensional comparisons [17].

5.2 Evaluation Orientation Centered on Actual Inference Scenarios

The performance evaluation of AI chips should prioritize focusing on the inference tasks of post-trained neural networks: on the one hand, it is necessary to select neural network models widely used in high-frequency user scenarios as test carriers; on the other hand, it is required to execute inference processes based on standard test sets, and combine quantitative indicators (such as AI computing power value, inference latency, throughput) and qualitative indicators (such as SDK compatibility, usability, and functional integrity) to build a comprehensive performance evaluation dimension.

Table 2. Comparison of Test Objects.

Standard	Test Object
YD/T 3944-2021 Evaluation method for artificial intelligence chip benchmark	AI acceleration cards or computing cards, modules specifically designed to handle massive computing tasks in AI applications. Their forms include but are not limited to GPU, FPGA, and ASIC.
T/ CESA 1121-2020 AI chips-test metrics and test method of deep learning chips for terminal side	Edge-side AI processors, in specific forms of: Control hosts with edge-side AI processor chips (cards/sticks): Edge-side deep learning chips used in the form of chips, cards, or sticks (e.g., AI chips/cards/sticks such as GPU, FPGA, and ASIC), which can be connected to the test host via interfaces like PCIe and USB.
T/ CESA 1120-2020 AI chips-test metrics and test method of deep learning chips for edge side	Training: Edge-side infrastructure, including but not limited to private cloud instances and public cloud instances. Inference:Tested systems with built-in edge-side deep learning chips (or boards): AI chips (cards) such as GPUs, FPGAs, and ASICs used in the form of chips or boards. These chips/cards can be connected to the tested system via interfaces like PCIe and interact with the test host to complete the test.
T/ CESA 1119-2020 AI chips-test metrics and test method of deep learning chips for cloud side	Training: Cloud infrastructure suitable for deep learning models, including but not limited to private cloud instances and public cloud instances. Inference: Tested systems with built-in cloud-side deep learning chips (or boards): AI chips (e.g., GPU, FPGA, and ASIC) used in the form of chips or boards, which can be connected to the tested system via interfaces like PCIe and further interact with the test host to complete the test; Private cloud instances equipped with AI processors.
ITU-T F.748.11-2020 Metrics and evaluation methods for a deep neural network processor benchmark	Deep neural network processors for AI systems, including but not limited to GPU, NPU, FPGA, and ASIC. Devices under test may be in the form of chips, accelerator cards, or modules, designed to support large-scale neural network training and inference tasks. Typical application scenarios cover image classification, object detection, segmentation, super-resolution, face recognition, machine translation, speech recognition, and recommendation systems.
ISO/IEC TS 25058:2024 Systems and software engineering-Systems and software Quality Requirements and Evaluation (SQuaRE)-Guidance for quality evaluation of artificial intelligence (AI) systems	Artificial intelligence systems of various types and scales, including but not limited to machine learning, reasoning, planning, and perception systems. Test objects encompass AI software, integrated AI solutions, and AI-enabled platforms—focusing on quality attributes such as functional suitability, performance efficiency, compatibility, and usability.

5.3 Optimization and Iteration of Test Models and Datasets

Limitations in the hardware architecture and operator support of AI chips can prevent specific operators within typical neural network models from execut-

Table 3. Comparison of Test Evaluation Indicators.

	Evaluation Indicator	YD/T 3944-2021	T/ CESA 1121-2020	T/ CESA 1120-2020	T/ CESA 1119-2020	ITU-T F.748.11-2020	ISO/IEC TS 25058:2024
Train	Training Latency	✓	×	✓	✓	✓	✓
	Accuracy	✓	×	×	×	✓	✓
	Training Power Consumption	✓	×	✓	✓	×	✓
	Linear Speedup Ratio	✓	×	×	×	×	×
	Training Computing Cost	✓	×	×	×	×	✓
Test	Inference Latency	✓	✓	✓	✓	✓	✓
	Throughput	✓	✓	✓	✓	✓	✓
	Inference Power Consumption	✓	✓	✓	✓	✓	✓
	Accelerator Utilization	✓	×	×	×	✓	×
	Energy Efficiency Ratio	✓	✓	✓	✓	✓	✓
	Load Usage Statistics of Main Control Core	✓	×	×	×	×	✓
	Inference Computing Cost	✓	×	×	×	×	✓
	Average Forward Inference Rate	×	✓	✓	✓	×	×
	Inference Accuracy	×	✓	✓	✓	✓	✓

Table 4. Comparison of Test Scenario.

Test Scenario		YD/T 3944-2021	T/ CESA 1121-2020	T/ CESA 1120-2020	T/ CESA 1119-2020	ITU-T F.748.11-2020	ISO/IEC TS 25058:2024
Machine Vision Tasks	Image Classification	✓	✓	✓	✓	✓	×
	Object Detection	✓	✓	✓	✓	✓	×
	Super-Resolution	✓	✓	×	×	✓	×
	Image Semantic Segmentation	✓	✓	✓	✓	✓	×
	Face Recognition	×	✓	✓	✓	✓	×
Speech Processing Tasks	Local Speech Wake-Up	✓	✓	✓	✓	×	×
Natural Language Processing	Speech Recognition	×	×	×	✓	✓	×
	Reading Comprehension	×	×	×	✓	✓	×
	Machine Translation	✓	×	×	×	×	×
Edge Gateway	Load	×	×	✓	×	×	×
Industrial IoT Tasks	Identification	×	×	×	✓	×	×

ing correctly on the target chip. This challenge prompts the need for continuous research into benchmark models and their corresponding datasets. Efforts should focus on two key areas: first, expanding the coverage of the model library by incorporating lightweight and specialized models adapted to diverse chip architectures [16,18]; second, optimizing the representativeness of datasets to ensure they accurately reflect the data distribution of real-world application scenarios, thereby preventing the distortion of evaluation results due to constraints in the models or datasets.

5.4 Expansion and Construction of Multi-Dimensional Evaluation Systems

Existing evaluation schemes predominantly focus on technical performance. In the future, it is necessary to further incorporate cost-effectiveness (e.g., cost per unit computing power, energy efficiency) and social impact (e.g., computing power accessibility, technological inclusiveness) into the evaluation scope, thereby forming a "technical performance-cost effectiveness-social value" trinity evaluation research system. It should be clarified that objective, fair, and scientific evaluation standards, systems, tools, and services serve as the core cornerstone and key driving force for advancing the technological iteration of AI chips and facilitating the healthy development of the industry.

6 Conclusion

There is a significant discrepancy between the rapid development of AI chips in the fields of neural networks and machine learning, and the immaturity of their derived evaluation systems and frameworks. Currently, AI chip evaluation faces challenges such as the diversity of systems, frameworks, scenarios, and models built on top of hardware. By means of hardware-software collaboration, open-source ecosystem construction, and joint participation from the industry, establishing an authoritative and unified test benchmark system can effectively guide the full-lifecycle development of AI models and products. By integrating the development status, characteristics, and standards of domestic and international AI evaluation benchmarks, this work puts forward relevant suggestions for the future research directions of AI chip evaluation methods, with the aim of providing references for the further development of this field.

Disclosure of Interests.. The authors have no competing interests to declare that are relevant to the content of this article.

References

1. Kevitt, P.M., Hegner, S.J., Norvig, P., Wilensky, R.: Artificial intelligence review. Sensors **3**, 95–99 (2018)
2. Gwennap, L.: AI benchmark remain immature. Mcroprocessor Rep. **33**(1:10-13), (2019)
3. Darney, P.E.: A review on artificial intelligence chip. Recent Res. Rev. J. **1**(1), 99–109 (2022). https://doi.org/10.36548/RRRJ.2023.1.009
4. Pang, G.: The AI chip race. IEEE Intell. Syst. **37**(2), 111–112 (2022). https://doi.org/10.1109/MIS.2022.3165668
5. Gao, R., Song, M.: Performance comparative analysis of artificial intelligence chip technology. In: 2021 2nd International Conference on Computer Engineering and Intelligent Control (ICCEIC), pp. 149–153. IEEE, Chongqing, China (2021). https://doi.org/10.1109/ICCEIC54227.2021.00037
6. Al-Ali, F., Gamage, D., Nanayakkara, H., Mehdipour, F., Ray, S.: Novel casestudy and benchmarking of AlexNet for edge AI: From CPU and GPU to FPGA. In: 2020 IEEE Canadian Conference on Electrical and Computer Engineering (CCECE), pp. 1–4. IEEE, London, ON, Canada (2020). https://doi.org/10.1109/CCECE47787.2020.9255739

7. Jayanth, R., Gupta, N., Prasanna, V.: Benchmarking edge AI platforms for high-performance ML inference. In: 2024 IEEE High Performance Extreme Computing Conference (HPEC), pp. 1–7. IEEE, Wakefield, MA, USA (2024). https://doi.org/10.1109/HPEC62836.2024.10938499
8. Adolf, R., Rama, S., Reagen, B., Wei, G. Y., Brooks, D.: Fathom: reference workloads for modern deep learning methods. In: 2016 IEEE International Symposium on Workload Characterization (IISWC), pp. 1–10. IEEE (2016)
9. Coleman, C., et al.: Dawnbench: an end-to-end deep learning benchmark and competition. Training **100**(101), 102 (2017)
10. Ignatov, A., et al.: AI benchmark: running deep neural networks on android smartphones. In: European Conference on Computer Vision (2019)
11. AI Matrix, https://aimatix.ai/zh-cn/, https://real-ai.cn/
12. AImark, https://www.ludashi.com/page/aimark.php
13. AIIA DNN benchmark overview, https://github.com/AIIABenchmark/AIIA-DNN-benchmark
14. Ren, Z., et al.: AIPerf: automated machine learning as an AHPC benchmark. Big Data Min. Analytics **3**, 208–220 (2021)
15. AI-Rank, https://github.com/wanghuacoder/AI-Rank
16. Luo, C., He, X., Zhan, J., Wang, L., Gao, W., Dai, J.: Comparison and benchmarking of ai models and frameworks on mobile devices. arXiv preprint arXiv:2005.05085 (2020)
17. Luo, C., et al.: AIoT bench: towards comprehensive benchmarking mobile and embedded device intelligence. In: International Symposium on Benchmarking, Measuring and Optimization, pp. 31–35 (2018)
18. Tang, F., et al.: AIBench training: balanced industry-standard AI training benchmarking. In 2021 IEEE International Symposium on Performance Analysis of Systems and Software, pp. 24–35 (2021)

Phys-TSGAIN: A Physics-Informed Generative Imputation for Data Completeness Governance of Lithium-Ion Battery Time Series

Wei Zuo[1], Xinyue Jin[2], Meng Xu[1], Yue Liu[1(✉)], and Siqi Shi[3(✉)]

[1] School of Computer Engineering and Science, Shanghai University, Shanghai, China
yueliu@shu.edu.cn
[2] Materials Genome Institute of Shanghai University, Shanghai University, Shanghai, China
[3] School of Materials Science and Engineering, Shanghai University, Shanghai, China
sqshi@shu.edu.cn

Abstract. Data completeness is a prerequisite for accurate life prediction and health management of Lithium-ion Batteries (LIBs). However, real-world battery time series often suffer from complex missing patterns due to sensor malfunctions, transmission errors, or human oversight. Existing imputation methods, which largely rely on statistical patterns, often fail to maintain physical consistency and lack domain knowledge guidance. To address this, we propose Phys-TSGAIN, a physics-informed generative imputation framework for LIBs data completeness governance. Unlike purely data-driven approaches, this method explicitly embeds electrochemical degradation mechanisms into a Generative Adversarial Network (GAN) through a novel Physics-Informed Knowledge Module and a Dual-Channel Hint Mechanism. Theoretically, we provide rigorous derivations to guarantee the unbiasedness, effectiveness, and convergence of the proposed algorithm. Extensive experiments across five datasets demonstrate that Phys-TSGAIN significantly outperforms traditional and state-of-the-art baselines under various missingness scenarios (MCAR, MAR, and MNAR). Specifically, the method achieves an average RMSE of 0.076 and MAE of 0.069 in downstream prediction tasks, reducing the error by approximately 73% compared to competing methods. Phys-TSGAIN effectively bridges the gap between data-driven learning and physical priors, providing high-quality data support for reliable battery modeling.

Keywords: Domain knowledge · Time series completeness · Lithium battery · Generative model

1 Introduction

The completeness of time series data is a prerequisite for reliable analysis and accurate life prediction in Lithium-ion Battery (LIB) management systems. How-

J. Zhan et al. (Eds.): Bench 2025, LNCS 16471, pp. 221–237, 2026.
https://doi.org/10.1007/978-981-95-9694-2_16

ever, in real-world scenarios, data collected from Battery Management Systems (BMS) are often incomplete due to sensor malfunctions, transmission errors, or human oversight [1,2]. These missing values, if not properly handled, obscure temporal patterns and significantly degrade the performance of downstream prognostic tasks.

To address this issue, existing approaches can be broadly categorized into three types: statistical methods, machine learning methods, and deep learning methods.

Statistical methods, such as mean/median imputation [1,2], Last Observation Carried Forward (LOCF) [3], and various interpolation techniques (linear, B-spline, polynomial) [4–6], are widely adopted due to their simplicity and low computational cost. These approaches are effective when the missing proportion is small or the series exhibits local smoothness. However, they often fail to capture long-range dependencies or nonlinear dynamics, inevitably introducing bias when gaps are large or degradation patterns are complex.

Machine learning methods treat missing value imputation as a predictive modeling task. Models such as Support Vector Regression (SVR) [7], Random Forests (RF) [8], and Ridge Regression [9] leverage historical data to infer missing points. While strategies like ensemble learning and clustering-based imputation [10–12] improve robustness, these methods remain sensitive to feature engineering and are often limited in modeling the inherent temporal sequence of battery aging.

Deep learning has emerged as a powerful paradigm by automatically extracting temporal representations. Discriminative approaches, including LSTM-based [13,14] and Transformer-based models [15,16], excel in capturing long-range dependencies but face challenges with irregular sampling and uncertainty quantification. Generative approaches, particularly those based on Generative Adversarial Networks (GANs), provide a complementary path. The GAIN framework [17] pioneered GAN-based imputation, inspiring extensions such as E^2GAN [18], Pix2Pix-based [19] and ImputeGAN [20]. These models achieve state-of-the-art performance by generating realistic distributions. However, purely data-driven generation may overlook domain constraints, occasionally producing physically implausible imputations (e.g., capacity regeneration without charging). Table 1 summarizes the suitability of these methods.

Motivated by these limitations, this work proposes **Phys-TSGAIN**, a physics-informed generative adversarial network for time series imputation. Unlike prior methods that rely solely on statistical patterns, Phys-TSGAIN explicitly embeds electrochemical domain knowledge into the adversarial learning process. Our specific contributions are as follows:

1. We design a novel hybrid architecture that couples a physical degradation model (bi-exponential decay with linear drift) with the generator. This constrains the imputation search space within domain-feasible boundaries.
2. We provide theoretical derivations to guarantee the unbiasedness, effectiveness, and convergence of the algorithm, proving that the optimal generator distribution aligns with the true data distribution.

Table 1. Literature Review of Time Series Data Completeness Governance Methods

Classification	Method	Related Work	Ref.	Suitability	Domain Knowledge
Statistical-based method	Statistical filling	MEAN	[1]	Low	–
		MEDIAD	[2]	Low	–
		Backfill (BF)	[3]	Middle	–
	Statistical prediction	LOCF	[4]	Middle	–
		Interpolation	[5]	Middle-High	–
		Polynomial	[6]	Middle	–
Machine learning-based methods	Independent prediction	B-splines	[7]	Middle	Low
		SMA	[8]	Middle	Low
		SVR	[9]	Low-Middle	Low
	Combination prediction	RF	[10]	Middle	Low
		Ridge	[11, 12]	Middle-High	Low
Deep learning-based methods	Discrimination model	LSTM-based	[13, 14]	High	Low
		Transformer-based	[15, 16]	High	Low
	Generative model	GAN-based	[17–20]	High	–
		Proposed method	–	**High**	**High**

3. We conduct extensive experiments on five real-world battery datasets. Results demonstrate that Phys-TSGAIN reduces the error of downstream prediction tasks by approximately 73% compared to competing methods, showing robust generalization across MCAR, MAR, and MNAR missingness mechanisms.

2 Problem Definition and Model Design

Overview of the Framework. To address the challenge of data incompleteness in lithium-ion battery time series, we propose **Phys-TSGAIN**, a physics-informed generative framework. As illustrated in Fig. 1, the architecture consists of three key components: (1) a **Physics-Informed Knowledge Module** (Φ) that provides domain-specific degradation priors; (2) a **Dual-Channel Hint Mechanism** that combines random masking with physics-based uncertainty; and (3) a **WGAN-GP-based Imputation Network** that learns to generate statistically consistent and physically plausible values. The interplay between these modules ensures that the imputed data not only fits the observed distribution but also adheres to electrochemical degradation laws.

2.1 Problem Definition

Let the true complete sequence of length T be denoted as $X = \{X_1, X_2, \ldots, X_T\} \in \mathbb{R}^T$, and the mask vector as $M = \{M_1, M_2, \ldots, M_T\} \in \{0,1\}^T$. The mask indicates the missingness status: if X_t is observed, then $M_t = 1$; if X_t is missing, then $M_t = 0$.

Consequently, the masked sequence $\tilde{X} = X \odot M$ can be defined as:

$$\tilde{X}_t = \begin{cases} X_t, & \text{if } M_t = 1 \\ 0, & \text{if } M_t = 0 \end{cases} \quad (1)$$

Suppose we observe n independent sequence samples, denoted as $\mathcal{D} = \{(\mathbf{x}_i, \mathbf{m}_i)\}_{i=1}^n$. The objective of our model is to generate multiple samples for each missing position from the conditional distribution $P(X|\tilde{X}, M)$, thereby capturing imputation uncertainty through a multiple imputation strategy.

2.2 Physics-Informed Knowledge Module Φ

Lithium-ion battery degradation typically exhibits a nonlinear trend characterized by a gradual decline in the early stage followed by accelerated aging in the later stage. To embed this domain knowledge, we assume that the observed sequence $x_{obs} = x \odot m$ follows a *bi-exponential decay with a linear trend model.*

For each time step t, we introduce learnable parameters and define the physics-informed predicted value x_{phy} as:

$$x_{phy}(t) = A_1 \exp(-\alpha_1 t) + A_2 \exp(-\alpha_2 t) + \beta t + b, \quad t = 1, 2, \ldots, T \tag{2}$$

Here, α_1, α_2 control the decay rates, while A_1, A_2 determine the weights of the exponential components. The parameter β captures the linear drift, and b represents the intercept term. All six parameters ($\theta_{phy} = \{A_1, A_2, \alpha_1, \alpha_2, \beta, b\}$) are learnable and are automatically optimized during the training process to fit the observed data points.

2.3 Dual-Channel Hint Mechanism (DHint)

To strengthen the discriminator's ability to distinguish between observed and imputed values, we propose a **Dual-Channel Hint Mechanism**. This incorporates the standard random hint mechanism H_{rand} from the original GAIN framework and a novel physics-based uncertainty hint H_{phys}.

Specifically, the random hint mechanism H_{rand} reveals partial mask information to the discriminator. It is generated by discarding entries of M with a probability λ_{hint}, where B_t follows a Bernoulli distribution:

$$H_{rand}(t) = M_t \cdot B_t, \quad B_t \sim \text{Bernoulli}(\lambda_{hint}) \tag{3}$$

The physics-based uncertainty hint H_{phys} is determined by the residual between the physics-informed prediction x_{phy} and the observed value x_{obs}. It provides the network with information about how much the current data deviates from the physical prior:

$$H_{phys}(t) = \frac{|x_{obs}(t) - x_{phy}(t)|}{|x_{obs}(t)| + \epsilon}, \quad \epsilon = 10^{-6} \tag{4}$$

By concatenating these two channels, we obtain the final Dual-Channel Hint vector:

$$DHint_t = [H_{rand}(t), H_{phys}(t)] \in \mathbb{R}^2 \tag{5}$$

2.4 WGAN-GP Adversarial Network

The core of Phys-TSGAIN is a Generative Adversarial Network (GAN) optimized using the Wasserstein distance with Gradient Penalty (WGAN-GP).

Generator. The generator takes as input the observed values x_{obs}, the mask M, the physics-informed predictions x_{phy}, a random noise vector Z, and sinusoidal positional encoding P. Its architecture utilizes LSTM layers to capture temporal dependencies, producing the imputation output. The input vector U_t and the generation process are defined as:

$$U_t = [x_{obs}(t), M_t, x_{phy}(t), Z_t, P_t] \tag{6}$$

$$H = \text{Dropout}(\text{LSTM}(U; \theta^G_{lstm})) \tag{7}$$

$$\Delta = \text{Tanh}(\text{FC}(H; \theta_{fc})) \tag{8}$$

$$\hat{X}_t = M_t x_{obs}(t) + (1 - M_t)(x_{phy}(t) + \Delta_t) \tag{9}$$

Here, the generator learns the residual term Δ_t, which represents the deviation from the physical prior x_{phy}. This design improves both training efficiency and interpretability.

Discriminator. The discriminator takes the completed sequence $\hat{X}$ and the dual-channel hint $DHint$ as input. It aims to distinguish which values are truly observed and which are imputed.

$$V_t = [\hat{X}_t, DHint_t] \tag{10}$$

$$H_D = \text{Dropout}(\text{LSTM}(V; \theta^D_{lstm})) \tag{11}$$

$$s = \text{SN}(WH_D + b) \tag{12}$$

where SN($\cdot$) denotes Spectral Normalization, ensuring the Lipschitz constraint required by WGAN is satisfied.

Loss Functions. To address the issue of variable missing rates, we introduce an observation propensity weight ω_t:

$$\omega_t = \begin{cases} \frac{1}{\pi(M_t|x_{obs})}, & \text{if } M_t = 1 \\ \frac{1}{1-\pi(M_t|x_{obs})}, & \text{if } M_t = 0 \end{cases} \tag{13}$$

The generator loss $\mathcal{L}_G$ combines adversarial loss, reconstruction loss, and physics-consistency loss:

$$\mathcal{L}_G = \mathcal{L}_G^{adv} + \lambda_{rec}\mathcal{L}_G^{rec} + \lambda_{phy}\mathcal{L}_G^{phy} \tag{14}$$

where $\mathcal{L}_G^{phy} = \mathbb{E}[\|\hat{X} - x_{phy}\|^2]$ enforces physical plausibility.

The conceptual architecture is shown in Fig. 1.

The training procedure is summarized in Table 2.

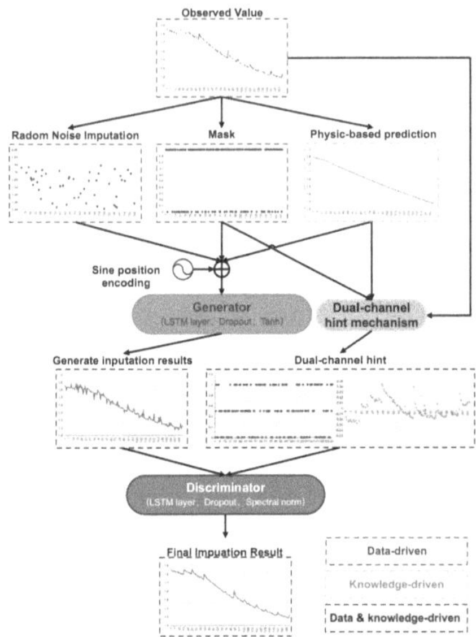

Fig. 1. Conceptual architecture of Phys-TSGAIN. The framework integrates a physics-informed module, a dual-channel hint mechanism, and an LSTM-based WGAN generator.

Table 2. Pseudocode of Phys-TSGAIN Training Procedure

Input: Dataset $\mathcal{D}$, Hyperparameters $\lambda_{rec}, \lambda_{phy}, \lambda_{hint}$
Output: Trained Generator G

1. **Initialize:** Physical model Φ, Generator G, Discriminator D.
2. **Pre-train:** Optimize Φ on observed data to obtain initial α, β.
3. **While** $J - J_{min} > \epsilon$ **do**:
   //—Discriminator Optimization —
   a. Sample minibatch $\{(\mathbf{x}_j, \mathbf{m}_j)\}_{j=1}^{k_D}$.
   b. Generate noise Z and hints H_{rand}, H_{phys}.
   c. Compute imputed data $\hat{X} \leftarrow G(\mathbf{x}, \mathbf{m}, \Phi(\mathbf{x}), Z)$.
   d. Compute Gradient Penalty (GP).
   e. Update D by minimizing: $\mathcal{L}_D = -\mathbb{E}[D(\mathbf{x})] + \mathbb{E}[D(\hat{X})] + \lambda_{gp}\text{GP}$.
   //—Generator Optimization —
   f. Sample minibatch $\{(\mathbf{x}_j, \mathbf{m}_j)\}_{j=1}^{k_G}$.
   g. Compute imputed data $\hat{X} \leftarrow G(\dots)$.
   h. Update G by minimizing $\mathcal{L}_G = -\mathbb{E}[D(\hat{X})] + \lambda_{rec}\mathcal{L}_{rec} + \lambda_{phy}\mathcal{L}_{phy}$.
4. **End While**

3 Theoretical Proof and Analysis

In this section, we provide a rigorous theoretical analysis of the proposed Phys-TSGAIN framework. We explicitly derive the properties of unbiasedness, effectiveness, and convergence to demonstrate that embedding physical priors does not compromise the statistical validity of the generative model.

3.1 Unbiasedness of the Algorithm

Lemma 1 (Unbiasedness). *Let the distribution of the true complete sequence be denoted as $p_{data}(\mathbf{x})$, and the mask generation probability as $\pi(\mathbf{m}|\mathbf{x}_{obs})$. The observed distribution is defined as $p_{obs}(\mathbf{x}_{obs}, \mathbf{m}) = p_{data}(\mathbf{x})\pi(\mathbf{m}|\mathbf{x}_{obs})$. For any integrable function $f(\mathbf{x})$, the expectation weighted by the inverse propensity score ω over the observed data is an unbiased estimator of the true expectation:*

$$\mathbb{E}_{\mathbf{x}_{obs},\mathbf{m}}[\omega f(\mathbf{x})] = \mathbb{E}_{\mathbf{x}\sim p_{data}}[f(\mathbf{x})] \tag{15}$$

Proof. Recall the definition of the observation propensity weight $\omega(\mathbf{x}_{obs}, \mathbf{m}) = 1/\pi(\mathbf{m}|\mathbf{x}_{obs})$. We expand the expectation on the left-hand side of Eq. (15) by integrating over the joint distribution of observations and masks:

$$\begin{aligned}
\mathbb{E}_{\mathbf{x}_{obs},\mathbf{m}}[\omega f(\mathbf{x})] &= \sum_{\mathbf{m}\in\{0,1\}^T} \int \omega(\mathbf{x}_{obs}, \mathbf{m}) f(\mathbf{x}) p_{obs}(\mathbf{x}_{obs}, \mathbf{m}) d\mathbf{x} && (16)\\
&= \sum_{\mathbf{m}\in\{0,1\}^T} \int \frac{1}{\pi(\mathbf{m}|\mathbf{x}_{obs})} f(\mathbf{x}) p_{data}(\mathbf{x})\pi(\mathbf{m}|\mathbf{x}_{obs}) d\mathbf{x} && (17)\\
&= \sum_{\mathbf{m}\in\{0,1\}^T} \int f(\mathbf{x}) p_{data}(\mathbf{x}) d\mathbf{x} && (18)\\
&= \int f(\mathbf{x}) p_{data}(\mathbf{x}) \left(\sum_{\mathbf{m}\in\{0,1\}^T} 1 \right) d\mathbf{x} && (19)
\end{aligned}$$

Note that in the imputation context, the marginalization over masks for a complete data point sums to 1 naturally in the expectation framework defined by the GAIN theory. Thus, we recover:

$$\mathbb{E}_{\mathbf{x}_{obs},\mathbf{m}}[\omega f(\mathbf{x})] = \int f(\mathbf{x}) p_{data}(\mathbf{x}) d\mathbf{x} = \mathbb{E}_{\mathbf{x}\sim p_{data}}[f(\mathbf{x})] \tag{20}$$

This completes the proof.

Remark. Lemma 1 demonstrates that the propensity weighting effectively eliminates the bias introduced by the missingness mechanism, enabling the model to handle not only MCAR but also MAR and MNAR scenarios where missingness is correlated with data values.

3.2 Effectiveness of the Algorithm

Lemma 2 (Effectiveness). *Let $p_{G_\theta}(\hat{\mathbf{x}})$ denote the generated distribution. Let $\mathcal{D}_1$ be the set of all 1-Lipschitz functions. The Wasserstein-1 distance $W_1(p_{data}, p_{G_\theta})$ is bounded by the weighted adversarial objective:*

$$W_1(p_{data}, p_{G_\theta}) = \sup_{D \in \mathcal{D}_1} \left(\mathbb{E}_{\mathbf{x}_{obs},\mathbf{m}}[\omega D(\mathbf{x}_{obs})] - \mathbb{E}_{\hat{\mathbf{x}},\mathbf{m}}[\omega D(\hat{\mathbf{x}})]\right) \tag{21}$$

Proof. Based on Lemma 1, we can substitute the weighted expectations over observed/imputed data with expectations over the true/generated distributions:

$$\mathbb{E}_{\mathbf{x}_{obs},\mathbf{m}}[\omega D(\mathbf{x}_{obs})] = \mathbb{E}_{\mathbf{x} \sim p_{data}}[D(\mathbf{x})] \tag{22}$$

$$\mathbb{E}_{\hat{\mathbf{x}},\mathbf{m}}[\omega D(\hat{\mathbf{x}})] = \mathbb{E}_{\hat{\mathbf{x}} \sim p_{G_\theta}}[D(\hat{\mathbf{x}})] \tag{23}$$

Substituting these into the right-hand side of Eq. (21):

$$\text{RHS} = \sup_{D \in \mathcal{D}_1} \left(\mathbb{E}_{\mathbf{x} \sim p_{data}}[D(\mathbf{x})] - \mathbb{E}_{\hat{\mathbf{x}} \sim p_{G_\theta}}[D(\hat{\mathbf{x}})]\right) \tag{24}$$

According to the Kantorovich-Rubinstein duality theorem, this supremum is exactly the definition of the Wasserstein-1 distance $W_1(p_{data}, p_{G_\theta})$. Thus, maximizing the discriminator's objective is equivalent to estimating the Wasserstein distance between the true and generated distributions.

Remark. Lemma 2 clarifies that the proposed loss function effectively measures the discrepancy between the generated and true distributions[cite: 118]. It implies that by maximizing the weighted adversarial objective, the model minimizes the Wasserstein distance, thereby achieving optimal distributional alignment even in the presence of missing values.

3.3 Convergence of the Algorithm

Theorem 1 (Convergence). *The generator loss function $\mathcal{L}_G$ reaches its global minimum if and only if three conditions are simultaneously met:*

1. *The generated distribution equals the true distribution: $p_{data} = p_{G_\theta}$.*
2. *The imputed values achieve the optimal trade-off residuals $\mathbf{x}^*$.*
3. *The physical model parameters achieve their optimal values (α^*, β^*).*

Formally:

$$\min \mathcal{L}_G \iff p_{data} = p_{G_\theta} \wedge \mathbf{x}^* = \frac{\lambda_{rec}\mathbf{m}\mathbf{x}_{obs} + \lambda_{phy}\mathbf{x}_{phy}}{\lambda_{rec}\mathbf{m} + \lambda_{phy}} \wedge (\alpha^*, \beta^*) = \arg\min \|\mathbf{x} - \mathbf{x}_{phy}\|^2 \tag{25}$$

Proof. The total generator loss function is defined as:

$$\mathcal{L}_G = \mathcal{L}_G^{adv} + \lambda_{rec}\mathcal{L}_{rec} + \lambda_{phy}\mathcal{L}_{phy} \tag{26}$$

where $\mathcal{L}_G^{adv} = -\mathbb{E}_{\hat{\mathbf{x}}}[\omega D(\hat{\mathbf{x}})]$. From Lemma 2, minimizing the adversarial component (in the context of the minimax game) is equivalent to minimizing the Wasserstein distance $W_1(p_{data}, p_{G_\theta})$. Since W_1 is a distance metric, its global minimum is 0, achieved if and only if $p_{data} = p_{G_\theta}$.

Now consider the reconstruction and physical consistency terms. Let us define the joint auxiliary loss function $F(\hat{\mathbf{x}})$ for a specific imputed sample $\hat{\mathbf{x}}$:

$$F(\hat{\mathbf{x}}) = \lambda_{rec}\|\mathbf{m} \odot (\mathbf{x}_{obs} - \hat{\mathbf{x}})\|^2 + \lambda_{phy}\|\hat{\mathbf{x}} - \mathbf{x}_{phy}\|^2 \tag{27}$$

Since $\lambda_{rec}, \lambda_{phy} > 0$, $F(\hat{\mathbf{x}})$ is a strictly convex quadratic function with respect to $\hat{\mathbf{x}}$. To find the global minimum, we take the derivative with respect to $\hat{\mathbf{x}}$ and set it to zero:

$$\frac{\partial F}{\partial \hat{\mathbf{x}}} = -2\lambda_{rec}\mathbf{m}(\mathbf{x}_{obs} - \hat{\mathbf{x}}) + 2\lambda_{phy}(\hat{\mathbf{x}} - \mathbf{x}_{phy}) = 0 \tag{28}$$

$$\lambda_{rec}\mathbf{m}\mathbf{x}_{obs} - \lambda_{rec}\mathbf{m}\hat{\mathbf{x}} = \lambda_{phy}\hat{\mathbf{x}} - \lambda_{phy}\mathbf{x}_{phy} \tag{29}$$

$$(\lambda_{rec}\mathbf{m} + \lambda_{phy})\hat{\mathbf{x}} = \lambda_{rec}\mathbf{m}\mathbf{x}_{obs} + \lambda_{phy}\mathbf{x}_{phy} \tag{30}$$

Solving for $\hat{\mathbf{x}}$, we obtain the unique optimal solution $\mathbf{x}^*$:

$$\mathbf{x}^* = \frac{\lambda_{rec}\mathbf{m}\mathbf{x}_{obs} + \lambda_{phy}\mathbf{x}_{phy}}{\lambda_{rec}\mathbf{m} + \lambda_{phy}} \tag{31}$$

Finally, the physical loss term implicitly depends on the physical parameters. The term $\|\mathbf{x} - \mathbf{x}_{phy}\|^2$ is minimized when the physical model parameters (α, β) best fit the data, i.e., $(\alpha^*, \beta^*) = \arg\min \|\mathbf{x} - \mathbf{x}_{phy}(\alpha, \beta)\|^2$.

Since the three terms (Adversarial, Reconstruction, Physics) are non-negative and their minima do not conflict, the global minimum of $\mathcal{L}_G$ is attained when all three conditions are satisfied.

Significance. Theorem 1 ensures that Phys-TSGAIN is mathematically grounded. It proves that the model learns an optimal balance between "restoring the data distribution" (via GAN) and "respecting physical laws" (via the trade-off solution $\mathbf{x}^*$).

4 Experiments and Discussion

4.1 Experimental Setup

This section details the comprehensive experimental framework designed to evaluate the proposed Phys-TSGAIN model. We introduce the diverse datasets used, the hardware and software environment, and the specific mechanisms for simulating missing data scenarios.

Datasets. To validate the robustness and universality of the proposed model across different battery chemistries and operational conditions, five publicly available lithium-ion battery time series datasets were selected. These datasets, labeled D1 through D5, represent a wide spectrum of data characteristics:

- **D1 (NASA Battery Dataset):** Sourced from the NASA Prognostics Center of Excellence. This dataset consists of 168 cycle records and is characterized by a relatively stable degradation trend with low variance, making it an ideal baseline for validating basic imputation capabilities.
- **D2 (CS35 Dataset):** Sourced from the CALCE Battery Research Group. It contains 932 cycle points and exhibits a heavy-tailed distribution, testing the model's ability to handle non-Gaussian data features.
- **D3 (HUST Dataset):** A large-scale dataset containing 1,504 data points with significant variance (Variance > 6000). This dataset represents high-dynamic range scenarios, challenging the model's stability in handling large value fluctuations.
- **D4 (MIT Dataset):** A dataset with a tight, left-skewed distribution, focusing on rapid degradation phases where capturing the steep slope of capacity fade is critical.
- **D5 (EV Dataset):** Real-world electric vehicle operation data containing 2,785 timestamped entries. Unlike lab data, D5 is characterized by high noise and irregular sampling, testing the model's practical applicability in real-world BMS.

Figure 2 visually illustrates the degradation curves of these five datasets, highlighting the varying degrees of non-linearity and noise. The diversity in mean, variance, skewness and other statistical characteristics across these datasets poses high requirements for the generalization ability of the imputation model.

Experimental Conditions. The experiments were conducted on a high-performance workstation running Ubuntu 20.04, powered by an Intel Xeon Gold 6254 CPU and 2x NVIDIA RTX A6000 GPUs. The deep learning framework used was PyTorch 2.0.

Since ground truth for missing values is rarely available in real-world scenarios, we artificially injected missingness into the complete datasets to simulate three distinct failure modes:

1. **MCAR (Missing Completely at Random):** 10%–50% of data points were randomly removed. This simulates random packet loss in data transmission.
2. **MAR (Missing at Random):** Random block deletion (30% of the sequence). This simulates prolonged sensor outages or communication interruptions.
3. **MNAR (Missing Not at Random):** Deletion probability was set proportional to normalized capacity values (30% rate). This simulates scenarios where sensors are more likely to fail as the battery degrades (e.g., due to unstable voltage near end-of-life).

The model parameters were fine-tuned for each dataset to ensure optimal performance. Common hyperparameters included a hint rate of 0.5, physics-consistency weight $\lambda_{phy} = 0.5$, and reconstruction weight $\lambda_{rec} = 5.0$. Specific settings are detailed in Table 4 (Table 3).

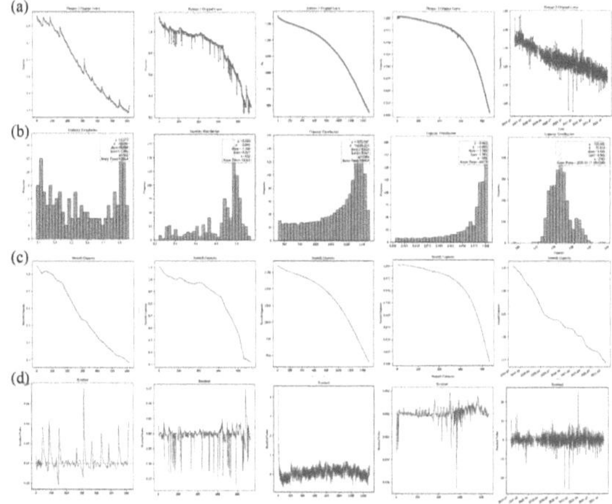

Fig. 2. Visual description of the experimental dataset D1-D5. The degradation trends vary significantly from linear (D1) to highly non-linear (D4) and noisy (D5).(a) Original data ; (b) Statisitical characteristics; (c) Smooth fitting;(d) Residual between Original data and smooth fitting

Table 3. Characteristics Parameters Related to the Dataset

Dataset	Gen. LR	Disc. LR	Batch Size	Epoch	Hidden Layer	LSTM Layer
D1	2e–4	1e–4	2	100	64	2
D2	2e–4	1e–4	2	150	64	2
D3	6e–4	3e–4	4	200	128	3
D4	6e–4	3e–4	4	150	128	3
D5	2e–4	1e–4	1	200	128	3

4.2 Result Discussion

This subsection provides a detailed analysis of the experimental results, verifying the accuracy, component contributions, comparative superiority, and generalization capability of Phys-TSGAIN.

Accuracy Validation. To establish a baseline for performance, we first conducted accuracy validation under a 30% completely random missingness (MCAR) scenario across all five datasets.

(1) Accuracy Validation Based on Internal Statistics A key requirement for valid imputation is that the generated data must preserve the statistical properties of the original distribution. Table 5 compares the internal statistics of the imputed sequences against the ground truth.

The results in Table 5 indicate a high degree of statistical fidelity. The mean deviations for all datasets are within 1%, and the variance shifts are minimal,

Table 4. Accuracy Verification Results Based on Internal Statistics

Dataset	Status	Mean	Variance	Skewness	Kurtosis	Autocorr.	Knee-point
D1	Completed	1.573	0.036	0.048	−1.496	0.998	idx=61
	Imputed	1.565	0.036	0.038	−1.493	0.990	idx=56
D2	Completed	0.842	0.048	−1.188	0.267	0.989	idx=617
	Imputed	0.836	0.046	−1.187	0.205	0.984	idx=602
D3	Completed	1072.947	6649.993	−0.823	-0.547	1.000	idx=888
	Imputed	1075.382	6556.357	−0.819	-0.600	0.995	idx=830
D4	Completed	0.963	0.002	−1.566	1.503	1.000	idx=641
	Imputed	0.964	0.002	−1.545	1.346	0.993	idx=616
D5	Completed	122.601	31.823	0.546	0.566	0.844	idx=419
	Imputed	122.650	29.442	0.610	0.723	0.857	idx=442

suggesting that the imputation does not introduce artificial noise or smoothing. More importantly, the Autocorrelation coefficients remain extremely high (> 0.98 for D1–D4), confirming that the LSTM-based generator successfully captures the long-term temporal dependencies of battery degradation. Critically, the Knee-points–which indicate the onset of rapid accelerated aging and are vital for safety management–are accurately preserved. For instance, in D1, the knee-point shifts by only 5 cycles (61 vs. 56), well within an acceptable margin for prognostic applications. This validates that Phys-TSGAIN maintains the physical consistency of the degradation trajectory.

Figure 3 further quantifies the reconstruction accuracy using standard regression metrics.

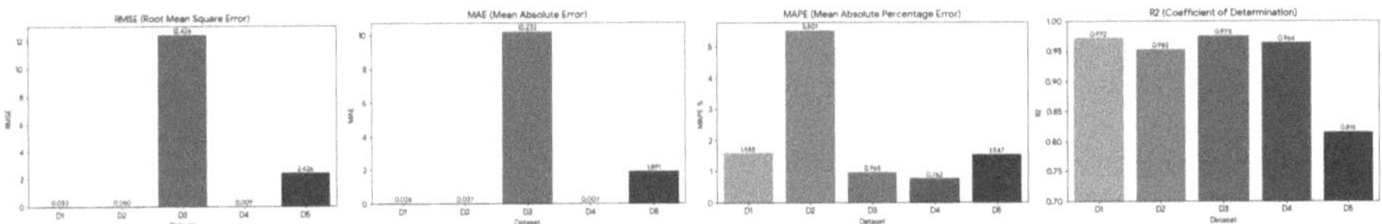

Fig. 3. Accuracy Verification Results Based on Statistical Indicators from D1 to D5.

The high R^2 values (> 0.95 for D1-D4) confirm that the imputed curves closely match the ground truth. Even for the highly noisy dataset D5, the model maintains an R^2 of 0.815, demonstrating robust performance under challenging conditions.

(2) Accuracy Validation Based on Downstream Tasks The ultimate test of imputation utility is whether it improves the performance of downstream applications. We trained six different regression models (LASSO, GPR, Ridge, SVR, KNN, RF) on both the original (completed) and imputed datasets to predict capacity.

Table 5. Accuracy verification results based on downstream tasks (RMSE)

Dataset	Status	LASSO	GPR	Ridge	SVR	KNN	RF	Avg RMSE
D1	Completed	1.042	1.075	0.966	0.882	0.989	1.008	0.994
	Imputed	0.063	0.044	0.079	0.141	0.065	0.064	**0.076**
D2	Completed	0.126	0.151	0.114	0.122	0.123	0.122	0.126
	Imputed	0.120	0.115	0.102	0.108	0.088	0.084	**0.103**
D3	Completed	1054.96	1054.98	1054.92	1054.88	1054.98	1054.98	1054.95
	Imputed	34.650	34.632	58.038	51.710	31.394	30.808	**40.205**
D4	Completed	0.073	0.091	0.120	0.060	0.113	0.114	0.095
	Imputed	0.035	0.027	0.024	0.034	0.023	0.023	**0.028**
D5	Completed	120.283	120.283	120.134	120.207	120.227	120.235	120.228
	Imputed	2.762	2.762	6.841	4.060	2.775	2.738	**3.656**

As illustrated in Tables 6, the imputation significantly enhances downstream task performance. For D1, the average RMSE drops dramatically from 0.994 to 0.076, representing an error reduction of over 90 %. This trend is consistent across all datasets, with D3 showing a reduction from $\sim$1054 to $\sim$40, which suggests that Phys-TSGAIN successfully restores the underlying physical manifold of the data, rather than just optimizing for a specific prediction task.

Comparative Evaluation of Imputation Methods. To demonstrate superiority over existing solutions, we benchmarked Phys-TSGAIN against 18 baselines, categorized into statistical, machine learning, and deep learning methods. Table 7 shows the results on D1.

Phys-TSGAIN outperforms all baselines by a wide margin. Traditional statistical methods (LOCF, Splines) perform consistently around 0.29 RMSE, limited by their inability to model non-linear global trends. Pure deep learning approaches like ImputeGAN (RMSE 2.828) suffer from instability and mode collapse due to the lack of physical constraints. Phys-TSGAIN achieves an RMSE of 0.076, which is approximately 73% lower than the best competing method (E2GAN-RF, RMSE 0.290), proving the necessity of integrating domain knowledge into generative models.

Generalization Validation. Finally, we evaluated the robustness of the model under varying conditions, confirming the theoretical claims of unbiasedness.

Table 6. Comparison of Effects of Different Imputation Methods (Dataset D1)

Category	Algorithm	LASSO	GPR	Ridge	SVR	KNN	RF	Avg RMSE
Baseline	Missing	1.042	1.075	0.966	0.882	0.989	1.008	0.994
Statistical	MEAN	–	–	–	–	–	–	–
	MEDIAD	0.944	0.754	0.732	0.820	0.778	0.901	0.821
	BF	0.365	0.298	0.146	0.679	0.124	0.121	0.289
	LOCF	0.363	0.299	0.143	0.682	0.127	0.132	0.291
	Interpolation	0.364	0.298	0.138	0.694	0.121	0.116	0.289
	Poly. Interp.	0.362	0.298	0.144	0.673	0.124	0.119	0.286
	B-splines	0.361	0.298	0.152	0.696	0.133	0.139	0.296
	SMA	0.365	0.299	0.141	0.697	0.134	0.140	0.296
Machine Learning	Fuzzy KM	1.389	1.263	1.721	0.877	1.389	1.591	1.372
	Ensemble	0.930	0.737	0.713	0.848	0.758	0.884	0.812
Deep Learning	HybridLSTM	0.976	0.792	0.772	0.839	0.821	0.948	0.858
	Moment	0.938	0.745	0.743	0.839	0.845	1.112	0.870
Generative	Pix2Pix GAN	8.530	8.503	8.611	1.042	9.838	11.533	8.009
	E2GAN-RF	0.364	0.298	0.139	0.696	0.123	0.119	0.290
	ImputeGAN	2.876	2.828	3.260	1.042	3.218	3.742	2.828
Proposed	**Phys-TSGAIN**	**0.063**	**0.044**	**0.079**	**0.141**	**0.065**	**0.064**	**0.076**

Generalization under Different Missingness Mechanisms. Table 8 presents the results under MCAR, MAR, and MNAR mechanisms.

Remarkably, the model performs consistently well even under MNAR (value-dependent missingness), which typically introduces significant bias in standard imputation. This result empirically validates Lemma 1 (Unbiasedness), showing that the propensity weighting mechanism effectively corrects for selection bias.

Besides, Generalization under Different Missing Rates Fig. 5 presents the performance under MCAR with missing rates from 10% to 50%.

Ablation Study. To systematically evaluate the contribution of each component in the Phys-TSGAIN framework, we performed an ablation study involving four variants:

- **Missing:** Baseline with no imputation.
- **GAIN:** Standard Generative Adversarial Imputation Network.
- **TSGAIN:** GAIN with LSTM-based generator/discriminator (Temporal structure only).
- **Phys-GAIN:** GAIN with physical consistency loss (Physics only).
- **Phys-TSGAIN:** The proposed full model.

Figure 4 presents the detailed results.

Table 7. Generalization Effect under Different Missing Conditions

Dataset	Condition	LASSO	GPR	Ridge	SVR	KNN	RF	Avg RMSE
D1	MCAR	0.063	0.044	0.079	0.141	0.065	0.064	**0.076**
	MAR	0.070	0.054	0.159	0.141	0.059	0.055	**0.090**
	MNAR	0.063	0.044	0.079	0.145	0.066	0.062	**0.077**
D2	MCAR	0.120	0.115	0.102	0.108	0.088	0.084	**0.103**
	MAR	0.117	0.123	0.155	0.119	0.094	0.094	**0.117**
	MNAR	0.118	0.118	0.112	0.102	0.093	0.093	**0.106**
D3	MCAR	34.65	34.63	58.04	51.71	31.39	30.81	**40.20**
	MAR	24.40	24.40	69.89	46.66	25.20	25.03	**35.93**
	MNAR	33.62	33.61	56.52	50.26	30.74	30.15	**39.15**
D4	MCAR	0.035	0.027	0.024	0.034	0.023	0.023	**0.028**
	MAR	0.034	0.026	0.036	0.034	0.021	0.021	**0.029**
	MNAR	0.035	0.027	0.024	0.034	0.022	0.022	**0.028**
D5	MCAR	2.762	2.762	6.841	4.060	2.775	2.738	**3.656**
	MAR	3.121	3.121	6.718	3.542	2.605	2.536	**3.607**
	MNAR	2.798	2.798	6.832	4.059	2.881	2.797	**3.694**

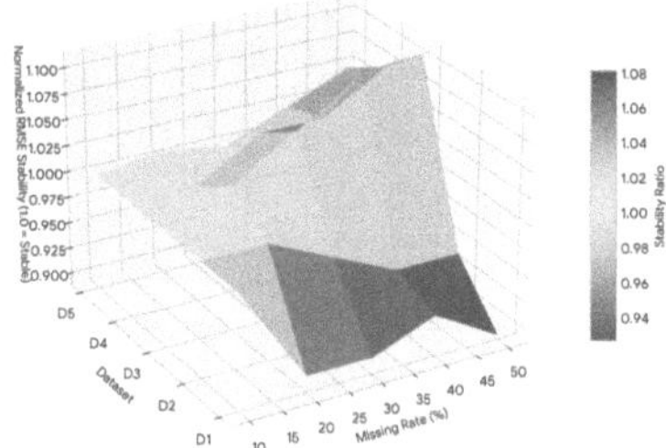

Fig. 4. Robustness analysis under varying missing rates (10%–50%).

The results reveal a clear incremental improvement. While the basic GAIN model reduces error significantly compared to the baseline, it lacks the continuity constraints needed for time series. Introducing TSGAIN addresses this by using LSTMs, improving RMSE from 0.265 to 0.196 on D1. However, the most dramatic improvement comes from Phys-GAIN (D1 RMSE $\rightarrow$ 0.083), proving that domain knowledge is the most critical factor in constraining the generator's search space. Finally, Phys-TSGAIN combines both strengths to achieve the lowest error across all datasets.

The qualitative difference is further highlighted in Fig. 5, where Phys-TSGAIN (blue) aligns much closer to the ground truth line than the physics-only model (orange), which tends to drift.

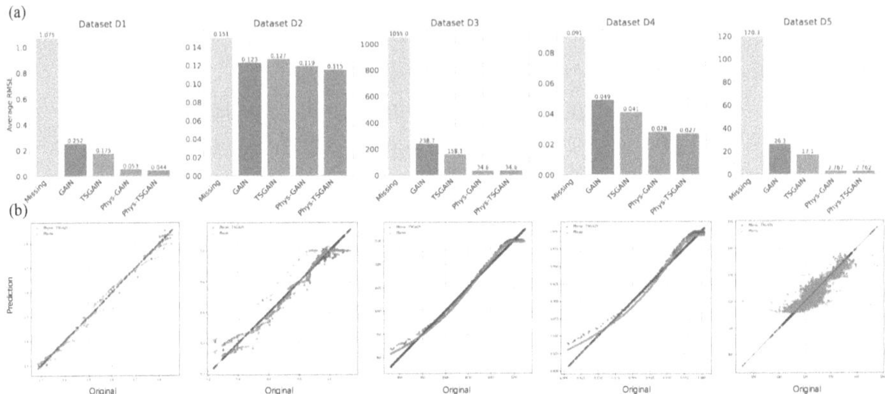

Fig. 5. Results of the ablation study. (a) Average RMSE of ablation experiments with MCAR, MAR and MNAR ; (b) Scatter plot of Physic imputation and Phys-GAIN imputation with 30% MCAR

5 Conclusion

In this paper, we proposed **Phys-TSGAIN**, a physics-informed generative imputation framework designed to address the data completeness challenge in lithium-ion battery management. By bridging the gap between data-driven learning and domain knowledge, the proposed method achieves robust data governance under complex missingness scenarios.

Our main contributions are summarized as follows:

1. **Theoretical Foundation:** We provided rigorous theoretical derivations to guarantee the *unbiasedness*, *effectiveness*, and *convergence* of the proposed algorithm. These proofs confirm that embedding physical priors into the generative process does not compromise the statistical validity of the distribution recovery.
2. **Methodological Innovation:** We designed a novel dual-channel hint mechanism and a physics-informed knowledge module. This hybrid architecture effectively constrains the generator search space, ensuring that imputed values are both statistically consistent and physically plausible.
3. **Experimental Superiority:** Extensive experiments on five real-world datasets demonstrate that Phys-TSGAIN significantly outperforms 18 baseline methods. Specifically, it reduces the average RMSE in downstream prediction tasks by approximately **73%** compared to state-of-the-art generative models. Furthermore, the method exhibits strong robustness across varying missing rates (10%–50%) and mechanisms (MCAR, MAR, MNAR).

In conclusion, Phys-TSGAIN offers a reliable and interpretable solution for time series data quality governance in the new energy sector, paving the way for more accurate battery health prognostics.

Acknowledgments. This work was supported in part by the Training Program of the Major Research Plan of the National Natural Science Foundation of China (No. 92270124) and the National Key Research and Development Program of China (Grant No. 2021YFB3802101).

Data and Code Availability. The authors declare that the main data supporting the findings of this study are available from the corresponding author upon reasonable request.

References

1. Singh, S.: Estimation of missing values in the data mining and comparison of imputation methods. Math. J. Interdiscip. Sci. **1**(2), 75–90 (2013)
2. Prtama, I., et al.: A review of missing values handling methods on time-series data. In: Proceedings of the ICITSI, pp. 1–6 (2016)
3. Amiri, M., Jensen, R.: Missing data imputation using fuzzy-rough methods. Neurocomputing **205**, 152–164 (2016)
4. Gupta, S., Gupta, M.K.: A survey on different techniques for handling missing values in dataset. Int. J. Sci. Res. Comput. Sci. Eng. Inf. Technol. **4**(1) (2018)
5. Wold, S.: Spline functions in data analysis. Technometrics **16**(1), 1–11 (1974)
6. Yodah, W.O., et al.: Imputation of incomplete non-stationary seasonal time series data. Math. Theory Model. **3**(12), 142–154 (2013)
7. Van Buuren, S., Groothuis-Oudshoorn, K.: MICE: multivariate imputation by chained equations in R. J. Stat. Softw. **45**(3), 1–67 (2010)
8. Zhang, X., et al.: Xgboost imputation for time series data. In: IEEE ICHI, pp. 1–3 (2019)
9. Peña, M., et al.: A novel imputation method for missing values in air pollutant time series data. In: IEEE LA-CCI, pp. 1–6 (2019)
10. Vaishnav, R.L., Patel, K.M.: Analysis of various techniques to handling missing value in dataset. Int. J. Innov. Emerg. Res. Eng. **2**(2) (2015)
11. Jegadeeswari, K., et al.: Missing data imputation using ensemble learning technique: a review. Adv. Intell. Syst. Comput. **1428** (2023)
12. Isil, B.E., et al.: MetaLIRS: meta-learning for imputation and regression selection. In: IDEAL 2024, Part I, pp. 155–166 (2024)
13. Cao, W., et al.: Brits: bidirectional recurrent imputation for time series. NeurIPS **2018**, 6775–6785 (2018)
14. Almeida, M.M., et al.: Univariate time series missing data imputation using Pix2Pix GAN. IEEE Lat. Am. Trans. **100** (2023)
15. Yildiz, A.Y., et al.: Multivariate time series imputation with transformers. IEEE Signal Process. Lett. **29**, 2517–2521 (2022)
16. Goswami, M., et al.: MOMENT: a family of open time-series foundation models. arXiv:2402.03885 (2024)
17. Yoon, J., et al.: GAIN: missing data imputation using generative adversarial nets. In: ICML 2018, PMLR vol. 80, pp. 5689–5698 (2018)
18. Zhang, Y., et al.: Missing value imputation in multivariate time series with end-to-end generative adversarial networks. Inf. Sci. **551**, 67–82 (2021)
19. Mauricio, M.A., et al.: A meta-learning based neural network and LSTM for univariate time series missing data imputation. Appl. Soft Comput. **172**, 112845 (2025)
20. Qin, R., Wang, Y.: ImputeGAN: generative adversarial network for multivariate time series imputation. Entropy **25**(1), 137 (2023)

Empirical Bias in Theoretical Frameworks: Validation of Distance and Load Assumptions in ICAO Aviation Carbon Emissions Calculation Methodologies

Jianxiong Chen, Jingtao Wang(✉), Yating Wei, and Lin Zou(✉)

Civil Aviation Flight University of China, Guanghan, Sichuan, China
1377821202@qq.com , zoulin@cafuc.edu.cn

Abstract. This study investigates the International Civil Aviation Organization's (ICAO) methodology for calculating aviation carbon emissions, focusing on empirical validation and bias analysis of its assumptions regarding flight distance and payload. Using full-sample operational data from January 1, 2023, to July 31, 2024, the research examines routes between Kunming airport (KMG) and Mangshi airport (LUM), Shuangliu airport (CTU), Xianyang airport (XIY), and Daxing airport (PKX), analyzing the impact of directional, seasonal, and airline-specific operational factors on load factors, baggage weights, and cargo strategies. Findings reveal that ICAO's current method—relying on a fixed assumption of 100kg per passenger, overlooking return-trip load imbalances, and ignoring variations in airline cargo strategies—introduces systematic biases in emission attribution. The study concludes that the static, average-based framework lacks scientific robustness under dynamic operational conditions, and calls for methodological adjustments to address multi-dimensional uncertainties.

Keywords: Aviation carbon emissions · ICAO methodology · payload assumption · empirical bias · dynamic operations

1 Introduction

The decarbonization of civil aviation has become an imperative in the context of global climate governance [1]. The standardized aviation carbon emissions calculation methodology established by the International Civil Aviation Organization (ICAO), with its globally unified accounting framework, has become the core measurement benchmark for aviation carbon offset mechanisms [2]. This methodology constructs a three-layer theoretical model through aircraft type energy consumption mapping, passenger-cargo responsibility separation, and cabin space equivalence. Its predefined equivalent aircraft database covers

J. Zhan et al. (Eds.): Bench 2025, LNCS 16471, pp. 238–253, 2026.
https://doi.org/10.1007/978-981-95-9694-2_17

93% of commercial aircraft worldwide, and, combined with route-group statistical parameters, forms a domain-specific methodological paradigm. While this standardized scheme has cemented ICAO's authoritative position in global aviation carbon governance, its core assumptions remain subject to systematic scientific verification and comparative evaluation [3,4].

An increasing body of research has placed growing emphasis on the accounting of aviation carbon emissions [5,6]. However, the core assumptions of this authoritative methodology are facing both theoretical and practical challenges [3]. The central debate concerns the simplified treatment of dynamic operational environments. The flight distance calculation employs a static great circle distance (GCD) model with fixed correction values, which fails to reflect variations in actual flight paths. Simultaneously, by using average load factors and passenger-to-cargo ratios to assume uniform payload distribution, this approach neither accounts for the real-time variability of individual flight load factors nor recognizes the significant transport imbalance between outbound and return directions, while its fixed benchmarks for passenger and baggage mass fail to reflect the seasonal variations and route-specific differences in actual baggage weights. These theoretical deficiencies expose the lack of scientific robustness of the current methodology under dynamic operational conditions, thereby highlighting the necessity of using more precise flight-level ADS-B data for improved carbon emission accounting [4].

This study systematically quantifies the empirical biases of the ICAO methodology in China's complex airspace environment by integrating high-precision radar trajectory data with detailed flight operation records. Based on full-sample operational data from January 1, 2023 to July 31, 2024, the research reveals for the first time the systematic deviation characteristics of both distance models and payload parameters. Regarding distance deviations, actual flight distances during the rainy season exceed ICAO reference values by 4.8% to 8.6% for outbound segments and 8.0% to 12.3% for return segments, with the short-haul KMG-LUM route exhibiting the maximum deviation of 38.2% during rainy season return segments. Concerning payload parameters, the study identifies that directional differences in passenger-cargo-freight factor (PCF) reach up to 4.14% points, reflecting significant directional imbalance in cargo transport; actual monthly average baggage weights consistently fall within the 2.5 to 7.5 kg range, presenting substantial divergence from ICAO's assumed standard of 100 kg (including passenger weight and baggage); different airlines demonstrate notable heterogeneity in cargo strategies, with major carriers focusing on passenger density while regional carriers actively developing belly cargo operations, yet ICAO's route-group averaging model cannot capture these structural differences. In response to these findings, this study proposes improvement directions: establishing a dynamic distance correction model based on real-time ADS-B trajectory data that accounts for airspace control and weather deviations; constructing a bidirectional load factor system distinguishing outbound-return directions, introducing seasonal dynamic baggage weight parameters, and establishing a classification system reflecting airline transport strategy differences; exploring the integration of flight-level actual operational data into carbon accounting systems to achieve a paradigm shift from statistical averaging to individual flight accounting.

To validate the aforementioned theoretical framework, this study focuses on Kunming Changshui Airport (KMG) as the core hub, selecting four typical routes including flights to and from Mangshi Airport (LUM), Chengdu Shuangliu Airport (CTU), Xi'an Xianyang Airport (XIY), and Beijing Daxing Airport (PKX). The study systematically quantifies dynamic deviations of the distance model and analyzes the error mechanisms of payload parameters across directional, temporal, and airline dimensions. Through empirical evaluations in Chinese scenarios, the study aims to drive innovation in domain-specific methodologies and provide scientific foundations for developing dynamic distance correction models and refined payload parameter systems.

2 ICAO Carbon Emissions Calculation Framework: Static Models and Theoretical Limitations

2.1 Core Framework

The aviation carbon emissions calculation system established by ICAO employs a three-tier mapping mechanism for implementation:

- **Aircraft Type-Energy Consumption Mapping**: Identify the types of aircraft based on the OAG flight plan database, correlate with ICAO fuel consumption formulas using 336 equivalent aircraft models, and address the issue of incomplete performance data for existing aircraft types.
- **Load allocation mechanism**: Utilize route group seat utilization rates and cargo-passenger quality ratios to separate the responsibility for carbon emissions associated with freight operations.
- **Cabin space equivalent**: Utilize the Y_{seat} system to quantify the proportion of different cabin space resources (with economy class as the baseline at 1.0). Combine this with Ch-Aviation's passenger cabin configuration data to achieve differentiated emissions allocation.

The aforementioned three-layer mapping mechanism forms the "black box" framework of the ICAO methodology: it packages aircraft performance, payload distribution, and cabin configuration differences into reusable computational modules using standardized parameters, while excluding the actual dynamic operational disturbances. To specifically reveal how this framework is invoked and how it generates systematic errors, the following sections will provide a detailed analysis of each module's input assumptions, mathematical transformations, and output boundaries.

2.2 Carbon Emission Calculation Method

ICAO uses the great circle distance (GCD) computation of coordinates of takeoff and landing airport as the reference flight distance, and compensates the route

Table 1. Route redundancy correction values

GCD	Correction value
Less than 550 km	+50 km
Between 550 km and 5500 km	+100 km
Above 5500 km	+125 km

redundancy caused by airspace control and meteorological deviation through the static segment correction shown in Table 1.

The fuel consumption calculation phase quantifies energy consumption through the mapping of equivalent aircraft models and the integration of multiple models. It identifies the types of aircraft operating from the OAG flight database, mapping them to 336 predefined equivalent aircraft types. The fuel consumption for each type of equivalent aircraft is calculated using the ICAO formula, which integrates performance data from aircraft manufacturer manuals with U.S. DOT Form 41 operational records. This formula outputs the unit segment fuel consumption for a given corrected distance. When there are multiple aircraft types flying the same route over the same city, the total fuel consumption is integrated using an off-take frequency weighting algorithm.

$$\text{Total fuel (kg)} = \sum_{k=1}^{n} \left(\text{Fuel}_k \times \frac{\text{Departures}_k}{\text{Total departures}} \right) \tag{1}$$

where k represents the specific model of the device. Fuel_k represents the actual fuel consumption of equivalent models in category k for a given flight range. Departures_k represents the number of departure flights for model k, and Total departures represents the total number of departure flights for all models.

The emission responsibility allocation mechanism consists of two core components: the separation of passenger and cargo responsibilities and the differentiation based on cabin classes. The separation of passenger and cargo responsibilities is based on a fixed weight assumption: passengers and their luggage are assigned a benchmark weight of 100 kg per person, while seat amenities are assigned a benchmark weight of 50 kg per seat. Together with the weight of the cargo and mail, these weights form the total mass.

$$\begin{aligned} \text{Total Mass (tonnes)} = & \frac{(\text{Passengers} \times 100) + (\text{Seats} \times 50)}{1000} \\ & + \text{Cargo (tonnes)} + \text{Mail (tonnes)} \end{aligned} \tag{2}$$

The passenger/cargo scale factor (PCF) is derived from the passenger relative mass fraction, i.e.:

$$\text{PCF} = \frac{\left(\frac{(\text{Passengers} \times 100) + (\text{Seats} \times 50)}{1000} \right)}{\text{Total Mass}} \tag{3}$$

The Passenger Load Factor (PLF) is the ratio of the actual number of passengers transported to the number of seats available within a route group.

$$\text{PLF} = \frac{\text{Passengers Transported}}{\text{Seats Available}} \tag{4}$$

This value originates from the ICAO Flight Segment Traffic Statistics (TFS) database, which provides aggregated regional data. The allocation of different cabin classes is achieved through the Y_{seat} factor, which quantifies the occupancy of spatial resources: first, the proportion of each cabin class is calculated horizontally, and combined with the vertical seat spacing (Pitch) to obtain the relative area; based on the economy class area as a benchmark (Y_{seat} factor = 1.0), a coefficient for equivalent cabin space is generated; finally, the weight of cabin emissions is calculated by combining the seat occupancy rate.

$$w_i^{cabin} = \frac{Y_{seatfactor_i}}{\sum(Seats_i \times Y_{seatfactor_i} \times PLF)} \tag{5}$$

The final passenger carbon emissions are allocated based on cabin class.

$$CO_2 \text{ per Pax}_i \text{ (kg)} = \left[\frac{\text{Total fuel (kg)} \times \text{PCF}}{\text{Total occupied } Y_{seat}} \times Y_{seatfactor_i}\right] \times 3.16 \tag{6}$$

2.3 Limitations of the ICAO Carbon Emissions Calculation Method

As a benchmarking framework for aviation carbon accounting, ICAO methodology enables comparable measurement of global flight carbon emissions through a standardized three-tier mapping mechanism, providing an operational methodological basis for the division of responsibilities. Its equivalent system of model libraries and route groups significantly reduces the complexity of large-scale aviation data processing and has theoretical validity in static scenarios. However, the framework's adaptability to dynamic operating environments has theoretical accuracy bottlenecks - when actual flights encounter complex airspace structures or when the load presents strong space-time heterogeneity. Its static correction model and mean parameters will cause significant systemic errors that need to be improved through precision modeling and validation mechanisms. The core assumptions are considered to have significant limitations:

- **Range calculation bias:** The static correction model which depends on the GCD is difficult to accurately quantify the actual flight distance fluctuation. Especially under China's complex airspace structure, air corridor control, meteorological circumnavigation and dynamic avoidance of military exclusion zones resulted in significantly higher actual ranges than the revised values.
- **Distortion of load parameter:** The annual statistical mean of PLF and PCF can not reflect the real-time load fluctuation of single flight, which results in the deviation of emission responsibility allocation of individual flight; Monthly fluctuations in the share of shipments and mail were also not dynamically captured.

The above analysis shows that although the ICAO carbon emission calculation method builds a standardized accounting framework, its statically revised range model and aggregated load parameters have significant theoretical weaknesses in dynamic operational environments: distance calculation does not cover trail fluctuations due to airspace regulations and meteorological avoidance. The PLF and PCF of airline group level cover up the spatial and temporal heterogeneity of single flight load.

3 Coupling Effects of Meteorological and Airspace Dynamics on Flight Distance Variability

This chapter aims to empirically test the theoretical deviation of the flight distance assumption in the ICAO carbon emissions calculation framework through high-resolution actual flight data. Focusing on typical Chinese airspace environments, target routes include LUM, CTU, XIY and PKX. To establish a baseline, Table 2 summarizes the core geographical parameters for each airport and the ICAO distance correction values. The table details the latitude and longitude coordinates of the airport taking off and landing, the GCD from KMG, and the static redundancy correction value superimposed by ICAO based on the length of the flight.

Table 2. Contrast table of the latitude and longitude of each airport, along with the GCD distance and correction values compared to KMG

Airport	Lon (°)	Lat (°)	ICAO GCD(km)	ADS-B GCD(km)
KMG	102.93094	25.09848	-	-
LUM	98.532412	24.399322	450	500
CTU	103.95157	30.559105	615	715
XIY	108.76482	34.438157	1180	1280
PKX	116.42052	39.5426	2040	2140

This study visualizes the distribution characteristics of flight paths using ADS-B radar data, as illustrated in Figs. 1, 2, 3, and 4, where trajectories marked with "(R)" originate from monsoon data from August 1–10, 2023. Red and blue lines represent inbound (from various airports to KMG) and outbound (from KMG to various airports) flight paths, respectively. Complex weather conditions (heavy rain) and airspace restrictions lead to significant dispersion of flight paths, exhibiting systematic circling behavior. Trajectories from the dry season (August 26–31, 2023), not marked with "(R)", are highly concentrated along planned routes. This weather sensitivity is universally applicable across all routes within the KMG hub, providing a basis for future quantification of flight distance deviations.

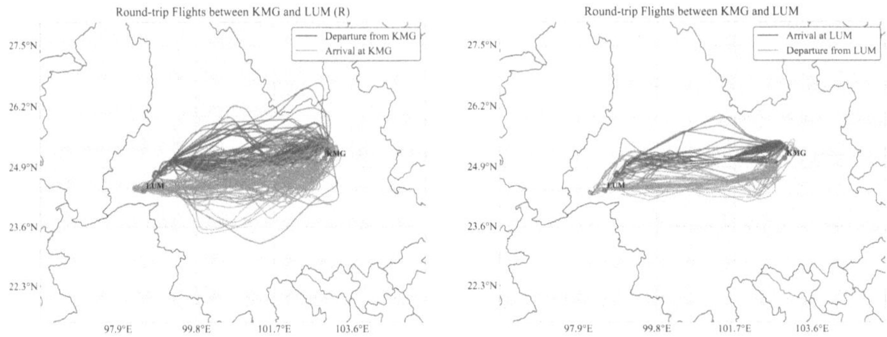

Fig. 1. The Impact of Meteorological Conditions on the Distribution of Approach and Departure Routes at KMG-LUM Airport (Left: Rainy Season; Right: Dry Season)

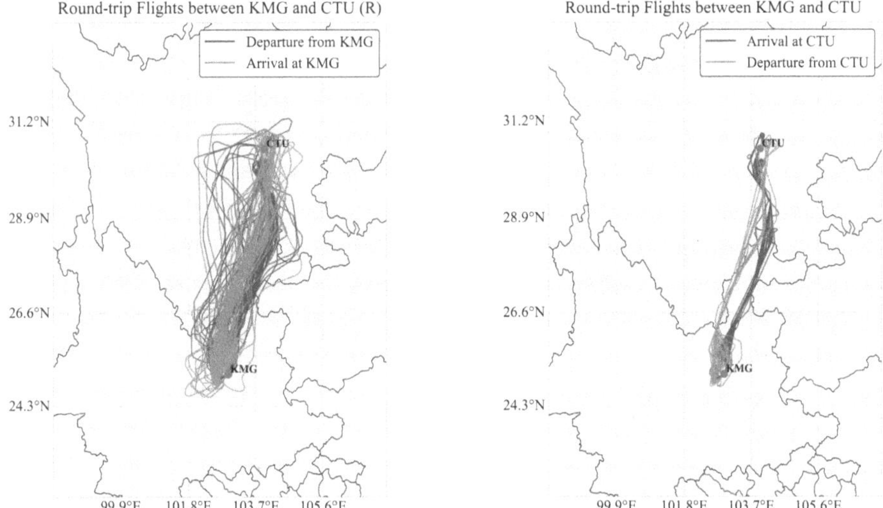

Fig. 2. The Impact of Meteorological Conditions on the Distribution of Flight Paths at KMG-CTU Airport (Left: Rainy Season; Right: Dry Season)

In order to extract the "true" flight distance from the original ADS-B series of latitude, longitude and altitude, three dimensional space distance accumulation algorithm is used to calculate the flight distance based on the ADS-B data. The curvature of Earth and the variation of flying height are taken into account.

For adjacent track points $P_i(\text{lat}_i, \text{lon}_i, \text{alt}_i)$ and $P_j(\text{lat}_j, \text{lon}_j, \text{alt}_j)$, the three dimensional space distance d_{ij} is calculated by the following formula:

$$d_{ij} = \sqrt{d_{\text{ground}}^2 + (\text{alt}_j - \text{alt}_i)^2} \tag{7}$$

where d_{ground} is the distance to the ground taking into account the curvature of the Earth, calculated using the Haversine equation:

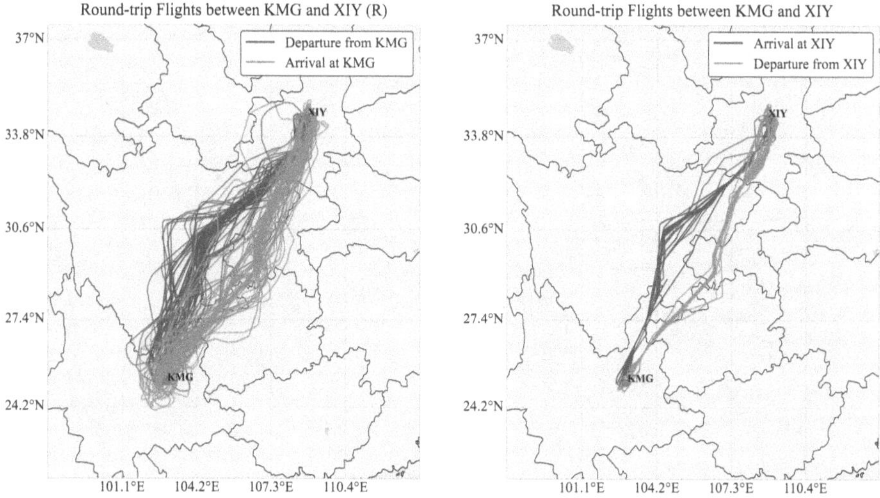

Fig. 3. The Impact of Meteorological Conditions on the Distribution of Flight Paths at KMG-XIY Airport (Left: Rainy Season; Right: Dry Season)

$$d_{\text{ground}} = 2R \cdot \arctan 2\left(\sqrt{a}, \sqrt{1-a}\right) \tag{8}$$

$$a = \sin^2\left(\frac{\Delta\phi}{2}\right) + \cos(\phi_i) \cdot \cos(\phi_j) \cdot \sin^2\left(\frac{\Delta\lambda}{2}\right) \tag{9}$$

Within the formula, $R = 637\text{KM}$ (Radius of the Earth), $\Delta\phi = \phi_j - \phi_i$ (Latitude difference, radian), $\Delta\lambda = \lambda_j - \lambda_i$ (Longitude difference, radian), $\phi = \frac{\pi}{180} \times$ latitude (Convert angles to radians).

The total flight distance of a flight is the cumulative sum of the distances between all adjacent points along the flight path.

$$D = \sum_{k=1}^{n-1} d_{k,k+1} \tag{10}$$

Table 3 summarizes the measured flight distances for the four routes between KMG during both the rainy and dry seasons. Compared to the ICAO static correction values, all samples exhibit systematic positive deviations: the mean departure segments during the rainy season are 4.8% to 8.6% higher than the ICAO reference values, while the return segments are generally 8.0% to 12.3% higher; the deviations during the dry season are generally lower but still generally exceed the reference values by 1.6% to 7.0%. The departure segments show both positive and negative fluctuations. Short-haul routes exhibit significantly greater deviations and volatility compared to long-haul routes, with the return segment of the KMG-LUM route during the rainy season showing the largest deviation of up to 38.2%, resulting in a variance spike of 3,110 km^2. This underscores the

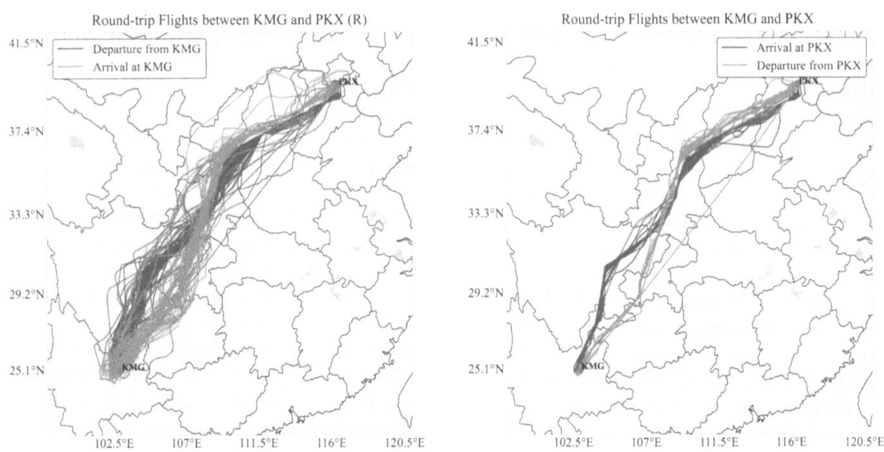

Fig. 4. Distribution of Flight Routes Connecting Different Airports in KMG (Left: Rainy Season; Right: Dry Season)

Table 3. Statistical values for flights to and from KMG at different airports

Route	Sample Size	Min	Max	Median	Average	Variance	ICAO Ref.
KMG → LUM	61	469.39	616.80	525.71	525.99	764.77	500
LUM → KMG	65	448.43	615.40	502.69	508.13	1387.57	500
KMG → LUM(R)	114	457.39	664.49	538.10	542.92	1322.08	500
LUM → KMG(R)	111	440.27	691.09	528.43	540.61	3110.36	500
KMG → CTU	59	648.03	837.95	683.05	698.49	1452.61	715
CTU → KMG	54	667.22	809.16	774.04	765.36	1214.43	715
KMG → CTU(R)	96	633.91	924.42	682.83	703.08	3027.51	715
CTU → KMG(R)	95	659.67	944.13	793.72	803.08	3219.99	715
KMG → XIY	72	1277.65	1404.59	1311.72	1316.94	674.77	1280
XIY → KMG	50	1220.62	1400.57	1363.08	1341.18	3473.63	1280
KMG → XIY(R)	113	1257.30	1521.62	1337.45	1348.06	3697.01	1280
XIY → KMG(R)	94	1244.17	1588.60	1401.99	1410.75	5875.16	1280
KMG → PKX	78	2144.55	2284.90	2196.14	2205.55	921.61	2140
PKX → KMG	60	2179.92	2303.88	2264.16	2257.19	750.70	2140
KMG → PKX(R)	126	2142.86	2468.72	2231.26	2242.84	4416.66	2140
PKX → KMG(R)	105	2163.98	2476.45	2291.46	2310.91	4993.94	2140

more pronounced circling behavior of short-haul routes under complex meteorological conditions and airspace regulations. The ICAO fixed compensation model struggles to dynamically capture the characteristics of Chinese airspace, necessitating the introduction of a weather-airspace coupled distance correction mechanism to reduce discrepancies in carbon emissions accounting.

4 Directionality, Seasonality, and Heterogeneity Deviations in Load Parameters Across Airlines

Based on the ICAO load factor calculation framework, the load factors of KMG to and from LUM, CTU, XIY and PKX were systematically dissected on the basis of full-sample operational data from 1 January 2023 to 31 July 2024. Focusing on the potential limitations of the ICAO approach at the parametric level, the following three problems in science are questionable:

- **Directional asymmetry:** ICAO regards round-trip routes as a symmetrical system, but does not answer whether differences in directional loads cause a systematic shift in carbon liability.
- **The time-varying characteristics of the load:** ICAO fixed the PLF and PCF at an annual average, and has not yet verified whether "seasonal fluctuations will amplify or dilute the emission allocation of individual flights at different times."
- **Air transport characteristics:** ICAO unified the PCF according to the regional average, and did not explore whether "differences in carrier cargo strategies lead to emissions allocation deviations that cannot be ignored on similar routes."

4.1 Directional Imbalance

Table 4 summarizes the passenger and cargo-mail transportation data for flights between KMG and the North Fourth Route during the study period. The results show significant "cargo-mail directional differences" among the four routes: the total cargo-mail weight from flights departing from KMG reached 18,636 tons, accounting for 99.3% of the total cargo-mail volume, while return flights carried only 130 tons, making up less than 0.7%. Specifically, the return cargo-mail volume for PKX and XIY routes is nearly zero, further confirming KMG's one-way flow characteristics as a hub for cargo-mail distribution in the southwestern region.

Figure 5 further visualizes the dual manifestation of directional differences in flight volume and occupancy rates. The bubble diagram shows that the number of round-trip flights is basically balanced among the cities; However, there is a systematic deviation in the seating factor as indicated by the broken line: the seating factor of outbound flights in KMG is on average 1.5 to 14.9% points lower than that of the return flight, and the deviation increases with the shortening of the flight. Among them, the KMG-LUM route is the most outstanding, the departure load rate is only 66.3%, while the return trip is as high as 81.2%, the difference reaches 14.9% points, which confirms the remarkable characteristics of "one-way passenger flow, one-way freight and mail" in the short-distance leisure route.

Based on the original passenger, seat and cargo data, further processing calculation, as shown in Table 5: KMG outbound flight average cargo weight

Table 4. Statistics on Passenger and Cargo Operations for Four Typical Routes with Round Trips from KMG

Route	Adult Pop.	Total Seats	Cargo & Mail Weight	Flights
PKX-KMG	1,145,424	1,445,617	0	7,732
CTU-KMG	823,905	1,014,599	0	6,056
KMG-PKX	1,069,778	1,442,778	7,739,292	7,711
KMG-CTU	807,389	1,012,855	3,370,678	6,044
KMG-LUM	874,558	1,319,762	1,320,148	8,947
KMG-XIY	1,231,035	1,465,497	6,205,646	8,402
LUM-KMG	1,065,548	1,311,869	130,321	8,899
XIY-KMG	1,273,227	1,466,941	37	8,409

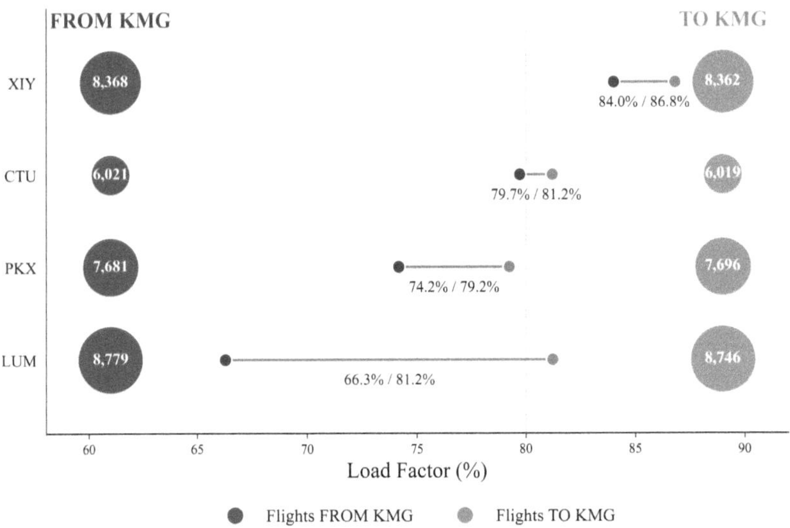

Fig. 5. Visualization of Directional Differences in Flight Volume and Occupancy Rates

was significantly higher than the return, resulting in the maximum difference in PCF in the direction of 4.14% point; PLF direction difference is more prominent, KMG-LUM route is particularly significant. The ICAO annual route group mean model does not distinguish the directional characteristics, and does not reflect the uneven distribution and real-time fluctuations of cargo and mail, which may cause significant emission liability deviation on one-way cargo and mail distribution routes.

Based on the above data, Fig. 6 quantitatively reveals a strong positive correlation between the GCD and the average cargo weight per flight ($R^2 = 0.842$). The scatter plot shows a significant increase from 147.6 kg to 1,003.7 kg with a

Table 5. Measured Load Factor Results for Four Routes with Round Trips from KMG

Route	Avg. Passengers	Avg. Seat Cap.	Avg. Cargo & Mail	PLF (%)	PCF (%)
PKX-KMG	148.14	186.97	0	79.23	100
CTU-KMG	136.05	167.54	0	81.20	100
KMG-PKX	138.73	187.11	1,003.67	74.15	95.86
KMG-CTU	133.59	167.58	557.69	79.71	97.50
KMG-LUM	97.75	147.51	147.55	66.27	99.15
KMG-XIY	146.52	174.42	738.59	84.00	96.94
LUM-KMG	119.74	147.42	14.64	81.22	99.92
XIY-KMG	151.41	174.45	0.004	86.79	100

standard deviation of 44.1–158.4 kg, reflecting a higher volatility for longer haul routes.

However, freight volumes have always been low as a proportion of total load: for example, on the KMG-PKX route, which has the largest freight volume, 1,003.7 kg of freight mail is equivalent to the total weight of 10 adult passengers under ICAO standards, highlighting the marginal contribution of freight forwarding to the allocation of carbon emissions responsibilities.

This finding echoes the empirical findings in Table 5 - cargo and mail-dominated outbound flights accounted for only 3.06% to 4.14% of the PCF bias when converted, reflecting a significant underestimation of the directional responsibility of ICAO mean processing.

4.2 Load-Time Variable Characteristics

This study analyzed time series data from four routes and found that the average weight of luggage per passenger per month consistently falls within the range of 2.5 to 7.5 kg. Figure 7 shows that even during peak travel periods such as the Spring Festival (TSID 1–3, 13–15, purple) and summer (TSID 7–9, 19, gray), the peak luggage weight only reaches 7 to 8 kg, which is less than 45% of the typical free baggage allowance of most airlines (approximately 20 kg).

This contrasts significantly with the ICAO estimate of a total passenger and luggage weight of 100 kg. The consistent annual fluctuation trends across the four routes in the chart indicate that the ICAO standard does not accurately reflect the actual luggage loads carried by passengers, particularly overlooking the lightweight characteristics of shorter routes and off-peak travel periods. This phenomenon embodies a dual contradiction:

- **Seasonal bias:** The ICAO standard does not account for the diluting effect of increased child passenger numbers during holidays (with generally fewer and lighter bags), focusing solely on "peak" periods while neglecting the fact that actual peaks remain relatively low.

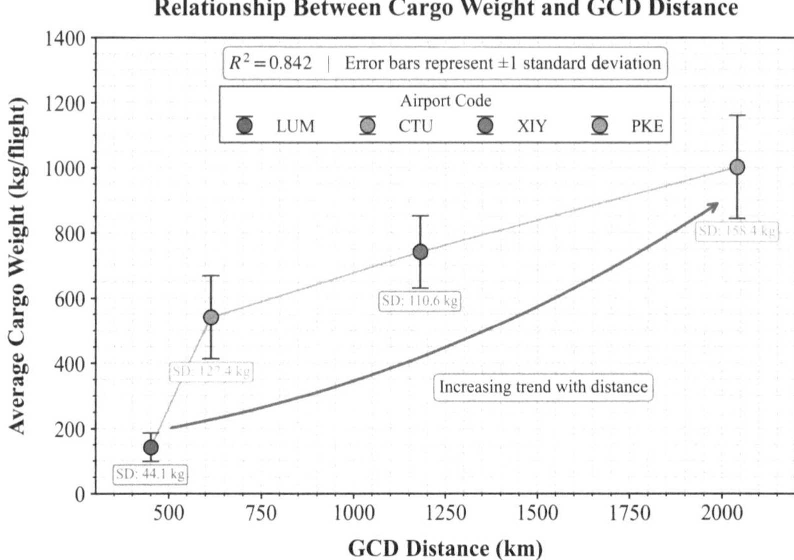

Fig. 6. Validation of the Correlation between Route Distance and Cargo Weight

- **Route specificity:** Apart from LUM as an international transit hub, as the flight distance increases within China's route network, the average weight of passengers' luggage also tends to rise, and it lacks rationality for ICAO to apply a uniform standard across all scenarios.

4.3 Shipping Characteristics of the Airline

The ICAO carbon emissions calculation method defaults that all flights carry cargo mail, but this is not in line with the actual situation of Chinese flights. In the radar diagram in Fig. 8, the line indicates the proportion of freight and mail flights carried out by each airline, and the size and color of the scatter points correspond to the total number of flights.

It can be seen that the route from KMG to various destinations shows a significant fault in the proportion of freight and mail flights. Eastern Airlines (MU), the largest carrier on all four routes, has a freight ratio of 0.5%. In contrast, KMG local and regional airlines such as Ruili Airlines (DR), Kunming Airlines (KY), Sichuan Airlines (3U), and Chang'an Airlines (9C) account for a higher proportion of flights with cargo despite the small number of flights.

Key observations include:

- Large airlines focus on passenger traffic density
- Regional airlines rely on local logistics network to actively develop belly cargo
- The ICAO's current regional average PCF algorithm ignores this structural difference, which will lead to a distortion of carbon liability attribution

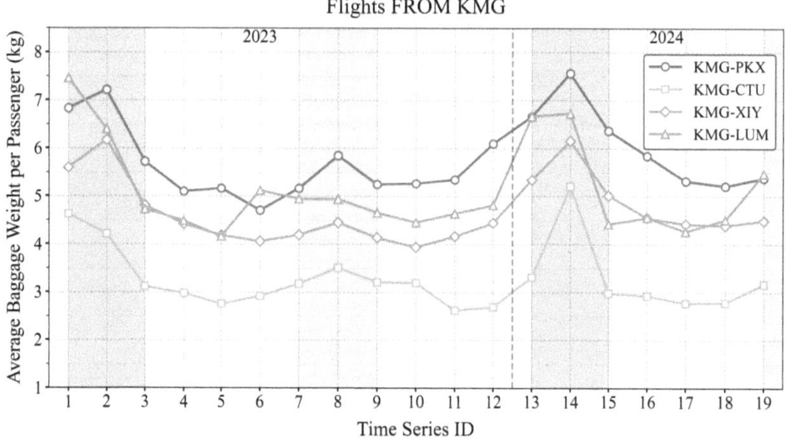

(a) Flights FROM KMG

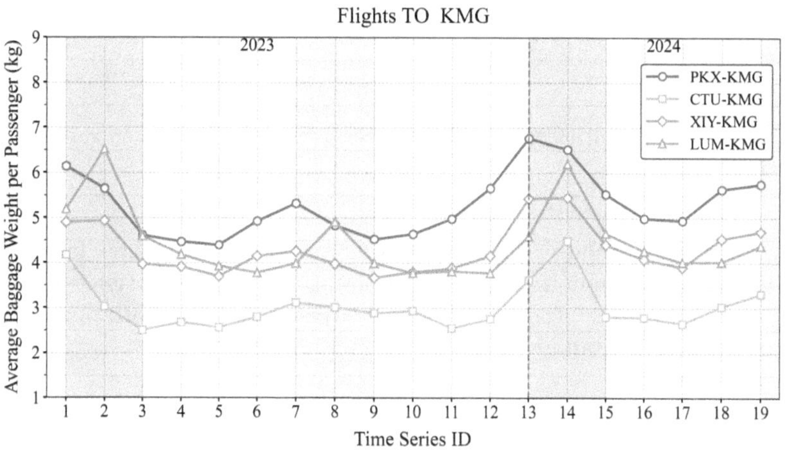

(b) Flights TO KMG

Fig. 7. Monthly Average Luggage Weight Sequences

When the cargo and mail capacity of a flight is zero, the responsibility for the carbon emissions of the aircraft is fully borne by the passengers. Take Eastern Airlines, for example:

- Each route accounts for more than 50% of flights
- Cargo and mail shipments are zero
- The actual carbon emission intensity of passengers will increase significantly

The above analysis results indicate that cargo and mail transportation exhibit significant directional clustering, with baggage weight being influenced by both seasonal variations and route-specific attributes, and there are notable differences

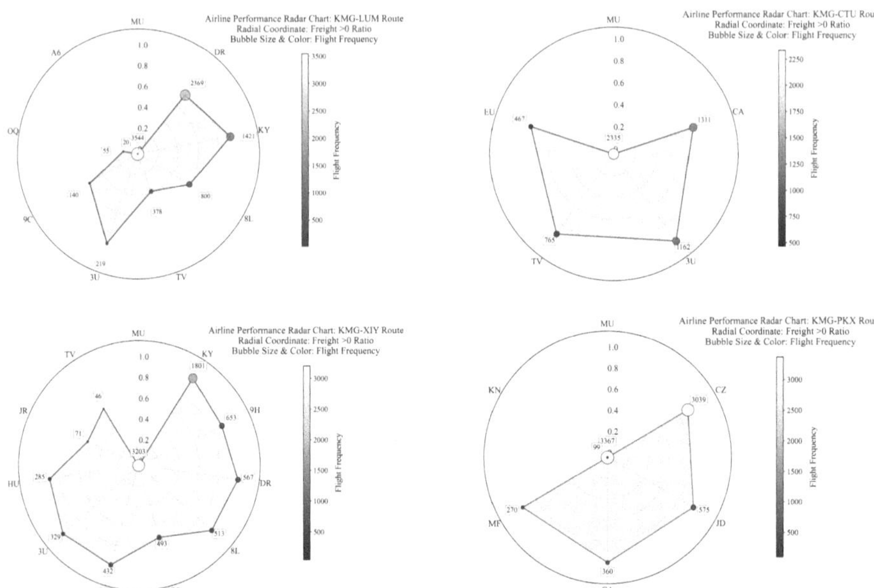

Fig. 8. Cargo capacity utilization rates for passenger flights operated by various airlines on different routes

in cargo strategies among airlines. The combination of these three factors leads to systematic deviations from the ICAO static load assumptions in Chinese routes, highlighting the need for a dynamic adjustment framework that considers direction, seasonality, and carrier-specific factors.

5 Conclusion

This study uses high-resolution operational data from typical Chinese routes to test the core assumptions of the ICAO aviation carbon emission methodology on flight distance and payload parameters. Although widely adopted as the global standard, the ICAO framework has rarely been empirically scrutinized, leaving few comparable studies. This gap underscores the relevance of our analysis, which evaluates the method's robustness under real-world conditions. Results show that ICAO's static flight distance correction model underestimates fluctuations caused by weather avoidance and airspace control in complex Chinese airspace. Its reliance on annual mean payload parameters obscures marked spatial and temporal heterogeneities: cargo and mail transport are asymmetric between outbound and inbound directions, passenger occupancy rates vary, baggage weights are often below the 100 kg per person assumption and shift with season and route, and airline-specific cargo strategies distort emission responsibility allocation. These issues reveal systematic biases in applying ICAO's static, average-based approach to dynamic operational environments.

In summary, while the current ICAO carbon emission calculation method provides a standardized framework for accounting, its simplifications in handling dynamic variations in flight distances and spatial-temporal heterogeneity of loads undermine the accuracy and fairness of carbon emission responsibility allocation, particularly in regions with complex airspace structures and significant transportation imbalances, such as China. The findings of this study call for critical improvements in the ICAO methodology, including the development of a dynamic flight distance correction model that integrates real-time meteorological and airspace data, the introduction of a refined mechanism for obtaining load parameters that distinguish between return journeys, account for seasonal fluctuations, and reflect specific carrier transportation strategies, and the reassessment and potential lowering of the quality benchmark assumptions for passengers and baggage. Future research should expand to more diverse airspace environments globally and explore the feasibility of incorporating high-resolution actual operational data into the carbon accounting system to build a more spatially and temporally accurate system for measuring aviation carbon emissions with fair responsibility attribution.

References

1. Haag, K.: International action and the role of ICAO. In: Aviation and Climate Change, pp. 104–116. Routledge (2020)
2. International Civil Aviation Organization: ICAO carbon emissions calculator methodology (version 13) (2024). https://www.icao.int/environmental-protection/CarbonOffset/Documents/Methodology%20ICAO%20Carbon%20Emissions%20Calculator_v13_Final.pdf
3. Kammila, A.: ICAO's approach to address aviation pollution: a critical analysis. Lex ad Coelum **3**(II) (2023)
4. Wang, J., Wang, Y., Zhang, S., et al.: Accounting of aviation carbon emission in developing countries based on flight-level ADS-B data. Appl. Energy **358**, 122600 (2024). https://doi.org/10.1016/j.apenergy.2023.122600
5. Wang, Z., Bai, Y.: Prediction of international aviation carbon emissions and offsetting based on ICAO mechanisms. In: Proceedings of the 2023 5th International Conference on Power and Energy Technology (ICPET), pp. 1349–1353. IEEE (2023). https://doi.org/10.1109/ICPET59380.2023.10367631
6. Yu, H., Bao, S., Man, Q., et al.: A study on the measurement and prediction of airport carbon emissions under the perspective of carbon peak. Eng. Proc. **80**(1), 43 (2025). https://doi.org/10.3390/engproc2024080043

Auto-tuning Compiler Flags with Pretrained Language Models and Surrogate-guided Search

Yinjun Pan, Junqing Lin, Jingwei Sun(✉), and Guangzhong Sun

School and Computer Science and Technology, University of Science and Technology of China, Hefei, China
{panyj609,linjunqing}@mail.ustc.edu.cn, {sunjw,gzsun}@ustc.edu.cn

Abstract. Compiler optimization is a crucial step in software development, aiming to enhance program performance by selecting the most suitable optimization flags. However, the vast search space of compiler flags, often exceeding hundreds, poses significant challenges for developers. This paper introduces a novel framework that leverages pretrained language models (PLMs) to extract rich code representations for compiler auto-tuning. A lightweight surrogate model predicts program performance based on these representations and optimization flag settings, while GASM (Genetic Algorithm via Surrogate Model) efficiently explores the configuration space through adaptive fine-tuning of the surrogate model. Experiments on PolyBench and CBench demonstrate that our approach achieves up to 2x faster optimization with comparable or better speedups than state-of-the-art methods like RIO, OpenTuner, and BOCA. The surrogate model achieves a 6% Mean Absolute Percentage Error, ensuring accurate performance predictions. This work establishes a scalable and efficient foundation for future research in automated compiler optimization.

Keywords: Compiler Optimization · Pretrained Language Models · Auto-tuning · Performance Prediction

1 Introduction

Modern compilers like GCC [2] and LLVM [1] provide a wide range of optimization flags, allowing developers and users to fine-tune program performance, memory usage, and code size. For instance, GCC 11 provides 252 optimization flags. While these flags offer significant flexibility and control, determining the optimal combination for a given application can be a daunting and time-consuming task.

To simplify the optimization process, compilers also provide preconfigured optimization levels (e.g., -O1, -O2, -O3). These levels aggregate carefully selected sets of flags designed to meet common optimization goals, offering a

J. Zhan et al. (Eds.): Bench 2025, LNCS 16471, pp. 254–271, 2026.
https://doi.org/10.1007/978-981-95-9694-2_18

practical and efficient alternative to manual flag customization. Yet, as demonstrated by prior studies [7,10,12,14,28,39], preconfigured optimization levels often fail to achieve the best possible performance. Consequently, developers are frequently compelled to manually experiment with various flag combinations, a process that is resource-intensive and error-prone. This underscores the need for automated approaches to compiler flag tuning [7,8,20]. However, designing an effective compiler auto-tuner entails addressing several fundamental challenges:

1. **High-Dimensional and Irregular Optimization Space.** Modern compilers provide hundreds of optimization flags, leading to an exponentially large configuration space [1,2]. This explosion in dimensionality makes it infeasible to evaluate every combination exhaustively. Moreover, the optimization space is highly irregular, with complex dependencies between flags wherein enabling one optimization might require disabling another to achieve the best synergy [7,14,28]. These characteristics demand advanced search strategies capable of efficiently navigating the space and identifying promising configurations without exhaustive enumeration.
2. **Time-Consuming Compilation and Testing.** Evaluating a single configuration requires compiling the target program and running benchmarks to measure performance metrics. This process can be time-intensive, especially for large-scale applications or when targeting multiple hardware platforms [7,12,14]. The cost of evaluating numerous configurations within a reasonable timeframe remains a significant bottleneck in auto-tuning workflows.
3. **Diverse Program Characteristics and Behaviors.** Programs exhibit substantial variability in their code structures, data access patterns, control flow complexities, and performance bottlenecks [12,15,40]. For instance, a configuration that delivers optimal results for a computation-intensive program may perform poorly for a memory-bound program. This diversity further complicates the auto-tuning process, as it necessitates adaptable strategies that can generalize across a wide range of programs while still identifying program-specific solutions.

Existing studies have proposed effective approaches to explore the complex search space of compiler flags, incorporating with black-box optimization techniques like Random Iterative Search(RIO) [14], Genetic Algorithms(GA) [21], Monte Carlo Search Trees(MCST) [28], Bayesian Optimization(BO) [12], Particle Swarm Optimization(PSO) [40], etc. Despite their effectiveness, the inherently time-intensive processes of compilation and testing still hinder the search speed. While some studies attempt to mitigate this issue by using surrogate models to approximate program performance [8–10,12,40], their models, such as Bayesian Networks, Random Forest, and Gaussian Process, remain limited in performance estimation accuracy. Moreover, to better capture the diverse characteristics and behaviors of programs, recent efforts have explored deep learning techniques, such as Graph Neural Networks (GNNs) [15,18,35] and Long Short-Term Memory (LSTM) networks [4,16], to extract syntactic and semantic features from code. However, their code understanding ability is constrained by the limited size of training datasets, reducing their ability to generalize across a wide variety of programs and adapt effectively to program-specific optimization requirements.

To address the challenges and limitations of existing compiler flag autotuning methods, this paper introduces a novel framework that leverages pretrained language models (PLMs) for compiler flag optimization, taking both generalizable code representation and efficient program-specific optimization into account. By utilizing the structural and semantic understanding capabilities of PLMs, our approach extracts rich program representations as high-dimensional feature vectors. These feature vectors are then integrated into a lightweight surrogate model for performance prediction and avoiding repetitive performance measurements. This surrogate model plays the role of a base model that can serve different programs. We further introduce GASM (Genetic Algorithm via Surrogate Model), combining adaptive genetic algorithms with the surrogate model to efficiently explore the high-dimensional optimization space. Given a specific program, GASM dynamically fine-tunes the base surrogate model using feedback from few actual measurements, achieving fast convergence to optimal configurations.

We validate the proposed framework on two widely used benchmarks, PolyBench and CBench. The results demonstrate that our approach achieves superior performance compared to RIO [14], OpenTuner [5], and BOCA [12]. Our framework reduces the search time by up to 2x while achieving comparable or better program speedups. The surrogate model exhibits strong predictive capability, achieving a Mean Absolute Percentage Error (MAPE) of approximately 6%, ensuring accurate evaluations of optimization flags.

Our work makes the following contributions:

- We propose leveraging PLMs to extract rich code characteristics for optimizing compiler flags, addressing the limitations of existing approaches in capturing program semantics and structure.
- We design a lightweight surrogate model to predict program performance and integrate it into a genetic algorithm, enabling efficient exploration of the optimization space.
- The proposed solution can be fine-tuned with minimal calibration data, enabling rapid adaptation to new programs and reducing the overhead of re-training.

2 Background and Related Work

2.1 Program Characteristics

Program characteristics refer to the intrinsic properties and execution behaviors of a program that significantly influence its performance and optimization potential. These characteristics can be broadly classified into two categories: static and dynamic. Static characteristics, such as control flow, data dependencies, and program structure, can be determined at compile time through static analysis techniques. In contrast, dynamic characteristics, including runtime behavior, resource usage patterns (e.g., memory access, CPU utilization, I/O usage), and performance metrics (e.g., cache hit ratios), emerge during program execution and require profiling or dynamic analysis to capture. Together, these characteristics provide critical insights for performance tuning.

In this work, we focus primarily on static analysis, as it enables the extraction of program characteristics directly from source code without requiring program execution. Static analysis approaches typically fall into three main categories:

Traditional Compiler-Based Analysis. Classical compiler analysis techniques leverage lexical, syntactic, and semantic analyses to extract program features. For example, lexical and syntax analysis generate abstract syntax trees (ASTs), while control flow analysis and data flow analysis are applied to construct control flow graphs (CFGs), data flow graphs (DFGs), and program dependency graphs. Tools like Tree-sitter can efficiently generate ASTs, which serve as a foundation for further semantic and dependency analyses. These techniques remain central to many static analysis workflows.

Graph Neural Networks (GNNs). Some recent studies employ GNNs to extract program characteristics by representing code as graphs [3,11,15,25]. For instance, ProGraML [15] transforms programs into graph representations, such as DFGs, and applies GNNs to learn feature embeddings. These embeddings are then used for downstream tasks such as compiler optimization and heterogeneous device mapping. GNN-based approaches have demonstrated strong potential in capturing the structural dependencies within programs.

Language Models (LMs). Advances in natural language processing (NLP) have led to the development of neural language models, such as RNNs [38], LSTMs [22], and Transformers [37], which have also been applied to program analysis [16,18]. However, traditional LMs often require extensive task-specific data to effectively model program characteristics. Their limited size also reduces their ability to generalize across a wide variety of programs.

2.2 Pretrained Language Model

Pretrained language models (PLMs) are a class of large-scale neural networks that undergo unsupervised or self-supervised training on extensive corpora to capture general language features. Following this pretraining phase, PLMs can be fine-tuned on domain-specific datasets for particular tasks. Since the introduction of the Transformer architecture [37], PLMs have become the cornerstone of modern NLP, with notable examples including BERT [17], GPT [30], and Llama [36].

PLMs excel in capturing linguistic features such as grammar, semantics, and context due to their large-scale training on diverse datasets. In code analysis, these capabilities have been extended to specialized code language models, such as CodeBERT [19], GraphCodeBERT [23], and CodeLlama [31], which are pretrained on code corpora. These models have shown promise in tasks like code completion, generation, and bug detection.

In the context of performance optimization, recent studies have adapted PLMs to compiler and runtime tasks. For example, MIREncoder [18] combines semantic features from PLMs with structural features extracted via GNNs to improve performance optimization tasks. Similarly, Taneja et al. [34] propose a vectorization generation tool based on LLMs, utilizing GPT-4 to generate vectorized code and introducing a verification method for correctness and equivalence validation.

In our work, we choose the fine-tuned CodeBERT to extract program features. It is a lightweight model with 110 million parameters and is capable of performing code extraction tasks effectively.

2.3 Compiler Auto-tuning

Compiler auto-tuning addresses the challenge of identifying optimal compiler flags for program performance, a task complicated by the vast and irregular optimization space. Existing methods can be broadly divided into two categories: direct search-based approaches and surrogate model-based approaches.

Search-based methods rely on strategies including random search [14], genetic algorithms [21], Monte Carlo tree search [28], and particle swarm optimization [40]. These techniques iteratively explore the optimization space and utilize feedback from prior evaluations to refine their search strategy. While they are effective for navigating high-dimensional spaces, their reliance on repeated measurements makes them computationally expensive. Surrogate model-based approaches attempt to alleviate this cost by predicting program performance using models such as Gaussian processes [12], random forests [40], or neural networks [7,13,27,32]. These models reduce the number of actual program evaluations required, accelerating the tuning process.

Our work is based on genetic algorithms, which are capable of handling irregular search spaces. Additionally, we modify traditional genetic algorithms to address the compiler auto-tuning problem.

3 Methodology

3.1 Method Overview

The proposed framework for compiler flag auto-tuning consists of two primary stages: an offline pretraining stage and an online search optimization stage, as illustrated in Fig. 1. These stages work synergistically to leverage PLMs for program feature extraction and dynamic optimization, ultimately discovering high-quality compiler configurations efficiently.

Offline Stage. The offline stage is designed to prepare the foundational components required for efficient online optimization. It comprises three main steps:

The first step focuses on enhancing the capability of the PLM. Specifically, as illustrated in Fig. 1, we adopt CodeBERT [19] as our chosen PLM and fine-tune it on the CodeNet [29] dataset.

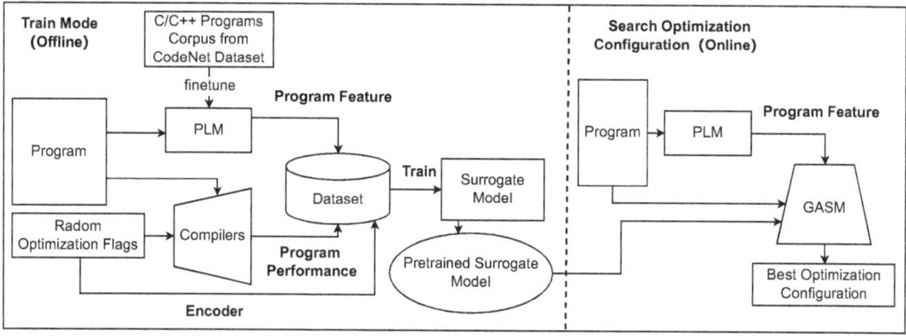

Fig. 1. Method Overview.

In the second step, we collect extensive performance data by executing benchmark programs in the early stage. This data is then used to train the surrogate model. CodeBERT is employed to extract code feature vectors from a benchmark suite. For each program, a set of random optimization configurations is generated, and their corresponding performance is evaluated in terms of the speedup ratio, defined as the ratio of the original program's execution time to the optimized program's execution time. The extracted code features and the measured performance data are then combined to construct a dataset, which serves as the input for training the surrogate model.

In the third step, a surrogate model is trained to predict the speedup ratio of a program given its code features and a specific optimization configuration. This regression model takes the program's feature vectors and optimization flags as input and outputs the predicted performance. By approximating the performance evaluation process, the surrogate model eliminates the need for expensive compilation and runtime measurements during the online optimization stage. The design of the surrogate model will be detailed in Sect. 3.3.

Online Stage. The online stage focuses on applying the pretrained model to dynamically search the optimal compiler flag configuration for a given program. It involves two key tasks:

First, we use PLM to extract feature vectors that capture the program's structural and semantic properties. These features serve as input to the surrogate model, enabling it to evaluate the performance of various optimization configurations.

Second, we integrate the surrogate model into a GASM to efficiently explore the high-dimensional space of compiler flags. It leverages the surrogate model to estimate the performance of candidate configurations and selects the most promising ones for actual measurement. After each search iteration, a small subset of configurations is evaluated through actual runtime measurements. The measured data is then used to fine-tune the surrogate model, progressively improving its predictive accuracy and guiding the search towards better configurations. By combining surrogate model predictions with iterative refinement,

GASM achieves rapid convergence to high-quality optimization setups. Detailed procedures of GASM will be introduced in Sect. 3.4.

3.2 Code Feature Extraction

CodeBERT treats the $[CLS]$ token as a special token at the beginning of each input sequence. The final hidden state of this token is designed to encapsulate the semantic and contextual information of the entire sequence, making it a natural choice for sequence-level representation.

The maximum token length supported by CodeBERT is 512. For programs whose source code exceeds this limit, we adopt a segmentation-based approach. The program is split into multiple segments, each containing up to 512 tokens. Each segment is then processed independently by CodeBERT, resulting in a 768-dimensional hidden vector for the $[CLS]$ token of each segment. These segment-level representations are subsequently averaged to generate a unified vector representation for the entire program. This averaging strategy ensures that the final feature vector retains information from all code segments while maintaining a fixed dimensionality.

For programs comprising multiple source files, we extend the averaging process to account for all files. Each file is independently tokenized, segmented (if necessary), and processed by CodeBERT to generate its 768-dimensional representation. The representations of all files are then averaged to produce a single feature vector for the entire program. This hierarchical approach ensures that the final program representation comprehensively captures the characteristics of multi-file projects while maintaining computational efficiency.

The final output of the code feature extraction process is a single 768-dimensional vector for each program, regardless of its length or the number of source files. This fixed-size representation is designed to be compatible with the input requirements of the surrogate model. By using a single, compact vector for each program, we ensure that the surrogate model can efficiently process the program features while maintaining scalability for large datasets.

3.3 Surrogate Model

The surrogate model is a pivotal component of our framework, designed to approximate program performance under various compiler optimization configurations. This model acts as a cost-effective alternative to direct program execution by predicting the speedup ratio based on the program's code features and selected optimization flags. The detailed design of the surrogate model is illustrated in Fig. 2a.

The surrogate model processes two distinct inputs: the code representation vector and the optimization configuration vector. These inputs are carefully encoded to ensure that the model captures both the semantic richness of the program code and the combinatorial impact of optimization flags. For the code representation vector, using the pretrained CodeBERT model, we extract a 768-dimensional vector that encapsulates the structural and semantic features of the

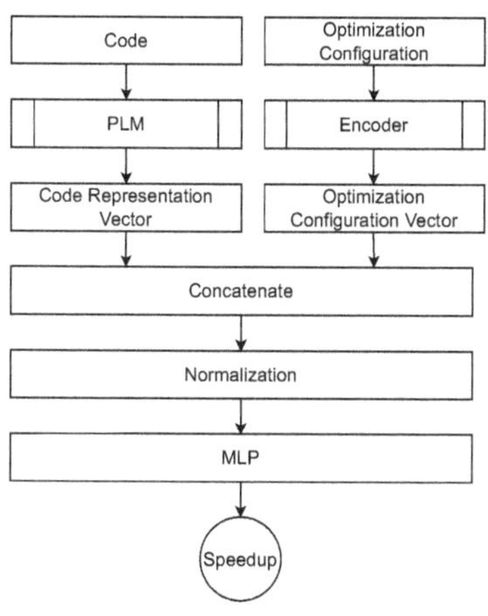

(a) Design of Surrogate Model

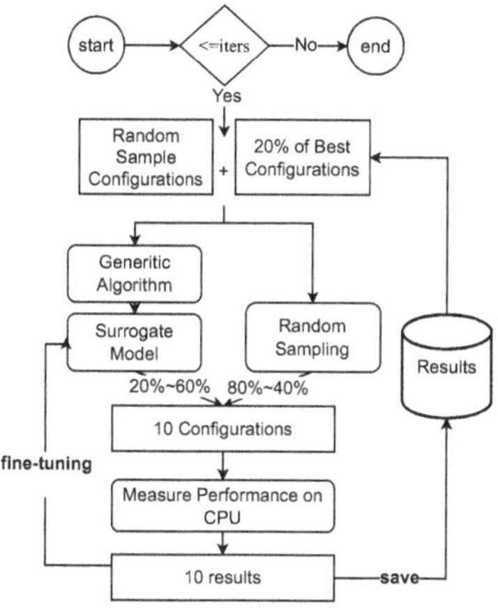

(b) GASM: Genetic Algorithm via Surrogate Model

Fig. 2. (a) Design of Surrogate Model (b) GASM: Genetic Algorithm via Surrogate Model

input program. This representation, derived as described in Sect. 3.2, serves as a compact and expressive encoding of the program's inherent characteristics. For the optimization configuration vector, each compiler optimization flag is represented as a categorical variable with two mutually exclusive states: enabled and disabled. To avoid introducing feature prioritization bias, we use one-hot encoding for these flags. This ensures that the surrogate model treats all flags equitably, preserving the integrity of its predictions. The resulting vector represents all selected flags for a given configuration.

To effectively combine information from the two inputs, the code representation vector and the optimization configuration vector are concatenated into a unified feature vector. As these inputs may have differing value ranges and distributions, a normalization operation is applied to standardize the concatenated vector. The fused feature vector is passed through a Multi-layer Perceptron (MLP), which serves as the core predictive model. The MLP is structured as a regression model, optimized to predict the speedup ratio directly. It is trained using the dataset generated in the offline pretraining stage. Each training example consists of the code representation vector (generated by CodeBERT), the one-hot encoded optimization configuration vector, and the observed speedup ratio (measured through actual program execution). The model is optimized using the Mean Squared Error (MSE) loss function, which minimizes the discrepancy between the predicted and observed speedup ratios. We employ the Adam optimizer with a learning rate scheduler to ensure stable and efficient convergence during training.

3.4 GASM: Genetic Algorithm via Surrogate Model

We propose GASM, a search strategy specifically designed for efficient and scalable compiler flag optimization. GASM builds upon the principles of genetic algorithms (GAs) while incorporating surrogate modeling and dynamic fine-tuning mechanisms to address the challenges of high-dimensional optimization spaces and expensive evaluation costs. The framework of GASM is illustrated in Fig. 2b.

Hybrid Population Initialization. Each iteration of GASM begins by initializing the population using a hybrid approach that combines elite sampling and random sampling. The elite sampling strategy selects the top 20% of past configurations with the highest actual performance, ensuring that high-quality solutions from previous iterations are retained. The remaining individuals in the population are generated through random sampling within the optimization space, introducing diversity and avoiding premature convergence. This combination balances exploitation of known high-performing solutions with exploration of new regions in the search space.

Surrogate Model-Driven Evaluation. A surrogate model replaces direct measurements during the evaluation phase, significantly reducing the computational cost of assessing optimization configurations. The surrogate model predicts the performance (in terms of speedup ratio) of candidate configurations based on their code features and optimization flag settings. By enabling rapid evaluation of a large number of configurations, the surrogate model allows GASM to efficiently explore the vast and irregular optimization space. This approach also enhances the algorithm's ability to make informed selection decisions.

Dynamic Model Fine-tuning Mechanism. To maintain the accuracy of the surrogate model and adapt it to the search process, GASM incorporates a dynamic fine-tuning mechanism. After each iteration, a subset of configurations is selected for actual performance measurement to update the surrogate model. The selection strategy employs a weighted combination of population sampling and random sampling. Specifically, 20% of the candidate configurations are drawn from the current population, ensuring the model remains aligned with recent search progress. Meanwhile, 80% of the candidate configurations are randomly generated to introduce diversity and prevent local optima. The balance between population and random sampling is dynamically adjusted across iterations. In the early stages, a higher proportion of random sampling broadens the search scope, addressing the surrogate model's lower initial accuracy. As the model becomes more reliable in later stages, the weight shifts toward population sampling, guiding the algorithm toward convergence with greater precision.

Genetic Operators for Candidate Generation. GASM employs classic genetic operators, including mutation and crossover, to generate new candidate configurations from the population. Mutation introduces small random changes to individual configurations, promoting diversity, while crossover combines features from pairs of configurations, enabling the algorithm to explore combinations of promising traits. The offspring generated by these operators are evaluated using the surrogate model, and the top-performing configurations are retained for the next iteration.

4 Evaluation

We designed three experiments to address the following questions: (1) the capability of PLM in code understanding, (2) the effectiveness of the surrogate model, and (3) the efficiency of our optimization algorithm.

4.1 Setup

Datasets. The datasets used in this study are as follows:

1. CodeNet [29] and POJ-104 [26]: These datasets are used to fine-tune CodeBERT
2. Exebench [6]: This dataset contains a large number of executable C functions. We use these functions to collect performance data under various optimization configurations, gathering approximately 480,000 data points from 5,830 functions.
3. CBench [33]: This dataset is used to evaluate the efficiency of our method.

Environment. CodeBERT is fine-tuned on an *Nvidia 4090*, and the surrogate model is trained on an *Nvidia 2080 Ti*. In this study, GCC 15 is used as the compiler, and the computing environment is equipped with an *Intel i5-12400* CPU and 16 GB of memory. Performance evaluation, data collection for the model and algorithm, and testing of the optimization settings are all conducted within this development environment.

Baseline. We compare our approach against the following widely used methods in compiler optimization. Random Iterative Optimization (RIO) [14] randomly samples configurations and selects the best based on actual measurements. Simple yet effective, it serves as a suitable baseline. OpenTuner [5] is a flexible, open-source framework for parameter tuning, widely applied in compiler optimization and performance tuning tasks. BOCA [12] is a Bayesian optimization-based framework that uses a random forest model to predict program performance and guide the search process.

4.2 Capability of the PLM in Code Understanding

Since CodeBERT was pretrained on CodeSearchNet [24], a dataset that lacks sufficient coverage of C/C++ programs, We conduct two tasks to fine-tune CodeBERT and use two different metrics to evaluate its capability. The first task is

Masked Language Modeling (MLM), using the CodeNet dataset, with perplexity as the evaluation metric. Perplexity measures a language model's ability to predict the next token in a sequence, with lower perplexity indicating better performance. The second task is Clone Detection, where we use the POJ-104 dataset to fine-tune the model, and evaluate it using Mean Average Precision at R (MAP@R). MAP@R measures the model's recall and ranking accuracy for "all relevant items" among the "top R recommended/retrieved results". After fine-tuning, the model achieves a perplexity of 1.04 and a MAP@P of 0.82.

In other words, we also evaluate the effectiveness of different fine-tuning methods in the surrogate model training task. We use regression metrics (e.g., MAE, MAPE, and R^2) to assess the surrogate model and compare the fine-tuning methods (see Table 1). We compare the model without fine-tuning and the model fine-tuned using two different methods to extract code features and train the surrogate model. From this, we conclude that the PLM demonstrates code understanding capability and, even without fine-tuning, can recognize C programs.

Table 1. Regression evaluation metrics of surrogate model

	MAE	MAPE	R2
CodeBERT-base	0.13	6.22	0.69
CodeBERT-mlm-finetune	0.13	6.19	0.68
CodeBERT-base-finetune	0.13	6.25	0.69

4.3 Effectiveness of Surrogate Model

The surrogate model's accuracy is evaluated by comparing predicted speedup ratios with actual measurements. As a regression model, it predicts program performance by processing feature vectors of the program and flag vectors of optimization settings. To visually demonstrate the predictive efficacy, we plotted a scatter diagram comparing predicted values against actual values (see Fig. 3). The results indicate a general linear trend between the two variables. Although the fitted line exhibits a non-zero intercept, this deviation does not significantly affect the model's ranking capability, since our study only requires distinguishing the relative merits of different flag configurations and thus can be reasonably neglected. In other words, quantitative metrics in Table 1 also validate the model's performance.

To further validate the surrogate model, we integrate it into a surrogate-model-enhanced random search algorithm. The specific process is as follows: in each search iteration, 1000 groups of optimization flag combinations are first generated through random sampling, and the surrogate model is used to predict the speedup ratio corresponding to each group of flags; subsequently, the flag combination with the optimal prediction result is selected for actual measurement

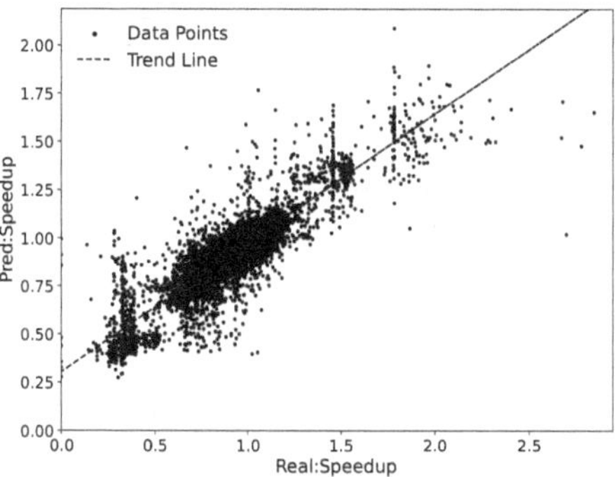

Fig. 3. The relationship between the values predicted by the surrogate model and the real values.

verification, and the measured results are fed back to the surrogate model for iterative learning. The above process terminates after iterating a certain number of rounds. We designed comparative experiments between this algorithm and the surrogate-free random search algorithm. Since this algorithm only adds the process of model evaluation compared to the random algorithm, comparing the results of the two groups of experiments can effectively verify the evaluation effectiveness of the surrogate model in speedup ratio prediction.

We conducted ten independent experimental repetitions for each program within the CBench benchmark suite, documenting the optimal speedup achieved in each search iteration and generating speedup variation profiles.

Table 2. Comparison of speedup between RIO and RIO with the model.

	RIO	RIO + model	O3 baseline
automotive_bitcount	1.47 ± 0.03	1.50 ± 0.04	1.00
automotive_susan_c	1.01 ± 0.04	1.00 ± 0.02	1.00
automotive_susan_e	1.04 ± 0.03	1.03 ± 0.01	0.99
automotive_susan_s	1.15 ± 0.01	1.15 ± 0.01	0.87
bzip2e	1.01 ± 0.01	1.02 ± 0.01	1.02
consumer_jpeg_c	1.05 ± 0.01	1.06 ± 0.02	0.95
security_sha	1.17 ± 0.03	1.21 ± 0.05	0.62
consumer_tiff2rgba	1.10 ± 0.02	1.12 ± 0.02	1.24
telecom_adpcm_c	1.40 ± 0.07	1.40 ± 0.06	1.01
office_rsynth	3.95 ± 0.23	4.05 ± 0.13	2.30

Figures 4 and Table 2 present the runtime performance of the tuned programs. For the optimization tasks of most programs, the algorithm using the model outperforms the one without the model in both convergence time and optimal speedup. This result demonstrates that the surrogate model can effectively evaluate the advantages and disadvantages of different optimization settings to a certain extent. In other words, we can conclude that even the program using O3 has significant potential for further improvement.

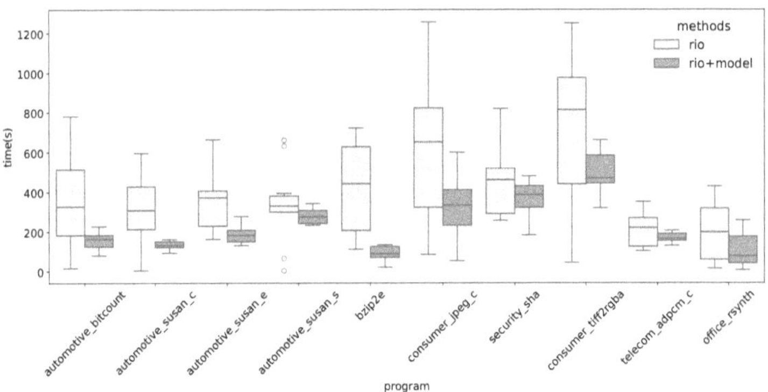

Fig. 4. Convergence time comparison between surrogate-assisted and surrogate-free random iterative algorithms

4.4 Efficiency of GASM

To verify the effectiveness of the newly designed search strategy, we selected Random Iterative Optimization (RIO), OpenTuner [5], and BOCA [12] as comparison baselines. For each program, ten repeated experiments were conducted, and the optimal speedup obtained under each scheme was statistically analyzed (see Table 3 for details). Experimental results demonstrate that our algorithm achieved the highest optimal speedup in over half of the tested programs. However, for programs with inherently limited acceleration potential, the performance gap between our approach and other baselines remained negligible. Analysis reveals that program-specific characteristics–such as structural complexity and inherent parallelism–significantly influence optimization outcomes, leading to divergent performance across algorithms. For instance, in automotive_bitcount, our method yielded a peak speedup of 1.50$\pm$ 0.03, outperforming **RIO**(1.47 $\pm$ 0.03), **OpenTuner**(1.44 $\pm$ 0.13) and **BOCA**(1.42 $\pm$ 0.01). Conversely, for consumer_jpeg_c, our speedup of 1.11 $\pm$ 0.02 mar-ginally trailed **OpenTuner**(1.12 $\pm$ 0.08) and **BOCA**(1.11 $\pm$ 0.03). These findings highlight the algorithm's efficacy in unlocking performance for programs with substantial optimization headroom.

Additionally, we statistically analyzed the results of ten experimental trials for each program across different methods, examining the distribution of convergence times. We visualized these findings using boxplots (Fig. 5). Furthermore,

Table 3. Comparison among different approaches in terms of speedup

	RIO	GASM	OpenTuner	BOCA
automotive_bitcount	1.47 ± 0.03	1.50 ± 0.03	1.44 ± 0.13	1.42 ± 0.01
automotive_susan_c	1.01 ± 0.04	1.00 ± 0.01	1.00 ± 0.03	1.00 ± 0.01
automotive_susan_e	1.04 ± 0.03	1.02 ± 0.01	1.03 ± 0.02	1.02 ± 0.02
automotive_susan_s	1.15 ± 0.01	1.15 ± 0.005	1.15 ± 0.01	1.13 ± 0.02
bzip2e	1.01 ± 0.01	1.02 ± 0.01	1.01 ± 0.01	1.00 ± 0.02
consumer_jpeg_c	1.05 ± 0.01	1.06 ± 0.02	1.04 ± 0.04	0.99 ± 0.02
security_sha	1.17 ± 0.03	1.21 ± 0.05	1.17 ± 0.04	1.07 ± 0.06
consumer_tiff2rgba	1.10 ± 0.02	1.11 ± 0.02	1.12 ± 0.08	1.11 ± 0.03
telecom_adpcm_c	1.40 ± 0.07	1.40 ± 0.06	1.40 ± 0.09	1.24 ± 0.00
office_rsynth	3.95 ± 0.23	4.05 ± 0.13	3.95 ± 0.25	2.38 ± 0.09

our algorithm demonstrates a clear advantage in convergence time, as illustrated in Fig. 5: it converges faster than all baselines in most programs, particularly those with higher optimization potential.

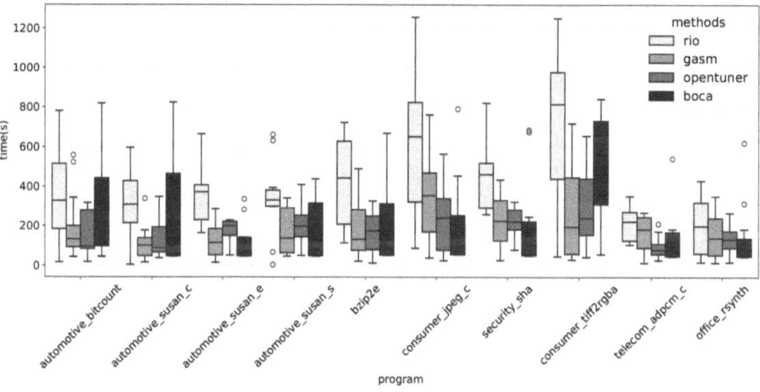

Fig. 5. Convergence time distributions across optimization methods

Analysis of the Table 3 reveals that the optimal flags identified by different methods yield comparable performance gains. In practice, any reasonably designed optimization approach can converge to effective flag configurations within acceptable time limits. However, convergence efficiency varies significantly across methods: as shown in Fig. 5, our method demonstrates a substantial advantage in convergence time, consistently identifying optimal flags in shorter iterations. Moreover, the standard deviation of our method's convergence times across programs is relatively low, indicating robust and predictable performance.

5 Conclusion

In this paper, we proposed a framework for compiler auto-tuning that combines PLMs, a lightweight surrogate model, and GASM, an adaptive genetic algorithm. By leveraging PLMs to extract semantic and structural code features, the surrogate model effectively predicts program performance, reducing the need for expensive runtime measurements. GASM dynamically fine-tunes the model for efficient exploration and rapid convergence to optimal configurations.

Evaluation on PolyBench and CBench benchmarks shows our approach consistently outperforms RIO, OpenTuner, and BOCA in speedup and convergence time, while maintaining robust performance across diverse programs. This work addresses key challenges in compiler optimization and provides a scalable, efficient solution for future research and practical applications in automated tuning.

Acknowledgments. This work was supported by the Industry-University-Research Cooperation Project of the Ministry of Education of China (No. 230906392304024)

References

1. LLVM's analysis and transform passes — LLVM 20.0.0git documentation, https://llvm.org/docs/Passes.html
2. Optimize options (using the GNU compiler collection (GCC)), https://gcc.gnu.org/onlinedocs/gcc/Optimize-Options.html
3. Allamanis, M., Brockschmidt, M., Khademi, M.: Learning to represent programs with graphs. CoRR **abs/1711.00740** (2017), http://arxiv.org/abs/1711.00740
4. Amalou, A.N., Fromont, E., Puaut, I.: Catreen: context-aware code timing estimation with stacked recurrent networks. In: 2022 IEEE 34th International Conference on Tools with Artificial Intelligence (ICTAI), pp. 571–576 (2022). https://doi.org/10.1109/ICTAI56018.2022.00090
5. Ansel, J., et al.: OpenTuner: an extensible framework for program autotuning. In: Proceedings of the 23rd International Conference on Parallel Architectures and Compilation, pp. 303–316. ACM. https://doi.org/10.1145/2628071.2628092, https://dl.acm.org/doi/10.1145/2628071.2628092
6. Armengol-Estapé, J., Woodruff, J., Brauckmann, A., Magalhães, J.W.D.S., O'Boyle, M.F.P.: Exebench: an ml-scale dataset of executable c functions. In: Proceedings of the 6th ACM SIGPLAN International Symposium on Machine Programming, MAPS 2022, pp. 50–59. ACM, New York, NY, USA (2022). https://doi.org/10.1145/3520312.3534867, https://doi.org/10.1145/3520312.3534867
7. Ashouri, A.H., Bignoli, A., Palermo, G., Silvano, C., Kulkarni, S., Cavazos, J.: MiCOMP: mitigating the compiler phase-ordering problem using optimization sub-sequences and machine learning **14**(3), 1–28. https://doi.org/10.1145/3124452, https://dl.acm.org/doi/10.1145/3124452
8. Ashouri, A.H., Killian, W., Cavazos, J., Palermo, G., Silvano, C.: A survey on compiler autotuning using machine learning **51**(5), 1–42. https://doi.org/10.1145/3197978, https://dl.acm.org/doi/10.1145/3197978
9. Ashouri, A.H., Mariani, G., Palermo, G., Park, E., Cavazos, J., Silvano, C.: COBAYN: compiler autotuning framework using bayesian networks **13**(2), 1–25. https://doi.org/10.1145/2928270, https://dl.acm.org/doi/10.1145/2928270

10. Ashouri, A.H., Mariani, G., Palermo, G., Silvano, C.: A bayesian network approach for compiler auto-tuning for embedded processors. In: 2014 IEEE 12th Symposium on Embedded Systems for Real-time Multimedia (ESTIMedia), pp. 90–97. IEEE. https://doi.org/10.1109/ESTIMedia.2014.6962349, http://ieeexplore.ieee.org/document/6962349/
11. Brauckmann, A., Goens, A., Ertel, S., Castrillon, J.: Compiler-based graph representations for deep learning models of code. In: Proceedings of the 29th International Conference on Compiler Construction, CC 2020, pp. 201–211. ACM, New York, NY, USA (2020). https://doi.org/10.1145/3377555.3377894, https://doi.org/10.1145/3377555.3377894
12. Chen, J., Xu, N., Chen, P., Zhang, H.: Efficient compiler autotuning via bayesian optimization. In: 2021 IEEE/ACM 43rd International Conference on Software Engineering (ICSE), pp. 1198–1209. IEEE. https://doi.org/10.1109/ICSE43902.2021.00110, https://ieeexplore.ieee.org/document/9401979/
13. Chen, P., Gong, J., Chen, T.: Accuracy can lie: on the impact of surrogate model in configuration tuning. IEEE Trans. Software Eng. **51**(2), 548–580 (2025). https://doi.org/10.1109/TSE.2025.3525955
14. Chen, Y., et al.: Deconstructing iterative optimization **9**(3), 1–30. https://doi.org/10.1145/2355585.2355594, https://dl.acm.org/doi/10.1145/2355585.2355594
15. Cummins, C., Fisches, Z.V., Ben-Nun, T., Hoefler, T., O'Boyle, M.F.P., Leather, H.: ProGraML: a graph-based program representation for data flow analysis and compiler optimizations. In: Proceedings of the 38th International Conference on Machine Learning, pp. 2244–2253. PMLR, https://proceedings.mlr.press/v139/cummins21a.html, ISSN: 2640-3498
16. Cummins, C., Petoumenos, P., Wang, Z., Leather, H.: End-to-end deep learning of optimization heuristics. In: 2017 26th International Conference on Parallel Architectures and Compilation Techniques (PACT), pp. 219–232. IEEE. https://doi.org/10.1109/PACT.2017.24, http://ieeexplore.ieee.org/document/8091247/
17. Devlin, J., Chang, M.W., Lee, K., Toutanova, K.: BERT: pre-training of deep bidirectional transformers for language understanding, http://arxiv.org/abs/1810.04805
18. Dutta, A., Jannesari, A.: MIREncoder: multi-modal ir-based pretrained embeddings for performance optimizations. In: Proceedings of the 2024 International Conference on Parallel Architectures and Compilation Techniques, pp. 156–167. ACM. https://doi.org/10.1145/3656019.3676895, https://dl.acm.org/doi/10.1145/3656019.3676895
19. Feng, Z., et al.: Codebert: a pre-trained model for programming and natural languages. CoRR **abs/2002.08155** (2020), https://arxiv.org/abs/2002.08155
20. Fursin, G., et al.: Milepost GCC: machine learning enabled self-tuning compiler **39**(3), 296–327. https://doi.org/10.1007/s10766-010-0161-2, https://doi.org/10.1007/s10766-010-0161-2
21. Garciarena, U., Santana, R.: Evolutionary optimization of compiler flag selection by learning and exploiting flags interactions. In: Proceedings of the 2016 on Genetic and Evolutionary Computation Conference Companion, pp. 1159–1166. ACM. https://doi.org/10.1145/2908961.2931696, https://dl.acm.org/doi/10.1145/2908961.2931696
22. Graves, A., Graves, A.: Long short-term memory. In: Supervised Sequence Labelling with Recurrent Neural Networks, pp. 37–45 (2012)
23. Guo, D., et al.: Graphcodebert: pre-training code representations with data flow. CoRR **abs/2009.08366** (2020), https://arxiv.org/abs/2009.08366

24. Husain, H., Wu, H.H., Gazit, T., Allamanis, M., Brockschmidt, M.: CodeSearchNet challenge: evaluating the state of semantic code search. https://doi.org/10.48550/arXiv.1909.09436, http://arxiv.org/abs/1909.09436
25. Li, Y., Gu, C., Dullien, T., Vinyals, O., Kohli, P.: Graph matching networks for learning the similarity of graph structured objects. In: Chaudhuri, K., Salakhutdinov, R. (eds.) Proceedings of the 36th International Conference on Machine Learning. Proceedings of Machine Learning Research, vol. 97, pp. 3835–3845. PMLR, 09–15 June 2019, https://proceedings.mlr.press/v97/li19d.html
26. Lu, S., et al.: Codexglue: a machine learning benchmark dataset for code understanding and generation (2021), https://arxiv.org/abs/2102.04664
27. Mithul, C., Abdulla, D.M., Virinchi, M.H., Sathvik, M., Belwal, M.: Exploring compiler optimization: a survey of ml, dl and rl techniques. In: 2024 8th International Conference on Computational System and Information Technology for Sustainable Solutions (CSITSS), pp. 1–6 (2024). https://doi.org/10.1109/CSITSS64042.2024.10816929
28. Park, S., Latifi, S., Park, Y., Behroozi, A., Jeon, B., Mahlke, S.: SRTuner: effective compiler optimization customization by exposing synergistic relations. In: 2022 IEEE/ACM International Symposium on Code Generation and Optimization (CGO), pp. 118–130. https://doi.org/10.1109/CGO53902.2022.9741263, https://ieeexplore.ieee.org/document/9741263
29. Puri, R., et al.: Project codenet: a large-scale ai for code dataset for learning a diversity of coding tasks. CoRR **abs/2105.12655** (2021), https://arxiv.org/abs/2105.12655
30. Radford, A., Narasimhan, K.: Improving language understanding by generative pre-training. https://api.semanticscholar.org/CorpusID:49313245
31. Roziere, B., et al.: Code llama: open foundation models for code. arXiv preprint arXiv:2308.12950 (2023)
32. Sajjadinasab, R., Arora, S., Drepper, U., Sanaullah, A., Herbordt, M.: A graph-based algorithm for optimizing gcc compiler flag settings. In: 2024 IEEE High Performance Extreme Computing Conference (HPEC), pp. 1–8 (2024). https://doi.org/10.1109/HPEC62836.2024.10938458
33. summerspringwei: GitHub - summerspringwei/cBench: Collective Benchmark (cBench). https://github.com/summerspringwei/cBench (2024)
34. Taneja, J., Laird, A., Yan, C., Musuvathi, M., Lahiri, S.K.: LLM-vectorizer: LLM-based verified loop vectorizer. In: Proceedings of the 23rd ACM/IEEE International Symposium on Code Generation and Optimization, pp. 137–149. ACM. https://doi.org/10.1145/3696443.3708929, https://dl.acm.org/doi/10.1145/3696443.3708929
35. TehraniJamsaz, A., Mahmud, Q.I., Chen, L., Ahmed, N.K., Jannesari, A.: Perfograph: A numerical aware program graph representation for performance optimization and program analysis. In: Oh, A., Naumann, T., Globerson, A., Saenko, K., Hardt, M., Levine, S. (eds.) Advances in Neural Information Processing Systems, vol. 36, pp. 57783–57794. Curran Associates, Inc. (2023), https://proceedings.neurips.cc/paper_files/paper/2023/file/b41907dd4df5c60f86216b73fe0c7465-Paper-Conference.pdf
36. Touvron, H., et al.: LLaMA: open and efficient foundation language models. https://doi.org/10.48550/arXiv.2302.13971, http://arxiv.org/abs/2302.13971
37. Vaswani, A., et al.: Attention is all you need. In: Advances in Neural Information Processing Systems, vol. 30 (2017), https://proceedings.neurips.cc/paper_files/paper/2017/file/3f5ee243547dee91fbd053c1c4a845aa-Paper.pdf

38. Zaremba, W., Sutskever, I., Vinyals, O.: Recurrent neural network regularization. CoRR **abs/1409.2329** (2014), http://arxiv.org/abs/1409.2329
39. Zhu, M., Hao, D., Chen, J.: Compiler autotuning through multiple-phase learning **33**(4). https://doi.org/10.1145/3640330, https://doi.org/10.1145/3640330, place: New York, NY, USA Publisher: Association for Computing Machinery
40. Zhu, M., Hao, D., Chen, J.: Compiler autotuning through multiple-phase learning **33**(4), 100:1–100:38. https://doi.org/10.1145/3640330, https://doi.org/10.1145/3640330

Examining TPC-C Characteristics on Modern E-Commerce Applications

Xueyuan Ren and Yang Wang(✉)

The Ohio State University, Columbus, OH, USA
{ren.450,wang.7564}@osu.edu

Abstract. TPC-C is widely used in evaluating transaction processing systems, due to its versatility and reasonable complexity to test different aspects of the database system. However, due to its age, it's questionable whether its workload still represents today's e-commerce applications. We compare the design of TPC-C with that of three popular online shopping applications. We observe a few key differences, including contention levels, use of complicated queries, imbalanced data and traffic, etc. Based on the study, we propose a few changes to TPC-C to better capture the performance characteristics of modern OLTP applications.

Keywords: TPC-C · OLTP · Benchmark

1 Introduction

Since its introduction in 1992, TPC-C [4] has become the de facto benchmark for online transaction processing (OLTP) systems, probably due to its versatility and reasonable complexity to test different aspects of the system. Despite the introduction of later OLTP benchmarks, such as TPC-E [5], SmallBank [10], YCSB+T [14], etc., TPC-C remains one of the most popular benchmarks for OLTP systems. Examples of works using TPC-C for evaluation include both research prototypes [11,16–19,21,22,25] and industrial systems [23,26,27].

As a result, TPC-C is guiding research in this field to some extent, since a corresponding work has to address the bottlenecks in TPC-C to demonstrate its benefits. Such an important role is also a source of concern, especially considering the age of TPC-C: If the characteristics of TPC-C deviate from the applications it represents, it may misguide us to address problems that are not prevalent or miss real problems.

This paper compares TPC-C with three popular online shopping applications. On the one hand, we find that, at a high level, these applications provide similar functions as the ones simulated by TPC-C, including creating orders, making payments, browsing histories, etc. On the other hand, we observe that, compared to TPC-C, these applications have made a few different design choices, leading to different performance characteristics. These include using shorter transactions and relying on application-specific logic or administrator's effort to address

J. Zhan et al. (Eds.): Bench 2025, LNCS 16471, pp. 272–289, 2026.
https://doi.org/10.1007/978-981-95-9694-2_19

atomicity and isolation issues, reducing contention levels with optimized implementations, using complicated OLAP-like queries in certain scenarios, etc.

Motivated by such observations, we have proposed changes to TPC-C so that it can better represent modern e-commerce applications.

2 Background of TPC-C

TPC-C simulates the database of a wholesale company, with a configurable number of warehouses. Each warehouse has 100,000 items to sell, and covers 10 districts each with 3,000 customers. It consists of nine tables (WAREHOUSE, DISTRICT, CUSTOMER, HISTORY, ORDER, NEW-ORDER, ORDER-LINE, STOCK, and ITEM) and five types of transactions:

```
TRANSACTION BEGIN
-- fetch customer data
1 SELECT c_discount,... FROM customer WHERE c_w_id=? AND c_d_id=? AND c_id=?;
-- fetch warehouse data
2 SELECT w_tax FROM warehouse WHERE w_id=?;
-- fetch district d_next_o_id for update
3 SELECT d_next_o_id,... FROM district WHERE d_w_id=? AND d_id=? FOR UPDATE;
-- increment d_next_o_id by one
4 UPDATE district SET d_next_o_id=d_next_o_id+1 WHERE d_w_id=? AND d_id=?;
-- insert order and new_order record
5 INSERT INTO oorder (o_w_id, o_d_id, o_id,...) VALUES (?,?,?,...);
6 INSERT INTO new_order (no_w_id, no_d_id, no_o_id) VALUES (?,?,?);
-- execute for each order_line item
for each order_line item:
    -- fetch item data
7   SELECT i_price, i_name, i_data FROM item WHERE i_id=?;
    -- fetch stock data
8   SELECT s_quantity,... FROM stock WHERE s_w_id=? AND s_i_id=? FOR UPDATE;
    -- insert order_line record
9   INSERT INTO order_line (ol_w_id,ol_d_id,ol_o_id,...) VALUES (?,?,?,...);
    -- update stock
10  UPDATE stock SET s_quantity = ?, ... WHERE s_w_id=? AND s_i_id=?;
TRANSACTION COMMIT
```

Fig. 1. TPC-C NEW-ORDER Transaction.

NEW-ORDER (Fig. 1). It simulates the procedure of a customer creating an order. A NEW-ORDER transaction randomly selects a district from a warehouse, selects 5 to 15 items based on an uneven distribution (some items have a higher probability of being selected), and randomly selects a quantity between one and ten for each item. It creates an order that includes all the selected items.

To create a unique order ID for each order, TPC-C maintains a per-district D_NEXT_O_ID value (i.e., the next available order number) in the DISTRICT table. NEW-ORDER retrieves this D_NEXT_O_ID value, uses it as the ID of the new order, and then increments the D_NEXT_O_ID value so that the next order can have a different ID (lines 3–4). NEW-ORDER inserts a new order record in both the NEW-ORDER table and the ORDER table. Then for each selected item, it retrieves the price from the ITEM table, updates the item count in the STOCK table, and inserts a record in the ORDER-LINE table.

In terms of performance characteristics, the per-district D_NEXT_O_ID value is a major contention point, since all NEW-ORDER transactions of the same district need to retrieve and update the same D_NEXT_O_ID value. The second contention point is the item count in the STOCK table when multiple NEW-ORDER transactions try to order the same item. As discussed above, TPC-C uses an uneven distribution to select items to order, so the contention chance is not small despite that there are 100,000 items.

```
TRANSACTION BEGIN
1 UPDATE warehouse SET w_ytd = w_ytd + ? WHERE w_id=?;
-- fetch warehouse data
2 SELECT w_street_1,... FROM warehouse WHERE w_id=?;
-- update district d_ytd with payment amount
3 UPDATE district SET d_ytd = d_ytd + ? WHERE d_w_id=? AND d_id=?;
-- fetch district data
4 SELECT d_street_1,... FROM district WHERE d_w_id=? AND d_id=?;
-- for simplicity, we only show fetch customer by id
5 SELECT c_credit,... FROM customer WHERE c_w_id=? AND c_d_id=? AND c_id=?;
-- for bad credit customer, fetch c_data and update
if c_credit == "BC":
6   SELECT c_data FROM customer  WHERE c_w_id=? AND c_d_id=? AND c_id=?;
7   UPDATE customer SET c_balance = ?, c_data = ?,...
      WHERE c_w_id=? AND c_d_id=? AND c_id=?;
-- for good credit customer, update customer balance
else:
8   UPDATE customer SET c_balance = ?,...
      WHERE c_w_id=? AND c_d_id=? AND c_id=?;
-- insert history record
9 INSERT INTO history (...) VALUES (...);
TRANSACTION COMMIT
```

Fig. 2. TPC-C PAYMENT Transaction.

PAYMENT (Fig. 2). It simulates the procedure of a customer making a payment. It updates the warehouse and district sales statistics (i.e., year-to-date amount) (line 1 and line 3). It then updates the customer's balance and payment values in the corresponding tables.

In terms of performance characteristics, the per-warehouse sales statistics is a severe contention point, as all PAYMENT transactions on the same warehouse need to update the same value.

ORDER-STATUS (Fig. 3). It simulates the procedure of a customer browsing past orders. It selects the customer's order with the largest order ID in the ORDER table (line 4). Then it retrieves item information by selecting rows from the ORDER-LINE table with the same order ID.

DELIVERY (Fig. 4). It simulates the procedure of the administrator making a delivery for an order. For each district, it selects the oldest order from the NEW-ORDER table, deletes this row, retrieves detailed information from the ORDER table, and then updates the ORDER-LINE table. It finally updates the balance in the CUSTOMER table.

```
TRANSACTION BEGIN
-- fetch the customer, the last order, and order_line data respectively
1 SELECT c_first,... FROM customer WHERE c_w_id=? AND c_d_id=? AND c_id=?;
2 SELECT o_id, o_carrier_id, o_entry_d FROM oorder
    WHERE o_w_id=? AND o_d_id=? AND o_c_id=? ORDER BY o_id DESC LIMIT 1;
3 SELECT ol_i_id, ol_supply_w_id,... FROM order_line
    WHERE ol_w_id=? AND ol_d_id=? AND ol_o_id=?;
TRANSACTION COMMIT
```

Fig. 3. TPC-C ORDER-STATUS Transaction.

```
TRANSACTION BEGIN
for each district to deliver:
  -- fetch oldest undelivered order
1 SELECT no_o_id FROM new_order WHERE no_w_id=? AND no_d_id=?
    ORDER BY no_o_id ASC LIMIT 1 FOR UPDATE;
  if no_o_id is not null:
    -- delete the new_order record
2   DELETE FROM new_order WHERE no_w_id=? AND no_d_id=? AND no_o_id=?;
    -- fetch the customer id for this order
3   SELECT o_c_id FROM oorder WHERE o_w_id=? AND o_d_id=? AND o_id=?;
    -- update the order carrier id
4   UPDATE oorder SET o_carrier_id=? WHERE o_w_id=? AND o_d_id=? AND o_id=?;
    -- update the order_line delivery date
5   UPDATE order_line SET ol_delivery_d = ?
      WHERE ol_w_id=? AND ol_d_id=? AND ol_o_id=?;
    -- fetch the total amount of this order
6   SELECT SUM(ol_amount) FROM order_line
      WHERE ol_w_id=? AND ol_d_id=? AND ol_o_id=?;
    -- update the customer balance
7   UPDATE customer SET c_balance = c_balance + ?, c_delivery_cnt =
      c_delivery_cnt + 1 WHERE c_w_id=? AND c_d_id=? AND c_id=?;
TRANSACTION COMMIT
```

Fig. 4. TPC-C DELIVERY Transaction.

In terms of performance characteristics, DELIVERY may contend with NEW-ORDER, as both may update the NEW-ORDER table. The actual contention rate may not be high, as NEW-ORDER adds new orders and DELIVERY retrieves and deletes the oldest order. Of course, this depends on how the database implements INSERT and SELECT.

STOCK-LEVEL (Fig. 5). It simulates the procedure of the administrator browsing the recently sold items whose stock level is under a threshold. Given a district, it first retrieves the D_NEXT_O_ID value from the DISTRICT table. It then selects order lines whose order IDs are greater than or equal to D_NEXT_O_ID - 20 from the ORDER-LINE table. For each item in these order lines, STOCK-LEVEL checks whether its quantity in the STOCK table is less than a threshold.

In terms of performance characteristics, STOCK-LEVEL contends with NEW-ORDER on D_NEXT_O_ID and maybe also on item quantity.

TPC-C further specifies the expected distribution of these five types of transactions: NEW-ORDER 45%, PAYMENT 43%, ORDER-STATUS 4%, DELIVERY 4%, and STOCK-LEVEL 4%. As a result, NEW-ORDER and PAYMENT are typically performance critical though others can get heavier in certain settings.

```
TRANSACTION BEGIN
-- fetch district next order id
1 SELECT d_next_o_id FROM district WHERE d_w_id=? AND d_id=?;
-- retrieve low-stock items in recent orders
2 SELECT COUNT(DISTINCT(s_i_id)) FROM order_line, stock
    WHERE ol_w_id=? AND ol_d_id=? AND ol_o_id<? AND ol_o_id>=?
    AND s_w_id=? AND s_i_id=ol_i_id AND s_quantity<?;
TRANSACTION COMMIT
```

Fig. 5. TPC-C STOCK-LEVEL Transaction.

TPC-C also specifies a keying time and a think time before each transaction to simulate the customer's behaviors. However, most research prototypes remove such time in their evaluation for various reasons [24].

3 Methodology

We select three e-commerce applications to investigate: Spree [2], WooCommerce [7], and PrestaShop [1]. These applications are popular open-source e-commerce platforms with high Github stars (Spree: 15k, WooCommerce: 10k, PrestaShop: 8.8k as of writing). They are also widely used in the industry and have a large user base [8,9], claiming thousands to millions of active stores, making them suitable candidates for our study. They also represent different approaches to e-commerce, with Spree built on Ruby on Rails, WooCommerce as a widely used plugin for WordPress that enables e-commerce functionality, and PrestaShop built on PHP.

For each application, we create a deployment including the web server running the corresponding application and a backend database (MySQL in our experiments). We first act as a seller to set up a sample store, then using a customer account to interact with the store through the webpages. We perform typical e-commerce operations, such as searching for items, creating orders, making payments, and browsing order histories, and then act as the seller again to confirm deliveries, browse item stocks, etc.

The development environments for these applications often output logs to the console, which include application transactions triggered by customer and seller operations. We can also enable database tracing during the procedure to record SQL statements issued by each of those actions. We analyze the recorded SQL traces to understand their intentions. We also cross-check with the application source code to understand application-level logic that is not captured by SQL traces. After analyzing the SQL traces and source code, we summarize the main functions and their corresponding transactions for each application. As a result, we collect a set of transactions for above typical operations in e-commerce applications.

4 Spree

Spree Commerce is an open-source e-commerce platform built with Ruby on Rails. It provides a flexible and modular architecture that allows developers to create custom online stores. Spree supports various features such as product management, order processing, payment integration, and shipping options.

A Spree deployment can include a number of "stores", which are similar to, but not exactly the same as, warehouses in TPC-C. A Spree store maps to a seller on online shopping websites like Amazon and Alibaba. As a result, different stores can have a vastly different number of items to sell and highly skewed traffic. In TPC-C, each warehouse has the same number of items and incoming traffic. The deployment has three roles: customer, seller (i.e., a store owner), and admin of the whole website. This study covers the customer and the seller, as their activities are similar to those in TPC-C.

Spree provides similar functions as TPC-C: A customer can create orders, make payments, browse past orders, etc. A seller can make deliveries, check stock levels, etc. However, Spree implements those functions in different ways.

4.1 Create Order

A customer in Spree can create orders with a NEW-ORDER and multiple ADD-ITEM transactions. In other words, a NEW-ORDER transaction in TPC-C maps to a NEW-ORDER and multiple ADD-ITEM transactions in Spree.

```
TRANSACTION BEGIN
-- validation and load information
SELECT 1 AS one FROM spree_orders
  WHERE spree_orders.number = 'R005887550' LIMIT 1;
SELECT 1 AS one FROM spree_orders
  WHERE spree_orders.number = CAST('R005887550' AS BINARY) LIMIT 1;
SELECT spree_users.* FROM spree_users WHERE spree_users.id = 2 LIMIT 1;
-- insert order record
INSERT INTO spree_orders (number, ......) VALUES ('R005887550', ......);
TRANSACTION COMMIT
```

Fig. 6. Spree NEW-ORDER Transaction.

Spree NEW-ORDER. This transaction creates a new order record for a customer when the customer adds her first item to her shopping cart. This order begins in the "cart" state and will hold all the items the customer adds until the customer either decides to checkout or to cancel the order.

Figure 6 shows the steps involved in creating a new order. Spree first generates a random order number (R005887550 in this example) and checks if an order with this exact number already exists in the spree_orders table. The second query performs a case-sensitive comparison to ensure the number is unique. If the order number is unique, it proceeds to the third query, which retrieves the customer information, particularly the customer's user ID, from the spree_users table. Spree will regenerate the order number until there is no same number existing. The final statement inserts a record for the new order in the spree_orders table. Compared to TPC-C NEW-ORDER, which generates a unique order ID by incrementing D_NEXT_O_ID, Spree's approach incurs almost no contention.

```
TRANSACTION BEGIN
-- load information
SELECT * FROM spree_prices WHERE ......;
SELECT * FROM spree_line_items WHERE ......;
......
-- compute item count
SELECT SUM(spree_stock_items.count_on_hand) FROM spree_stock_items
  INNER JOIN spree_stock_locations ON spree_stock_locations.deleted_at IS
      NULL AND spree_stock_locations.id = spree_stock_items.stock_location_id
  WHERE spree_stock_items.deleted_at IS NULL AND spree_stock_items.variant_id
       = 142 AND spree_stock_locations.deleted_at IS NULL AND
      spree_stock_locations.active = TRUE;
-- create line item
INSERT INTO spree_line_items (......);
-- set initial price
UPDATE spree_line_items SET pre_tax_amount = 71.99 WHERE id = 26;
-- compute adjusted price including tax, shipment, promo, etc.
SELECT SUM(quantity) FROM spree_line_items WHERE order_id = 4;
......
-- update order
UPDATE spree_orders SET ...... WHERE id = 4;
TRANSACTION COMMIT
```

Fig. 7. Spree ADD-ITEM Transaction.

Spree ADD-ITEM. The ADD-ITEM transaction in Spree adds an item to an existing order when a customer adds an item to her shopping cart.

Figure 7 shows the steps of ADD-ITEM. It first gathers the necessary information and performs a series of checks. Then, it retrieves the item information and runs a SUM query on spree_stock_items table to ensure the product is in stock and available for purchase before adding it to the cart. Here, Spree uses the SUM query to count items in all stock locations. If the product is available, it proceeds to create a new line item in the spree_line_items table thus adding the item to the cart. It then computes the order's total price by including each item's original price and adjusted cost such as tax, shipment, promo, etc. Finally, it updates the order information.

Compared to TPC-C NEW-ORDER, Spree ADD-ITEM does not update the item count, which is updated during CHECKOUT and discussed later. This means that different ADD-ITEM transactions do not contend, but ADD-ITEM may contend with CHECKOUT.

4.2 Checkout

The checkout process in Spree, which maps to PAYMENT in TPC-C, involves multiple transactions that handle various aspects of completing an order, such as addressing, delivery, payment, and order finalization. We will focus on the payment and order finalization transactions. These transactions include creating a payment record, updating the stock levels, and finalizing the order.

Separating them into multiple transactions may violate atomicity: A failure may cause payment to be made but stock level is not updated. Spree (or Ruby on Rails) has application-level logic to (help the seller) detect such incomplete checkout and resume the unfinished checkout, by logging necessary information. In other words, Ruby on Rails is implementing a redo log by itself. Prior studies have shown that real-world applications often use such "ad-hoc" transactions to improve performance at the cost of more complicated error handling [12,20].

```
TRANSACTION BEGIN
-- load information and validate
SELECT * FROM spree_payments WHERE ......;
SELECT * FROM spree_users WHERE ......;
......
SELECT spree_stores.id FROM spree_stores INNER JOIN
     spree_payment_methods_stores ON spree_stores.id =
     spree_payment_methods_stores.store_id WHERE spree_stores.deleted_at IS
     NULL AND spree_payment_methods_stores.payment_method_id = 3 ORDER BY
     spree_stores.created_at ASC;
-- create payment records
INSERT INTO spree_payments (..., state, ...) VALUES (..., 'checkout', ...);
......
TRANSACTION COMMIT
```

Fig. 8. Spree PAYMENT Transaction.

Spree PAYMENT. This transaction creates a payment record for the order when a customer selects a payment method during checkout. Note that the payment is actually processed later.

Figure 8 shows the steps of the PAYMENT transaction. It begins with a series of SELECT queries to load and validate data, including the customer's account, her addresses, and the payment method she chose. Then it inserts a new payment record in the spree_payments table. The record's initial state is set to 'checkout', indicating that the payment has been created but not yet processed.

```
TRANSACTION BEGIN
-- load information and validate
SELECT 1 AS one FROM spree_variants LEFT OUTER JOIN spree_stock_items ON ...
     AND spree_stock_items.variant_id = spree_variants.id WHERE ......;
......
-- create movement record
INSERT INTO spree_stock_movements ......;
-- load and update stock item
SELECT * FROM spree_stock_items WHERE ...... FOR UPDATE;
UPDATE spree_stock_items SET count_on_hand = 99, ..... WHERE id = 142;
TRANSACTION COMMIT
```

Fig. 9. Spree UPDATE-STOCK Transaction.

Spree UPDATE-STOCK. It creates a stock movement record and decreases the item count for the purchased item.

Figure 9 shows the main steps in UPDATE-STOCK. This transaction includes several validation steps to ensure that the product variant is available for purchase. It checks if the variant exists, retrieves product information, and verifies stock availability (omitting due to space). Note that Spree's model of items is more complicated than that in TPC-C. In Spree, each item can have multiple "variants", often due to their differences in colors, sizes, etc., and variant information is stored in a separate table. As a result, related queries often need to JOIN the item and the variant tables. Then, UPDATE-STOCK creates an audit record in the spree_stock_movements table, which logs the quantity change applied to the stock item. Afterwards, it updates the item count (count_on_hand) in the spree_stock_items table (from 100 to 99 in this example). The update first uses SELECT FOR UPDATE to retrieve current item count and lock the item count to prevent concurrent updates.

Compared to TPC-C PAYMENT, Spree UPDATE-STOCK does not update sales statistics like year-to-date amount in TPC-C. As a result, Spree UPDATE-STOCK transactions do not have heavy contentions like TPC-C PAYMENT, unless they target the same item. If a Spree seller wants to view sales statistics, she will incur transactions to compute the sum of all orders, which will contend with UPDATE-STOCK. Considering UPDATE-STOCK is probably more frequent than viewing statistics, we believe this is a reasonable design choice to reduce contentions.

```
TRANSACTION BEGIN
-- load information
SELECT 1 AS one FROM spree_orders WHERE ......;
-- update order states
UPDATE spree_orders SET shipment_state = 'pending', payment_state = '
    balance_due', updated_at = '...' WHERE id = 4;
TRANSACTION COMMIT
```

Fig. 10. Spree Finalize-Order Transaction.

Spree FINALIZE-ORDER. It finalizes the order by updating its state related to shipment and payment.

This final simple transaction updates the overall status of the order, moving it to the next step in the checkout process. Figure 10 shows the statements involved in finalizing the order. The update statement sets the shipment state to 'pending' and the payment state to 'balance_due'. This indicates that the inventory has been allocated for the order, but the item is not yet shipped. A payment record exists, but the funds have not been captured yet by the seller. This transaction moves the order to the fulfillment workflow.

4.3 Order-Status Transactions

The Order-Status transactions in Spree are responsible for retrieving the current status of orders. There are two types of transactions: one for retrieving a list of orders for order history and another for retrieving the details of a specific order.

```
-- check if there are completed orders
SELECT 1 AS one FROM spree_orders WHERE user_id = 2 AND completed_at IS NOT
    NULL AND store_id = 1 LIMIT 1 OFFSET 0;
-- retrieve the last 25 completed orders
SELECT spree_orders.* FROM spree_orders WHERE user_id = 2 AND completed_at IS
     NOT NULL AND store_id = 1 ORDER BY created_at DESC LIMIT 25 OFFSET 0;
-- retrieve the last pending order
SELECT spree_orders.* FROM spree_orders WHERE user_id = 2 AND store_id = 1
    AND completed_at IS NULL AND state NOT IN ('canceled', '
    partially_canceled') ORDER BY created_at DESC LIMIT 1;
```

Fig. 11. Spree ORDER-HISTORY Transaction.

Spree ORDER-HISTORY. It retrieve a list of orders (the most recent 25 orders by default) for a specific customer. This transaction is triggered when a customer wants to view their order history. Because this process is read-only, each single SELECT is executed as a transaction. We list the queries most relevant to the order status in Fig. 11.

These queries fetch a paginated list of a user's completed orders to display on their account page. The first query checks if there are any completed orders for the user. Then, it selects all completed orders for the current customer and orders them by creation date. The last query checks if there are any pending orders for the customer.

```
-- retrieve order by order number and line items for the order
SELECT * FROM spree_orders WHERE ......;
SELECT * FROM spree_line_items WHERE ......;
```

Fig. 12. Spree ORDER-DETAILS Transaction.

Spree ORDER-DETAILS. It retrieves the details of a specific order. This transaction is triggered when a customer clicks an order to view the details of this order. It will retrieve all the information to display a complete, detailed view of a single order.

To build the order details page, Spree needs to reconstruct the entire order by fetching data from multiple tables. Figure 12 shows the queries involved in retrieving the order details. This includes the order itself, line item details, shipment and address information, and payment data.

Compared to TPC-C ORDER-STATUS, Spree's implementation is more complicated, but we do not see a fundamental difference in performance characteristics.

```
TRANSACTION BEGIN
-- validation
SELECT 1 AS one FROM spree_shipments WHERE spree_shipments.number = ......;
......
-- update shipment status
UPDATE spree_shipments SET state = 'shipped', ... WHERE id = 3;
......
TRANSACTION COMMIT
```

Fig. 13. Spree SHIPMENT Transaction.

4.4 Shipment Transaction

After a seller verifies the payment information, she can start the delivery process and use the SHIPMENT transaction to mark an order as shipped. It has the similar role as DELIVERY in TPC-C. Figure 13 shows the details, which include some validation steps and a UPDATE statement to set the shipment status as 'shipped'.

```
SELECT spree_stock_items.* FROM spree_stock_items INNER JOIN spree_variants
    ON spree_stock_items.variant_id = spree_variants.id INNER JOIN
    spree_products ON spree_variants.product_id = spree_products.id INNER
    JOIN spree_products_stores ON spree_products.id = spree_products_stores.
    product_id INNER JOIN spree_variants variants_spree_stock_items ON
    variants_spree_stock_items.id = spree_stock_items.variant_id WHERE ... IN
     (SELECT spree_variants.product_id FROM spree_variants WHERE
    spree_variants.deleted_at IS NULL GROUP BY spree_variants.product_id
    HAVING (COUNT(spree_variants.id) = 1))) ORDER BY spree_stock_items.
    created_at DESC, spree_variants.position ASC LIMIT 25 OFFSET 0;
```

Fig. 14. Spree STOCK-LEVEL Transaction.

4.5 Stock-Level Transaction

A seller can incur the STOCK-LEVEL transactions to view the stock levels of all product variants.

The first group of statements is executed when a seller navigates to the stock management page to view the stock levels of all products in the store. Figure 14 shows the main queries involved in this process. The query is a complex SELECT statement that incorporates multiple JOINs, a subquery, and keywords like GROUP BY, HAVING, ORDER BY, etc. It builds a list of all product variants for the store. Then, it executes a series of queries to load the associated products, variants, stock locations, and count on hand for each variant. Since these are quite straightforward, we do not list details here.

Compared to TPC-C STOCK-LEVEL, Spree STOCK-LEVEL looks more like an OLAP transaction, which tests the database's capability for complicated queries. We have observed similar transactions in other seller-side transactions, such as SALES-REPORT and ANALYTICS-DASHBOARD.

4.6 Summary of Comparison with TPC-C

As a mature product, Spree is obviously more complicated than TPC-C, represented by its more complicated table designs, various kinds of validations, etc. Apart from such implementation-level differences, we observe the following major differences:

- Unlike warehouses in TPC-C, Spree's stores are probably highly imbalanced, in terms of both item number and traffic.
- Compared to TPC-C, Spree tends to use multiple shorter transactions to implement a function, and relies on application-specific logic or seller's effort to achieve atomicity.
- The design of Spree has reduced contention level compared to TPC-C. This includes not relying on D_NEXT_ORDER_ID to generate a unique order ID, and not maintaining the sales statistics.
- TPC-C updates the item count when a customer adds the item to the order. Spree updates the item count when the customer checks out the order.
- Spree uses JOIN in multiple transactions due to its table design. Some complicated queries combine multiple JOINs, subqueries, GROUP BY keywords, etc., which make them more close to OLAP transactions.

5 WooCommerce and PrestaShop

We perform the same study for WooCommerce and PrestaShop. At a high level, their designs are quite similar to that of Spree, though the detailed implementations are different. This section summarizes the key comparison with TPC-C:

- (Same as Spree) Both have the concept of "store". Again, stores are probably highly load imbalanced.
- (Slightly different from Spree) Both use short transactions. In fact, both only use single-statement transactions, as shown in the traces we collected.
- (Different from Spree) Both use the "auto increment" feature of the database to generate a unique order ID. This approach still has less contention than retrieving and incrementing D_NEXT_O_ID in TPC-C.
- (Slightly different from Spree) Both maintain a per-item sales statistics for each store. Compared to TPC-C's per-warehouse sales statistics, maintaining a per-store per-item sales statistics incurs less contention.
- (Same as Spree) Both update item count when the customer checks out her order.
- (Same as Spree) Both use JOINs in multiple transactions. Both have complicated OLAP-like transactions to browse histories and/or statistics.

6 Suggestions and Results

Based on our study, we have tried to incorporate the difference into TPC-C. We find some are easy to incorporate, but some require a significant change to TPC-C. Therefore, our suggestion is to incorporate those "easy" changes into TPC-C and maybe build a new benchmark to incorporate those significant changes in the long term. In this section, we discuss the easy changes we suggested to TPC-C, their potential impact on evaluation of transaction processing systems, and why other changes require a significant effort.

Suggested Changes to TPC-C. We find the following changes can be made to TPC-C without significant changes:

- We make warehouses imbalanced. Specifically, we use the zipf distribution to generate the number of items in each warehouse and the traffic to each warehouse. Data skew is also recommended by other works [15] and TPC-E [5].
- We split the NEW-ORDER transaction in TPC-C into one that creates an empty order, and multiple ADD-ITEM transactions, each adding one item to the order.
- We use the auto-increment feature of MySQL to generate a unique order ID.
- We remove the logic of updating the year-to-date sales statistics in PAYMENT.

Potential Impact on Evaluation. The suggested changes may affect the evaluation of transactional processing systems in the following ways:

- The imbalanced warehouses will test a database's capability to do load balancing, which is important for a distributed or multi-core database. Standard TPC-C does not have this capability.
- Due to using auto-increment to generate IDs and removing maintenance of sales statistics, modified TPC-C has less contention than standard TPC-C. Modified TPC-C contends only when customers purchase the same item from the same store. We can still tune this contention level by tuning the distribution of items to purchase.
- Shorter transactions and less contention make works that rely on code analysis more feasible.
- Shorter (and more) transactions may increase overhead when contention level is low, as the database system needs to pay more overhead for committing transactions and transferring messages. However, when contention level is high, shorter transactions can reduce contention duration.

To demonstrate some of such potential impact, we compare the results of standard TPC-C and our modified TPC-C on MySQL. We ran our experiments on CloudLab [13], using c220g5 machines. Each machine is equipped with two Intel Xeon Silver 4114 10-core CPUs (20 virtual cores with hyperthreading), 192 GB of RAM, and one Intel DC S3500 480 GB 6G SATA SSD. The machines are interconnected by a dual portIntel X520-DA2 10Gb NIC. We run MySQL server version 8.0.42 and configure it with 8 GB buffer pool size and 4 GB redo log.

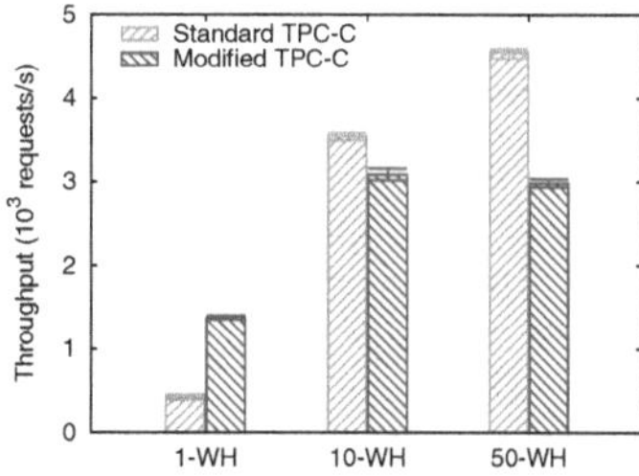

Fig. 15. Throughput of standard and modified TPC-C. For modified TPC-C, we count one NEW-ORDER and its corresponding ADD-ITEM as one transaction for a fair comparison with standard TPC-C.

Figure 15 shows the effects of using shorter transactions and removing contention points. When there is one warehouse, the throughput of modified TPC-C is significantly higher than that of standard TPC-C. This is because, with one warehouse, standard TPC-C has severe contention on per-warehouse sales statistics and per-district D_NEXT_O_ID, and modified TPC-C has removed such contention points. With more warehouses, the trend is the opposite: As the contention level gets lower with more warehouses, standard TPC-C gets higher throughput. Modified TPC-C suffers more from the overhead of processing more shorter transactions, and thus has lower throughput than standard TPC-C.

Effect of Contention Level. We tune the skewness of item hotness to change the contention level of modified TPC-C, since multiple NEW-ORDER transactions contend if they target the same item. Note that in standard TPC-C, the item access is non-uniform by default, but the contention level is different from that of our tuned item skewness. Figure 16(a) shows that, with a single MySQL server and one warehouse, tuning the skewness of item hotness can decrease throughput by up to 75%, but with 10 or more warehouses, such tuning does not have a significant impact on throughput. However, when running the 10-warehouse setting with three-way replication and with increased network latency, as shown in Fig. 16(b), increasing such skewness can reduce overall throughput by 56%, since replication increases the duration of contention. This means, compared with standard TPC-C, modified TPC-C allows us to tune contention level under the same number of warehouses, enabling more flexible experiment settings.

Effect of Traffic Skewness. As discussed, in practice, the stores may be highly imbalanced. We simulate such an imbalance by introducing a skewness into store traffic. We run our experiments on a 4-node cluster where tables are partitioned by the warehouse ID. Our experiments show that, compared to the uniform distribution, a skewed distribution can reduce overall throughput by 11%. Of course, the throughput of a distributed setting may be affected by the number of nodes, the policy to partition tables, and load balancing strategies, which can be the targets of further optimization.

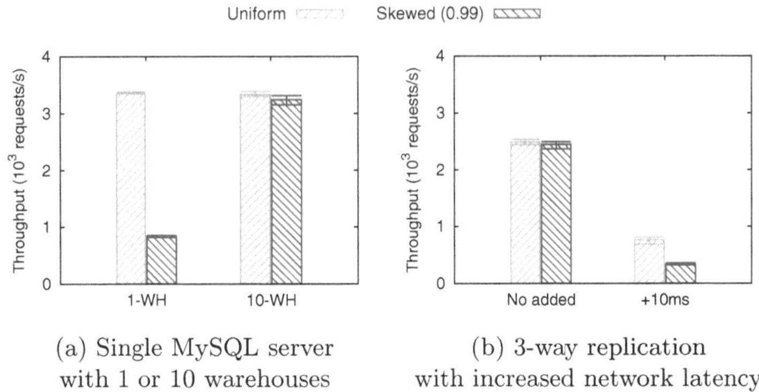

(a) Single MySQL server with 1 or 10 warehouses

(b) 3-way replication with increased network latency

Fig. 16. Throughput of modified TPC-C for varying item skewness (uniform and skewed) under different settings.

As shown in these results, modified TPC-C indeed shows quite different performance characteristics compared to standard TPC-C, which shows the importance of such a study.

Changes that Require Significant Effort. We do not add more JOINs or complicated OLAP-like queries, since they require a significant re-design of TPC-C's table structure. We tried to move the logic of updating stock level from NEW-ORDER to PAYMENT, but that is harder than we thought. The reason is that in standard TPC-C, PAYMENT does not connect to any specific order and instead only generates some random payment. If we wanted to let PAYMENT update the stock level, we needed to let it connect to a specific order, retrieve the item and purchase count from the order, and then update the item count. Such changes require a significant re-design of PAYMENT. As a result, we do not incorporate these changes in modified TPC-C but recommend building a new benchmark to incorporate them.

7 Related Work

In addition to TPC-C, the database community has developed several other benchmarks for evaluating OLTP systems. For example, the SmallBank benchmark models a banking application in which transactions operate customers' accounts [10]. The Voter Benchmark simulates a voting system in which users vote on their favorite contestant, updating the total number of votes [6]. The TATP benchmark simulates a mobile carrier database, which provides high-speed transactions to retrieve and update information for callers [3]. The YCSB+T benchmark extends YCSB, a key-value benchmark, to encapsulate multiple key-value operations in a transaction [14]. TPC has also introduced another OLTP benchmark TPC-E [5] in 2007.

However, we observe that despite its age, TPC-C remains one of the most popular OLTP benchmarks in both academia and industry, possibly due to its reasonable complexity (benchmarks like SmallBank and Voter only use simple SQL statements while TPC-E may be too complex) and the fact that online shopping demands high throughput under potential high contentions, which creates challenging problems.

A number of works have analyzed TPC-C and/or proposed changes to TPC-C [24,28]. To the best of our knowledge, this is the first work to compare TPC-C with real-world online shopping applications.

8 Conclusion

This work compares TPC-C with three online shopping applications to understand the representativeness of TPC-C. We have identified a few key differences in the design choices of TPC-C and others, which can lead to different performance characteristics. Based on this study, we have proposed changes to TPC-C so that it can better represent modern e-commerce applications.

Acknowledgments. We thank the anonymous reviewers for their valuable feedback. This material is based in part upon work supported by the National Science Foundation under Grant Numbers CCF-2118745.

References

1. PrestaShop. https://github.com/PrestaShop/PrestaShop
2. Spree. https://github.com/spree/spree
3. TATP Benchmark. https://tatpbenchmark.sourceforge.net/
4. TPC-C Benchmark. https://www.tpc.org/tpcc/
5. TPC-E Benchmark. https://www.tpc.org/tpce/
6. Voter Benchmark. https://github.com/cmu-db/benchbase/wiki/Voter/
7. WooCommerce. https://github.com/woocommerce/woocommerce
8. Spree Commerce Documentation (2024). https://spreecommerce.org/docs/user/what-is-spree-commerce
9. The State of Ecommerce in 2025 (2025). https://storeleads.app/reports
10. Alomari, M., Cahill, M., Fekete, A., Rohm, U.: The cost of serializability on platforms that use snapshot isolation. In: 2008 IEEE 24th International Conference on Data Engineering, pp. 576–585 (2008). https://doi.org/10.1109/ICDE.2008.4497466
11. Cai, Q., et al.: Efficient distributed memory management with RDMA and caching. Proc. VLDB Endow. **11**(11), 1604–1617 (2018). https://doi.org/10.14778/3236187.3236209
12. Cheng, C., Han, M., Xu, N., Blanas, S., Bond, M.D., Wang, Y.: Developer's responsibility or database's responsibility? Rethinking concurrency control in databases. In: 13th Annual Conference on Innovative Data Systems Research (CIDR'23), 8–11 January 2023, Amsterdam, The Netherlands (2023)

13. CloudLab. https://www.cloudlab.us
14. Dey, A., Fekete, A., Nambiar, R., Röhm, U.: YCSB+T: benchmarking web-scale transactional databases. In: 2014 IEEE 30th International Conference on Data Engineering Workshops, pp. 223–230 (2014). https://doi.org/10.1109/ICDEW.2014.6818330
15. He, H., et al.: Benchmarking distributed transactional database systems. In: International Symposium on Benchmarking, Measuring and Optimization, pp. 37–53. Springer (2024)
16. Lim, H., Kaminsky, M., Andersen, D.G.: Cicada: dependably fast multi-core in-memory transactions. In: Proceedings of the 2017 ACM International Conference on Management of Data. SIGMOD 2017, pp. 21–35. Association for Computing Machinery, New York, NY, USA (2017). https://doi.org/10.1145/3035918.3064015
17. Lu, Y., Yu, X., Cao, L., Madden, S.: Aria: a fast and practical deterministic OLTP database. Proc. VLDB Endow. **13**(12), 2047–2060 (2020). https://doi.org/10.14778/3407790.3407808
18. Lu, Y., Yu, X., Madden, S.: Star: scaling transactions through asymmetric replication. Proc. VLDB Endow. **12**(11), 1316–1329 (2019). https://doi.org/10.14778/3342263.3342270
19. Mu, S., Nelson, L., Lloyd, W., Li, J.: Consolidating concurrency control and consensus for commits under conflicts. In: 12th USENIX Symposium on Operating Systems Design and Implementation (OSDI 16), pp. 517–532. USENIX Association, Savannah, GA (2016). https://www.usenix.org/conference/osdi16/technical-sessions/presentation/mu
20. Tang, C., et al.: Ad hoc transactions in web applications: the good, the bad, and the ugly. In: Proceedings of the 2022 International Conference on Management of Data, SIGMOD 2022, pp. 4–18. Association for Computing Machinery, New York, NY, USA (2022). https://doi.org/10.1145/3514221.3526120
21. Thomson, A., Diamond, T., Weng, S.C., Ren, K., Shao, P., Abadi, D.J.: Calvin: fast distributed transactions for partitioned database systems. In: Proceedings of the 2012 ACM SIGMOD International Conference on Management of Data, SIGMOD 2012, pp. 1–12. Association for Computing Machinery, New York, NY, USA (2012). https://doi.org/10.1145/2213836.2213838
22. Tu, S., Zheng, W., Kohler, E., Liskov, B., Madden, S.: Speedy transactions in multicore in-memory databases. In: Proceedings of the Twenty-Fourth ACM Symposium on Operating Systems Principles, SOSP 2013, pp. 18–32. Association for Computing Machinery, New York, NY, USA (2013). https://doi.org/10.1145/2517349.2522713
23. Wang, D., et al.: TXSQL: lock optimizations towards high contented workloads. In: Companion of the 2025 International Conference on Management of Data, SIGMOD/PODS 2025, pp. 675–688. Association for Computing Machinery, New York, NY, USA (2025). https://doi.org/10.1145/3722212.3724457
24. Wang, Y., et al.: A study of database performance sensitivity to experiment settings. Proc. VLDB Endow. **15**(7), 1439–1452 (2022)
25. Wei, X., Shi, J., Chen, Y., Chen, R., Chen, H.: Fast in-memory transaction processing using RDMA and HTM. In: Proceedings of the 25th Symposium on Operating Systems Principles, SOSP 2015, pp. 87–104. ACM, New York, NY, USA (2015). https://doi.org/10.1145/2815400.2815419
26. Yang, X., et al.: PolarDB-MP: a multi-primary cloud-native database via disaggregated shared memory. In: Companion of the 2024 International Conference on Management of Data, SIGMOD 2024, pp. 295–308. Association for Computing Machinery, New York, NY, USA (2024). https://doi.org/10.1145/3626246.3653377

27. Yang, X., Zhang, Y., Chen, H., Sun, C., Li, F., Zhou, W.: PolarDB-SCC: a cloud-native database ensuring low latency for strongly consistent reads. Proc. VLDB Endow. **16**(12), 3754–3767 (2023). https://doi.org/10.14778/3611540.3611562
28. Zhang, H., et al.: Dike: a benchmark suite for distributed transactional databases. In: Companion of the 2023 International Conference on Management of Data, SIGMOD 2023, pp. 95–98. Association for Computing Machinery, New York, NY, USA (2023)

Author Index

J. Zhan et al. (Eds.): Bench 2025, LNCS 16471, pp. 291–292, 2026.
https://doi.org/10.1007/978-981-95-9694-2

Zeitfracht Medien GmbH
Ferdinand-Jühlke-Straße 7
99095 Erfurt, Deutschland
produktsicherheit@kolibri360.de